D0881234

# Earthbound

# Earthbound

## NEW INTRODUCTORY ESSAYS
## IN ENVIRONMENTAL ETHICS

WILLIAM AIKEN
ANNETTE C. BAIER
ALASTAIR GUNN
DALE JAMIESON
EDWARD JOHNSON
TIBOR R. MACHAN
MARK SAGOFF
K. S. SHRADER-FRECHETTE
ROBERT L. SIMON

### Edited by Tom Regan

North Carolina State University at Raleigh

TEMPLE UNIVERSITY PRESS
PHILADELPHIA

First Edition
Temple University Press, Philadelphia 19122
Copyright © 1984 by Random House, Inc.
Published 1984

**Library of Congress Cataloging in Publication Data**

Main entry under title:

Earthbound: new introductory essays in environmental
  ethics.

  Bibliography: p.
  Includes index.
  1. Human ecology—Moral and ethical aspects—Addresses,
essays, lectures.    I. Aiken, William, 1947–
II. Regan, Tom.
GF80.E16     1984        170        83–16012
ISBN 0–87722–351–3

Manufactured in the United States of America

*To Nancy's Parents,*
*Lucile and Charles Tirk*

# PREFACE

This anthology consists of original essays that explore issues in environmental ethics. Some of the essays focus mainly on the interplay between the environment and the interests of presently existing human beings while others place considerable importance on our environmental policies and our obligations to generations yet unborn. Some deal mainly with the environmental ties that bind us to the members of our own community whereas others discuss environmental questions against the backdrop of our duties to people who live in distant nations. Still others inquire into the moral status of the nonhuman denizens of the earth, both animals and plants; indeed, sometimes it is the earth itself whose moral status is the object of inquiry. The essays, in a word, examine a rich variety of concerns relating to and about the environment. Moreover, if there is one outstanding characteristic common to them all, it is that each essay abundantly confirms the impossibility of examining one idea at a time. Questions about the ethics of alternative approaches to agriculture or to controlling pollution, for example, soon spill over into deeper, more fundamental questions about equality and individual rights. More than is usually the case, therefore, it is difficult to fix an order in which to read these essays. There is, I am sure, no single "right way" to do this. Nevertheless, a few words about the present arrangement might indicate why I think the order in which I have arranged them is not arbitrary.

Philosophers writing in environmental ethics sometimes write as if "the environment" indicates wilderness but excludes Washington. The environment in which most of us live, however, is an urban environment —a large city, for example, or a college town. Since this is the environment most of us know best, it is natural to begin with "The City Around

Us," the title Dale Jamieson gives to the lead essay. To begin with the urban environment is not to dodge important environmental questions. As Jamieson explains, many of these questions not only arise within but their difficulty is increased by the complexities of urban life.

One of the problems Jamieson considers is pollution. Few people speak in its favor, but how can we control it? And how should we? These questions are keys that unlock some of the heaviest doors of moral and political theory, especially theories about the proper function of the state. As Tibor Machan argues in the second essay, "Pollution and Political Theory," we cannot have well-thought-out answers to questions about allowing and controlling pollution unless we first have thought carefully about the nature of a just social order. Machan's vision of that order, one that challenges the dominant vision in American society, will be found in his essay. Even now, however, we can begin to suspect that many of the questions of environmental ethics are not just about the environment. Many of them are about justice itself.

The next essay, "Ethics and Energy" by Kristin Shrader-Frechette, confirms this suspicion. The so-called energy crisis, she argues, is misnamed; the crisis is not so much about energy as it is about political and economic justice—and injustice. Only after we have come to realize this, she argues, will we be able to make an informed judgment about which we prefer: hard path energy technologies (for example, nuclear power) or the technologies of the soft path (for example, solar and geothermal). This does not mean that we can make an informed judgment while ignorant of *the facts* about these alternative approaches to energy production. It is only to insist that knowledge of these facts, while necessary, will not provide answers to the value questions we need to answer.

But how shall we answer questions of value? One answer that has found favor with important, powerful policymakers is examined at length in the essay by Mark Sagoff, "Ethics and Economics in Environmental Law." This answer is that value is reducible to economics or, more precisely, that one's values are established by what one would be willing to pay to get or avoid something. Is this a reasonable theory of value? What would be its environmental impact if it was accepted and implemented? And how would its results, if applied, square with our vision of ourselves as citizens of America—or, for that matter, of Canada, England, Australia, or New Zealand? If Sagoff is right, this economic theory of value is mistaken not only as a theory of the value the natural environment holds; it is equally, and perhaps more profoundly, mistaken in fostering a false picture of who and what *we* are.

The fifth essay, "Troubled Waters: Global Justice and Ocean Resources" by Robert L. Simon, carries the previously mentioned theme of political and economic justice a step further. Some areas of our natural environment (for example, the deep sea bed) contain important natural resources. Presently unowned, the benefits derivable from mining these resources promise to be very large indeed. Who should enjoy these benefits: Only those who have the technical and financial base required to carry out the mining operations, or does justice require that those able to do this must share some portion of these benefits with the citizens of nations who lack both the technology and money to participate? Who should say what everyone's "fair share" is, if everyone is entitled to one, and how should the distribution be carried out? Again, informed answers to these questions depend on our first having thought carefully about the nature of justice at a more fundamental level, a point that Simon brings to our attention throughout his essay.

As was mentioned earlier, a number of the essays touch on the issue of our obligations to future generations. This is now so central a theme in the literature in environmental ethics that no collection of essays would be adequate that failed to include a selection devoted to it. Annette Baier offers such a selection in her "For the Sake of Future Generations." A stock device in the rhetoric of politicians, the idea of "obligations to future generations" turns out to have challenging, subtle, and oft-neglected difficulties. Baier patiently explores the hurdles standing in the way of making sense of how we can have duties to nonexisting persons, and she examines alternative accounts of how stringent or weighty these duties are. The conclusions she reaches look backward and forward; that is, we can take her conclusions and ask of the essays that precede hers as well as of the ones that follow: "Do their views of our obligations to generations yet unborn conform or conflict with hers?"

This question can certainly be asked of the seventh essay—William Aiken's "Ethical Issues in Agriculture." Indeed, all the major themes alluded to in the foregoing—political and economic justice, obligations to distant strangers and to future generations, economic theories of value and the values of nature—all find a voice in Aiken's essay. Like a number of the other contributors, the conclusions Aiken reaches call for important changes in how we live. While many of the questions he and others examine are "theoretical," we should not lose sight of the practical implications of the answers given and defended. Like the others, Aiken enjoins us *to act* differently because he first endeavors rationally to persuade us *to think* differently.

With Aiken's essay we encounter for the first time a contributor to this volume asking whether we should broaden our moral concern and take the welfare or rights of animals into account. Alastair Gunn's essay, "Preserving Rare Species," presses for consideration of these matters. And more. Most of those species that are rare or endangered are species of plants, not animals, so the deep, foundational questions about the grounds of the obligation to preserve rare species must go beyond, even as it includes, considerations about the rights and welfare of animals. Rejecting arguments that our obligations are exclusively to humans, including future generations, Gunn inclines toward a more holistic understanding of the value of nature, where ecosystems rather than their individual members are thought of as the basic units of value.

To have gone this far in the readings is already to have gained some sense of the theoretical possibilities when one thinks about issues in environmental ethics. What better place to end, then, than with an essay devoted largely to a critical survey of these possibilities, including the holistic option favored by some? Edward Johnson's "Treating the Dirt: Environmental Ethics and Moral Theory" provides the needed critical summary. That his essay is positioned last should not lead us to conclude that it is of least importance. One might more reasonably infer the very opposite.

Here, then, is *a* way to read the essays, starting from what we know best (our urban environment); next working our way through the tangle of difficulties we face when we restrict our attention to the interrelationships between the environment and human interests and ideals (for example, economic and political justice between generations and nations); next examining the ethics of how our acts and institutions affect the nonhumans in our environment; and so on. Not the only way but, I hope, a fruitful one.

Finally, I should say that the Introduction has two principal aims. First, it attempts to explain some important assumptions shared by all the contributors—for example, some assumptions concerning how *not* to answer moral questions. Second, by tracing some of the major ideas current in moral philosophy, it formulates sets of questions that might help readers work their way more confidently through the essays themselves. The hope is that people will better understand the discussion of a particular issue in enviromental ethics when it is viewed against the backdrop of moral philosophy generally, and vice versa.

It is a pleasure to thank all the contributors for their help and cooperation; Steve Pensinger and Fred Burns of Random House for their help; my wife, Nancy, for her expert typing and other assistance; Ruth Boone and Ann Rives for their work in preparing the manuscript; and my children, Bryan and Karen, for their benign indulgence.

Tom Regan

*Raleigh, North Carolina*
*March 28, 1983*

# CONTENTS

## 3.  Pollution and Political Theory

## 4.  Ethics and Energy

## 5. Ethics and Economics in Environmental Law

MARK SAGOFF **147**

## 6. Troubled Waters: Global Justice and Ocean Resources

ROBERT L. SIMON **179**

## 7.  For the Sake of Future Generations
ANNETTE  BAIER                                              **214**

## 10.  Treating the Dirt: Environmental Ethics and Moral Theory    E D W A R D   J O H N S O N    336

# Earthbound

i

# I

# *Introduction*

## TOM REGAN

§1 WE ARE WHAT WE EAT

The concerns of environmental ethics might begin with the food on our plate. If "we are what we eat," that food should tell us a good deal about what we are, both individually and as a nation. Those of us who live in the United States are blessed with abundant food supplies and, thanks to modern transportation systems, agricultural innovations, and competitive retail stores we are able to select what we eat from a wide variety of tasty foods available throughout the year at low cost—at least the costs are low when compared with prices elsewhere! Popular national wisdom has it that we are the best fed, as well as the best dressed and housed, people in the world. Are we? And at what costs to the environment and others with whom we share it?

Some of the worries about our food concern the methods used to produce it. Modern agriculture is increasingly monocultural and chemically intensive. It is monocultural because a particular crop, say wheat or corn, soybeans or barley, is grown on the same land year after year; crops are not rotated, nor is acreage allowed to lie fallow so that the earth might renew itself. It is chemically intensive because of extensive use of fertilizers, herbicides, nematicides, pesticides, and the like. Though this form of agriculture has doubtless produced many benefits, it also leaves many serious questions in its wake.

One concerns pesticide residue in the food itself. At present there are approximately 400 different pesticides in agricultural use. Three different government agencies—the Environmental Protection Agency (EPA), the United States Department of Agricultural (USDA), and the Food and Drug Administration (FDA)—are charged with insuring that pesticide residue in food, including pesticides known to be carcinogens,

3

do not exceed the "tolerance levels" set by the government. Some critics of government policies and efficiency are skeptical, however, perhaps none more so than Lewis Regenstein who, in his recent book *America the Poisoned*, states that

> a review of the government's policy in setting and enforcing tolerance levels of toxic pesticides leads to the inescapable conclusion that the program exists primarily to insure the public that it is being protected from harmful chemical residues. In fact, the program, as currently administered, does little to minimize or even monitor the amount of poisons in our food, and serves the interests of the users and producers of pesticides rather than those of the public.[1]

If Regenstein is right, the food we eat could be poisoning us to death.

In addition to pesticide residue in our food serious worries also arise concerning the contamination of our water supplies from runoffs of pesticides and other chemicals commonly used in agriculture. Almost 50 percent of Americans use water from underground reservoirs, and approximately 40 percent of the water used in farm irrigation systems comes from this source. The purity of this water, which does not pass through filtration systems, is seriously jeopardized by the presence of toxic chemicals, including those employed as agricultural pesticides. Dibromochloropropane (DBCP), for example, widely used as a pesticide in California before it was banned in 1977, was found in half the irrigation and drinking wells surveyed in the San Joaquin Valley *two years later*. DBCP is a known carcinogen. Even water that comes from above ground sources (lakes, rivers, streams, and the like) and that passes through municipal filtration systems is not always free from toxic chemicals, including pesticide residue from agricultural use perhaps hundreds of miles away. "The drinking water of every major American city," writes Regenstein, "contains dozens of cancer-causing chemicals and other toxins,"[2] a number of which can be traced to the chemically intensive methods used to produce the food on our plate.

Pesticides, of course, and the other chemicals essential to monocultural agriculture do not occur in nature but are the products of the petrochemical industry. The food on our plate is, therefore, causally related to that industry and, in this respect, is indirectly related to the pollution caused by petrochemical plants. That pollution, critics like Regenstein claim, besides adversely affecting the quality of the water we drink and the food we eat, also impacts detrimentally, directly and indirectly, on the quality of the air we breathe. Directly, quality is affected by petrochemical plants by way of their release into the air of toxic substances, some of which are causally implicated in increased incidences of respiratory diseases, such as emphysema and bronchitis, as well as a variety of cancers, especially lung cancer. Indirectly, the petrochemical industry, pesticides, and the food on our plate are a party to a decline in air quality because industry runs on electrical power that is frequently generated by methods that are themselves detrimental to the quality of the air we breathe.

The phenomenon known as acid rain illustrates the tangled web of cause and effect. The chemistry seems fairly simple. Sulphur oxides and nitrogen oxides emitted into the air form acids when they combine with water vapor. These acids in turn fall to the earth when it rains or snows with the result that both land and water acidity increase. The acidity of rain falling in some parts of the United States, for example, is estimated by an EPA study to have increased fifty-fold in the last twenty-five years and is sometimes over 100 times more acidic than normal rainfall. Though estimates vary, perhaps as much as 80 percent of the sulphur emissions that are the first link in the chain of events that culminate in acid rain result from human activities. Along with the increase in the acidity of rain there is a predictable increase in the incidence of acute and chronic respiratory ailments, and there are also serious reasons to question the continued fertility of the earth itself. Even the products of human creation—buildings, monuments, and the like—are not immune to acid rain. To cite just one example: In 1883 Cleopatra's Needle, a granite obelisk, after spending some thirty-five centuries in the Egyptian desert, was placed in New York City's Central Park. Exposed to the scorching sun, to wind, to sand, the obelisk withstood the rigors of its desert environment for 3,500 years—better than it has its New York home, where in just 100 years it has lost several inches of its granite, in part because of the chemical fallout of acid rain. Human creations, our *urban* environment, not just nature and our bodies, can feel the bite of the acid in the rain.

Older coal-burning power plants along the Ohio River are among the principal causes of acid rain. But pollution travels, and the areas most affected by acid rain are across state and even national boundaries. "Dead" lakes—absent any plant or aquatic life—are found throughout the northeastern United States and southeastern Canada. A thousand lakes "dead" in Wisconsin, perhaps 10,000 endangered. There are "dead" lakes in Colorado and California, and in other countries, such as Sweden, which has lost approximately 15,000 lakes. Some experts predict that 50,000 or more lakes in Canada and the United States will "die" in the next fifteen years, all as a result of acid rain. How long the surrounding vegetation can withstand this onslaught and what the long-term effects for the earth's fertility will be is anyone's guess. Might the food on our plate turn out to be causally linked with forces which, if allowed to continue, will threaten the very possibility of growing food in the future?

The mention of the future takes us a step beyond concerns we are likely to have about our own health. Barring a catastrophic nuclear war, we will not be the last generation on this earth; an indefinite number of future generations will come after us. The effects of those practices we allow at present, including the effects of pesticides in the food chain and the petrochemical industry's contamination of the air, are likely to be here after we are gone. "Dead" lakes are likely to be here, and so is drinking water that is hazardous to anyone's health. The underground sources of water, mentioned earlier, move beneath the surface of the earth at a snail's pace. Some of the water we drink from these sources to-day fell as rain over a hundred years ago, and today's rain, absorbed into underground aquifers, may not resurface until the twenty-second century. With the increase in acid rain attributable to human activities, including the power plants that produce the energy to fuel the petrochemical plants that produce the pesticides that are used to produce the food on our plate, and even ignoring, if we may, the many other sources of chemical contamination of the earth's water supplies, are we doing what we should with respect to generations yet unborn? Would we be doing it if, instead of relying on power from coal we rely instead on nuclear plants, given the serious problems *for them*, our descendants, posed by storing nuclear wastes? The food on our plate that we eat today—does it include a message from future persons, condemning us for a failure of moral will and vision to act now to protect the vital interests of generations yet to come?

Except for descendants of the Marquis de Sade, few people are likely to look with enthusiasm on pollution of any kind. It is, as some have said, a *public evils* problem: *public* because pollution travels and, in doing so, harms, or puts at risk of harm, people in general (the "public at large"); *evil* because the effects of pollution on those who are exposed are either actually or potentially harmful. Few of us, then, are likely to be in favor of pollution as such, since this is tantamount to harming, or putting at risk of harm, people in general (perhaps even ourself!). If we consider matters from a political point of view (not "political" in the sense of this or that actual political party, but theoretically—from, that is, the point of view of those who aspire to say what is *the best* political arrangement under which persons can live), how should we deal with this public evils problem? To choose among the options is a daunting challenge. Some political theories will allow a lot of pollution; some might disallow any at all; in between these two extremes are subtly differing conceptions of the ideal state and their respective policies regarding pollution. That there is pollution in America at all, and that the history of the food on our plate involves the use of pesticides and other chemicals that everyone must agree *can* pollute and that some claim *do* pollute, tells us something about the political arrangements under which we in fact live. Should we tolerate pollutants? Should we be less concerned than we are? Or should we restrict their presence, possibly to the extent of banning them altogether? When we think about the food we eat, can we rationally avoid asking these questions? And once they are asked, can we rationally refuse to expend the effort to answer them as best we can?

Unless we happen to be one of the estimated 20 to 25 million people who are practicing vegetarians in the United States, that food on our plate is likely to include meat. Part of the national wisdom about Americans being "the best fed people in the world" includes our access to flesh foods—chicken, steak, ham, ribs, burgers, hot dogs, and the like. Not a few critics of the farm animal industry have argued that, from the point of view of our individual health, we would be better off if we ate no or far less meat. A major part of the health risk, so these critics claim, again involves chemicals. Like other forms of contemporary agriculture, farm animal agriculture tends to be chemically intensive, only the food sources receiving the chemicals in this case are not carrots and wheat but are hogs and chickens, cows and turkeys. Raised in close confinement systems or what are called "factory farms," farm animals increasingly live indoors in dense populations or in cages or stalls. These animals are fed a veritable diet of chemicals from birth to death—growth stimulants, for example, and drugs to prevent or control the outbreak of contagious diseases. Residues of these chemicals collect and are stored in various tissues and organs in the animals' bodies. Some are toxic and again pose serious health questions when consumed by humans. Others, such as antibiotics, could lose their restorative properties for people who, in consuming animal flesh or products, also consume unsuspected quantities of these "wonder drugs." That meat on our plate—perhaps there is more to it than meets the eye?

A second question related to meat consumption involves waste and human needs. Meat and animal products, such as eggs, milk, and cheese, are sources of complete protein, a nutrient essential to human health. Vegetable sources of protein are incomplete, considered individually, but when combined in various ways (for example, peanut butter on whole wheat bread) yield complete protein. So while complete protein is essential to human health, meat and animal products are not. Moreover, with comparatively few exceptions (mainly small family farms) the farm animals raised for human consumption are themselves fed vegetable foodstuffs, such as corn and barley, that provide the same nutrients to them as they would to humans who ate them. The amount of protein provided by slaughtered animals, however, is often a good deal less than the amount of vegetable protein they consume. Beef cattle, according to one estimate, consume eight to nine pounds of vegetable protein to return one pound, while the conversion rate for hogs might be as high as four to five pounds consumed for each pound supplied. One critic of the animal industry, Francis Moore Lappé, has characterized this use of more protein to produce less as "a protein factory in reverse."[3] Lappé views the system as woefully wasteful. Many see it is a case of *our* wasting while millions of *others* want.

These "others" are the estimated 10,000 people who starve to death every day and the millions more who are chronically malnourished. Might we not make a more efficient, a more humane use of our vegetable food resources if, instead of using them to fuel a "protein factory in reverse," we distributed them to those who truly need them—whose need for nutritious food is literally a matter of life and death? There is, or so many critics of the politics of food distribution argue, more than enough food to feed the human population, not only now but into the indefinite future. Most of those whose needs are greatest, it is true, are unknown to us and live beyond our national borders; most are what are sometimes referred to as *distant strangers*. Still, if we can have obligations to persons across temporal boundaries (duties to future generations), might we not also have duties across spatial boundaries (duties to distant strangers)? Do we owe it to these people to make changes in our own life-style to help them have a realistic chance of a minimally decent human existence? In particular, should we make a decision on principle to refuse to support the farm animal industry because of its alleged ties to the tragedy of massive global hunger? Are we morally obligated, for these reasons, to cease putting meat on our plate? And if we are obligated to do that, how *large* a change in the American way of life should we be willing to make in order to fulfill our duties to distant strangers? Do our obligations to them begin and end with the food on our plate—if, indeed, they begin there?

A further question about the meat on our plate concerns the animals that are raised in factory farms. What sort of creatures are hogs and cows, chickens and turkeys? Few today would agree with the philosopher-mathematician René Descartes (1596–1650) in viewing them as "nature's machines," void of any semblance of conscious awareness. Most would agree that, like us, they experience pleasure and pain, are aware of their surroundings, and have needs and consciously felt preferences that are frustrated by the confined conditions in which they are forced to live. To frustrate the desires of a human being who has done no wrong and poses no threat so that others might benefit seems, on its face, to be wrong, and to do this to not one but hundreds of millions of individuals annually seems to point to a practice that, however much it might be supported by those who benefit from it or enjoy its fruits, is morally dubious. Yet this is what is done to literally hundreds of millions of farm animals every year. If we are seriously to address the ethical implications concerning the animals that end up on our plate, creatures who do not belong to our species but who share the earth with us, must we not ask about the treatment of those animals whose final resting place takes the form of a Kentucky Fried Chicken or a Big Mac? In eating the flesh of these animals, do we act above moral reproach? Is it possible that we might be violating their rights?

Moral questions about the treatment of animals are by no means restricted to farm or other domesticated varieties. Wild animals also fall within the scope of moral inquiry, a point given sharp focus by the concern many people have in preserving endangered species. That concern often is selective, with a few exotic, mysterious, or symbolic species favored over others (including many species of plants) that are equally endangered. For Americans, the bald eagle gets a resounding "yes!," the snail darter, a politically vociferous "no!" Whatever we might or should say about the selectivity of concern about endangered species, a variety of causes—including, not surprisingly, the chemical contamination of the air, water, and earth to which, as has been noted, the food on our plate is related—place a large number of species at risk. Another, perhaps subtler relationship between our food and endangered species involves the destruction of their natural habitat. One pattern of destruction repeats itself on a global scale. Cities and their populations grow, pushing ever farther out from the center. Former agricultural lands are converted to residential and other urban uses, and wild areas, formerly home to delicately balanced systems of life (ecosystems), are cleared or plowed under to make room for new farms only to have urban growth encroach on agricultural lands again, and so on, and so on. Wild species caught in the spiral of urban expansion are threatened. Some hang on. Others do not.

The pressures of urban growth, then, are a principal contributing cause of endangering species. If this were a case of one good thing winning out over another, we could rest content that a kind of cosmic justice prevails. But there are problems on both sides of the contest as so described. Most of us live in an urban environment—a city or town of one size or another, or the outskirts (the "burbs"). Quite apart from the impact of urban growth on endangered species, how big is too big? Is there, that is, a limit to the size of the urban environment beyond which it is no longer *good for us* to live there? If there is (and many critics of urban and suburban sprawl think so), then we cannot automatically assume that urban growth is "a good thing." Nor can we breezily dismiss questions about what in our urban environments is worth saving when, as we often must, we have to choose between preservation and redevelopment. If there is a limit to how much outward growth of our urban centers we should allow, there are also important questions about which, if any, of our urban landmarks and neighborhoods we should preserve.

The idea that the survival of a species is itself "a good thing" poses fundamental questions of its own. To a large extent the industrial, technological, and agricultural development that has led to and now underlies the variety of foods available to us has proceeded on the tacit assumption that *human interests* are the measure of all things valuable—at least things of the earth. "Anthropocentrism" is the name usually given to this vision of value. To consider seriously that the continued existence of a species is "a good thing" is to force ourselves to question the credentials of anthropocentrism. Is it possible that *species themselves* have a kind of value that is not reducible to the degree to which they serve human interests? Many would deny this. Value, they say, is to be fixed in economic terms, measured by the yardstick of human satisfaction as determined by what we would be willing to pay for that satisfaction. The value of a car, a house, a coat is set by how much we would be willing to pay for it or, if we already are the owner, by how much we would be willing to take in exchange. To speak of "the value of endangered species," then, in such a view, is a roundabout way of referring to how much we would be willing to pay to have them survive. To establish the amount we would be willing to pay might be difficult but, so proponents of an economic theory of value believe, not impossible. *Species as such* have no value, given an economic theory of value, but neither does anything else, neither truth, nor beauty, nor (noneconomic) goodness.

Many people, including many concerned to protect endangered species, reject economic theories of value. Even among those who are of one voice in rejecting such theories, however, serious and possibly divisive questions remain. In what can the (supposed) value of species as such consist, and how does the value of a species, assuming that it has one, correspond to or depart from the value of individual members, assuming that each member has some kind of (noneconomic) value? Or again, if species as such have value that is independent of human interests, including human economic interests, is it possible that we owe it to species themselves to protect them against human agents and forces which, if they were allowed to operate, would bring about the extinction of these species? If, for example, people in certain localities, responding to population pressures, are destroying the natural habitat of the last known representatives of an endangered species—ought we to halt this human encroachment, not in the name of human interests but for the sake of the value of species themselves? Ought we perhaps to do this *no matter what* the costs to the humans most directly involved, those who need new agricultural land to feed the new mouths which otherwise are likely to go hungry? To dismiss this question out of hand is to run the risk of accepting anthropocentrism uncritically.

The food on our plate is, one might say, a symbol of our predecessors' "conquest of nature," a conquest made possible by the widespread acceptance of anthropocentrism. That food, then, should remind us of our debts to them. But it should also occasion our critical curiosity as we assess the anthropocentric moral vision they have passed down to us. To do so, in its way, is to pay the finest tribute to our predecessors, since one ideal they bequeathed to us (one needs only to think of those true revolutionaries, America's Founding Fathers) *is* to be curious, to question the received opinions and common practices of the day. Those opinions and practices operative today are, metaphorically speaking, part of what we eat when we eat as we do. If we are what we eat, then divining the food on our plate does promise to tell us a good deal about what we are, as individuals and as a nation. And perhaps a good deal more about what we can and should be.

## §2  ENVIRONMENTAL ETHICS

To begin to identify some of the questions that form the larger economic, political, technological, medical, and historical background of the food we eat is just that—a beginning. Questions raised are not questions answered, and the questions raised in §1 could be drawn out from considering virtually any aspect of our daily life, not just our eating habits. Still, to have a sense of the range of questions that can arise when one reflects on something as mundane as the food on our plate—questions examined at length in the several essays comprising this volume, including in particular William Aiken's "Ethical Issues in Agriculture"—goes some way toward conveying a sense of the character and aspirations of moral philosophers. Moral philosophers are persons who take a special interest in thinking carefully about right and wrong, good and bad, justice and injustice, duty and obligation. When this interest is focused primarily on environmental concerns, whether it be pesticide use in agriculture or the call to save endangered species, the preservation of wilderness or alternative sources of energy, the questions being asked are properly classified as questions in environmental ethics. As is true of internal divisions in other disciplines, the division between environmental ethics and other areas in moral philosophy is not set in concrete. Questions about duties to future generations, for example, arise in medical and business ethics as well as in environmental ethics; so "the wall" separating environmental ethics from other areas in moral philosophy should be viewed as being like a porous membrane through which fundamental ideas, ideas such as the value of the individual and the proper role of government, respect for justice and the scope of obligation, freely pass. It is the perspective in which such ideas are viewed and the real-life settings to which they apply, rather than the presence of the ideas themselves, that mark an essay, a book, a lecture as belonging to environmental ethics.

Like others who seek to replace opinion with understanding, moral philosophers do not always agree on what is true. The contributors to this volume prove no exception. Some affirm that individuals have value but deny that species or ecosystems do, for example; others think *both* have value. Some argue that people have rights where others fail to see them. So we must not expect to find unanimity on all important questions in the pages that lie ahead. But despite the presence of some vital disagreements, the contributors to this volume agree about many essential matters; for example, they think there are some tempting, though mistaken or confused, ways to answer moral questions. Agreement at this level is important. Without it the present collection of essays would have as much organization as Joe, Curley, and Moe have when they try to enter a door at the same time. The remainder of this Introduction attempts to highlight some of the shared assumptions the contributors bring to their work, assumptions that more often than not go unstated. The hope is that by understanding what they do not say we might better understand what they do.

# I. META-ETHICS

## §3 CONCEPTUAL ANALYSIS

The first idea that requires attention is that of conceptual analysis. Philosophers frequently use the words "conceptual analysis" to refer to the activity of clarifying our concepts or ideas. Since we use words to express our concepts, the goal of conceptual analysis is to reach a clearer understanding of the meaning of words. Achieving such clarity is absolutely vital. If we do not have a clear understanding of the meanings of words, we will not have a clear understanding of our questions. And if we do not understand our questions, we will not understand what count as answers to them. This is especially true in the case of questions that ask whether something is morally right or wrong—for example, whether it is wrong to destroy an urban landmark to make room for a parking lot. If we do not understand what a landmark is, how can we even begin to consider questions about whether it would be wrong to destroy one?

One way to think about conceptual analysis is in terms of necessary and sufficient conditions. If $x$ is a necessary condition of $y$, then $y$ cannot be the case if $x$ is not the case; in other words, if not $x$, then not $y$. Being a plane closed figure, for example, is a necessary condition of something's being a triangle. A sufficient condition is different. If $a$ is a sufficient condition of $b$, then $b$ will be the case if $a$ is the case; that is, if $a$, then $b$. Being a plane closed figure with three sides or three interior angles, for example, is a sufficient condition of something's being a triangle.

A necessary condition may not be sufficient, and *vice versa*. For example, while being a plane closed figure is a necessary condition of something's being a triangle, it is not sufficient: There are many plane closed figures that are not triangles—e.g., rectangles. Again, that something is a Cadillac Seville is a sufficient condition of its being a car, but being a Cadillac Seville is not a necessary condition of being a car: There are many cars that are not Cadillac Sevilles.

The ideas of necessary and sufficient conditions relate to the activity of conceptual analysis in the following way. Conceptual analysis can be understood as the attempt to state the necessary and sufficient conditions of the correct use of a given concept. The aims of conceptual analysis, in this view, are thus (1) to state, so far as possible, those conditions which, if they are *not* satisfied, prevent the concept in question from being correctly applied—the necessary conditions of correct use—and (2) to state those conditions which, if they *are* satisfied, permit the concept to be correctly applied—the sufficient conditions of correct use. In this view of conceptual analysis, an analysis is itself correct to the extent that it states the necessary and sufficient conditions of correct use.

Now, sometimes it is not possible to give a complete set of necessary and sufficient conditions, and sometimes the conditions given cannot be very precise. For example, though a triangle must have no more nor less than three interior angles, how many hairs a person must be missing to be bald is far less precise. We should not expect all concepts to be analyzable with the precision that concepts in mathematics are. Some "defy analysis" in the sense that it is not possible to give a complete set of quite precise necessary and sufficient conditions. Even in the case of these concepts, however, one ought to strive to reach the highest degree of completeness and precision possible. The more complete and exact we can make our understanding of a given concept, the more likely it is that we will understand those questions in which the concept figures.

If we think about the concepts that occupy center stage in the essays in this volume—the value of species, animal rights, obligations to future

generations, and duties to distant strangers, for example—we can anticipate some problems for conceptual analysis. These concepts are not as
precise as "triangle," and it is not unusual to find spirited debates over
how they should be understood. Take "risk." Some people offer an
analysis of this concept that identifies risk with probability of fatality
and then they use what is known or claimed about risk to defend a controversial thesis (for example, that nuclear power plants should be accepted because the risk associated with having them is less than the risk
associated with, say, coal mining). But is this a credible analysis of
"risk"? And if it is not, what then becomes of arguments that rely on this
analysis? This and related questions about risk are explored at length by
Kristin Shrader-Frechette in her essay "Ethics and Energy." To turn such
questions over carefully, examining them on all sides, is not idle seman-
tic curiosity. Important moral questions (for example, should we encourage the development of nuclear power plants?) are bound up with
how we answer conceptual ones.

The arguments for and against competing analyses of the concept of
risk must await a reading of "Ethics and Energy." And similar remarks
apply to alternative analyses of other important concepts that figure
prominently in the other essays. In the essay "Troubled Waters: Global
Justice and Ocean Resources," for example, Robert Simon considers the
view that nations cannot act immorally because (1) only individuals can
do what is wrong, and (2) nations are not individuals. Being an individual, in this view, in other words, is a necessary condition of being an appropriate object of moral judgment. Simon rejects this analysis. Or consider the concept of interests. Some philosophers analyze this concept in
ways that imply that only actual or presently existing people have interests, an analysis that implies that we cannot meaningfully consider the
interests of future people. Annette Baier disputes this analysis in her contribution, "For the Sake of Future Generations." As these examples illustrate, philosophers, even when they do not agree on how given concepts
should be analyzed, do agree on the need to analyze them. The merits of
a variety of analyses certainly is one thing that will have to be considered
in all of the essays that lie ahead.

## §4 IS THERE A CORRECT METHOD FOR ANSWERING MORAL QUESTIONS?

The conceptual analysis of key moral concepts is one part of what is called
"meta-ethics." The other major component of meta-ethics is the inquiry
into the correct method for answering moral questions. Such a method
would function in the case of moral questions in ways that are analogous
to how the scientific method functions in the case of scientific questions.
This latter method does not itself contain answers to particular questions
(for example, about what happens to the pressure of a gas when the temperature is raised). Rather, the scientific method can be understood as
specifying how we must approach particular questions *if we are to give*

*scientific answers* to them; it defines, one might say, what it is to think about questions "from the scientific point of view." Well, if there is a correct method for answering moral questions, similar things would be true of it: It would not itself contain answers to particular moral questions (for example, whether wilderness *or* urban landmarks should be preserved only if it is economically profitable to do so, questions explored, respectively, by Mark Sagoff in "Ethics and Economics in Environmental Law" and Dale Jamieson in "The City Around Us"); rather, it would specify how we must approach questions, *if we are to give moral answers* to them—if, that is, we are to give answers "from the moral point of view."

Whether there even exists such a method, not surprisingly, is a very controversial question. Some philosophers think there is; others think not. And among those who think there is, some think it is one thing while others think it is something different.

It will not be possible to examine this controversy in all the detail it deserves. Instead a rough sketch will be given of some of the central issues. Two ideas in particular are important. First, there is the matter of how *not* to answer moral questions; this idea is explored in §5. Second, there is the idea of an ideal moral judgment; this is discussed in §6. The relevance of these ideas to the essays will be explained as we proceed.

## §5 SOME WAYS NOT TO ANSWER MORAL QUESTIONS

*Moral Judgments and Personal Preferences*   Some people like classical music; others do not. Some people think bourbon is just great; others detest its taste. Some people will go to a lot of trouble to spend an afternoon in the hot sun at the beach; others can think of nothing worse. In all these cases disagreement in preference exists. Someone likes something; someone else does not. Are moral disagreements, disagreements over whether something is morally right or wrong, good or bad, just or unjust, the same as disagreements in preference?

It does not appear so. For one thing, when a person (say, Jack) says he likes something, he is not denying what another person (Jill) says, if she says she does not like it. Suppose Jack says "I (Jack) like bourbon," and Jill says "I (Jill) do not like bourbon." Then clearly Jill does not deny what Jack says. To deny what Jack says, Jill would have to say "You (Jack) do not like bourbon," which is not what she says. So, in general, when two persons express different personal preferences, the one does not deny what the other affirms. It is perfectly possible for two opposing expressions of personal preference to be true at the same time.

When two people express conflicting judgments about the morality of something, however, the disagreement is importantly different. Suppose Jack says, "Pollution should be allowed if this is necessary to increase the rate of production and employment," while Jill says, "Pollution should not be allowed for these reasons." Then Jill *is* denying what Jack affirms; she is denying that pollution should be allowed for the reasons Jack gives so that, if what she said were true, what Jack said would

have to be false. Some philosophers have denied this. They have maintained that moral judgments should be understood as expressions of personal preferences. Though this view deserves to be mentioned with
respect, it is doubtful that it is correct. When people say that something
is morally right or wrong, it is always appropriate to ask them to give
reasons *to support* their judgment, reasons for accepting their judgment
as *correct*. In the case of personal preferences, however, such requests
are inappropriate. If Jack says he likes to go to the beach, it hardly seems
apt to press him to give reasons to support his judgment; indeed, it hardly
seems that he has made a *judgment* at all. If he says pollution is acceptable if it is necessary to increase production and employment, however,
a judgment has been expressed, and it is highly relevant to test Jack's
judgment by examining the reasons he gives for thinking what he does.

This difference between expressions of differing personal preference
and conflicting moral judgments points to one way not to answer moral
questions. Given that moral judgments are not just expressions of personal
preference, it follows that moral right and wrong cannot be determined
just by finding out about the personal preferences of some particular person—say, Jack. This is true even in the case of our own preferences. Our
personal preferences are certainly important, but we do not answer
moral questions just by saying what we like or dislike.

*Moral Judgments and Feelings* Closely connected with personal preferences are a person's feelings, and some philosophers have maintained
that words like "right" and "wrong" are devices we use merely to express
how we feel about something. In this view, when Barbie says that we
ought to protect wilderness areas from commercial development, what
she conveys is that she has certain positive feelings toward policies that
protect wilderness; whereas when Ken says that it is wrong to exclude
these areas from commercial development, what he expresses is that he
has feelings of disapproval about such protection. It is as if what Barbie
says is, "Wilderness protection—hooray!" while what Ken says is, "Wilderness protection—boo!"

This position encounters problems of the same kind as those raised in
the previous section. It is not appropriate to ask for support in the case of
mere expressions of feeling. True, if Ken is sincere, one can infer that he
has strong negative feelings toward wilderness protection. But his saying
that wilderness ought not to be protected from commercial development
does not appear to be simply a way of venting his feelings (or of eliciting
ours). As in the case of a person's preferences, so also in the case of a person's feelings: Neither by itself provides answers to moral questions.

*Why Thinking It So Does Not Make It So* The same is true about what
someone thinks. Quite aside from her feelings, Bonnie, if she is sincere,
does think that we who are well off ought to make sacrifices to help feed
the many starving people in the world if she says that we ought to do so.
Nevertheless, if her judgment is a *moral* judgment, what she means cannot be "I (Bonnie) think we who are well off ought to make sacrifices to

help feed the many starving people in the world." If it were, then she would not be affirming something that Clyde denies, when he says "We who are well off ought not to make such sacrifices." Each would merely be stating that each thinks something, and it is certainly possible for it *both* to be true that Bonnie thinks that we ought to make sacrifices for those who are starving *and*, at the same time, that Clyde thinks we ought not. So if Clyde is denying what Bonnie affirms, he cannot merely be stating that *he* thinks that we ought not to make sacrifices for these people. Thus, the fact that Clyde happens to think what he does is just as irrelevant to establishing whether we ought or ought not to make sacrifices to help those who are starving as are Ken's feelings about wilderness preservation. And the same is true concerning what *we* happen to think. Our thinking something right or wrong is not what makes it so.

*The Irrelevance of Statistics*    Someone might think that though what one person happens to think or feel about moral issues does not settle matters, what all or most people happen to think or feel does. A single individual is only one voice; what most or all people think or feel is a great deal more. There is strength in numbers. Thus, the correct method for answering questions about right and wrong is to find out what most or all people think or feel. Opinion polls should be conducted, statistics compiled. That will reveal the truth.

This approach to moral questions is deficient. All that opinion polls can reveal is what all or most people happen to think or feel about some moral question—for example, "Should the government subsidize research and development of solar energy technology?" What such polls cannot determine is whether what all or most people happen to think about such an issue is reasonable or true, *or* that what all or most people happen to feel is appropriate. There may be strength in numbers, but not truth, at least not necessarily. This does not mean that "what we think (or feel)" is irrelevant to answering moral questions. Later on, in fact (§8), we will see how, given that certain conditions have been met, "what we think" provides us with a possible place from which to begin the search for what makes acts right or wrong, as well as a possible test of the adequacy of competing theories of right and wrong. Nevertheless, *merely* to establish that all (or most) people happen to think that, say, solar sources of energy should be preferred to nuclear power plants, is not to establish that the former should be preferred. In times past, most (possibly even all) people thought the world was flat. And possibly most (or all) people felt pleased or relieved to think of the world as having this shape. But what they thought and felt did not make it true that the world is flat. The question of its shape wasn't answered merely by finding out what most people happened to think or feel. There is no reason to believe moral questions differ in this respect. Questions of right and wrong cannot be answered just by counting heads. As Tibor Machan argues in his essay ("Pollution and Political Theory"), that the majority happens to favor a given pollution policy is no guarantee of its morality.

*The Appeal to a Moral Authority*   Suppose it is conceded that we cannot answer moral questions just by finding out what Jack or Jill or Ken or Barbie happen to think or feel; or by finding out what all or most people happen to think or feel. After all, single individuals like Jack or Jill, or most or all people like them, might think or feel one way when they should think or feel differently. But suppose there is a person who never is mistaken when it comes to moral questions: If this person judges that something is morally right, it *is* morally right; if it is judged wrong, it *is* wrong. No mistakes are made. Let us call such a person a "moral authority." Might appealing to the judgments of a moral authority be the correct method for answering moral questions we seek?

Most people who think there is a moral authority think this authority is not an ordinary person but a god. This causes problems immediately. Whether there is a god (or gods) is a very controversial question, and to rest questions of right and wrong on what an alleged god says (or the gods say) is already to base morality on an intellectually unsettled foundation. The difficulties go deeper than this, however, since even if there is a god who is a moral authority very serious questions must arise concerning whether people always understand what this authority says about right and wrong. The difficulties that exist when Jews and Christians consult the Bible can be taken as illustrative. Problems of interpretation abound. Some who think that we were created to be vegetarians think they find evidence in the Bible that God thinks so too; others think they find evidence that He does not. Some who think that God allows us to exploit nature without regard to its values cite what they think are supporting chapters and verses; others cite other chapters and verses they think show that God does not allow this, or they cite the same passages and argue that they should be interpreted differently. The gravity of these and kindred problems of interpretation should not be underestimated. Even if there is a moral authority, and even if the God Jews and Christians worship should happen to be this authority, that would not make it a simple matter to find out what is right and wrong. The problem of finding out what God thinks on these matters would still remain, and would be especially acute in areas where the Bible offers very little, if any, direct guidance, a point Annette Baier makes regarding the lack of Biblical direction on the matter of obligations to future generations.

Problems of interpretation aside, it is clear that the correct method for answering moral questions cannot consist merely in discovering what some alleged moral authority says. Even if there is a moral authority, those who are not moral authorities can have no good reason for thinking that there is one unless the judgments of this supposed authority can be checked for their truth or reasonableness without relying on these judgments themselves *as grounds* for their truth or reasonableness, and it is not possible to do this unless what is true or reasonable regarding right and wrong can be known independently of what this supposed authority says. An example from another quarter might make this point clearer. A plumber proves his "authority as a plumber," not merely by what he says but by the quality of his work, which can be verified independently of what he says in any particular case. *After* we have come to know, on independent grounds, that a particular plumber's judgment is reliable, *then* we have reason to rely on his judgment in the future. The same is true of the authority of one's judgment in, say, science, economics, the law, and morality. One's "credentials" can be established in the case of moral judgment only if there are independent ways of testing moral judgment against what is known to be true or reasonable. Thus, since in the nature of the case there must be some independent way of knowing what judgments are true or reasonable in order to test for the authority of another's moral judgments, to appeal to this or that "moral authority" cannot itself be the method that we seek for answering moral questions.

## §6  THE IDEAL MORAL JUDGMENT

The ideas discussed in §5 are relevant to the essays in this volume because the authors never argue that something is right or wrong merely on the grounds of their personal preferences, or merely because they personally feel one way or another, or just because they think it right or wrong, or only because all or most people happen to feel or think a certain way, or because some alleged moral authority has said or revealed that something is right or wrong. It is important to realize the ways that these philosophers do not argue; and it is also important to understand some of the arguments that can be given against arguing in these ways. This is what has been briefly explained in §5. What now needs to be described is an approach to moral questions that is not open to the objections raised against the methods considered so far.

The approach described in what follows turns on how the following question is answered: "What requirements would someone have to meet to make an ideal moral judgment?" Considered ideally, that is, what are the conditions that anyone would have to satisfy to reach a moral judgment as free from fault and error as possible? Now, by its very nature, an *ideal* moral judgment is just that—an ideal. Perhaps no one ever has or ever will completely meet all the requirements set forth in the ideal. But that does not make it irrational to strive to come as close as possible to fulfilling it. If we can never quite get to the finish, we can still move some distance from the starting line.

There are at least six different ideas that must find a place in our description of the ideal moral judgment. A brief discussion of each follows.

*Conceptual Clarity*   This idea was mentioned earlier (§3). Its importance is obvious. If someone asserts that animals have rights that are violated when we destroy their natural habitat, for example, we cannot determine whether that statement is true or reasonable before we understand what is meant by a *right*, a matter Alastair Gunn, among others, explores in his contribution, "Preserving Rare Species." Similar remarks apply to other issues. The German medical doctor and missionary Albert

Schweitzer (1875–1965) is famous for his view that we should practice "reverence for all life." Should we? Who can reasonably say without first taking the time to ask what "reverence for life" means, a question Edward Johnson examines in his essay, "Treating the Dirt: Environmental Ethics and Moral Theory." Clarity by itself may not be enough, but rational thought cannot get far without it.

*Information*    We cannot answer moral questions in our closets. Moral questions arise in the real world, and a knowledge of the real world settings in which they arise is essential if we are seriously to seek rational answers to them. For example, in the debate over alternative agricultural practices, some people claim that productivity is increased by relying on extensive use of monocultural planting (that is, planting the same crop on the same acreage year after year). Is this true? Is this a fact? In his essay "Ethical Issues in Agriculture" William Aiken reminds us that we have to come out of our closets to answer this (or to find the answer others have tried to reach on the basis of their research); and answer it we must if we are to reach an informed judgment about the ethical dimensions of alternative agricultural practices. The importance of getting the facts, of being informed, is not restricted just to this case, by any means. It applies all across the broad sweep of moral inquiry.

*Rationality*    Rationality is a multifaceted concept. The one aspect that concerns us here is when rationality is understood as the ability to recognize the connection between different ideas—the ability to recognize, that is, that if some statements are true, then some other statements must be true while others must be false. Now, it is in logic that rules are set forth that specify when statements follow from others, and it is because of this that a person who is rational often is said to be logical. When we speak of the need to be rational, then, we are saying that we need to observe the rules of logic. To reach an ideal moral judgment, therefore, we must not only strive to make our judgment against a background of information and conceptual clarity; we must also take care to explore how our beliefs are logically related to other things that we do or do not believe. For example, imagine that Ozzie thinks it is not wrong to expose people to risks if they voluntarily decide to run them; and suppose that his wife, Harriet, recently has taken a job at a nuclear plant that exposes her to risks she would otherwise not run. Then Ozzie is not being rational or logical if he claims that it is wrong for the company to expose Harriet to these risks. Rationally he *cannot* believe this while believing the other things we assume he believes. Logically, it is *impossible* for both the following statements to be true: (1) it is not wrong to expose people to risks if they voluntarily decide to run them, and (2) it is wrong of her company to expose Harriet to risks she has voluntarily decided to run. Whenever someone is committed to a belief or group of beliefs that cannot possibly all be true at the same time, that person is said to be committed to a *contradiction*. Ozzie, then, is committed to a contradiction. To fall short of the ideal moral judgment by committing oneself to a contradiction is to fall as short as one possibly can.

*Impartiality*   Partiality involves favoring someone or something above others. For example, if a father is partial to one of his children, then he will be inclined to give the favored child more than he gives his other children. In some cases, partiality is a fine thing; but a partiality that excludes even thinking about or taking notice of others is far from what is needed in an ideal moral judgment. The fact that someone has been harmed, for example, always seems to be a relevant consideration, whether this someone is favored by us or not. In striving to reach the correct answers to moral questions, therefore, we must strive to guard against extreme, unquestioned partiality; otherwise we shall run the risk of having our judgment clouded by bigotry and prejudice.

The idea of impartiality is at the heart of what is sometimes referred to as the formal principle of justice: Justice is the similar, and injustice the dissimilar, treatment of similar cases. This principle is said to express the *formal* principle of justice because by itself it does not specify what factors are relevant for determining what makes cases similar or dissimilar. To decide this, one must supplement the formal principle of justice with a substantive or normative interpretation of justice. More will be said on this matter (§10). Even at this juncture, however, we can recognize the rich potential the formal principle of justice can have in arguments about moral right and wrong. Were we to approve of practices that cause unnecessary suffering to farm animals while denouncing such practices when those who suffer are human beings it would be apposite to ask why the two cases are judged dissimilar. For they must be dissimilar if, as we are assuming, dissimilar treatment is allowed. If, in reply to our question, we were told that the difference is that human beings belong to one species while farm animals belong to others, it would again be apposite to ask how this difference in species membership *can* make any moral difference to the morality of the treatment in the two cases. To sanction practices that cause unnecessary suffering to farm animals while disapproving of similar practices in the case of humans because of species membership seems to be a symptom of unjustified partiality (what some call speciesism), a point made by a number of the contributors to this volume. While the formal principle of justice does not by itself tell us what are the relevant factors for determining when treatment is similar or dissimilar, that principle must be observed if we are to make the ideal moral judgment. Not to observe it is a symptom of prejudice or bias, rational defects that must be identified and overcome if we are to make the best moral judgment we can.

*Coolness*   All of us know what it is like to do something in the heat of anger that we later regret. No doubt we have also had the experience of getting so excited that we do something that later on we wish we had not done. Emotions are powerful forces, and though life would be a dull wasteland without them we need to appreciate that the more volatile among them can mislead us; strong emotion is not a reliable guide to doing (or judging) what is best. This brings us to the need to be "cool." "Being cool" here means "not being in an emotionally excited state, being in an emotionally calm state of mind." The idea is that the hotter (the more emotionally charged) we are, the more likely we are to reach a mistaken moral conclusion, while the cooler (the calmer) we are, the greater the chances that we will avoid making mistakes.

This position is borne out by common experience. People who are in a terribly excited state may not be able to retain their rationality; because of their deep emotional involvement, they may not be able to attain impartiality; and when they are in an excited, emotional state, they may not even care about what happened or why. Like the proverb about shooting first and asking questions later, a lack of coolness can easily lead people to judge first and ask about the facts afterward. The need to be "cool," then, seems to merit a place on our list.

*Valid Moral Principles*  The concept of a moral principle has been analyzed in different ways. At least this much seems clear, however: For a principle to qualify as a *moral* principle (as distinct from, say, a scientific or a legal principle), it must prescribe conduct for all moral agents. Moral agents are those who can bring impartial reasons (i.e., reasons that respect the requirement of impartiality) to bear on deciding how they ought to act. They are thus conceived to be both rational and autonomous. Individuals who lack the ability to understand or act on the basis of impartial reasons (e.g., young children) fail to qualify as moral agents. They cannot meaningfully be said to have obligations to do, or to refrain from doing, what is morally right or wrong. Only moral agents can have this status, and moral principles can apply only to the determination of how moral agents should behave. Normal adult human beings are the paradigmatic instance of moral agents.

How does the idea of a valid moral principle relate to the concept of an ideal moral judgment? In an ideal moral judgment, it is not enough that the judgment be based on complete information, complete impartiality, complete conceptual clarity, and so on. It is also essential that the judgment be based on a *valid* or *correct* moral principle. Ideally, one wants not only to make the correct judgment but to make it for the correct reason. The idea of correct moral principles will be discussed more fully below in Part II, Normative Ethics.

## §7 NO DOUBLE STANDARDS ALLOWED

The portrait of the ideal moral judgment drawn in §6, or something very like it, forms the background of the several essays in this anthology. The authors do not always explicitly say that, for example, impartiality or rationality are ideals worth striving for; but the manner in which they argue makes it clear that these ideals play an important role in their examinations of the views of others. Accordingly, these philosophers imply that it would be fair to apply these same ideals to their own thinking. In the case of each essay, therefore, we can ask:

1. Have important concepts been analyzed, and, if so, have they been analyzed correctly?
2. Does the author argue from a basis of knowledge of the real-life setting(s) in which a moral question arises?
3. Is the author rational? (Do the arguments presented observe the rules of logic?)
4. Is there a lack of impartiality? (Is someone, or some group, arbitrarily favored over others?)
5. Are things argued for in a state of strong emotion? (Are deep feelings rhetorically vented in the place of hard thinking?)
6. Are the moral principles used valid ones? (Is any effort expended to show that they meet the appropriate criteria?)

These six questions, then, though they do not exhaust all possibilities, at least provide a place to begin. It is pertinent to ask how our authors pose these questions of the persons whose views they examine. But fairness requires that these same questions be asked of each author's views too. No double standards are allowed.

## II. NORMATIVE ETHICS

Earlier, meta-ethics was characterized as the inquiry into the meaning of key concepts (for example, risk and rights) as well as the inquiry into whether there is a correct method for answering moral questions. Meta-ethical questions, however, by no means exhaust a moral philosopher's interest in ethics. A second main area of inquiry is commonly referred to as *normative ethics*. Philosophers engaged in normative ethics attempt to go beyond the questions concerning meaning and method that arise in meta-ethics; the goal they set themselves is nothing short of determining *what moral principles are valid*—those principles, that is, by which all moral agents ought morally to be guided. There is, then, an important connection between the goal of normative ethics and the concept of an ideal moral judgment. An ideal moral judgment, we have said, must be based on valid moral principles, and it is just the question, "What principles *are* the valid ones?" that is at the heart of normative ethics. Unless the normative ethical philosopher succeeds in disclosing what moral principles are valid, therefore, a vital part of the ideal moral judgment will be unfulfillable because unknown.

Which moral principals *are* valid? Not surprisingly, a variety of answers have been offered. Not all of them can be considered here, and no one can be considered in much detail. But enough can be said to make important ideas intelligible.

## §8 CONSEQUENTIALIST THEORIES

One way to begin the search for the valid moral principle(s) is to begin with our considered beliefs (also referred to by some as our "reflective intuitions"). These beliefs or intuitions are not to be identified with what we just happen to believe independent of our critical reflection; rather, our considered beliefs are those beliefs we have about right and wrong, good and bad, justice and injustice *after* we have made a conscientious effort to think about these beliefs with an eye to four of the five requirements of the ideal moral judgment explained in §6. Such beliefs are considered beliefs or reflective intuitions, in other words, only if we have made our best effort to think about them with maximal conceptual clarity, coolly and impartially, and against the backdrop of the ideal of complete information. Those moral beliefs we continue to hold or come to hold *after* we have thought about them in these terms are our considered beliefs, and it is at least in part by appeal to such beliefs, or so many moral philosophers think, that normative moral philosophy can get under way and against which its possible success can be fairly tested. Not all moral philosophers, it is true, possibly not even all those who have contributed to this volume, are in agreement on this fundamental methodological point. But let us see how this point of agreement in theory, where it obtains, might work in practice.

Suppose we could reach agreement about a body of considered beliefs; then we would believe, on reflection, that certain acts are right or wrong, just or unjust, and the like. Assuming this much we could then ask how this body of beliefs could be unified; we could ask, in other words, what general moral principle(s) unify these intuitions by identifying their plausible common ground. By way of example, suppose George and Gracie each operate farms and sell their produce at roadside stands. George's business has suffered of late because of the recent competition offered by Gracie's new stand, and he decides to eliminate the competition by hiring a professional arsonist with whom he has had dealings in the past. Fire inspectors rule that the fire that gutted Gracie's house was due to faulty wiring, George's business regains its former vitality, and Gracie, who barely had enough money to start her enterprise and had no insurance, is left in a state of abject poverty. Suppose we judge that what George did was wrong, and suppose we make this judgment not only initially but after we have made a conscientious effort to think about the case coolly, impartially, and so on. What could plausibly illuminate the wrongness of George's act? Well, Gracie experiences some unhappiness certainly. When she thinks about her former business she is distraught and frustrated, and the enjoyment she would have had, if the business had continued to grow, is cancelled. Gracie, then, is worse off than she would have been, both in terms of the unhappiness of her present condition and in terms of lost enjoyment. Thinking along these lines has led some philosophers to theorize that what makes George's (and the arsonist's) act wrong is that it is the cause of bad results, in this case the frustration, anger, disappointment, and general unhappiness caused Gracie.

Next imagine this case. Suppose people accepted a general rule whose observance gave unequal protection to male and female employees. This rule (R) requires that men be given protective clothing while in the presence of chemical toxins while denying such protection to female workers. Such a rule must strike us as radically unjust. But why? Well, imagine how women are likely to feel in such circumstances. It is not implausible to suppose that they will feel angry, resentful, and envious. These feelings (anger, resentment, envy) are not desirable. Moreover, because they are made more vulnerable to environmental dangers in the workplace, women employees are more likely to suffer from debilitating conditions, the results of which also are not good for them. As in the earlier example of George and Gracie, then, we again have a situation where (1) we would judge, on reflection, that something is wrong, and (2) what we judge to be wrong causes bad results.

Many philosophers have not stopped with just these sorts of cases. Roughly speaking, the one common and peculiar characteristic of every wrong action, they have theorized, is that it leads to bad results, whereas the one common and peculiar characteristic of every right action, again roughly speaking, is that it leads to good results. Philosophers who accept this type of view commonly are referred to as *consequentialists*, an appropriate name given their strong emphasis on results or consequences. Theories of this type also are called *teleological theories*, from the Greek *telos*, meaning "end" or "purpose," another fitting name since, according to these thinkers, actions are not right or wrong in themselves; they are right or wrong, according to these theories, if they promote or frustrate the purpose of morality—namely, to bring about the greatest possible balance of good over evil consequences. Acts are, as it were, arrows we shoot: Right acts hit the target (that is, cause the best results); wrong acts do not.

Now, in normative ethics, when someone advances a principle that states what makes all right acts right and all wrong acts wrong, they do so in the course of advancing a *normative ethical theory*. Considered abstractly, there are at least three different types of teleological normative ethical theories.

1. *Ethical egoism*: According to this theory, roughly speaking, whether any person (A) has done what is morally right or wrong depends solely on how good or bad the consequences of A's action are *for* A. How *others* are affected is irrelevant, unless how they are affected in turn alters the consequences for A.
2. *Ethical altruism*: According to this theory, roughly speaking, whether any person (B) has done what is morally right or wrong depends solely on how good or bad the consequences of B's action are *for everyone except* B. How B is affected is irrelevant, unless how B is affected in turn alters the consequences for anyone else.
3. *Utilitarianism*: According to this theory, roughly speaking, whether any person (C) has done what is morally right or

wrong depends solely on how good or bad the consequences of C's action are *for everyone affected*. Thus, how C is affected is relevant; but so is how *others* are affected. How *everyone* concerned is affected by the good or bad consequences is relevant.

These are not very exact statements of these three types of teleological normative ethical theories, but enough has been said about two of them—namely, ethical egoism and ethical altruism—to enable us to understand why most philosophers find them unsatisfactory. Both seem to fall far short of the ideal of impartiality, ethical egoism because it seems to place arbitrary and exclusive importance on the good or welfare of the individual agent, and ethical altruism because it seems to place arbitrary and exclusive importance on the good or welfare of everyone else. Moreover, both theories arguably lead to consequences that clash with a broad range of reflective intuitions. This is perhaps clearest in the case of ethical egoism. Provided only that, all considered, torching Gracie's house led to consequences that were as good *for George* as any that would have resulted had he acted otherwise, what he did was not morally wrong, according to ethical egoism. But that is something we would most likely deny, not only in a case involving arson but in many other sorts of cases (e.g., murder or rape, which also would not be wrong if the consequences *for the agent* were at least as good as those that would have resulted if the agent had acted otherwise). Faced with the choice between accepting ethical egoism or giving up a large class of considered beliefs, most philosophers choose to reject the theory and retain the convictions.

It is utilitarianism, then, that seems to represent the strongest possible type of teleological theory. Certainly it is the one that has attracted the most adherents; not unexpectedly, therefore, it is the one that figures most prominently in the essays in this volume. It will be worth our while, therefore, to examine it at slightly greater length.

## §9 UTILITARIANISM

"The Principle of Utility" is the name given to the fundamental principle advocated by those who are called utilitarians. This principle has been formulated in different ways. Here is a common formulation.

> Acts are right if they bring about the greatest possible balance of intrinsic good over intrinsic evil for everyone concerned; otherwise they are wrong.

Already it must be emphasized that utilitarians do not agree on everything. In particular, they do not all agree on what is intrinsically good and evil. Some philosophers (called *value hedonists*) think that pleasure and pleasure alone is intrinsically good (or good in itself), whereas pain, or the absence of pleasure, and this alone, is intrinsically evil (or evil in itself). Others (so-called preference utilitarians) believe that the satisfac-

tion of one's desires or preferences is what is good and their frustration
bad. The classical utilitarians—Jeremy Bentham (1748–1832) and John
Stuart Mill (1806–1873)—favor hedonistic utilitarianism. Most recent
utilitarians, especially those who seek to apply economic theory to
ethical issues, favor preference utilitarianism. Whether either of these
views regarding intrinsic value is adequate is a question we can bypass at
this juncture, since the ideas of special importance for our present purposes can be discussed independently of whether value hedonism, for example, is a reasonable position.

*Act- and Rule-Utilitarianism*   One idea of special importance is the difference   between   act-utilitarianism   and   rule-utilitarianism.   *Act-
utilitarianism* is the view that the Principle of Utility should be applied
to individual actions; *rule-utilitarianism* states that the Principle of Utility should be applied mainly to rules of action. The act-utilitarian says
that whenever people have to decide what to do, they ought to perform
that act which will bring about the greatest possible balance of intrinsic
good over intrinsic evil. The rule-utilitarian says something different:
People are to do what is required by justified moral rules. These are
rules, some rule-utilitarians maintain, that would lead to the best possible consequences, all considered, *if* everyone were to abide by them. The
rules recognized as valid by these rule-utilitarians, in other words, need
not be rules that most people *do* accept and act on—what we might call
conventional morality. Rules recognized as valid are those everyone
*should* act on because everyone's doing so would lead to the best results.
If a justified rule unambiguously applies to a situation, and if no other
justified moral rule applies, then the person in that situation ought to
choose to do what the rule requires, even if in that particular situation
performing this act will not lead to the best consequences. Thus, act-
utilitarians and rule-utilitarians can reach opposing moral judgments.
An act that is wrong according to the rule-utilitarian, because it is contrary to a justified moral rule, might not be wrong according to the act-
utilitarian's position.

*Some Problems for Act-Utilitarianism*   Is act-utilitarianism correct?
Many philosophers answer no. One reason given against this theory is
that act-utilitarianism clashes with a broad range of our considered
beliefs. Recall the arson example. According to act-utilitarianism,
whether George's hiring of the arsonist was wrong or not depends on this
and this alone: Were the net consequences for everyone affected by the
outcome at least as good as the net consequences that would have resulted if he had done anything else? It is not *just* the bad results Gracie
has to live with (her frustration, anger, and the like) that are relevant.
How *others* are affected also is relevant, given act-utilitarianism, and
there is no reason why, just because Gracie is made worse off than she
would have been as a result of George's decision, *the sum or total* of the
good and bad consequences for everyone involved might not "hit" the
utilitarian target. The benefits George derives from eliminating Gracie's

competition, the income the arsonist earns, and the possible pleasures and satisfactions others derive (for example, perhaps George's son can now go to college and the arsonist's wife can have her teeth capped) — these pleasures and satisfactions, too, not just Gracie's misery, have to be taken into account. In principle, then, there is no reason why the consequences, all considered, might not add up to the best balance of good over evil, or at least equal a balance that is as good as any other that would have resulted if George had acted otherwise.

Suppose the consequences are at least as good as any that would have obtained had George acted otherwise. Then act-utilitarianism implies that what he did was right. And yet his involvement in the destruction of Gracie's business is likely to strike us as wrong. Thus, we again seem to be faced with a choice between (1) retaining a considered belief or (2) accepting a particular normative ethical theory. And the same choice would recur in a host of other cases involving our reflective intuitions (e.g., intuitions about the wrongness of murder and rape, individual cases of which arguably could lead to the best balance of good results over bad, when the good and bad for the involved individuals are totaled). There are, that is, *many* sorts of cases where the implications of act-utilitarianism are or seem to be in conflict with our considered beliefs. In the face of such conflicts, many come down on the side of retaining our convictions and rejecting the theory.

Act-utilitarians actively defend their position against this line of criticism. The debate is among the liveliest and most important in normative ethics. The point that bears emphasis here is that *rule*-utilitarians do not believe that *their* version of utilitarianism can be refuted by the preceding argument. This is because they maintain that what George did was wrong because it violated a valid moral rule—the rule against destroying another's property. Thus, the rule-utilitarian holds that his position not only does not lead to a conclusion that clashes with the conviction that what George did was wrong; this position actually illuminates *why* it was—namely, because it violates a rule whose adoption by everyone can be defended by an appeal to the Principle of Utility.

*Some Problems for Rule-Utilitarians*   One success does not guarantee that all goes well, however, and many philosophers think that rule-utilitarianism, too, is inadequate. One of the most important objections turns on considerations about justice. The point of the objection is that rule-utilitarianism arguably could justify the adoption of rules that would be grossly unjust. To make this clearer, recall the rule that figured in our earlier example about employment: Men are to receive protective clothing while in the workplace but women are not. The injustice of this rule (R) jumps out at us. It is unjust to discriminate against people in the workplace in the way R requires. And yet might not this rule be justified by appeal to rule-utilitarianism? Certainly it seems possible that, when the good and bad consequences for each affected individual are taken into account and totaled, we might find that adopting R would bring about the best balance of good over bad results. Granted, the envy, resentment, and anger of the female employees must be taken into account. But so, too, must the benefits that males secure. So, *on balance*, the "minuses" for women might be more than offset by the "pluses" for men, especially if there are very few female workers, most of whom are married to men who earn an income adequate to support their dependents. If, then, rule-utilitarianism could sanction unjust rules, not only in employment but across the broad sweep of social policies (for example, in education, voting, and health care, where some might be denied benefits offered to others in the name of "the general welfare")—if this is true, then rule-utilitarianism is not the adequate ethical theory its proponents suppose.

Can rule-utilitarians defend their position against this line of attack? Philosophers are not unanimous in their answer. As was the true of the debate over the soundness of act-utilitarianism, this debate is too extensive to be examined further here. Nevertheless, enough has been said to suggest the importance of utilitarianism, an importance confirmed when we note that, though none of the philosophers in this volume *explicitly* endorses utilitarianism, that theory makes an appearance in each of the essays. In view of the historical and contemporary importance of utilitarian theory, and in light of the frequency with which it is discussed in the present collection, we are forearmed if we take the following set of questions to each of the essays.

1. Is the philosopher being read a utilitarian?
2. If so, of what kind—act or rule?
3. If the philosopher is a utilitarian, are persuasive arguments adduced in support of the utilitarian answers given?
4. Is the possible clash between justice and utility examined?
5. If the philosopher being read is not a utilitarian, what arguments, if any, are given against the validity of the principle of utility and how rationally compelling are these arguments?
6. If the philosopher is not a utilitarian, what other principle (or principles) is (or are) subscribed to?
7. How rationally compelling are the arguments, if any, that are given in support of the principle(s)?

## §10 NONCONSEQUENTIALISM

"Nonconsequentialism" is a name frequently given to normative ethical theories that are not forms of consequentialism. In other words, any theory that states that moral right and wrong are *not* determined *solely* by the relative balance of intrinsic good over intrinsic evil consequences commonly is called a nonconsequentialist theory. Theories of this type are also called *deontological* theories, from the Greek *deon*, meaning "duty." Such theories might be either (1) extreme or (2) moderate. An extreme deontological theory holds that the intrinsic good and evil of consequences are *totally irrelevant* to determining what is morally right or wrong. A moderate nonconsequentialist theory holds that the intrinsic good and evil of consequences *are relevant* to determining what is morally right and wrong but that they are not the *only* things that are relevant and may not be of the greatest importance in some cases. A great variety of nonconsequentialist theories, both extreme and moderate, have been advanced. Why have some philosophers been attracted to such theories?

*The Problem of Justice* A central argument advanced against all forms of consequentialism by many nonconsequentialists is that no consequentialist theory (no form of ethical egoism, ethical altruism, or utilitarianism) can account for basic convictions about justice and injustice—for example, that it is unjust to allow policies that discriminate against people on the basis of race or sex. The point these deontologists make is that such discrimination not only is wrong; it wrongs the people who are discriminated against. Fundamentally, according to these thinkers, it is because people are wronged when treated unjustly, quite apart from the value of the consequences for the victim or others, that all consequentialist theories ultimately prove to be deficient.

Suppose these deontologists are correct—a large assumption! Some deontological theory would then be called for. A number of such theories have been advanced. The one associated with the German philosopher Immanuel Kant (1724–1804) is unquestionably the most influential. In Kant's view, all persons (that is, all rational, autonomous individuals) have a distinctive kind of value, a unique worth or dignity. The value these people have, Kant may be interpreted to believe, is not reducible to the value of their mental states (e.g., their pleasure) and is, in fact, incommensurate with this latter kind of value; one cannot meaningfully ask how much pleasure the value of an individual is equal to. That would be like trying to compare apples and oranges. Moreover, the worth of a person is not reducible to that individual's talents (for example, at sports or music), nor to that individual's utility or service to others (a surgeon has neither more nor less worth than a dishwasher, a saint neither more nor less than a used car salesman), nor to how others relate to that individual (the loved and admired are neither more nor less valuable than the despised and forsaken). All who have worth or value as individuals, in short, have this value equally. Now, in order to treat such individuals as morality requires, we must never treat them in ways that fail to show proper respect for their unique value. Yet this is precisely what we would be guilty of if, in an effort to justify treating some people in a given way, we claimed that doing so gave rise to the best aggregate balance of pleasure over pain, or preference satisfactions over frustrations, for all affected by the outcome. For Kant, this is tantamount to ignoring the distinctive kind of value people have as individuals; it is to treat them as *mere means* to promote the ends others have, not as ends in themselves. Any and all such disrespectful treatment is wrong, for Kant, whatever the consequences.

This Kantian approach to moral questions offers a strikingly different interpretation of equality than the one offered by utilitarians. For Kant, it is *individuals* who are equal in value, whereas, for utilitarians, what is equal in value are similar pleasures or preference satisfactions. Moreover, Kant's position provides a very different way to approach questions of just treatment, something we can illustrate by recalling the rule (R): Men are to receive protective clothing while on the job but women are not. As was suggested earlier (§9), a utilitarian justification of adopting R is at hand *if* observing R would produce the best aggregate balance of good over bad for all those affected by the outcome, assuming that the preferences or pleasures of all have been considered and weighted equitably. The fact that, if this rule were adopted, women employees would run a greater risk of ill health than would men *by itself* is no objection to adopting it, given utilitarian theory. What each person is due is equal consideration and weighting of their pleasures or preferences, and as that is what each gets in this case there should be no cry of injustice.

Kant would be of a different mind. The very approach to R's justification prescribed by utilitarians is morally flawed from the word go. What all people are due is respect for their value *as individuals*, something we would fail to show if we attempted to decide the morality of acts or rules by asking which among them causes the best aggregate balance of good over bad (e.g., pleasure over pain) for all affected by the outcome. If, then, the justification of R is that its adoption "would promote the general welfare," those who follow Kant would descry its adoption. Conduct prescribed by the rule in question is wrong because it treats women with something less than the respect they are due, treating them *as if their value* as individuals can be ignored if doing so would bring about the best consequences.

## §11 LEGAL AND MORAL RIGHTS

Philosophers sympathetic with Kant can use his views concerning the unique value of the individual as a foundation on which to rest their positions about the rights of the individual. To make this clearer, it will be useful first to explain some of the differences between the concept of legal and moral rights.

First, moral rights, if there are any, are *universal*, while legal rights need not be. Legal rights depend upon the law of this or that country, and what is a matter of legal right in one country may not be so in another. For example, in the United States any citizen eighteen years old or older has the legal right to vote in federal elections; but not everyone in every nation has this same legal right. If, however, persons living in the United States have a moral right to, say, life, then *every* person in every nation has this same moral right, whether or not it is also recognized as a legal right.

Second, unlike legal rights, moral rights are *equal* rights. If all persons have a moral right to life, then all have this right equally; it is not a right that some (for example, males) can possess to a greater extent than others (for example, females). Neither, then, could this moral right be possessed to a greater extent by the inhabitants of one country (for example, one's own) than by the inhabitants of some other country (for example, a country poor in agricultural resources with a burgeoning human population and widespread famine).

Third, moral rights often are said to be *inalienable*, meaning they cannot be transferred to another—for example, they cannot be lent or sold. If Frankie has a moral right to life, then it is hers and it cannot become anyone else's. Frankie may give her life for her country, sacrifice it in the name of science, or destroy it herself in a fit of rage or despair. But she cannot give, sacrifice, or destroy her right to life. Legal rights, on the other hand, are paradigmatically transferable, as when Frankie transfers her legal right to an inheritance to Johnnie or gives him her car.

Fourth, moral rights are sometimes said to be "natural" rights, not in the sense that they are discoverable by closely studying nature from the scientific point of view, but in the sense that they are not conventional —are not, that is, as are legal rights, created by the acts of ordinary human beings.

Kant's view of the unique worth of persons dovetails with these four characteristics of the concept of a moral right. (1) All persons have unique worth (that is, this value is *universal* among persons); (2) no one person has this value *to any greater degree* than any other (that is, all who have this value have it *equally*); (3) those who have this unique value *cannot transfer* it to anyone else, or buy or sell it (that is, this unique value is *inalienable*); and, finally, (4) the value or dignity persons possess is theirs *independently of the acts or decisions of anyone else* (is, that is, "natural," in the sense explained). Small wonder, then, that those philosophers enamored of the view that individuals have moral rights should find a strong ally in Kant's views about the value of the individual.

## §12 LEGAL AND MORAL JUSTICE

Moral and legal rights are connected in important ways with moral and legal justice. Legal justice requires that one respect the legal rights of everyone, while moral justice demands that everyone's moral rights be honored. The two—legal justice and moral justice—do not necessarily coincide. Critics of "the law" frequently claim that certain laws are morally unjust. For example, a country might have a law that allows companies owned by whites to pollute but not those owned by blacks. Then *legal* justice might be done in this country if this law is enforced. If people have moral rights, however, it would not follow that moral justice is done. That would depend not on whether there is a particular law in this country, but on whether the law recognizes and protects the moral rights of the country's inhabitants. If it does, then the law is both legally and morally just; if it does not, then, though the law may be legally just, it lacks moral justice. Thus, this law in particular and "the law" in general are appropriate objects of moral assessment, a theme that characterizes a number of this volume's essays, including, for example, "Ethics and Economics in Environmental Law," by Mark Sagoff.

## §13 NEGATIVE AND POSITIVE RIGHTS

Even were we to agree that people themselves have a unique sort of value and moral rights grounded in this value, we might still disagree on what rights they have. One of the major sources of disagreement in this regard concerns what some call "welfare rights." Though the terminology frequently differs, philosophers who defend the validity of moral rights all seem to agree that some of these rights are *liberty rights*; in many cases, that is, to have a right is simply *to be at liberty* to act as one chooses (for example, to go to a concert, or to stay at home). Other rights are *claim rights*; those who have such rights *have a valid claim to be treated in certain ways* (for example, not to be injured, or have lies spread about them, or be killed). Both sorts of rights have correlative duties. If Eleanor is at liberty to have the chocolate cake rather than the strawberry yogurt, then Franklin has a duty not to deny her the exercise of her liberty when she makes her choice, something he would be doing if he coerced or forced her to choose as *he* wished. If, in addition, Eleanor has a right to life, then Franklin has a duty not to kill her except, perhaps, in quite exceptional circumstances (e.g., in self-defense).

Now, both those duties correlated with liberty rights and those correlated with claim rights are *negative duties*. They prescribe what people *are not to do*, how they *are not to act*, given that others have such rights. As such, it seems that we can fulfill these duties by doing nothing. If, that is, Franklin does not personally kill Eleanor, then he seems to do all that is required to respect her right to life, while if he does not personally interfere with the exercise of her liberty, then he seems to do all he is obliged to do to respect her right to liberty. The duties correlated with *welfare rights*, however, if there are such rights, differ fundamentally. If people have welfare rights, we have *a duty to help them*, not merely a duty not to harm them or not to interfere with their liberty. And the performance of this duty to help, if this duty is correlated with welfare *rights*, is something that we *owe* to those who need it, is something *they deserve*, and so is their due as a matter of moral justice.

Two examples will help make the importance of welfare rights clearer. The first concerns mining the deep sea bed, a matter mentioned earlier. Third World nations lack the technological and economic base to push forward in this enterprise. If the only rights people have are negative rights, then those nations who have the capacities to mine the deep sea bed, or individual corporations operating within the jurisdiction of such nations, do *not* owe any of the benefits secured from their mining operations, as a matter of individual rights, to those persons who inhabit the nations of the Third World. If all human rights are negative, those who reap the benefits of mining the deep sea bed of course *may* share some of their benefits with these people out of charity or good-heartedness, but they will not *owe* anything to them as a matter of justice or respect for individual rights. If, on the other hand, human beings everywhere have certain positive or welfare rights, then the moral case for the obligatoriness of sharing the benefits of mining the deep sea bed with those unable to mine these beds themselves is far more problematic. If people have welfare rights, we *owe* it to them to help them when they need it, assuming that we violate no one else's rights in the process. The peoples of the Third World *are* in need of much financial and other types of assistance. If people have welfare rights, do these people then have a *right* to share the benefits of deep sea bed mining? Or, even assuming that they have such a right, do those who have the ability to develop and put in place the exotic technologies required to carry out the actual mining have a greater right to keep what benefits they are able to secure by their own labors and initiative? Robert Simon explores these and related questions in his essay, "Troubled Waters: Global Justice and Ocean Resources." His examination illustrates well both the importance of the idea that people have welfare or positive rights and the complexities the introduction of this idea adds to our moral thought about a matter of current economic and political urgency.

By way of a second example, consider again the issue of pollution. If people have a range of welfare rights (for example, rights to employment, decent housing, and health care) then it is arguable that the proper role of government is to create and sustain laws and institutions that recognize and protect these rights. Suppose that, in order to achieve the high rate of employment necessary to show proper respect for its citizens' right to work, it is necessary for the government to allow relaxed antipollution laws. Some citizens, it is true, would then be more likely to suffer from the effects of industrial pollutants than they would if the laws were stiffer; still, all considered, it is possible that a larger number of people will secure jobs if increased pollution is allowed. Or so it can be argued. Should we accept this position? Much depends again on the thorny notion of welfare rights, a point Tibor Machan develops in his contribution, "Pollution and Political Theory." If, as Machan argues, people do not have any welfare rights, then the government cannot defend pollution policies on the grounds that these are necessary to protect such rights; in particular, relaxed pollution legislation cannot be justified on the grounds that it is necessary in order to respect the citizens' right to a job, *or* to health care or housing. Machan's own position regarding the government's proper role when it comes to pollution must await a careful reading of his essay, but that it will not depend on respecting anyone's welfare rights is something we can know before reading it.

## §14 THE RIGHTS OF ANIMALS

A final aspect of recent controversies about individual rights merits brief mention here. Traditionally, rights theories have limited moral rights to *human* beings. It is not always clear whether a given theory should be interpreted to hold that (1) *all* human beings have certain moral rights, or (2) only *some* human beings have these rights; more often it is clearer that given theories hold that *only* human beings have them. This latter assumption has come under sustained attack in recent years, and the idea that certain animals (for example, chimpanzees and pigs, wolves and cats) have certain moral rights, once rhetorically dismissed by even educated people, now receives respectful if not always supportive attention. What position we take on the issue of animal rights is certain to make an important difference to the stance we take on most of the issues discussed in this anthology. If animals have moral rights it seems likely that some of their rights are negative, and among the particular rights they are likely to have is the right not to be harmed—that is, not to have their individual welfare adversely affected by the acts of moral agents. It is, however, clear that many current societal practices, from commercial animal farming to hunting and trapping wild animals, cause such harm, and that fact is bound to, or at least should, make a difference to the moral judgment we make about the acceptability of these practices. This Introduction is neither the time nor the place to argue for or against recognizing the rights of animals, nor is it the proper occasion to offer moral assessments of the variety of practices harmful to animals that now characterize most of the world's societies. Much is said on these matters in, for example, Alastair Gunn's essay, "Preserving Rare Species."

## §15  MORAL ATOMISM AND HOLISM

Despite their many differences all of the normative ethical theories discussed so far are "atomistic"; that is, each thinks it is of crucial moral importance that *individuals* be considered equitably. Some of the theories, it is true, emphasize the importance of considering the rights or worth of individuals, while others emphasize consideration of individual interests or preferences. Still, all take the notion of the importance of the individual as a sort of moral datum in terms of which we must do our thinking about moral right and wrong. As so often happens in philosophy a widely shared assumption has given rise to a cadre of critics, persons who for a variety of reasons argue that the traditional importance attached to the individual in moral theory is misplaced at best and morally perverse at worst. In place of the pervasive "atomistic" emphasis in moral theory, these critics would have us develop a "holistic" vision, a vision that locates ultimate value in systems rather than in the individuals who comprise them. It is, on this view, the balance, sustainability, diversity, integrity—the beauty, even—of more or less large ecosystems or communities of living things that should be the focus of our moral thinking. The importance of the individual, like the emperor of lore, has no clothes.

This assault by holistic thinkers on the importance traditionally attached to the individual, and the growing debate over animal rights, are perhaps the most significant recent developments in the general area of environmental ethics. Non-anthropocentric well beyond those who argue for the rights of animals, these holistic thinkers are attempting to articulate a radical transformation of how we do ethics, or at least environmental ethics, and their possible success in this endeavor would, if it came to pass, have enormously important implications for virtually all of the issues discussed in this anthology. For example, a great deal of recent thought has been devoted to questions about the existence and stringency of our obligations to future generations. To the extent that we suppose that issues about environmental policy depend on obligations to future generations, however, to that extent at least it is arguable that we continue to perpetuate the "atomistic" vision of morality holistic critics are determined to replace. In their view, or so it seems, concern about the welfare and rights of the individual, even including those of our descendants (a concern we find assessed in, for example, Dale Jamieson's "The City Around Us" and in Kristin Shrader-Frechette's "Ethics and Energy"), is too narrow, focusing as it does on the rights, interests, or value of the individual rather than on the beauty, stability, balance, and sustainability of ecosystems. Should we accept this "paradigm shift" away from the individual to the ecosystem? It is not easy to say. But it should come as no surprise that the grounds and implications of this holistic approach to environmental ethics should be the object of critical scrutiny in a number of this volume's essays, including in particular Edward Johnson's "Treating the Dirt: Environmental Ethics and Moral Theory."

## §16 A FINAL SET OF QUESTIONS

The discussions of ideas in the preceding sections provide few, if any, answers, but like earlier discussions, they enable us to formulate a set of questions which we can take to the readings that follow. Here are some examples.

1. Does the author being read make use of the idea of individual rights and, if so, are the rights invoked legal or moral rights?
2. Is any effort expended to say what rights are (that is, how the notion of a right, whether moral or legal, is to be analyzed?) If so, how adequate is the analysis that is offered?
3. If moral rights are invoked, are they negative rights, or positive (welfare) rights, or both? And is any argument offered in support of recognizing the validity of the rights appealed to?
4. Does the author address the question of the scope of rights (that is, the question of who or what has rights)? For example, is the question concerning animal rights examined and, if so, how is it answered?
5. Does the author implicitly or explicitly subscribe to an anthropocentric vision of morality? Are human interests and rights, and *only* human interests and rights, assumed to be the measure of right and wrong?

6. Does the author implicitly or explicitly endorse an "atomistic" vision of morality, one that places the rights and interests of the *individual* at the center of our moral thinking, or is a "holistic" vision advocated, one that places value in the integrity and stability of whole systems or, perhaps, the entire biosphere? In either case, what arguments, if any, are offered to support the author's vision of the moral scheme of things, and how rationally compelling are these arguments?

As before, this final set of questions hardly exhausts those we can ask of the philosophers whose work we will be reading, when we put our questions in terms of, say, the rights of the individual or the value of ecosystems or their nonhuman inhabitants. Like the previous questions, however, those just given provide us with a map of sorts, helping to guide us through the thicket of ideas that lie ahead by reminding us of some of the questions we will need to ask if we are to understand where we are and where we are going. Philosophy, Aristotle remarks, begins in wonder, and to wonder is seriously to ask "What?", "Why?", "How?"—is, that is, seriously to question. To have a store of questions at our disposal, therefore, questions we will seriously pose of the essays that follow, is already to have begun the journey that is philosophy.

## §17 EARTHBOUND?

Introductions are first words, not last words, beginnings, not endings. The final words of the final essay in this collection make these truths all the more evident. "For good or evil," Edward Johnson writes, "we will not be earthbound forever." The threat of nuclear annihilation notwithstanding, there is some chance, perhaps even good odds, that humans will develop the technological capacities to move beyond the bounds of the earth in a more or less permanent way. Space stations, with a core of terrestrial denizens; mining operations on passing meteors; even settlements on other planets or orbiting agricultural satellites—all these, and more, might come to pass in the lifetime of those who read this book. Will these technological advances, if acted upon, be a blessing or a curse? Will they help solve the many environmental problems we face today or will these problems merely be moved to another place? Questions about pollution, welfare rights, energy efficiency, methods of agriculture production, and the others canvassed in this Introduction and in the essays that follow—these questions are unlikely to disappear if or as we take our needs and interests into outerspace. Whatever the future holds, whatever technological innovations await us, both history and proper humility urge us to view our current crop of problems as calling for a wisdom within the bounds of what we know best—a wisdom that sees the human species, indefinitely even if not forever, as bound to the earth. For there is, after all, little chance that we will sow the seeds of our wisdom throughout the cosmos if we are unable first to do so here, on that planet we say is the Mother of us all.

# *NOTES*

1.  Lewis Regenstein, *America the Poisoned* (Washington, D.C.: Acropolis Books, 1982) p. 86.
2.  *Ibid.*, p. 182.
3.  Frances Moore Lappé, *Diet For a Small Planet* (New York: Ballantine Books, 1971) p. 4.

# 2

# The City Around Us

## DALE JAMIESON

## I. INTRODUCTION

### §1 THE WAY WE ARE

It may seem odd to many people that a book devoted to environmental ethics includes an essay on the city. We often speak of the environment as if it is everywhere except where we live. The environment is Yellowstone, Estes Park, Cape Hatteras, and other vacation spots. It is the Amazon River basin, Alaska, East Africa, places that many of us care about preserving even though we will never visit them. Indeed, the very logic of wilderness preservation demands that most of us will never visit these areas. For if a great many of us were to visit, say, the Maroon Bells Wilderness Area in Colorado, it would soon take on the trappings of an urban park. That so many of us are willing to pay to preserve places that we never expect to visit confounds conventional economists and would-be developers. After all, what could the value of these areas consist in if not their extractable resources and their potential for recreational development? It is no wonder that such people have no better explanation for the rise of preservationism than that it is a conspiracy of wealthy "limousine liberals" who are out to deny the rest of us the benefits of economic growth. But this story is one that we cannot pursue in this essay. What is important here is that many of us think of the environment as including "the sea around us," in the words of the American naturalist Rachel Carson, but excluding the city around us, and this is a serious mistake. The environment in which most of us spend most of our time is the urban environment, and any deep understanding of our relationship to the environment cannot ignore this fact.

Increasing urbanization has been a worldwide trend for several centuries. In 1800 about 2 percent of the world's population lived in urban areas; by 1900 the figure had doubled to 4 percent; and by 1976 it was 38 percent. This trend has been even more dramatic in the United States. In 1800 only 6 percent of our population lived in cities; by 1900 the figure had increased to 40 percent; and by 1977, 74 percent of our population lived in cities.[1] Indeed, depending on how we define the key terms, it is arguable that almost no rural areas remain in the United States. When we think of rural life we often think of our forebears, real or imagined, living their lives almost completely untouched by urban influences. They worked on the land, educated their children at home, made their own household necessities, and joined with neighbors at quilting bees, dances, and hoe-downs for recreation. Today almost none of this exists. A drive in the country almost anywhere reveals factories, mines, and warehouses, the accouterments of the industrial functions associated with cities. Rural people today often commute to industrial jobs, gardening in their spare time. The farm, for the few who still own one, frequently is rented to someone who can afford the enormous capital investment needed to make it profitable. Except for rare exceptions, children are no longer educated at home; they are bussed to consolidated schools where they are taught from the same syllabus prescribed for children in towns and cities. Necessities are purchased on shopping trips to the city, or at the new K-Mart in what used to be the village. Entertainment is mostly television and the latest records from *Billboard's* "Hot 100." Almost the only remaining rural areas are those that are preserved by the federal government, and even some of these would have to be excepted. Yosemite, for example, is one of California's largest cities from May to September. It even has its own jail! And the amenities available there far exceed those that can be obtained in most small towns. But however we define the key terms, it is clear that the urban environment is pervasive. Cities are central in our lives, and despite this or because of it, we both love them and hate them.

## §2 VIEWS OF THE CITY

Americans have always had complicated and ambiguous attitudes toward cities. This is reflected in political rhetoric, literature, films, philosophy, and even architecture. Some intellectuals have been overtly antiurban. They have seen the city as decadent and depraved; it could corrupt even the best of people. Others have not been antiurban in principle, but they have viewed American cities as vastly inferior to those of Europe. According to these thinkers, American cities celebrate crass materialism and vulgar commerce at the expense of community, cultivation, and refinement.

The first important antiurban tract written in America was Thomas Jefferson's *Notes on the State of Virginia*, composed in 1781. Jefferson argued that cities were inimical to good government:

The mobs of the great cities add just as much to the support of pure government as sores do to the strength of the human body.[2]

In a letter to Benjamin Rush, Jefferson wrote:

I view great cities as pestilential to the morals, the health and the liberties of man.[3]

Jefferson thought that everyone should be a farmer; or work in an occupation whose services are needed by farmers, like carpenters, masons, and smiths.

Most of our leading nineteenth-century literary figures shared Jefferson's views. Emerson thought that only farmers create wealth, and that all trade rests on their labors. Emerson also shared Jefferson's views about the moral superiority of the farmer:

That uncorrupted behavior which we admire in animals and in young children belongs to him [the farmer], to the hunter, the sailor—the man who lives in the presence of Nature. Cities force growth and make men talkative and entertaining, but they make them artificial.[4]

Emerson's friend, Thoreau, disliked cities and their culture even more:

I wish to speak a word for Nature, for absolute freedom and wildness, as contrasted with a freedom and culture merely civil—to regard man as an inhabitant, or a part and parcel of Nature, rather than a member of society.[5]

Melville, Hawthorne, and Poe all depicted the city as a sewer of evil and wickedness. In a story set in the future, Poe portrays a New York so decimated that archeologists have trouble reconstructing the lives of its inhabitants. Finally, it is determined that nine-tenths of New York was covered by a series of pagodas devoted to the idols of Wealth and Fashion.[6] Although sometimes Henry James (1843–1916) tried to like American cities he ultimately failed, living most of his adult life as an expatriate in England. He hated the uniformity of New York's architecture and the diversity of its language and culture. He could never see the skyscraper-dominated skyline as anything other than a "pincushion in profile."

The views of the philosophers were, as we might expect, more subtle and complex. Although William James (1842–1910) did not share completely the views of his brother Henry, he was concerned about the "hollowness" and "brutality" of the large cities. He, along with John Dewey (1859–1952), advocated a decentralized city in which community is recognized as the prime virtue. James's Harvard colleague, California-born Josiah Royce (1855–1916), was more radical in his views. He lodged three charges against the great cities. First, they were so overwhelmed with large numbers of alienated and unassimilated people that the very fabric of society was stretched to the breaking point. Second, the centralization of culture bred conformity and intellectual stagnation. And third, the cities encouraged the "spirit of the mob" which is antithetical to the preservation of liberty.

In a characteristic passage Royce attacks large circulation newspapers on the grounds that they produce ". . . a monotonously uniform triviality of mind in a large proportion of our city and suburban population."[7] Royce's ideal of democracy was the New England town meeting in which

> men . . . take counsel together in small groups, who respect one another's individuality, who meanwhile criticize one another constantly.[8]

He feared that a highly centralized and urbanized nation would

> . . . fall rapidly under the hypnotic influence of a few leaders, of a few fatal phrases.[9]

But contrary to James and Dewey, Royce did not believe that decentralization within the city was a viable solution to urban problems. Rather, Royce advocated a thoroughgoing decentralization of American society in which cities would simply become less important.

> We need . . . a newer and wiser provincialism. I mean the sort of provincialism which makes people want to idealize, to adorn, to ennoble, to educate their own province; to hold sacred its traditions, to honor its worthy dead, to support and to multiply its public possessions. I mean the spirit which shows itself in the multiplying of public libraries, in the laying out of public parks, in the work of local historical associations, in the enterprises of village improvement societies . . . I mean also the present form of that spirit which has originated, endowed, and fostered the colleges and universities of our Western towns, cities and states, and which is so well shown throughout our country in our American pride in local institutions of learning.[10]

The views of the most important distinctively American architect, Frank Lloyd Wright, are especially interesting. Wright was raised in rural Wisconsin and never overcame his initial experiences in Chicago. Throughout his life he saw the city as ugly, brutal, and impersonal. He often drew an analogy between cities and malignant tumors, with the architect having the responsibility to

> . . . take away all urban stricture and depravity . . . and then—absorb and regenerate the tissue poisoned by cancerous overgrowth.[11]

Wright thought that technology would make traditional cities obsolete, and envisioned a utopian city he called Broadacre. Now, with the hindsight of almost four decades, it is depressing to realize that Wright's utopian city is much like the sprawling megalopolis of Los Angeles.

Although the antiurban tendencies of American thought are very striking indeed, it would be wrong to exaggerate them. Some Americans, like Walt Whitman, celebrated the city. And undoubtedly antiurban traditions exist in other societies as well. Still, surveys have indicated that most Americans feel great antipathy for cities, even if they live in them.[12] And since the American experience has been quite different from the European experience, it is not surprising that this should be so. Our ruling mythology teaches that we are descended from people who left the "old world" to escape poverty and oppression. Our forebears cames to America to begin anew on land of their own. The cities all too often have been seen as a remnant of the past that our forebears were escaping, as a part of the old world transplanted to the new. Undoubtedly much of this mythology is demonstrably false. But true or false, it is such ideas that have shaped our perceptions of the city.

One effect of our antiurban tradition is that we have been slow to develop an urban policy. This is especially surprising since almost as long as there have been cities in America there have been those who have thought them to be in crisis. The French observer Alexis de Tocqueville (1805–1859), in his classic *Democracy in America* published in 1835, wrote:

> The lower ranks which inhabit these cities [Philadelphia and New York] constitute a rabble even more formidable than the populace of European towns. They consist of freed blacks, in the first place, who are condemned by the laws and by public opinion to a hereditary state of misery and degradation. They also contain a multitude of Europeans who have been driven to the shores of the New World by their misfortunes or their conduct; and they bring to the United States all our greatest vices without any of those interests which counteract this baneful influence. As inhabitants of a country where they have no civil rights they are ready to turn all the passions which agitate the community to their own advantage; thus, within the last few months serious riots have broken out in Philadelphia and New York.

De Tocqueville went on to warn:

> The size of certain American cities and especially . . . the nature of their population . . . [is] a real danger which threatens the future security of the democratic republics of the New World.[13]

Perhaps de Tocqueville's gloomier predictions have not been realized. Still, who would deny that cities today face crushing problems, ranging from deterioration of basic services like transportation, education, and public safety to the problems of poverty, or that the quality of urban life has declined in recent years and continues to decline? Despite this, it was not until 1978 during the Carter administration that the federal government formulated an explicit urban policy.[14] Of course, from the very foundation of the republic there have been de facto urban policies. The decisions made in Washington concerning housing, health care, and so forth have greatly affected the cities. But all too often these decisions have been made with little sensitivity as to whether or not their impacts on urban areas have been coherent and consistent.

Although cities have been studied by economists, political scientists, sociologists, and geographers, and despite the fact that cities are the primary environment for most of us, fundamental questions about the cities around us frequently have been overlooked or ignored. Are cities good for us? Should we try to reform them, abolish them, or preserve them the way they are? How do cities affect our individual psychologies and our collective political and social systems? How do they affect our values? What influence do they have on our sense of justice, and on our efforts to create a better society? Obviously not all these questions can be addressed, much less answered, in this essay. What I hope to do is to raise some fundamental questions about the urban environment, and to show that these are not "technical" questions as conceived by social scientists, but rather fundamental value questions which go to the very core of what we are and how we live; and that, indeed, the "technical" questions can only be meaningfully addressed in the context of widespread discussion and debate concerning these more fundamental questions.

In Part II I try to make clear how I use some basic terms, for example, "city" and "urban area," and sketch some future trends in urban development. In Part III I discuss some urban problems and the economist's approach to them. Part IV focuses on one problem in some detail: the preservation of urban landmarks. Finally, in Part V, I discuss the nature and role of utopian thinking about cities. If, as is certainly the case, we can only scratch the surface of the ideas that are examined in what follows, the hope is that the scratch will start an itch to do more and better thinking in an area as important as it is neglected by recent writing in environmental ethics.

## II. DEFINITIONS

### §3 WHAT ARE CITIES?

Before we can come to any systematic understanding of the city around us, we must be clear about what we mean by "city." Most of us seem willing to use the term "city" interchangeably with "urban area." If we make a distinction at all it is this one: The city is the city proper; an urban area includes suburbs and other areas touched by the city proper. In the past the distinction between cities and urban areas was much sharper. The term "city" was formerly reserved for the citizens of a community, while "urban area" referred to the place which they inhabited. In this sense cities, like nations, can be in exile, and it is this sense in which St. Augustine spoke of the community of believers, widely scattered as it is, as "the city of God." These considerations are important because they remind us that any assessment of the quality of life in a city cannot ignore the importance of community. We shall return to this theme in §14 and 15, but for present purposes I shall follow ordinary usage in speaking of cities both as people and as places.

The main problem in developing an adequate definition of the term "city" is that a very wide range of things have been called by that name. A very small city in Illinois seems to have little in common with Tokyo or Singapore. The ancient cities of the Middle East could hardly have been more different from Los Angeles. I shall not try to give necessary and sufficient conditions for being a city. Our purposes will be well enough served by sketching three characteristics or "symptoms" which most cities —ancient or modern, Eastern or Western—exhibit to some degree.

When we think of cities most of us think of areas that are very crowded; and indeed, population density is one of the marks of a city. But there is no magic number such that everything which reaches a certain threshold of density is a city and everything which fails to reach this threshold is not. The population density of cities varies greatly. San Francisco is almost seven times as dense as Dallas, and Manhattan is four times as dense as San Francisco. Rural areas in the Far East often have population densities of 2,000 per square mile, while some American cities, for example Jacksonville and Oklahoma City, have population densities of 600 to 700 people per square mile.[15] This shows that cities are not areas of "absolute" high density; rather they are areas of "relative" high density. What is characteristic of cities is that they are significantly more dense than the regions which surround them. Another feature of cities that comes rapidly to mind is their occupational structure. When we think of cities we think of people who earn their living buying, selling, and trading, rather than farming. And indeed, the second mark of a city is that its inhabitants work mainly in nonagricultural occupations. Finally, the third characteristic of cities is that they are important cultural, religious, economic, and administrative centers for the regions that surround them.

## §4 FUTURE TRENDS

Cities have changed enormously since the time of the Greeks, and there is no question that they will change enormously in the future. The international trends are clear. World population will continue to increase, and the urban population will increase even more. The social structure of the world will be dominated increasingly by huge urban concentrations like those of Mexico City and Tokyo. And the problems with which we must be concerned as global citizens will increasingly be their problems.

The prospects for the United States, however, are not quite so clear, as a look at our own recent history shows. The process of suburbanization began in a major way during the prosperity of the 1920s. During that decade the suburban population of the seventeen largest cities increased almost 40 percent, a much higher rate of growth than that of the central cities.[16] The Great Depression and the Second World War inhibited the tendency toward suburbanization, but encouraged by federal housing and highway programs, it exploded in the post–World War II period. The census figures tell the story well. The suburban share of the population was 33 percent in 1950. By 1960 it had increased to 43 percent, and by 1970 it was 50 percent. During this period the suburbs gained in population mainly at the expense of rural areas. As a result, the country became increasingly urbanized. Since 1970, however, there have been dramatic shifts. In the last decade more Americans have left the cities than have moved to them. Small towns with populations of less than 2,500 are the fastest growing demographic unit, and many rural areas, particularly those in the sunbelt, have been experiencing unprecedented growth. It is far from clear what, if anything, these trends mean. They may be short-term statistical anomalies with very little significance in the long run. Or they might reflect an important long-term change in environmental preferences. But even if the latter is true, it is still not easy to say precisely what this trend foreshadows about our future.

Some geographers and planners have speculated that we are witnessing a shift from an epoch dominated by cities to an epoch dominated by "urban fields."[17] Until the electronics revolution of the last decade it was necessary for people and businesses to reside in close proximity to each other and to sources of relevant information. These circumstances gave rise to hierarchial cities with a central core devoted to business and administration. But with improved transportation and communication it is no longer necessary for people and business to be located close to each other in space. For this reason the traditional city with its dominant central core is redundant and unnecessary, or so some have argued. The central city can and is being replaced by a decentralized urban field, with no single region dominant over the others. If this hypothesis is correct, the flight from the central cities may not be antiurban at all; it may be the first step in the creation of a new kind of urban area.

Whatever the future holds for America's cities, it is clear that many people no longer want to live in them, and the number is increasing. In the pages ahead we shall discuss a range of questions about the city and urban problems with the view of putting them in philosophical perspective.

## III. URBAN PROBLEMS AND ECONOMIC THEORY

Cities confront us with several different kinds of problems. Some are unique to cities, while others exist in rural areas as well but are exacerbated by the urban environment. Some urban problems are rooted in what it is to be a city. For example, one of the characteristics of a city, as we saw in §3, is that it is an area of relatively high population density. It is not surprising, then, that cities have very high levels of noise and air pollution. Historically, cities have also been associated with high rates of infectious disease, and even today cities have a great many public health problems, ranging from high rates of cancer and ulcers to high rates of suicide and drug addiction. Cities also have high rates of violent death. In both the United States and Western Europe, the rates of traffic death and violent crime increase as population density increases.[18]

It should be evident to even the casual observer that cities face some unique problems, as well as some very severe instances of some familiar ones. Moreover, urban problems often resist the conventional solutions proposed by economists and policymakers. To see why, we must enter the thicket of their terminology.

## §5  INTERNALIZING EXTERNALITIES

Economists are happiest with what they call private goods. A private good is something to which some assignable individual, whether corporate or not, has an entitlement. He can sell it, or buy more of it. He can exclude people from using it, or he can charge people for using it at his discretion. Private goods are the capitalist's ideal; he would like everything to be a private good. In our society private goods include my Hawaiian shirts, your copy of *Earthbound*, and Ronald Reagan's ranch. Sometimes conflicts arise over how individuals use their private goods. The problem is that individuals do not always bear all of the costs associated with producing or consuming these goods. Consider a trivial but real example.

My neighbor has a wood stove which she uses to heat her house. Since Colorado averages 300 days of sunshine per year, I prefer to dry my laundry on the clothesline even in winter. But I cannot, for the smoke and soot from my neighbor's chimney invades my property and would soil my laundry if I were to hang it out to dry. From an economist's point of view, my neighbor is getting off cheap. I am bearing part of the cost of her heating with wood. She is "externalizing" these costs to me, in the form of the smoke and soot which fouls my yard. The economist's solution is to "internalize" these "externalities" by requiring my neighbor to install smoke abatement equipment, or by requiring her to compensate me for giving up my right to dry laundry on my clothesline in winter. This approach is potentially very powerful, as can be seen from another example which is more serious and just as real.

According to a government study, two million asbestos-related cancer deaths will occur in the next thirty-five years due to exposures that have already taken place.[19] This is an average of more than fifty thousand deaths per year. Monetary losses from illness caused by asbestos exposure are estimated in the hundreds of millions. These losses are part of the cost of producing and consuming asbestos, yet they are not borne by the companies involved nor their consumers. Rather, these costs are externalized into the bodies of asbestos workers and into the society as a whole in the form of higher insurance premiums and health care costs. If these costs were internalized, the price of asbestos would be much higher, reflecting the true cost of producing and consuming this substance, and much less asbestos would be used and many fewer people would die. In this case it is easy to see what is to be gained by some and lost by others by internalizing externalities.

## §6  SOME PROBLEMS FOR THE ECONOMIST

Requiring individuals and corporations to internalize externalities is potentially a powerful approach to many environmental problems. Unfortunately, however, this approach has some problems of its own. First, it is more difficult even in theory to identify externalities than it might at first seem. Consider an example. Some people are very sensitive to the clothes worn by others. They find Hawaiian shirts, or mismatched colors, or white socks with black shoes, offensive and upsetting. Still, I doubt that many people would say that I ought to compensate the sensitive soul who dislikes my clothes. We do not think of the annoyance caused to others by dressing unconventionally as an externality that should be internalized. What is different about this case and that of my neighbor's wood stove is that I have a right to dress as I like but she doesn't have a right to foul my air. This suggests that the identification of externalities rests on some prior conception of how rights are distributed—that is, who has what rights. But the determination of who has what rights is far from settled, not only in practice but also in theory, and anyway, it is a job for a philosopher and not an economist. In short, the economic approach to environmental problems must ultimately rest on some controversial philosophical view about what constitutes a just society.

Another example might make the point clearer. It used to be the case that smokers smoked anywhere with impunity. It was a widespread belief that smokers had the right to fill the air, not just their lungs, with smoke, and if someone else didn't like it, that other person should leave. Nowadays most of us think that nonsmokers have a right to clean air, and that those who smoke in public violate the rights of nonsmokers. The smoker is now typically viewed as externalizing the costs of smoking into the air of nonsmokers, rather than as exercising rights in a legitimate way. This is because our conception of the initial distribution of rights has changed. So long as nonsmokers were viewed as lacking a right to clean air, smokers were not viewed as externalizing the costs of smoking as they exhaled. Once nonsmokers are viewed as having a right to clean air, however, the picture changes. But who has what rights is not decided by the economist's call for internalizing externalities; instead that call assumes that we have already answered this prior question about the distribution of rights.[20]

A second problem with the economist's approach becomes especially apparent in the city. Almost everything an urban dweller does impinges on others. Noise, conversation, and music are ubiquitous. Hundreds of passersby cannot fail to note the state of my house. How I dispose of my garbage, how often I use my air conditioner, and when I drive my car, all affect others. How can the economist deal with a situation in which externalities are everywhere? The problem is this. The economist's approach suggests a picture in which the usual situation is one in which if I were to exercise suitable restraint, then my use of my private goods would affect only me. In those few cases when it does affect others, I should be forced to internalize these effects. But this picture does not conform very well to urban life. There, it seems, it is rare when, with suitable restraint, one's use of a private good affects only one's self. I enjoy the taste of my Szechuan eggplant alone, but I share the aroma with my neighbor.

## §7  PUBLIC GOODS: THE ECONOMIST'S REJOINDER AND A REPLY

In an effort to deal with these problems and others, economists have developed the notion of a public good. Public goods tend to fall into two categories. First, there are some goods that just do not have the logical characteristics of private goods. Everyone benefits from them, though it is difficult to say how much; and it is difficult or impossible to deny benefits to those who are unwilling to pay. Police and fire protection, and access to the legal system fall into this category. But second, there are goods, which although they could be denied to those who are unwilling or unable to pay, we believe everyone is entitled to anyway. Education and health care are in this category. Public goods of both varieties are typically provided by governments and financed by taxes.

The introduction of public goods, necessary though it is, creates new problems that cannot easily be resolved. Consider an example. Although there is considerable dispute over how to define "clean air," almost no one doubts that clean air is a public good and that Denver's air is dirty. It is also clear that dirty air causes severe health problems and even death. One study has shown that current levels of carbon monoxide in Denver probably cause 100 to 125 heart attacks per year.[21] These heart attacks are not "acts of God"; they are caused by people driving cars. Of course there is no single driver who causes all of these heart attacks, or perhaps even one of them. And we cannot say with certainty which of the thousands of heart attacks which occur in Denver each year are caused by carbon monoxide. It also should be said that drivers in Denver are not wicked people. They do not drive with the intention of causing their neighbors' heart attacks. Rather, they use their cars for the same reasons we do: in order to get to work, to go shopping, and so forth. The "extra" heart attacks are an unintended, though foreseeable, consequence of their individual actions, taken collectively. It should also be said that undoubtedly some of those who suffer heart attacks themselves drive cars. They are not simply the innocent victims of other people's behavior. On the other hand it also should be noted that in all likelihood some of the victims do not drive, and many of those who do might well prefer other means of transportation were they available. These considerations are relevant in morally evaluating those who drive in Denver. They might lead us to soften the judgments we might otherwise make. Still, whatever we might say about the character of those individuals who drive, it must be acknowledged that our collective behavior sometimes seriously harms and perhaps even kills innocent people (e.g., young children). They are wronged even if as individuals we don't wrong them. This should lead us to ask: How should a morally conscientious person respond to this?

Some might argue that we should refrain from driving. They might reason in a way that is reminiscent of the eighteenth-century German philosopher Immanuel Kant: I should only use an automobile if I am willing that everyone should use an automobile. But if everyone were to use an automobile, then some innocent people will be seriously harmed. Since I am unwilling to permit innocent people to be seriously harmed, I should not use my automobile. Although this argument follows a familiar pattern of reasoning, it seems to go wrong here. After all, if only half as many people used cars as do now, perhaps no heart attacks would be caused by air pollution. From the fact that I don't want everyone to drive it doesn't follow that I want no one to drive. But the problem with this response to the argument is that just as I might reason in this way to the conclusion that I have no moral duty not to drive, so might everyone reason to this conclusion. And the result is that 100 or so innocent people suffer heart attacks as a consequence of our actions.

One way of trying to escape this conclusion is to deny that any innocent people are wronged. It might be suggested that environmental problems, like air pollution, do not by and large result in the deaths of particular individuals who are identifiable in advance. Rather, high levels of air pollution impose additional risk on a large pool of individuals, and only a small number of them suffer heart attacks. What we should do in such situations, it might be argued, is to offer people a deal. Suppose that it would cost automobile owners $500 each to eliminate the risk of heart attack caused by air pollution. By voting, cost-benefit analysis, or some other procedure we could present people with a choice: Either take your chances with heart attack and pay nothing, or eliminate the risk of pollution-caused heart attack and pay $500. From this perspective the moral problem seems to vanish. Those who suffer heart attacks caused by air pollution are just the losers in a democratic decision.

But there are a great many problems with this approach. First, those who suffer the heart attacks may not have been those who were willing to take the risk. This is especially important in view of the magnitude of the losses. Ordinarily we think that if the risks of a policy or a decision that is really a gamble are very great, people should be permitted to opt out. Most of us would not object too strenuously if a dollar were deducted from our weekly pay and used to purchase a lottery ticket. It is likely that we would lose a dollar a week this way. But a dollar a week isn't much to lose, and there is always the chance that we may win. But suppose instead that we stood to lose our houses. Suppose that a majority of our neighbors had agreed to wager the entire neighborhood on the outcome of the Super Bowl. Even though there is a chance that we might win and win very big, we would be indignant at being compelled to risk so much. The air pollution case is like this one in some important respects. Those who lose the air pollution bet lose quite a lot indeed. They forfeit their health and perhaps even their lives. It is wrong for a majority to require everyone to play this high-risk game.

A second and perhaps more fundamental objection to this way out is that the distinction between individual and statistical heart attacks is really bogus. Statistical heart attacks just are individual heart attacks about which we know very little. But we do know this: In both cases the victim has a life with friends, family, relatives, acquaintances, a job, a hobby, a pet, and so forth. Our ignorance concerning which individuals will suffer from air pollution makes no moral difference. But whether or not we can identify in advance the victims of our policies in no way determines whether there are such victims. The moral price is the same in each case.

The preceding discussion has unearthed two characteristic features of environmental problems as they arise in the city around us: (1) they often concern the provision and preservation of public goods, and (2) they often arise because individuals find it rational to behave in a way that is collectively irrational. I have tried to show that it is the very nature of the city to exacerbate such problems. I have also argued that these problems cannot be adequately treated from a purely economic point of view. In the next section I shall discuss a specific urban environmental problem. It involves issues in which the limitations of a purely economic analysis are readily apparent. It is an issue which involves conflicting values. It is the problem of preserving landmarks.

## IV. PRESERVING LANDMARKS

In the city in which I live there is a movie theater which was built in 1936. For an entire generation, this ornate, art deco theater was a home away from home. It was where kids spent Saturday afternoons, where teenagers would go on dates, and where their parents would enjoy an evening out. But in the 1970s the Boulder Theater fell upon hard times. It was no longer profitable to operate this large, downtown building as a movie theater. In the age of the automobile everyone owned cars. New theaters sprang up in shopping centers which offered cheaper rents. The Boulder Theater became a dilapidated building on a valuable piece of land, a prime candidate for demolition.

The story that I tell is typical. Some version of it has been played out in most cities and towns in America. And it is not just a story about movie theaters. Entire neighborhoods are "redeveloped" out of existence in order to make way for freeways or office buildings. In the late 1960s in San Francisco, a Japanese neighborhood was razed so that a Japanese Cultural Center, catering mostly to tourists, including those from Japan, could be constructed. The story that I tell, then, is not just the story of one movie theater in one town in Colorado. It is an example of an issue which is increasingly important in virtually every city in the country.

### §8 ECONOMIC THEORY AND PRESERVATION

Having set the stage, we may now ask: What should be done with the Boulder Theater? For those who draw their policy prescriptions solely from economic considerations the answer is simple: Use it in the most economically efficient way possible. Under prevailing conditions this is equivalent to saying that the Boulder Theater should be torn down and the land used as a parking lot. In recent years all across America a great number of landmarks have been replaced by parking lots. Downtown real estate is very expensive. Parking lots produce high revenue with low overhead at almost no risk.

Sometimes preservation can be made commercially successful, however. San Francisco's Ghiradelli Square and Denver's Larimer Square are often cited as examples of economically successful preservations. Many believe that such preservations are and must be the wave of the future. James Biddle, former president of the National Trust, has written:

> We must show that preservations can be good for business. We can elaborate on aesthetic values, but we need to talk cold, hard cash.[22]

Still, some would deny that the models of economically successful preservation cited above are real preservations. Except for the building facades, very little has been preserved in either case. But even if the success of these examples is granted, as I think it should be, it is obvious that preservations cannot always be made commercially successful. For example, a thoroughgoing preservationist wants to preserve historic ethnic communities, however poor and deprived. Most of these areas will never be transformed into handsome tourist attractions.

Those who wish to preserve neighborhoods, buildings, and other landmarks must, at some point, resolutely face their opponents and say that they reject economic efficiency as the ultimate criterion for social policy. In the current political climate such a declaration sounds shocking when put so boldly. Still, there is ample evidence that most Americans do reject economic efficiency as the sole criterion for social policy. Most Americans are committed to preserving endangered species and cleaning up the air and water even if this means that economic growth will be inhibited.[23] Psychological research has indicated that in experimental situations people are willing to trade increments of efficiency for equality, fairness, and other values.[24] What this means is that most people are irrational from the point of view of the economist. But we ordinary folk should not be too deeply stung by this charge. Economists use the terms "rational" and "efficient" in peculiar ways that are tailormade to fit their favored theory of rationality. Moreover, we can ask an economist some difficult questions about the importance he attaches to efficiency. That efficiency is a good cannot be doubted by any reasonable person. But some economists and the policymakers and analysts that are influenced by them would justify all economic and social arrangements in terms of efficiency. What makes efficiency the primary virtue of social policies? The answer cannot be that efficient policies are efficient, for that reply would lead to a vicious circle. It must be that the economist believes that there are independent grounds for the primacy of efficiency. It is hard to imagine what they might be. And against this view, there are arguments that have been developed over thousands of years for the primacy of justice, respect, equity, and other moral virtues. We common folk who believe that sometimes efficiency must take a back seat to other values should not be cowed by the epithets of economists.

The gospel of efficiency, then, can be rejected in a principled way by the preservationist. But this rejection of efficiency does not in itself show that the Boulder Theater or any other landmark ought to be preserved. That task requires some positive arguments on behalf of preservation.

## §9  WHAT IS A LANDMARK?

Before considering these arguments we should be clear about what we mean by "landmark." I have been using the term very broadly so that it encompasses buildings, neighborhoods, monuments, and so forth. But of course not all such things are landmarks. The tract house in Southern California in which I was raised is not a landmark. Nor is the suburb of which it is a part. Another difficulty is that some definitions of "landmark" imply that they are now being preserved or that they ought to be. Some even include the reasons for such preservation as part of the definition. For example, the *American Heritage Dictionary of the English Language* defines "landmark" as "a building or site *having historical significance and marked for preservation* by a municipal or national government" [italics added]. Since we want to discuss some buildings, neighborhoods, and so forth that have not been marked for preservation by a government, and since we want to examine a wide range of arguments for such preservation, and not just historical ones, it is clear that we must use "landmark" in a slightly different sense than that specified in the dictionary. Two points about our use of "landmark" should be noted particularly. First, we shall count as a landmark anything that is a plausible candidate for preservation, relying on a stock of common sense examples for purposes of discussion. Thus in our sense of "landmark" it makes sense to say that something is a landmark but it ought to give way to something else. Second, we shall separate the question of whether something is a landmark from the grounds that might be cited for preserving it. We do not want it to be true by definition that landmarks must be preserved for historical or cultural reasons. With these emendations in mind, we can go on to consider some arguments for preservation.

There are at least three kinds of arguments that can be given for preservation. The first kind appeals to characteristics of the landmarks themselves. I shall consider two examples: the Argument from the Rights of Landmarks, and the Argument from Aesthetic Features. A second kind of argument for preservation rests on duties to persons other than ourselves. The Argument from Duties to Future Generations and the Argument from Duties to Past Generations illustrate this kind of argument. A third kind of argument for preservation is rooted in considerations about those who presently exist. The Argument from Cultural Identity and the Argument from Common Wisdom will be my examples.

## §10  THE ARGUMENT FROM THE RIGHTS OF LANDMARKS

The first kind of argument that we distinguished appeals to characteristics of the landmarks themselves as the grounds for why we should preserve them. The most far reaching of these arguments is the Argument from the Rights of Landmarks. This argument purports to show that it is wrong to destroy landmarks because *they have a right to exist* independently of human desires or preferences. This argument strikes some people as ludicrous and others as obvious. But to properly evaluate it, we must view it from the perspective of contemporary theories of rights.

In recent years rights to almost everything have been posited by someone. And almost every class of entity has its champions. Two decades ago most people would have ridiculed the claim that animals have rights. But today advocates of animal rights are an important influence on contemporary thought and action. Also in the last two decades environmentalists have begun to argue that natural objects like rivers and trees have rights as well. Legal theorist Christopher Stone argued that rights could be extended to natural objects on the basis of well-established legal principles. Although Stone remains a minority voice, his arguments were sympathetically received by the late Supreme Court justice William O. Douglas.[25] Some have tried to carry Stone's argument even further, arguing that artifacts like works of art also have rights.[26] Perhaps it is absurd to ascribe rights to urban landmarks, but if it is, at least it is an absurdity that is in keeping with the tenor of the times.

How might one argue that urban landmarks have rights? The first stage of the argument would establish some favorable condition that is sufficient for having rights. A long tradition in both moral and legal philosophy holds that *having interests* is sufficient for having rights. This condition seems more favorable to the preservationist than the oft-cited alternatives of being autonomous or being a party to a contract. It can be argued on the basis of this "interest principle" that infants and comatose humans have rights. It is also easy to see how rights could be extended to nonhuman animals on the basis of this principle; just as humans have an interest in a long and pleasant life, so do the other higher animals. But what about artifacts like paintings and buildings? Do they have interests? It is true that we often speak of them as if they do. We might say that we "feel sorry" for the house next door since it has been purchased by an irresponsible owner who does nothing to keep it in repair. Or we might say that it was "a good thing" for the paintings in the National Gallery in London that they were evacuated to the countryside before the German bombing began. But on reflection I think we can see that these are not literal uses of language. When a raccoon is hit by a car, we may or may not be disturbed by it; but it is clearly bad for the raccoon. But if a historical landmark is razed and we are not disturbed by it, either for ourselves or for future or past generations, there seems little sense in saying that it was bad for the landmark that was razed. To put the point another way, if there were no other sentient beings in the universe it would still be a bad thing that an animal suffered and died, but it would not be a bad thing that an earthquake swallowed up the ruins of the Roman Coliseum.

The argument I have presented against supposing that artifacts have rights is mainly intuitive and therefore not overwhelming in its strength.

But on the other hand the only argument that I have seen in favor of this view rests on an equivocation, as I have tried to show. That is, it rests on supposing that artifacts have interests in the same sense in which humans and other animals do. Until better arguments are presented, the intuitive considerations that I have given seem strong enough to carry the day.

## §11 THE ARGUMENT FROM AESTHETIC FEATURES

A second example of an argument which grounds the duty of preservation in characteristics of the landmarks themselves is the Argument from Aesthetic Features. This argument is often cited in everyday discussions of preservation. It gains plausibility from the fact that some of the legislation concerning landmark preservation directly appeals to the aesthetic features of landmarks as the grounds for their preservation. For example, the criteria of eligibility for being listed in the *National Register of Historic Places* explicitly lists high artistic value as one consideration. This suggests that perhaps landmarks ought to be preserved because they embody valuable aesthetic features.

There are two problems with this argument even if it is viewed in a favorable light. First, this argument fails to provide grounds for preserving many landmarks that many people believe ought to be preserved. Houses in which presidents were born rarely embody valuable aesthetic features. Inner city neighborhoods seldom have much in common with works of art. Secondly, rather than motivating preservation, this argument only challenges developers to do better. If our interest in landmarks is an aesthetic one, then no one can complain if we destroy a landmark, so long as we replace it with a structure that is aesthetically more pleasing. Such a policy might lead to an environment which is aesthetically more rewarding but one which many of us would believe had lost something important.

There are two more problems with this argument. First, many philosophers believe that aesthetic judgments are objective, but they have not done a good job of convincing other people of this. As a matter of practice, when aesthetic value is debated in the realm of public policy there is a strong tendency for anyone's opinion to be regarded as the equal of anyone else's. As the proverbial (but possibly false) saying goes, "There is no disputing matters of taste." Many people seem to like the Golden Arches, and find the clean austere look of modern office buildings vastly more pleasant than the aesthetic qualities of crumbling warehouses. Second, most people, and certainly most decisionmakers, regard aesthetic value to be commensurable with other values. That is, most people would trade an increment of aesthetic value for an increment of some other value, say convenience or economic welfare. Thus someone might admit that an office building from the 1920s is aesthetically superior to the one that has been proposed to replace it, but at the same time prefer the proposed building because of the greater convenience it would afford (e.g., better lighting, better plumbing, better electricity, and so forth). Although the Argument from Aesthetic Features provides some reason for preserving some landmarks, it is only of slight help in establishing a thoroughgoing preservationist position.

## §12  THE ARGUMENT FROM DUTIES TO FUTURE GENERATIONS

The second category of arguments for preservation appeals to our duties to those who are not now alive. The first example of such an argument that we shall consider is the Argument from Duties to Future Generations. The basic idea is that we deprive members of future generations from experiencing the landmarks that we destroy. The fact that they come after us in time gives us no warrant to deny them these pleasures. Therefore, it is wrong for us to destroy landmarks.

Two criticisms of this argument merit our attention. First, it must be recognized that virtually everything we do deeply affects members of future generations. Indeed what we do even affects the identity of who will exist in the future.[27] The slightest change in the remote past would have made it highly unlikely that *we* would now exist. Look at it this way. A necessary condition for my existing is that I originated in the union of a unique sperm and a unique egg. If my mother had stubbed her toe on the way to bed on the night of my conception, I would not have been conceived. For if a child would have been conceived an instant later it would have originated from a different sperm uniting with the egg. The result might have been someone very much like me, as much like me as my brother is, but still a different person. Once we see the radical contingency of our existence, it is obvious that different policies concerning historical preservation would result in different people being born in the future. If we raze a building instead of preserving it, some construction worker has a job who would not otherwise have one. Instead of staying home and conceiving a child he is out destroying a building. The child whom he does conceive when he returns home from work, who would not otherwise have existed, marries and has children. Her children would not have existed had she not existed. It is easy to see that after several generations the planet would be populated by people who would not have existed had we adopted a different policy concerning historic preservation. But that is to say that the people who would live in a world with preservation are not the same people who would live in a world without preservation. Those people who do exist in the future cannot complain, then, or so a critic of the Duties to Future Generations Argument might contend, that they are harmed by our razing of landmarks, since if we had *not* razed our historical landmarks they would *not* have existed.

On the face of it, this argument undercuts the Argument from Duties to Future Generations. The problem is that this argument, if successful, would seem to show that we have *no duties at all* to future generations; an implication many would find unacceptable. (As for why, see the discussion of the Doomsday device in §13.) It would take us too far afield to properly evaluate this argument, but whether or not it is sound, there is a second argument that serves to diminish the force of the Argument from Duties to Future Generations; one that does not imply that we have *no* duties to them.

I have already argued that preservation is, to a great extent, economically inefficient. If that were not the case we could trust preservation to the free market, since the free market, at least under certain ideal conditions, guarantees efficient outcomes.[28] Whenever we preserve a landmark for future generations which would otherwise be destroyed if the market were permitted to operate freely, we are effectively depriving future generations of some economic advantage. It is one thing for us to say that if *we* lived in the future *we* would prefer an increment of preservation to an increment of economic welfare, but how do we know which *people who live in the generations after us* will prefer? Doubtless they will prefer many of the same things we do—health rather than sickness, for example, and clean water rather than muck. So, assuming that we have some duties to future generations, we can allow that we have the duty not to leave them a world that seriously jeopardizes their health or is devoid of clean water. But our degree of certainty on these matters is not easily transferable to convictions about the preferences of future people for landmark preservation rather than extra increments of economic welfare. Posterity might view our landmarks as symbols of a rapacious and disgusting civilization. They might prefer to begin anew. We simply do not know and, in the nature of the case, we can never know.

It might be objected that I have overstated our uncertainty about the preferences of future generations. We know that we are happy that landmarks have been preserved for us, and therefore, it might be argued, we have good inductive evidence for supposing that future people will be happy if landmarks are preserved for them. It is important to remember, however, that cultural preferences can and do change radically, often in a very short time. One example concerns our preferences with respect to wilderness. The contemporary historian Roderick Nash has documented the radical shift in American perceptions of wilderness over the last three centuries. For the Puritans wilderness was "poor, barren, hideous, boundless, and unknown"; for the contemporary environmentalist it is a source of wisdom which "holds answers to questions man has not yet learned how to ask."[29] Even in the case of urban preservation popular attitudes have changed dramatically in the last decade. In the 1960s urban renewal programs destroyed large numbers of important buildings in the downtown sections of most American cities. What opposition there was to these programs came mostly from political conservatives objecting to the role of government in these projects. But nowadays many people, regardless of their views on other issues, see the urban renewal of the 1960s as a great national tragedy. Moreover, our lack of knowledge concerning the preferences of future generations is particularly troublesome when coupled with the fact, already noted, that to a great extent preservation is a good that is provided to future generations at the price of some increment of their economic welfare. Perhaps there is a strong inductive case for the urgency of people's preference for preservation, but there is an even stronger case for the urgency of their preference for economic welfare. In the end, then, the Argument from Duties to Future Generations fails to be convincing because of the indeterminacy of the preferences of future generations, even if it is true, as we have allowed, that we have *some* duties to those who will live after us.

At this point, it might be countered that it doesn't matter what future generations would prefer, what matters is what is good for them; and preservation of landmarks would be good for them. This argument is really a version of two other arguments, the Argument from Cultural Identity and the Argument from Common Wisdom, and it will be taken up when we discuss those arguments (in §14 and 15, respectively).

## §13 THE ARGUMENT FROM DUTIES TO PAST GENERATIONS

The second argument that we shall consider which locates our obligation to preserve landmarks in duties to persons other than ourselves is the Argument from Duties to Past Generations. The basic argument is very simple. When people construct buildings, create neighborhoods, make public sculptures, and so forth, they do these things with an eye to their creations continuing beyond their deaths. Although there is no explicit intergenerational agreement to preserve the creations of the past, still, we have a duty to respect the preferences and desires of our ancestors.

One objection to this argument should first be put to rest. It might be thought that we do not have duties to the dead because the desires of the dead die with them. Consider an example. My father is on his deathbed. I promise him that I will never sell a family heirloom. As soon as he dies I rush to the antique shop and cash in. Have I violated a promise? No, it might be suggested, it doesn't make sense to think of the promise as existing after the death of my father. If I have an obligation to someone it must be the case that the person in question exists, and though my father once existed he doesn't exist now. Thus, a necessary condition for having an obligation does not obtain and there can be no obligation.

This line of argument is very tempting. It does seem strange to suppose that interests, desires, preferences, intentions, or hopes survive the deaths of their subjects. But supposing they do not is stranger still. If, for example, a promise dies with the person to whom the promise is made, what could be the point of promising someone that you will take care of his children or protect his art collection? At best such "promises" are exercises in collective self-deception. At worst they are a cruel hoax. But in addition to making nonsense of our commitments to the dying, this view threatens to make nonsense of duties to future generations as well. If a necessary condition for having a duty to someone is that she exists, then surely we can have no duties to future people since they do not exist now any more than do the dead. But if we were now to construct a Doomsday device that would explode in the year 2100, surely it is plain that by our actions here and now we would have wronged future people. These considerations suggest that a "timeless" view of morality might be correct. Just as someone's location in space is not in itself sufficient for removing him from the domain of moral concern, so it is with his location in time.

That the dead *were once* alive and that future people *will be* alive is enough to make them the proper objects of moral concern.

Although this objection against the Argument from Duties to Past Generations founders, there are other objections which fare better. First, it is often far from clear what the intentions and desires of those who lived in the past were. Not every architect and builder cared whether or not his work lived on after his demise; indeed, some continue to build and design with an eye to planned obsolescence. Moreover, even if without exception all of the geniuses of the past cared about the persistence of their creations, a difficult question would remain concerning how their hopes, wishes, and desires generate duties on our part. This difficult question can be illustrated by the following examples.

Suppose that you are sunbathing by a lake on a fine summer day. Several feet from shore there is a child drowning. Suppose that you could save the child with very little risk or even inconvenience to yourself. Moreover, only you are in a position to save the child; there is no one else around. It seems clear that in this case you have a duty to save the drowning child, even though you never agreed to undertake this duty. Now consider a quite different case. You return home one day to find my bicycle parked on your porch. There is a note saying that I have decided to sell it to you and that you owe me $300. You might justly protest, denying that you owe me this money on the grounds that you never agreed to buy my bike. After all, I cannot impose an obligation on you simply by intending that you acquire it and behaving accordingly.

Which of these cases is most similar to the supposed duty to preserve the creations of the past? It is difficult to say. Like the first case, only we are in a position to save the creations of our ancestors. But unlike the first case, it seems that in order to do this we sometimes would have to be willing to pay quite a price. How important is the interest that our ancestors have in the preservation of their creations? Is it a very deep and serious interest, like the interest in life that the drowning child has? Or is it a relatively frivolous interest, like my interest in selling you my bike? These are difficult questions which cannot be easily answered. It is clear, however, that it is very problematical to suppose that the intentions and desires of those who lived in the past are sufficient for imposing on us a duty to preserve their creations.

It is also worth noting that even if these considerations about past generations do generate duties of preservation on our part, it is not clear that they lead to conclusions consistent with our considered judgment about the relative stringency of these duties. Most of us believe that whatever duties we have to past generations become weaker with the passage of time. If we owe anything to past generations at all, we owe more to the last generation than the one which lived in 5000 B.C. I may have a stringent duty to my father not to sell the family jewels, but my duties to my ancestors seventeen generations removed are surely not so stringent. Yet for the preservationist, the urgency of preservation seems to increase with the passage of time. If, then, the duty to preserve is grounded in obligations to past individuals, it would seem that the most stringent duty would be to preserve the most recent landmarks even if this would mean destroying more ancient ones—for example, preserving the Athens Holiday Inn at the price of the deterioration of the Acropolis. There is a counterargument that one might give, however. It might be suggested that our duty is often to preserve older landmarks at the expense of newer ones because we have duties to *more* people concerning old landmarks than we do concerning new ones. We owe it to the builders of the Acropolis to preserve it, but we also owe this duty to all who have lived between then and now who have wanted the Acropolis preserved. For this reason the duty to preserve old landmarks is often more stringent than the duty to preserve new ones, even though duties do become less stringent with the passage of time.

These considerations are, so far, inconclusive. I have rejected one plausible objection to the Argument from Duties to Past Generations. In addition I have suggested that it is unclear whether the intentions and desires of our ancestors are sufficient for imposing on us duties to preserve their creations. I then pointed out that even if this argument were successful it might imply that landmarks ought to be preserved in roughly the reverse order of priority that most preservationists would urge. There is one remaining objection to the Argument from Duties to Past Generations. It is the one which I believe has the most force.

If it were the case that we have a duty to preserve the creations of our ancestors because of their preferences and desires, then we would have a duty to preserve everything and anything that they wanted us to preserve. If, for whatever reasons, they wanted us to preserve their outhouses and storm cellars, but didn't care at all whether we preserved their paintings and cathedrals, then we would be dutybound only to preserve these mundane objects. Similarly, if we desired that toxic waste dumps and automobile burial grounds should be our gift to future generations, then those who come after us would have a duty to preserve them. This seems perverse. After all, it is the present generation who must live with the legacy of the past. Perhaps respecting the preferences of our ancestors is a good "first cut" at determining what ought to be preserved. Perhaps it would even be very nice of us to preserve what they want us to preserve. But it cannot be that we have a duty to them to do this. For what ought to be preserved surely turns on *the properties of the things in question and their impacts on the lives of those living now*. To suppose otherwise is to enslave those now alive to the known tastes and preferences of those who have gone before or to the unknown tastes and preferences of those who will come afterward.

In short, then, although in principle those who live in the present have duties to the dead, there is no good reason for supposing that we have any specific duty to preserve the creations of the past because we owe it to those who have gone before. The Argument from Duties to Past Generations fails to provide a convincing foundation for preservation.

## §14 THE ARGUMENT FROM CULTURAL IDENTITY

The final category of arguments that I shall consider roots our obligation to preserve landmarks in considerations about people who are now alive. One such argument frequently heard in popular discussion is that preserving landmarks is necessary for preserving our cultural identity. The usually unargued assumption that lies in the background is that preserving our cultural identity is a good thing.

We might begin by asking what it means to have a cultural identity. Perhaps the words of Josiah Royce quoted earlier in this essay (§1) suggest an answer. People with a cultural identity "idealize," "adorn," and "ennoble" their communities. They educate their children in the history and traditions of their culture. They preserve and protect their language, literature, and native arts. They do what they can to help those who are also members of their culture.

Assuming that this is roughly what it means to have a cultural identity, we may then go on to ask why it is a good thing to have one. This is not an easy question to ask, much less answer, in the contemporary climate. In the 1960s the promotion of cultural identity was widely considered to be an important step in the liberation of America's oppressed minorities. In the 1970s the fascination with cultural identity spread beyond Afro-Americans, Hispanics, and Native Americans to encompass people of virtually every ethnic and cultural background. Many of our recent novels, films, and television programs, ranging from *Roots* to *Mean Streets*, assert the importance of cultural identity. Perhaps even the current religious revival, exemplified by the Moral Majority, can be explained in part by a yearning for a common cultural identity in a pluralistic and fragmented society.

If we seriously ask why cultural identity might be a good thing, two answers suggest themselves. The first focuses on the individual. It might be argued that cultural identity is important for human happiness and welfare. Humans are, after all, cultural animals. When we have no strong cultural background to identify with we tend toward the dysfunctional. We become rootless and unstuck. Though we may survive, we do not flourish. The second answer focuses on the society rather than the individual. A society in which individuals have a cultural identity is one in which people are more likely to cooperate and pursue common goals. A society which is unified in purpose and principle is one which is better for everyone to live in.

The first of these answers involves a difficult empirical claim. Whether or not people with a cultural identity are happier or more functional than those without such an identity is a matter for psychological investigation. It would not be an easy investigation to undertake, however, for such murky notions as "having a cultural identity," "being functional," and "being happy" would have to be made operational—that is, we would have to know what counts as evidence for and against each of these attributions. Since there is reason for despair about the possibility of empirically verifying or falsifying this claim, we might as well do some speculating.

There is some reason to believe that people with a cultural identity might be happier and more functional than those without one. People with a cultural identity have more clearly defined roles. What is expected of them is not in doubt. What is of meaning and significance is given by shared cultural norms. But just as there is reason for supposing that cultural identity is conducive to happiness and being functional, so there is reason for believing that it is not. Societies in which people have a strong sense of cultural identity are often intolerant and repressive. Such societies force individuals into molds not of their own choosing. It is important to remember that cultural identity, which has the ring of something good, is the near neighbor of chauvinism and jingoism, both of which are clearly evils.

The second answer to our question is that a society in which people have a cultural identity is one in which people are more likely to cooperate and to pursue common goals. Two very different kinds of societies in which people might have a deep sense of cultural identity must be distinguished, however. The first kind is one which is homogeneous, and most people share a common cultural identity. Contemporary Poland, a country with few ethnic minorities in which almost everyone is Roman Catholic in religion, might be an example of this kind of society. The second kind of society is one which is pluralistic. In this kind of society most people have a cultural identity, but there is no common cultural identity which they share. Perhaps the United States is, or once was, an example of this kind of society. It could be argued that Italians, Jews, Blacks, and so forth all have a strong sense of cultural identity, but that their identities are as Italian-Americans, Jewish-Americans, Afro-Americans, and so forth. It is easy to see why cultural identity in the first kind of society would be conducive to widespread cooperation and the pursuit of common goals. It is difficult to see why this would be so in the second kind of society, however.

Some would surely wish to question the very idea that widespread cooperation and the pursuit of common goals is a good. They would point out that those societies with evil purposes and corrupt goals are all the worse for the unity they exhibit. If there must be a Nationalist Japan or a Nazi Germany better they should be fragmented and disunited. Some would go even further and say that except in extraordinary circumstances it is better for all societies to lack widespread cooperation and the pursuit of common goals. They would say that a good society is one which permits individuals to realize their own projects and life-plans. Since there is a richness and diversity in the projects and life-plans of individuals, a good society would create conditions in which many such projects and plans may thrive. For a society to be unified, cooperative, and in pursuit of common goals implies that it is suppressing, overtly or covertly, the individual goals and projects of its citizens. In this view the role of a society is to enable those within them to flourish. There is no further mission for the society as a whole.

It should be clear that the Argument from Cultural Identity raises some interesting questions that are not easily resolved. The most important of these questions center on (1) whether cultural identity is a good, (2) if it is, why it is, and (3) how important a good it is. Until we get a more convincing affirmative answer to the first, and compelling answers to the second and third questions, this argument remains unpersuasive.

One further question about this argument is worth asking. We have seen that the case for supposing that cultural identity is important for human happiness and welfare is inconclusive, and that the case for cultural identity as conducive to cooperation and the pursuit of societal goals is most plausible when there is a common cultural identity widely shared within the society. What policy regarding landmark preservation would be advocated by someone who believed that engendering cooperation and the pursuit of common societal goals were important goods?

The most general answer is that he would favor a policy of preferring landmarks associated with the dominant culture over those associated with minority cultures. Indeed, if he considered cultural uniformity a very great good, he might advocate the destruction of minority landmarks, since they contribute to maintaining minority cultures which inhibit social unity. Historical landmarks commemorating national leaders and the major events in the history of the nation would be a major priority for preservation since, in this view, they help to define a culture. In the case of the United States, it is hard to see what else in the way of landmarks serves to define a common culture. Perhaps it is not entirely silly to suggest that the first MacDonald's hamburger stand in Des Plaines, Illinois, the first casino built in Las Vegas, and the largest used car lot in Texas would be landmarks worthy of preservation if we were to follow this policy, while the sacred burial grounds of Native American peoples and the architecture of the Shakers would be allowed to pass from view.[30]

All of this taken together suggests that the Argument from Cultural Identity does not support a strong presumption in favor of landmark preservation.

## §15 THE ARGUMENT FROM COMMON WISDOM

The final argument that I shall consider is the one which I think provides the most powerful reason for preserving landmarks. But before developing this argument, we need to take stock of what already has been done.

So far I have argued that we have no duty to past or future people to preserve landmarks. If we ought to preserve them it is because such preservation is good for us. I have further suggested that preservation is often not economically efficient, that appeals to the aesthetic features of landmarks are insufficient to support much preservation, and that considerations about cultural identity do not provide a clear and unambiguous case for preservation. We must rethink what our policy concerning landmarks should be. In order to do this in a way that results in a sensible landmarks policy, we must develop a sensible urban policy; and in order to do that we must ask again what we want from our cities.

If we ask this question, I think the answer is obvious: We want our cities to provide an environment that is conducive to the good life. There are, of course, many different and competing conceptions of the good life. But most plausible conceptions share the view that the good life consists in qualitative goods as well as quantitative ones. To put the point in a different way, the good life cannot plausibly be defined just in terms of access to flush toilets or police protection; it must consider quality of life considerations as well. Although amenities like flush toilets probably bear on the quality of life for most of us, social, psychological, and emotional factors are at least as important. What I am suggesting is that we value cities not only for the material amenities they provide, but also for the possibilities they present for living a life of high quality, where high quality of life includes but does not exhaust the following: security, community, self-respect, self-esteem, adequate housing, adequate nutrition, adequate health care, opportunities for education, recreation, cultural development, and so forth. The question of whether landmarks should be preserved ought to be answered by reference to the impact of such preservation on the quality of life of those who live among and within them.[31]

The view that I wish to urge is that there is a strong presumption in favor of preserving landmarks because there is reason to believe that they are often part of a physical and cultural ecology which is conducive to the living of high quality lives. Before trying to say what might follow from this about landmarks policy, it is important to consider what arguments can be given for the view. Like most arguments that concern landmark preservation, they are fragmentary and less conclusive than one might wish. Still, they seem to me to carry considerable weight.

The first argument is really a negative one. As long as there have been cities, most attempts at central planning and redevelopment have only made things worse; and therefore, generally speaking, it is better to let well enough alone. The recent American experience is an instructive example.

As we noted in the introduction, as long as there have been cities in America there have been those who have thought them to be in crisis. By the end of World War II many people thought the situation had become intolerable. People and wealth were increasingly moving to the suburbs. The central cities could not compete successfully with suburban shopping centers, and their economic base was declining. The housing stock in the central cities was inferior to that of the suburbs and was rapidly degenerating. In 1949 Congress passed the Housing Act which for the first time guaranteed a "decent home" for every American family. The mechanism was to be an unprecedented partnership between the public and private sectors. The Housing Act provided for the creation of urban renewal authorities empowered to assemble large tracts of urban land by negotiation or condemnation. The authorities would develop land use plans, and then sell these tracts to private developers who were willing to build in accordance with the plans. In 1954 urban renewal authorities were also granted the power to develop commercial areas as well as housing.

From the beginning urban renewal was plagued by controversy. Political conservatives objected to the cost of the program, the role of government in planning, and the power of urban renewal authorities to condemn land. Many liberals saw urban renewal as a program designed to bring middle and upper class people back to central cities, rather than as a program designed to improve the lot of the city's working-class inhabitants. Some people saw urban renewal as a mechanism for distributing wealth away from small landowners and business executives to large corporations and developers. Others simply thought the projects were ugly. Although many well-intentioned and compassionate people favored urban renewal at the outset, the consensus now seems to be that this program was at best a mistake and at worst a tragedy.[32]

The problem, quite simply, is that, like natural ecosystems, urban networks are very complicated and interdependent; and it is extremely difficult to anticipate all of the consequences of one's actions. Very often urban renewal disrupted and displaced stable neighborhoods that were old and traditional. It destroyed small businesses and dispersed friends and relatives. Corner drugstores, taverns, churches, social halls, and other places that provided the focus for community life were destroyed. Often people whose homes were demolished were not adequately relocated. And all too often when they were, they wound up in large housing projects designed for efficiency and cost-effectiveness, rather than community and security. Although the following passage by the contemporary social critic, Jane Jacobs, is perhaps extreme in its rhetoric, it is largely correct about the effects of urban renewal:

> Look what we have built with the first several billions: low-income projects that become worse centers of delinquency, vandalism, and general hopelessness than the slums they were supposed to replace. Middle-income housing projects which are truly marvels of dullness and regimentation, sealed against any buoyancy or vitality of city life. Luxury housing projects that mitigate their inanity . . . with a vapid vulgarity. Cultural centers that are unable to support a good bookstore. Civic centers that are avoided by everyone but bums. . . . Expressways that eviscerate great cities. This is not the rebuilding of cities. This is the sacking of cities.[33]

The problem with the urban renewal program and others like it is not that the planners were ill-intentioned or malevolent. They simply did not know enough to carry out the projects which they had undertaken. As a society, we were quite ignorant about the character of urban life in the early days of the program. But even if everything were known that could be known, there would still be reason to be skeptical of large-scale redevelopment. Human communities are fragile and sensitive. It is easier to destroy them than to create them. It is as difficult to transplant a traditional inner-city community to a high-rise housing project as it is to transplant an entire biological ecosystem (e.g., the Everglades) to an alien environment (e.g., Montana).

This brings us to our second argument. Some might be tempted to dismiss the story about urban renewal that I have told as a special case. The problem is that the projects were not well done, it might be said, not that they were undertaken. Much has been learned from these failures. We will do better next time, and indeed we are doing better even now. Such optimism is not well founded. Were we to look at a number of such programs in a variety of countries, we would see that the fate of urban renewal in the United States is the norm rather than the exception. Large-scale redevelopment typically works only when planners have something in mind other than the maintenance of human communities and the pursuit of a high quality of life. An example is the redesign of Paris after the revolutions of 1848. Napoleon III was disturbed at how the narrow winding streets of Paris made it difficult to suppress urban uprisings with modern armies. He commissioned Haussmann to redesign the city in such a way that would make it difficult for the people ever again to control the city in defiance of the government. Haussman's design was very successful. It has stood succeeding governments in good stead ever since, most recently in May of 1968. Had Haussmann been commissioned to redesign Paris with a view to enhancing the quality of life of its inhabitants, the failures of other planners are an omen of his chances of success. Like willfully setting out in pursuit of happiness, the intention seems almost certain to guarantee its own frustration.

It is no accident that most ambitious redevelopment programs fail. Traditional buildings and neighborhoods are the results of many small decisions by many ordinary people. Buildings have been constructed with the purpose of their users in mind. And when they have not been, over a long period of time people turn these buildings to their ends. A *common wisdom* is expressed in vernacular architecture and "unplanned" cities. It is the collective wisdom of several generations. It is not easy for any single individual to grasp and articulate this wisdom. The "planning" that is implicit in these traditional structures is likely to embody more subtle distinctions and make possible more worthwhile connections, like the rugs woven by entire families in Afghanistan and Tibet, than any comparable structures that are invented by a planning firm after a month or year of thought. The traditional structures have, after all, stood the test of time. They have survived as long as they have because, at least to some degree, they are adequate to the purposes of the people who have made them and use them. This is more than we can be sure of when we commission planners to rebuild our cities.

The best reason for preserving landmarks, then, is that they embody the common wisdom of those who have built them, lived in them, worked in them, and played in them. They are likely to permit greater community, liberty, security, and so forth, and to make possible a higher quality of life than anything we might invent. This is not to say that the last word in urban planning ought to be the preservation of what has survived. It is to say that it should be the first word, and a word to which we all too often have been deaf.

I have suggested that there is a presumption that urban landmarks should be preserved because they are part of a pattern of life which is more conducive to a high-quality human existence than anything we are likely to invent to replace them. This perspective suggests that, whenever possible, landmarks should be preserved as part of an urban system and not just as idle curiosities. What is valuable about landmarks is their role in human life, and that can be destroyed as effectively by isolating them as by razing them. For all its publicity and acclaim, the French Quarter of New Orleans, for example, is a heart without a body, a mere shadow of its former self. It is a place to visit; it is not a place to live. If we must choose between preserving a landmark that is part of a viable living system or one that is of greater aesthetic value but is not part of such a system, it may well be best to prefer the former. Landmarks are more than the sum of their own parts; they are also, in part, the sum of their relations to the ways of life around them.

It is well to remember that the considerations that have been given create only *a presumption* in favor of preservation. There are many other concerns which we have, ranging from distributive justice to environmental protection. These concerns might weigh against preservation in particular cases. A viable, comprehensive policy concerning landmark preservation would have to provide a mechanism for weighting these competing interests. To develop such a policy is beyond the more modest ambitions of the present essay. Even so, one can say that the argument I have given does not give preservationists everything they want. Nevertheless, it gives them as much as they are entitled to; and, I think, it makes the strongest case for preservation that can reasonably be sustained.

In conclusion, it should be recognized that the Argument from Common Wisdom, in addition to making the strongest case for preservation that can reasonably be sustained, also encompasses many of the concerns reflected in the other arguments which we have considered. What more respect can we show for the dead than a deep appreciation for the fundamental structures of human life which they have bequeathed to us? What better gift could we give to the future than cities which are not just livable, but also make possible the development of all that is best in human life, taken both individually and collectively? And surely nothing could be a better symbol of our cultural identity than cities which protect diversity but also encourage community. Since we are creatures with an aesthetic sensibility, we can be confident that what permits us to thrive will not deeply transgress our sense of beauty. Finally, although landmarks do not have rights, their contribution to the good life is so basic and pervasive that they should enjoy relative autonomy from the passing whims and fancies of urban design.

## V. THE PLACE OF UTOPIAN THINKING

Throughout this essay I have argued that, at least when it comes to urban problems, it is usually better to trust the everyday decisions of ordinary people than the social engineering of the experts. I have argued that the tools of economic analysis, so well-entrenched in the bastions of policy-making, are not always adequate for constructive and creative thinking about urban environmental problems. I have argued in particular that the strongest reason for preserving landmarks is not any of the reasons commonly cited, but rather it is because the common wisdom of generations of builders and users working on a piecemeal basis is likely to result in structures that are more conducive to human flourishing than anything that city planners are likely to come up with in their armchairs or at their drawing tables. These conclusions might suggest that there is no place for "unordinary" people, those with utopian visions about what cities ideally can and should be. But that would be wrong.

Utopian thinking about cities is important for a number of reasons. Before discussing these reasons, however, it is important to understand the character of such thinking. Utopian thinking about cities is a form of social theorizing and social criticism. The idea that there is a connection between the physical structures of communities and their social lives is an ancient one. This idea has been especialy influential in the United States. During the nineteenth century, many different sects, including the Shakers, the Mormons, and the True Inspiration Congregations, developed distinctive forms of architecture and community planning that were regarded as specially related to the moral and religious beliefs of the community. Even the communal movement of the 1960s was associated with its own distinctive architecture and planning, most notably the geodesic dome and the "Blueprint for a Communal Environment," a document produced by members of several Berkeley community organizations.[34] Generally speaking, architecture and planning in the twentieth century have been dominated by thinkers with a utopian vision. Some were crackpots like Hitler, tinkering with his models and sketches of a new Berlin while the old one was bombed to pieces by the Allies. Others seem merely fatuous, like Paoli Soleri, who labors on in his attempt to create the utopian city of Arcosanti in the middle of the Arizona desert. But others have been very influential on practicing architects and planners, perhaps none more than the French architect Le Corbusier and the English planner Ebenezer Howard.

Le Corbusier's vision in the 1920s, like many of his contemporaries in painting, sculpture, and interior design, was the Modernist one. Existing cities were crowded, confused, unsanitary, and irrational. They were to be swept away. We would begin anew building in concrete and steel, exploiting the possibilities for efficiency and standardization created by new technologies. Le Corbusier's vision is revealed most clearly in his plan for the reconstruction of central Paris. Everything was to be destroyed, save only a handful of isolated historic landmarks. The new centerpiece was to be a series of sixty-floor office buildings, each stripped of any ornamental detail, each sited on its own piece of land. This complex of office buildings was to be serviced by a number of high-speed transportation routes carrying workers to their jobs. Outside the central core was to be a series of apartment buildings, each of the same height, every one the same. Le Corbusier conceived of the city as a "tool for living." The purpose of design and planning was to make these tools as efficient as possible. This could be done by making everything as uniform and geometrically perfect as could be. Le Corbusier also saw the need for interaction with nature. For that reason each building was to be sited on its own patch of green. There is a vision of human life and society in Le Corbusier's utopian dreams. It is the vision of uniformity and efficiency. It is the vision of human life as just another job to be completed. It may not be a vision we like very much, but it is one that has been extremely influential in this century.

Ebenezer Howard's vision was quite different. He was shocked by the ugliness and blight of the British industrial cities at the turn of the century. He thought nothing could be done with the old cities. The solution was to build new ones that were more adequate to human needs and desires. Howard proposed new cities of about 30,000 situated on approximately 1,000 acres of land, surrounded by a greenbelt of farms and gardens. Beyond the greenbelt were the factories that provided the residents with employment. All the land was to be held in common and rented to its users.

The architecture and planning of Le Corbusier and Howard were rooted in different views about human life and human society. Le Corbusier was inspired by breakthroughs in science and engineering. Problems of planning were, for him, technical problems. A viable aesthetic would follow from the study of efficiency. Howard, on the other hand, was influenced by the tradition of utopian socialism. His mission was to harmonize capital and labor, city and country, factory and farm, in practice and not just in theory.

For all of their genius, the influence of Le Corbusier and Howard has not always been salutary. The monuments to Le Corbusier are the cold, faceless skyscrapers that now dominate the downtown sections of most of our cities. Howard's legacy is the sprawling suburbs that surround them.

Still, there is a place for utopian thinking about cities. While our traditional patterns of building, our collective wisdom, often embody diversity and tolerance, they often embody less noble characteristics as well. After all, today's innovation becomes part of what preservationists might seek to preserve and protect tomorrow. Here is an example. Most people today would say that we should "design with nature." It would be best for our streets to follow the natural contours of the land and to respect the prominent features of the natural environment. Yet most American cities were originally laid out according to a grid, regardless of the topography. If a hill or a swamp or a river got in the way, it was filled or bulldozed or dynamited. If that was impossible, an uneasy and often unworkable truce was established. Preserving the original plans of most American cities would often mean preserving these attempts to dominate nature rather than to coexist with her. Not everything new is good; but neither is everything old. We must learn from the sins of our ancestors, and not complacently bequeath them to our children. Utopian thinkers, one might say, are the conscience of the ages speaking to us now.

How, practically, are utopian thinkers important? Their visions are important, first of all, because they sometimes result in ideas we can use. Le Corbusier made us acutely aware of the possibilities of new materials. Howard gave us the greenbelt, a concept which has become very important in the plans of many middle-sized communities. We need not buy everything these thinkers are selling in order to find something helpful.

Second, utopian thinking is valuable because it forces us to clarify our views about what cities are for and where we want them to go. Consider an example. In the introduction to their book *Communitas*, Percival and Paul Goodman write:

> For thirty years now, our American way of life as a whole has been subjected to sweeping condemnation by thoughtful social and cultural critics. . .
>
> In this book we must add, alas, to the subjects of this cultural criticism the physical plant and the town and the regional plans in which we have been living so unsatisfactorily. We will criticize not merely the foolish shape and power of the cars but the cars themselves, and not merely the cars but the factories where they are made, the highways on which they run, and the plan of livelihood that makes those highways necessary.[35]

This passage should make us think. Do we share the Goodmans' view of the automobile? Or is this just another example of pathological hatred of this symbol of middle-class life? If we disagree with the Goodmans, we should know why. If we agree with them, perhaps their book will extend and deepen our belief.

Finally, utopian thinking is important because it gives us a yardstick by which to measure our progress. It reminds us that we ought not to be satisfied with things as they are. Utopian thinkers remind us of what is possible, and of how far we have to go to make human life even remotely as good as it can be.

In conclusion, however, it is important to remember the major theme of this essay. In the end, the cities around us are the creations of ourselves and of our ancestors. They are the primary environments in which most of us live, and they are one of the most important gifts we will give our children. Although we are often told that urban problems are beyond our competence to control, we must not alienate our power and forfeit our responsibility to those who might mystify us with their techniques. For all too often they twist the problems in order to fit their methods, rather than tailoring their methods to the problems that need to be solved. In its own way, urban life is as fragile as the ecosystems of the oceans and the environment of the California condor. Just as a proper humility is necessary for one who wishes to save a species or an ocean, so it is required for one who wishes to preserve what's best in urban life.

# NOTES

I would like to thank Professor Dana Cuff, now of the Rice Institute School of Architecture, for her many helpful suggestions, not all of which I have been able to follow; and Lori Gruen who has been enormously helpful in assisting with my research. In addition, I am grateful to the Organized Research Fund of the Colorado Commission on Higher Education for the grant that supported this project in its early stages.

1.   The international statistics are taken from 1976 *World Population Data Sheet* (Washington, D.C.: Population Reference Bureau, 1976). The American statistics are from Bureau of Census, *Census of Population:* 1970 (Washington, D.C.: U.S. Government Printing Office, 1971).

2.   Thomas Jefferson, *Notes on the State of Virginia* (New York: Harper and Row, 1964), 158.

3.   Thomas Jefferson, *Works of Thomas Jefferson*, vol. 4, ed. P. Ford (New York: G. P. Putnam's, 1905), 146–7.

4.   Ralph Waldo Emerson, *Society and Solitude* (Boston: Houghton, Mifflin, and Company, 1883), 148.

5.   Henry David Thoreau, *The Writings of H. D. Thoreau*, vol. 9 (Boston: Houghton, Mifflin and Company, 1906), 51.

6.   Edgar Allan Poe, "Mellonta Tauta," in *Collected Works of Edgar Allan Poe*, vol. 3, ed. T. Mabbott (Cambridge, Mass.: Harvard University Press, 1978).

7.   Josiah Royce, *Race Questions, Provincialism and Other American Problems* (New York: The Macmillan Company, 1908), 77.

8.   *Ibid.*, 87.

9.   *Ibid.*, 95.

10.  Josiah Royce, *The Philosophy of Loyalty* (New York: The Macmillan Company, 1908), 245–6.

11.  Frank Lloyd Wright, *The Living City* (New York: Bramhall House, 1958), 97.

12.  W. R. Catten, J. C. Herdee, and T. W. Steinburn, *Urbanism and the Natural Environment: An Attitude Study* (Seattle: Institute for Sociological Research, University of Washington, 1969); and Louis Harris Associates, *A Survey of Citizen Views and Concerns about Urban Life* (Washington, D.C.: Department of Housing and Urban Development, 1978).

13.  Alexis de Tocqueville, *Democracy in America*, vol. 1, trans. P. Bradley (New York: Alfred A. Knopf, 1945), 289–90.

14.  See U.S. Department of Housing and Urban Development, *The President's National Urban Policy Report* (Washington, D.C.: U.S. Government Printing Office, 1978).

15.  These statistics are taken from lectures by Professor Jean Gottman of Oxford University.

16.  See M. Costello, "Future of the City," in Hoyt Gimlin, ed., *Editorial Research Reports on the Future of the City* (Washington, D.C.: Congressional Quarterly Inc., 1974), 12.

17. See, for example, the essays by Melvin M. Webber in *Daedalus* 97 (1968), and in Lowdon Wingo, Jr., ed., *Cities and Space* (Baltimore: Johns Hopkins Press, 1963).

18. For discussions of the urban problems mentioned in this paragraph see the following: G. Harrison and J. Gibson, eds., *Man in Urban Environments* (Oxford University Press, 1976); D. Elgin, T. Thomas, T. Logothetti, and S. Cox, *City Size and Quality of Life* (Stanford: Stanford Research Institute, 1974); Department of Housing and Urban Development, *op. cit.*; and Claude S. Fischer, *The Urban Experience* (New York: Harcourt Brace Jovanovich, 1976).

19. This projection is taken from U.S. Department of Health, Education and Welfare, *Asbestos Exposure* (Washington, D.C.: National Cancer Institute, 1980). For a general account of the issues see Samuel S. Epstein, *The Politics of Cancer* (Garden City, N.Y.: Doubleday, 1979).

20. Those who are inspired by the economic analysis of the law might wish to go so far as to advocate distributing all rights on the basis of economic efficiency. For general background see Richard A. Posner, *The Economics of Justice* (Cambridge, Mass.: Harvard University Press, 1981).

21. This data was made available to me by researchers at the National Center for Atmospheric Research. Although there is very little data in this area which can be regarded as definitive, the concerns of this section, which are fundamentally moral, are not affected by the exact details of the nature and extent of the connections between carbon monoxide and heart attack.

22. As quoted in M. Cohn, "Historic Preservation," in Hoyt Gimlin, *op. cit,* 163.

23. R. Anthony, "Polls, Pollution and Politics," *Environment* 24 (1982).

24. G. McLelland and J. Rohrbaugh, "Who Accepts the Pareto Axiom? The Role of Utility and Equity in Arbitration Decisions," *Behavioral Science* 23 (1978).

25. See Christopher Stone, *Should Trees Have Standing?* (Los Altos, Calif.: William Kaufman, 1974); and Justice Douglas's dissent in *Mineral King* v. *Morton,* 405 U.S. 727, 742 (1972).

26. For criticism of this view, see Martin and Naomi Golding, "Why Preserve Landmarks? A Preliminary Inquiry," in K. E. Goodpaster and K. M. Sayre, *Ethics and Problems of the 21st Century* (Notre Dame, Ind.: University of Notre Dame Press, 1979).

27. The argument in this paragraph is Derek Parfit's. His forthcoming book investigates its implications for moral philosophy, economics, and decision theory.

28. This is a well-known result in general equilibrium theory. See, for example, Paul Anthony Samuelson, *Economics*, 10th ed. (New York: McGraw-Hill Book Company, 1976), 634.

29. These passages are quoted by Roderick Nash in his *Wilderness and the American Mind* (New Haven: Yale University Press, 1967), 37, 259.

30. Shortly after writing these words the following news item came to my attention.

> **Threatened:** The first McDonald's fastfood restaurant, a sleek drive-in hamburger stand in Des Plaines, Ill., was opened by Ray Kroc in 1955. Nearly 7,000 McDonald's and 60 billion hamburgers later, the parent corporation says that the seatless facility is too small and outmoded and will be replaced in the spring. However, McDonald's may move the building to create a museum of fast food. It also may be nominated to the National Register of Historic Places, *Preservation News* (February, 1983), p. 12.

31.   For more on the concept of quality of life see D. Jamieson and J. Sneed, "What Is Quality of Life?", a Working Paper available from the Center for the Study of Values and Social Policy, University of Colorado, Boulder CO 80309.

32.   See, for example: Charles Abrams, *The City Is the Frontier* (New York: Harper and Row, 1965); Scott A. Greer, *Urban Renewal and American Cities* (Indianapolis: Bobbs Merrill, 1965); Martin Anderson, *The Federal Bulldozer* (Cambridge, Mass.: The MIT Press, 1964); Herbert J. Gans, *People and Plans* (New York: Basic Books, 1968), Chap. 18; Bernard J. Frieden, *The Future of Old Neighborhoods* (Cambridge, Mass.: The MIT Press, 1964); and P. Kessler and C. Hartman, "The Illusion and Reality of Urban Renewal: A Case Study of San Francisco's Yerba Buena Center," *Land Economics* 44 (1974).

33.   Jane Jacobs, *The Death and Life of Great American Cities* (New York: Vintage Books, 1961), 4.

34.   "Blueprint for a Communal Environment," in Theodore Roszak, ed., *Sources* (New York: Harper and Row, 1972).

35.   Paul and Percival Goodman, *Communitas* (New York: Vintage Books, 1960), 4.

## SUGGESTIONS FOR FURTHER READING

Any serious thinking about cities must begin with the work of Lewis Mumford, especially *The Culture of Cities* (New York: Harcourt Brace and Company, 1938), and *The City in History*, published in 1961 by the same company. The philosophical literature on cities is both sparse and disappointing, but see A. K. Bierman, *The Philosophy of Urban Existence* (Athens: Ohio University Press, 1973), and Lawrence Haworth, *The Good City* (Bloomington: Indiana University Press, 1963).

See the following sources in addition to those cited in the notes for further discussion of some of the main themes of this essay.

§§1–4.   Any good textbook in urban geography will supply the basic information concerning the comparative history of urbanization and forecasts about present trends. I have found Ray M. Northam, *Urban Geography* (New York: John Wiley, 1979) to be particularly useful. Concerning attitudes toward the city in American intellectual history, there is no substitute for reading original sources; still, Morton and Lucia White, *The Intellectual Versus the City* (Cambridge, Mass.: Harvard University Press and The MIT Press, 1962) is certainly the best secondary source available.

§§5–8.   The view that I have called the economist's view is really only the view of some economists. It is even perhaps more characteristic of policy analysts and others in government and business who are deeply influenced by economists. The most useful short introduction to the basic concepts and their justification is that of A. Myrick Freeman, III, "The Ethical Basis of the Economic View of the Environment," a Working Paper available from the Center for the Study of Values, University of Colorado, Boulder CO 80309. A helpful textbook is by E. J. Mishan, *Elements of Cost-Benefit Analysis*, 2d ed. (Boston: George Allen and Unwin, 1976). Influential criticisms of this approach include those of Amartya Sen, "Rational Fools: A Critique of the Behavioral Foundations of Economic Theory," *Philosophy and Public Affairs* 6 (1977); Laurence Tribe, "Policy Science: Analysis or Ideology," *Philosophy and Public Affairs* 2 (1972); and several articles by Mark Sagoff, for example, "Economic Theory and Environmental Law," *Michigan Law Review* 79 (1981).

The conventional approach to valuing lives which I criticize is amply represented in Steven E. Rhoades, ed., *Valuing Life: Public Policy Dilemmas* (Boulder, Colo.: Westview Press, 1980). A devastating critique of the conventional approach is by J. A. Broome, "Trying to Value a Life," *Journal of Public Economics* 9 (1978).

§11.  For the views of several philosophers on the objectivity of aesthetic value see W. E. Kennick, ed., *Art and Philosophy*, 2d ed. (New York: St. Martin's Press, 1979), Parts 5–6; and the references cited therein.

§12.  On the general topic of duties to future generations see Ernest Partridge, *Responsibilities to Future Generations* (Buffalo, N.Y.: Prometheus Books, 1981).

§13.  The problem of duties to past generations has not received the attention it deserves, but see: Thomas Nagel, *Mortal Questions* (New York: Cambridge University Press, 1979), Chapter 1; Joel Feinberg, *Rights, Justice and the Bounds of Liberty* (Princeton: Princeton University Press, 1980), Chapter 3; Ernest Partridge, "Posthumous Interests and Posthumous Respect," *Ethics* 89 (1979); and George Pitcher, "The Misfortunes of the Dead," forthcoming in the *American Philosophical* Quarterly.

§14.  Considerations concerning the importance of cultural identity are often introduced in popular debates over such issues as bilingual education, aboriginal whaling, and the distribution of foreign aid. Surprisingly there has been very little philosophical investigation of the importance of cultural identity. A notable exception is the work of Peter Wenz of Sangamon State University. See his forthcoming essays, "Human Rights and Ethnic Integrity" and "What Good Is Ethnic Diversity?".

§15.  Although the Argument from Common Wisdom has, to my knowledge, never before been explicitly formulated and applied to the problem of landmark preservation, it is related to the general view of cities sketched by Richard Sennett in *The Uses of Disorder* (New York: Random House, 1970). I was led to construct this argument by reflecting on some remarks of J. L. Austin's concerning the wisdom embodied in ordinary language. See his *Philosophical Papers*, second edition (New York: Oxford University Press, 1970), pp. 181–182. This view is related to the conservative traditionalism of Edmund Burke, most famously expressed in his *Reflections on the Revolution in France* (Chicago: Gateway Editions, Inc., 1962).

Part V.  A fascinating discussion of American utopian architecture may be found in Delores Hayden, *Seven American Utopias* (Cambridge: The MIT Press, 1976). For the views of Le Corbusier see *The Ideas of Le Corbusier on Architecture and Planning*, edited by J. Guitan and translated by M. Guitan (New York: George Braziller, 1981). For Ebenezer Howard's views see *Garden Cities of Tomorrow* (London: Faber and Faber, 1951). Murray Bookchin's *The Limits of the City* (New York: Harper and Row, 1974) is an extremely stimulating discussion of the limits of urban planning.

# 3

# Pollution and Political Theory

## TIBOR R. MACHAN

《 〉》

## I. INTRODUCTION

The concept of pollution is problematic from the start. Dictionaries differ as to what it means. One says pollution is "the act of defiling or rendering impure, as pollution of drinking water."[1] Another states that it "occurs when materials are accumulated where they are not wanted."[2] Yet another says that to pollute is "to corrupt or defile" and identifies pollution with "contamination of soil, air and water by noxious substances and noises."[3] In the end a sensible definition of pollution will have to cover air and water pollution from materials, nuclear particles, noise, light, and anything else that is the result of human activity and can be shown to cause harm to another human being or damage to property. Such a definition would preclude anything like "natural" pollution. Nature may render things impure, but only human beings can pollute.

The central problem associated with pollution, as far as the general public is concerned, has to do with the difficulty—perhaps even the impossibility—of confining harms to particular people and places. For example, air pollution occurs when people dump materials into the air which others do not want there and which at the same time harms others or puts them at risk of harm. Were it possible to confine these materials in some definite location, the polluter could perhaps release them without inflicting the pollution on others. But as things are now, pollution usually is not controllable in this way. The airborne contaminants from Birmingham's smokestacks can end up in New England's lakes—can, indeed, render these lakes "dead."

It is by no means clear just how permanent or inescapable this problem is. Those with a robust sense of reality are not likely to be optimistic

74

on this score, however, and, in any event, the kind of problem it is—a kind of *public evils* problem—could well be a permanent one. It is important, therefore, to examine what different political theories would say with respect to handling pollution, important both because their respective answers might help us understand how best to cope with the problem of pollution and because the merits of their respective approaches to this problem might help us choose which one among these theories is the best, all considered.

There is a further point to be made, before proceeding. In our day-to-day life there is an understandable inclination to focus attention upon particularly noxious examples of pollution (e.g., Love Canal or nuclear fallout from early atomic testing in the American Southwest). Convinced that a grave injustice has been done, we are unlikely to ask about the grounds of justice themselves. And yet a moment's reflection should direct our attention in this more theoretical though not less important direction. Particular acts, laws, or practices are unjust. To find a given act unjust thus is to commit oneself to the view that other acts like this one in the relevant respects also are unjust. But what are these relevant respects? That is a question that must be answered by *thinking about* those particular acts we judge unjust, not merely by issuing our judgment that they are. Thus arises, not by a philosopher's trick or ruse, the need to think about the nature of justice generally—its grounds and scope. Indeed, once we feel the logic of the pull of ideas, we soon realize that questions about what is just in particular cases will lead us, if we will but follow, to questions about the nature of a just social order. The question about how to deal with the problem of pollution justly, therefore, cannot and should not be answered in a theoretical vacuum. If we are to command a clear view of the problem, we must see it against the backdrop of competing visions of a just society.

Although virtually every known and distinct political theory is in force to some degree somewhere on our globe, we will concern ourselves only with those operative in the more powerful, influential societies. These societies provide the effective leadership in matters of problem solving, including how the problems created by pollution are approached worldwide. Though selective, we are not arbitrary when we limit our attention to these political alternatives.

Four distinct political theories will concern us. These are (1) capitalism (or libertarianism), (2) socialism (democratic and centrist), (3) the welfare state, and (4) fascism (military or one-party dictatorships). Though distinct, in actual political systems elements of one can mix with elements of others. Elements of capitalism are found in fascist and welfare states, for example, just as the welfare state contains features that we will see evident in socialist societies. Considered theoretically, however, the systems are distinct and importantly different. We shall examine each with special reference to the problem of pollution. But we shall also want to assess their respective merits (or lack of them) at a deeper level.

## II.  FASCISM: RULE BY INSPIRED LEADERSHIP

Most of us associate fascism with Adolf Hitler's Germany and Mussolini's Italy, both of which are held in contempt by most decent people. But there are many people who hold capitalism and socialism in contempt as well, and there are those who regard the welfare state as a pitiful excuse for a just social order. The objective here is not to stress how most of us *feel* about these systems but to examine, in impartial, fair terms, what the tenets of the systems are and what implications those tenets hold for handling the problem of pollution.

What is crucial about fascism is that it is a system of government that relies on the leadership of those who are taken to be great, inspired individuals in a society. In this respect the fascist system assumes it is possible to identify who such a great leader is or would be. It is not a concern of ours now to question whether this basic idea is sound. Suffice it to mention that it is not unusual for us to expect to find someone in some area of human concern who is more highly qualified than others to understand the relevant issues. In such special areas as physics, chemistry, sociology, psychology, economics, and the like, we often assume that someone will achieve the status of the most informed, even wisest. Fascism merely pushes this natural assumption into the realm of politics.

### §1  SELECTING THE LEADER

The main theoretical difficulty with this idea concerns how the leader is to be identified. In a fascist system there can be no reliance on the democratic method—although in some actual fascist systems there sometimes is an official bow, so to speak, to democracy, as when "elections" are conducted to give the appearance of widespread public participation in the political process. In an outright fascist system, however, no such pretense can be found since, so far as fascist political theory is concerned, there is no need to rely on the democratic process to identify the appropriate person who would lead the community in question. Instead, the leader would be *self-selected* and would inspire support through the clear superiority he or she has when it comes to political wisdom.

In a fascist system there is more reliance on what is most accurately called intuition than on any other method of reaching an understanding about political methods. The intuition in question has to do with the leader's apprehension of what is right and wrong for the entire human community—with, that is, the leader's intuition of how the state can progress toward the goals which, in his or her wisdom, the leader selects.

Intuition is familiar to us as a kind of unanalyzed understanding or knowledge. The sexist expression "woman's intuition" refers to a woman's presumed ability to know certain facts without extensive reflection, research, analysis, or inference. Women (supposedly) *just know* what is the case, what is right or important, unaware of any way they came by this knowledge. In more technical terms, intuition is a kind of *immediate understanding* of some matters for which no other avenue of discovery is available. Such a mode of understanding is often taken to apply most especially to moral and political matters.

In the history of philosophy it has often been maintained that knowledge about matters of right and wrong is not like knowledge about matters of fact. This is the essence of the so-called is/ought gap, the contention that no judgment as to what *should* be the case or what *should* be done can be derived from or based on what *is* the case. Lacking ordinary ways of gaining knowledge, it has been proposed that a different way to knowledge is available when it comes to knowledge of values, whether moral, political, or aesthetic. And fascism, whether based on this historical problem or not, relies on this intuitionist approach to value, at least in the case of the intuitions of those who are to be the leaders of society.

All this can be seen to be problematic, especially from the point of view of those who have great confidence in systematic methods of gaining knowledge—e.g., the biological and social sciences. Yet even among those who find fascism a very questionable political system, there are many who accept its underlying method of reaching truth and understanding about values. Indeed, there are many today, working in democratic societies, who believe that there is no right method for reaching truth of any kind, not even in science, let alone in morality or politics. So at its foundations, fascism's view of how we know any "fundamental" truth has *some* intellectual support in our own culture, even among philosophers of science.[4]

## §2 SAME STRUCTURE, DIFFERENT FORMS

The structure of a fascist political regime would be dictatorial. One might imagine that structure to take the form of an upright pyramid, with the heroic leader at the very top, guiding all elements of human life beneath. And there is no question that throughout human history something along these lines has been the status quo for many societies, including some widely admired systems of human community life such as, for example, American Indian tribes that relied on the leadership of tribal chiefs.

Do we then conclude that as far as handling various problems of society, including those associated with pollution, the approach would have to be regarded as pretty much arbitrary? Not quite. Although the goals chosen by the leader would be grasped by intuition—something that is not possible to explain and defend by reference to familiar standards of truth and value—there is no reason that once these goals were chosen, the leaders could not rely on less esoteric resources. Argentina, Chile, Brazil, and Libya have all made attempts, with various degrees of success, at tapping nuclear power generation as a source for industrial develment. (It is not in these societies that we witness the outpouring of protests against the use of nuclear power generation, whether it has to do with peaceful or military technology.) From this alone it is clear that some societies that are more or less modeled on the fascist theory—and it is rare that any society is fully consonant with any one political view-point—are committed to using scientific means to achieve technological progress.

Though a fascist state need not be opposed to science and the technological progress this reliance makes possible, it might be. To the extent that a fascist system is committed to inspired leadership, the goals to be pursued would be dependent on the dictates of the inspiration experienced by the hero leader. Inasmuch as some fascist societies are religiously based, their progress is frequently envisioned as spiritual, not scientific or technological. Of course, there need be no conflict between spiritual and scientific/technological progress, if the leader "sees" no conflict. Yet it is possible that in societies which stress spiritual matters, technological advancement would be relegated to a subordinate level. Such concerns might be checked by priorities such as overall environmental well-being, aesthetic quality, and similar matters. Those could keep science and technology at a relatively low level of development.

Now what is crucial for our purposes is that in fascist societies *the harm caused by pollution* would be made a function of the kind of progress that would be pursued in light of the inspiration of the hero leader. Just what inspiration such a leader would be motivated by is not possible to ascertain in general terms. A particular leader could be inspired to pursue any of such familiar goals as religious purity, moral excellence, artistic superiority, scientific/technological development, military power, or economic advancement. That being so, the problem of pollution in general would reduce to familiar questions about means and ends. In other words, as to the ends a fascist state would pursue, this is quite indeterminate. In general, however, such states would aim at superiority or excellence with regard to whatever end that was selected. And the questions concerning pollution, then, would be those that dealt with whether the end in view would be enhanced or ill served by allowing pollution to occur and, if so, to what extent.

## §3  FASCISM AND POLLUTION

Put in formal terms, a fascist state would take a purely pragmatic view of pollution. Given a certain objective, only the practical problem of whether this is helped or harmed by certain levels of pollution would arise. And, assuming the leader failed to "see" the rights of the individual, there would be no problem about various rights individuals might have against having pollution imposed upon them. Except for a concern about the well-being of individuals as a function of some envisioned progress of the state, what burden would fall upon members of that state, or the members of *other* states, from having to endure a certain level of wasteful emission would be entirely unproblematic. Given certain objectives, of course, various technical difficulties would still have to be faced. A kind of cost-benefit analysis would have to be carried out with respect to the level of various sorts of pollution or wasteful emission that is acceptable. Some of these difficulties would probably be more serious in religiously inspired fascist states than in states that engage in public policy determination on the basis of modern scientific/technological analysis, mainly because the former's concerns do not lend themselves to measurable weighing of costs and benefits. And this would introduce a special feature of fascist states, namely that aside from the determination of the goals to be pursued by the state, even the *methods* by which those goals are to be attained would be identified through spiritual inspiration.

In essence, then, the problem of handling pollution in a fascist society would, like all problems, be left to the judgment of the hero leader in whatever (inspirational or inspirationally dictated) way he or she would find appropriate. To say anything more would be to attempt to inject into fascism a degree of determinateness regarding public policy that is inimical to it.

## §4 A CRITIQUE OF FASCISM

It would be useful to consider just a few of the challenges which can be leveled at fascism from what we have seen of it above. Of course, all the other political theories would amount to challenges of one another anyway, so we will not cover everything at this stage of the discussion. (In any case, we can only *begin* to raise the difficulties which the systems that we will be discussing will have to face up to.)

There surely are numerous features about fascism that are questionable, but concerning our topic some matters of special concern come immediately to mind. Whether some substance is highly toxic or in some other manner harmful in less immediately obvious ways (e.g., causes eventual biological degeneration) depends on facts which *are* facts *quite independently* of an inspired leader's accepting the legitimacy of the scientific or other means of establishing this. Indeed, if there is a problem of pollution as such, it is one that exists as an objective, independent feature of reality, quite apart from what we believe. From research in biology and chemistry, for example, it is found that certain substances are harmful to human organisms. That is either true or false, regardless of any inspirations or visions anyone may or may not have. If we deny this we deny that there *is* a problem of pollution that faces political theories.

As soon as we admit the above, however, the central features of fascism, as a distinctive approach to organizing and administering a human community, come into question. At all stages of community life we rely on factual information. It may even be argued, as some philosophers do, that questions of value, including morality, politics, and aesthetics, amount to questions about a rather complex type of fact, not about something mystical, mysterious, elusive, and ineffable. For example, the value of health is based on the basic fact that life for the living is better than its termination (except in some very rare cases where death may be a relief). Public policy may be argued to be closely tied to this idea, and public policy regarding pollution is surely directly tied to it. Fascism, by its extreme reliance on mysterious ways of knowing—what goals should governments pursue, and how these goals should be pursued—is undercut, it appears, from the start, when the possibility of the requirement for factual knowledge is brought home to us. The sort of whimsical, though no doubt often enthusiastic and vehement (that is, "inspired"), approach to politics fascism takes simply flies in the face of what human living seems to require at every turn, namely, reasonableness, careful study of issues, science, and technology.

Regarding the explicit moral and political issues that are of interest to us, fascism of course offends the sensibilities of most of us, even those who may embrace some of its epistemological features, by showing absolutely no regard for the human individual. It is a system that allows, indeed can require, that individuals be used as mere means toward the realization of some greater collective good. There is not even a general requirement of treating members of the human community with equal regard for their worth as human beings, their dignity. The absence of values such as these would appear to call into question fascism's moral legitimacy, whatever else, if anything, could be said in its favor. Even though there are difficulties surrounding the demonstration of the values fascism thoroughly neglects, fascism's flagrant disregard for them, even as problems to contend with, must thwart any prospect of this system's success as a theory of a just social order.

## III. SOCIALISM: COLLECTIVE OR CENTRAL DECISIONMAKING

The essence of socialism is that a human community is to be viewed as a whole, an organic whole, the governance of which is to be carried out by way of *either* a democratic *or* a centrally planned approach. How would pollution be construed in such a system? Like every other question of public policy, this one is to be addressed by making reference to the central principle that should guide a human society from a socialist perspective—namely, that the well-being of society as a whole is to be promoted. This requires a discussion of alternative ways to approach this objective. Two answers can be found within socialist literature.

### §5 DEMOCRATIC SOCIALISM

First, democratic socialism requires that the standards of well-being for a human community should be identified by means of maximum political participation—elections, public debates, full representation of all those who comprise the membership of a society, and so on. But while these standards would have to emerge from political participation, some standards are embedded in the socialist framework itself. Democratic socialism seeks the well-being of a human community by relying on the presuppositions underlying democratic theory. The central presupposition is that, when it comes to reaching a decision concerning public matters, every individual is to count as one equal participant. Democracy is *rule of the people* and each member of the group considered to be "the people" counts for *just one*. Socialism need not be democratic, but to the extent that it is, it relies in part on the central features of democracy. A crucial one is simply that individual members of a society are equal in respect to being authorized to contribute to public decisionmaking. The point is not that everyone's wishes, wants, desires, choices, and so forth count equally, since the results of a democratic decisionmaking process (e.g., the adoption of a given public policy) could place more importance on some people's wishes than on those of others. Moreover, whether a majority or a plurality carries the decision, some members of the community will probably be left unsatisfied—*their* wishes, wants, choices, or judgments very likely will be frustrated on some occasions. Democracy means only that as far as input into decisions involving the public is concerned, everyone is entitled to an equal say.

Democratic socialism construes the public realm very broadly. Virtually all important matters are subject to public decisionmaking. Decisions concerning the use and disposal of valued items—e.g., land, factory equipment, medical facilities, educational institutions, and so forth—are all public decisions within the framework of socialism. For certain democratic socialists human labor is the most important resource in society and, accordingly, its use and disposal must also be subject to the democratic decisionmaking process.[5] In democratic socialist systems, then, all decisions concerning matters of significance to the society as a whole are ultimately subject to the democratic process.

Of course questions still will arise concerning what standard members of a community should use *as individuals* when deciding how valued items and services are to be governed. When a person goes to the voting booth, he or she would already have some ideas as to what is to be done about something. Democracy is not a complete decisionmaking mechanism. The individuals who comprise the public need to have ideas of their own and the content of these ideas cannot itself be the outcome of a prior voting process.

Within democratic socialism, individuals do not possess any right to own items of great social value on their own, items which instead are owned by the public at large; they do possess the right to partake in the debates concerning what should be done collectively with what is owned collectively. The idea is that problems would be raised and everyone would be entitled to make a contribution to the discussion. And the source of each person's contribution would be that person's interests, desires, wishes, wants, choices, and so on. In democratic theory there is an assumption that everyone has individual interests which through suitable aggregation will make up the general or the public interest. It is from the intellectual and political collision of these individual interests, during public debate, that the public interest arises.

Another assumption of democratic theory is that there is value to social life for every individual, even if not every individual's private desires, wishes, and so forth can be satisfied on every occasion. This assumption is necessary because otherwise—that is, without it—there would be little reason to assume that individuals who make up a human community would be committed to the superiority of the public interest, an interest which may in any given case contradict their individual interests.

## §6 DEMOCRATIC SOCIALISM AND POLLUTION

With the foregoing as background, we can now consider the implications of democratic socialism for handling the problem of pollution. Let us admit, from the start, however, that although there is a general commitment to social life and rule by election, there is ample reason to assume that the individual members of any human community do not generally desire to be harmed. Therefore, it makes good sense to assume that whatever the beneficial consequences of any polluting process might be, individuals would not wish to be the victims, at least in significant measure, of severe pollution. This needs to be noted from the outset because, despite the assumption that the ultimate source of standards of choice in a democratic socialist system will include consideration of the individual's very possibly idiosyncratic interests, it need not be assumed that individuals differ in *all* important aspects. There is no denial in democratic theory of the general similarity among human beings, especially when it comes to interests in health, nutrition, and other common needs. (Indeed, one reason why democracy is egalitarian is that people *are* assumed to be largely similar.) So we can take it without much argument that no one in a democracy is interested in wanton injury to himself. Pollution is a form of harm and its effects bring a kind of injury that we may assume people would not welcome without serious compensation. Any pollution that would be accepted in a democratic socialist system, therefore, would have to reap considerable benefits for the public as a whole. This means that pollution would not be accepted without widely recognized social benefits.

Ultimately, the basis of public policy concerning pollution in a democratic socialist system would be a calculus of benefits versus harms associated with any polluting process. Furthermore, the measurement of benefit and harm would have to be such that it could be generalized. In other words, some unit of measurement would be required which could be agreed upon. Only factors that are generally accepted to carry significance—e.g., improved shelter, health, nutrition, employment, or increased life expectancy—would figure in weighing the value of some process versus the disvalue of the pollution associated with it.

A case in point would be the necessity to balance the heavy costs of controlling pollution against an increase in unemployment. When the production process is very costly, the resulting products or services are more expensive and so fewer people can purchase them. Something has to give in order to gain something else. Pollution can be allowed in a socialist system only if something else of value to the public at large otherwise would be lost or made more difficult to obtain.

The situation may be looked upon along lines of what any group faces —be it a team, a choir, a family, a sorority—when it has limited resources and these resources can be used for some purposes but not others. In a socialist human community the available resources can be devoted to efforts to reduce pollution, *or* to efforts to increase the production of various valued items, *or* to increasing services by neglecting pollution, *or* to trying to reach some compromise.

Under democratic socialism the final determination of the degree of allowable pollution would emerge by way of the electoral process. It is generally assumable that pollution will not be wantonly accepted (self-inflicted). It is also true that people who are aware of the cost-benefit nature of the pollution process will often be willing to accept some pollution so that they may enjoy some other value, e.g., employment or shelter or better technology. To arrive at a publicly acceptable balance of values, the fullest possible participation of the members of the public would be required. By this means, the public policy that emerges will have registered the widest possible expression of individual interests.

There is no pretense in such a system that a result satisfactory to everyone will emerge from the electoral process. Indeed, it has been argued by some decision theorists that sometimes conflicting results can emerge from the very same democratic electoral process, and complicated mathematical proofs have suggested that many matters submitted to a democratic decisionmaking process will end in inherently inconsistent outcomes.[6] Nevertheless, others have argued that even this is preferable to the abandonment of democracy. As one spokesperson for democracy has put it, "In political theory as in life one can't always enjoy all good things together. All too often we must sacrifice one to save another."[7] A democratic socialist system rests on the idea that the value to be achieved through community life is worth the sacrifice of some other values, possibly including, if need be, the value of a fully consistent, nonconflicting set of public policies.

## §7 A CRITIQUE OF DEMOCRATIC SOCIALISM

Democratic socialism would appear to be a decided improvement on fascism, at least judged by standards which are widely cherished in modern political thought. For example, no *arbitrary* distinctions among members of the community is permitted, at least at the level of political participation: Where each person has an equal say, the "intuitions" of an inspired leader carry no greater weight. Thus democratic socialism is decidedly more egalitarian than fascism, something that at a certain level is accepted as a virtue for any human community.

Yet democratic socialism also faces some basic troubles. For one, even though the theory's application relies on the generation of social values from individuals' interests, wishes, wants, and so forth, there is no satisfactory account of how individuals *as individuals* are rationally to determine their own interests. Although *social* policy will emerge from debate, how can individuals make a rational contribution to this debate if they have no standards by which to judge the merits of what they personally might wish to contribute? As a general theory of human values, that is, this theory is importantly incomplete.

Furthermore, while democracy requires widespread participation in a community's political process, this may not amount to a great deal in the end. The implications of the theory not only allow, they sanction the "tryanny of the majority," in that policies sanctioned by this theory can harm a given individual or group as a mere means to (that is, merely in order to advance) collective goals of the society at large. So while democratic socialism does not dismiss the role of individuals in public decisionmaking, in the last analysis it can easily overwhelm the interests, wishes, wants, and choices of individuals. To that extent the participatory democracy of democratic socialism might be no more than a kind of foil to hide the ultimate injustice. When the rhetorical dust about equality settles, individuals can still be the innocent victims of policies that advance the general welfare. In the case of pollution this could mean that persons who have done nothing to deserve it could be made to suffer harm by way of pollution simply because they have been outnumbered. Or, on the other hand, entirely harmless waste emission might be prohibited simply because, for example, the majority finds it aesthetically displeasing.

So, although democratic socialism has only a trace of the epistemological problems of fascism—both are incomplete in that both fail to provide standards of value for the "ordinary" individual—it does encounter the same serious problem as fascism vis-à-vis the treatment it would allow for some of the members of society. In both, some persons could be made to share an inequitable (and so unjust) amount of harm, including harm caused by pollution, in order to advance the general welfare. Perhaps central planning socialism will provide a more successful approach than democratic socialism to the problem of pollution, as well as to other public policy problems.

## §8  CENTRAL PLANNING SOCIALISM

Central planning is another way that a socialist system can approach decisionmaking. Sometimes called democratic centrism—to indicate that despite the central planning it is advancement of the interests of the people as a whole that is being aimed at by those who do the planning—this system relies on expert leadership. Certain individuals are taken to possess the capacity and wisdom, as well as the will, for determining the public interest and are therefore regarded as properly authorized to implement what they determine it to be.

The main difference between democratic and centrist socialist systems is that public policies concerning the use of socially valued items emerge from the electoral process in the former while in the latter they are the product of the wisdom of the leadership. The crucial question, then, concerning the centrally planned socialist society, is how rationally to set such policies in the absence of information about the desires, interests, and so on, of individual citizens that would be acquired from citizen involvement in the electoral or some other participatory process. Indeed, a principal theoretical criticism of nondemocratic forms of socialism is that central planning is impossible because the information needed for making decisions for the public needs to be obtained by observing the members of the public making their own decisions (either in a marketplace or in the voting booths), decisions made *in the absence* of a socially planned society.

It is in the context of centrally planned socialism that a scientific approach to public policy comes to fruition. The idea is that the leader of a human community would be able to consult the "laws of history" and make decisions on the basis of such consultation. Just as engineers rely on the laws of physics for purposes of, so to speak, governing the process of construction, so social engineers are to rely on the laws of history (and economics, sociology, psychology, etc.) in their effort to arrive at the correct decisions concerning public affairs.

Such an approach would still involve cost-benefit analysis. It would rely less on the input of private interests, however, and more on some theories of social welfare, the nature of man as a social being, and the requirements of human (social) health. It is not the individuals (who comprise the membership of the community) who would make the primary contribution to the determination of public policy but the leaders of the community, guided by their knowledge of the relevant "laws," who would do so. The implication for public choice, including the determination of how to handle the problem of pollution, as we shall see in §9, is not difficult to imagine.

In socialist theory individuals are conceived of as part of a whole which transcends but is, nevertheless, composed of them. Most socialist theorists do not see a basic difference between the interests of society and those of its individual members. Indeed, they regard the fulfillment of the interests of society as a necessary condition of the fulfillment of the interests of the individuals who comprise that society. This must, however, be understood in a somewhat special way. Unlike those systems of political organization that take the individual as the central value to be promoted or protected in a society—thus insisting on the protection of individual rights to life, liberty, and private property, for example—under socialism there is no way to conceive of the individual apart from other individuals. This requires that in virtually all respects the individual's goals, interests, and so on are to be understood inseparably from those of other individuals. In democratic socialist systems the way this is achieved is by the fullest possible participation of all individuals in the establishment of public policy. In centrally planned socialist systems a theory of the interests of human individuals as integral members of society must guide the decisions of the central planners.

Although the version of socialism associated with Karl Marx (1818–1883) is of the scientific type, tending to deemphasize norms (duties, obligations, moral virtues, moral character, etc.) in favor of historical laws (the force of dialectics, the determinate powers of economic factors, the principles of class conflict, etc.), centrally planned and governed socialist societies usually draw on Marxism for the theories by which they determine what *ought* to be done to promote the individual's and the public's interests. This is understandable; despite the purported scientific character of Marxism, there is a good deal of what would best be called political value judgments at the heart of the system. Not only is Marx often willing to praise and blame various features of various social institutions and events in social history, he has an explicit theory of what is of value to human life. Based on this theory, central planners can derive, so it is assumed, various policy judgments.

In Marx's writings, human nature is viewed principally in terms of *conscious production*.[8] This means that unlike other animals that engage in activities to satisfy needs and desires, human beings fulfill their needs and desires by working according to a plan—working by giving their work conscious, thoughtful direction. To put the matter somewhat simply, people are the sort of beings who are first and foremost *thinking workers*, at least when they are fully matured. In addition, Marx, because he conceived of work as a social process, viewed human beings as necessarily involved in social life, again at least when fully matured or emancipated. And for Marx, the rational, fulfilling, and ultimately emancipating form of life for each individual therefore must involve full involvement in society. Only because of the incomplete development of human nature—which, according to Marx, is still undergoing a process of growth but will reach full realization in communist society—are members of society often (and unnaturally) separated into private spheres or special groups (classes).

This outlook provides the central planner—even one who is not fully Marxist in his or her viewpoint—with an idea of what human nature is and how it should be fulfilled in a good human community. Human nature is fulfilled by ensuring that everyone is a conscious worker, and by organizing society in such a way that each individual is treated in compliance with this idea. Central planners must, therefore, see to it that there is full participation in labor, especially since, as the contemporary socialist economist Robert Heilbroner claims,[9] *labor itself* is a public commodity to be organized by those responsible for planning the economy.

## §9 CENTRAL PLANNING SOCIALISM AND POLLUTION

What are the implications of this theory for the issue of pollution? In most socialist societies—not one of which is purely socialist and many of which are regarded as socialist by some but not by other advocates of socialism—we find ample evidence of pollution in the form of harmful waste emissions from numerous production processes. There is a problem, however, with construing these emissions as ultimately harmful if, as will often be the case, the harm from them is considered to be indispensable for achieving the benefits which a centrally planned socialist society seeks—namely, the full emancipation of human nature as characterized by conscious production. The situation would probably be best looked at along the following lines.

Let us imagine that a society is an individual person. Does it make sense to think that one has harmed oneself when one achieves, say, physical fitness or artistic enlightenment if, in pursuit of these chosen goals, one has engaged in activities that are taxing on parts of oneself? The answer is clearly: No! So long as the overall result of such exercise is good for oneself, the "costs" one pays (e.g., pain and exhaustion) cannot be regarded as harmful. A composer of music may indeed hurt his or her eyes in the process of creating a great song or symphony, but so long as that achievement is in fact something that promotes the composer's interests overall, the injury to the eye cannot be regarded as harmful *to the person as a whole*.

In roughly the same way, if a society is conceived of as a whole entity which is to flourish, its planners cannot view the various efforts required to bring about that flourishing as a form of harm. To the objection that some individual members of society might be harmed by allowing pollution at the level necessary for the well-being of society considered as a whole, central planning socialists will reply that the objection misfires. Since the fulfillment of the individual's life mission is inseparable from the fulfillment of the goal(s) of society, any "harm" that may befall the individual would have to be construed as something indispensable in the process of the individual's proper life and thus as *no harm* really. The analogy with parts of the body again is apt. If to do its work as an organ of a person the eye must experience injury now and then, this cannot be regarded as harmful; rather it must be seen as an indispensable condition of serving the interests of the person in question.

Accordingly, the central planners of a society would not conceive of all pollution in the way understood at the outset of our discussion, namely, as a type of harm. Or if they would, they would not regard any necessary byproduct of the production process as an instance of pollution. By this account, then, there would be no pollution, properly conceived, in a properly governed socialist society, that is, no pollution that harms the body politic *considered as a whole*, only some necessary (perhaps very unpleasant) byproduct of the proper running of society. One might think of pollution as one views the excretion of wasteful materials from a well functioning human body. It may be unpleasant, to be sure, but it certainly cannot be taken to be harmful.

The central planners of a socialist society would therefore need to make sure only of one thing, namely, that whatever is done in their community—whatever production process is undertaken—is necessary for the development of that society. Of course this still leave the planners with many technical difficulties. But, in theory, the position seems clear enough. In a centrally planned socialist society we would see a type of cost-benefit approach to the problem of pollution where the determination of cost and benefit would not rely so much on democratic input as on the implications of a supposedly adequate theory of human nature. Guided by such a theory, central planners could presumably determine how much and what kind of pollution or injurious waste emission is required to achieve the necessary level of production in a human community.

## §10  A CRITIQUE OF CENTRAL PLANNING SOCIALISM

The main and distinctive feature of central planning socialism concerns its reliance on a theory of human nature in terms of which the interests of society as a whole and, therefore, the individual members of society, would be determined and public policy, including concerns about pollution, would be guided. This theory involves, as has been observed, what might be called a conception of historical progress governed by laws of history.

The determination of these laws is a thorny problem, however. It is especially difficult to tell how we could come to know where these laws are leading humanity or various societies. In the case of individual animals or human beings, we have had ample experience with the process and results of maturation, so we have a clear enough idea about a fully realized, healthy, mature *member* of, for example, the human species. It is quite another thing, however, to speak of the full development or maturation of humanity as a collective whole, or any segment of it (e.g., American or Russian society). Difficult as this would be, to derive or otherwise obtain a coherent, effective public policy for a society, a policy based on something so elusive as the projected realization of humanity's nature, would be far more difficult, if not entirely impossible.

Even if it is possible to know what humanity might be like when (and if) it reaches its highest stage of development, one must ask why *current* public policy should be based on that projected picture. Don't we want solutions to problems faced by us now? And how, exactly, do our legitimate interests mesh, or fail to mesh, with those of some future (and presumably rather different) kind of "human being"? By way of analogy, many of the problems of an adolescent are not fairly or reasonably solved by reference to the interests of a mature adult. It would appear, then, that central planning socialism lacks a standard for setting *current* public policy, ignoring, as seems fair, the preferences, judgments, whims, and choices of the central planners. Of course, some of these preferences, for example, may well be in accord with wisdom or the opinions of many members of the community. But justifying central planning socialism by reference to this would not be sufficient, since then *democratic* socialism, with its commitment to maximal canvassing of the interests, desires, and so on of the public as a basis for public policies, would be more appropriate.

In addition to the preceding objections central planning socialism is clearly vulnerable to the charge that it could not only allow but require that some be made to suffer a lot in the name of "human progress," not because this is the outcome of a democratic procedure but because of the judgment of a mere handful of persons who comprise the planners (e.g., members of the central committee of the Communist party of the USSR). And here the issue of violating the rights of individuals arises quite obviously, since there is no good reason why we should disregard consideration of those rights in favor of some projected "advance" of humanity (and, through it, the gradual development of every individual as a species-being, to use one of the key ideas of Marx when he discusses these matters).[10] Of course, central planning socialists, even more so than democratic socialists, deny that individuals have any rights. Marx himself castigated the doctrine of individual rights as wrongheaded because it focuses on persons as selfish individuals separated from others.[11] But this stormy denunciation lacks the power to persuade to the extent that his own theory of human nature and humanity's eventual emancipation remains in serious doubt. So the familiar idea that the rights of individuals deserve consideration in public policy decisionmaking should not be overthrown just yet. Why should some, the planners, possess the full authority to govern, while others, the citizens, are subject to their will? Lacking adequate reasons for this, the alternative— namely, that all persons have the same moral rights, *as individuals*, including the right to have a voice in the formulation of public policy— retains its rightful place in our moral thought. And central planning socialism clearly violates this idea head on.

## IV. THE WELFARE STATE

Of all the political systems dealing with human community life, the welfare state is perhaps the most familiar to us today. It is also that system in which some of the main faults of democratic and central planning socialism might find an effective remedy.

Two widely regarded goals are generally taken to be the objectives of this political and economic system, namely, liberty and happiness, or well-being. We saw how all the previous systems have aimed, in some fashion, toward securing some type of happiness or well-being. And we saw that all of them faltered, to various degrees, when it came to making provisions for individual human rights and, with this, human dignity.

The welfare state may be construed as an important departure from those other systems because it gives a prominent place to individual liberty and other rights.

That a certain sort of happiness is the proper goal that human beings should pursue in life has been argued by a number of very prominent thinkers throughout at least Western intellectual history. Two of its founders, Plato (427?–347? B.C.) and Aristotle (384–322 B.C.), assert this, and in a certain but different sense many more recent leading figures in human thought (e.g., Thomas Hobbes [1588–1679], John Locke [1632–1704], Jeremy Bentham [1748–1832], John Stuart Mill [1806–1873], and Marx) follow suit. What they take to be happiness or human well-being is often diverse but not the implied importance of achieving happiness, not only in one's own case, but also in the case of others. Such a view is bound to have important implications about the proper role of government, as we shall shortly see.

Liberty, too, has been an objective of sorts for many ethical and political systems, though, as with happiness, what liberty has been taken to be has differed. Two major types of liberty have been of concern, namely, positive and negative. We are considering the former when we speak of the *freedom to* do something—for example, freedom to overcome temptation, hardship, alienation, deprivation, and so forth. We acquire such freedom by obtaining the ability to do something. We are considering the second type of freedom when we speak of *freedom from* other people's interference. Of course, the two types of freedom frequently are related. We can, for example, add to our abilities (our freedom to do various things) by removing some obstacle placed before us by other people (thus securing our *freedom from* their interference). The two types of freedom, in other words, are not mutually exclusive. In the case of the welfare state the liberty usually emphasized is the negative sort—*freedom from* others' intrusions upon one's sphere of authority. Along with the claimed importance of the value of happiness, then, the welfare state also stresses a certain level of human autonomy for everyone.[12]

## §11  A DELICATE BALANCING ACT

The welfare state is the political attempt to do some degree of justice to both of these widely supported values—both to human happiness and human liberty. It is, therefore, something of a delicate balancing act, an attempt to keep some ideal proportion between a concern for individual liberty and welfare. This is fairly evident in the United States. Neither of the two major political parties, for example, can discount the ideal of liberty or the ideal of well-being, at least for the needy, as political objectives the government must pursue.

But just what kind of balance is to be pursued by the government of a welfare state? On some interpretations, though by no means by all, we must look to the United States Constitution to answer this question. The Constitution stresses both negative liberty and welfare. Whether this stress is laid in such a way as to be more in line with those thinkers who favor negative liberty more than well-being, or vice versa, as objectives of government policy, we can imagine that one way to attempt to strike a balance is to let the Constitution be our guide: As a matter of law, Congress *may not do* certain things but also *must do* others. Legally, that is, various powers are kept away from the state as far as the U.S. Constitution is concerned, but the government is constitutionally empowered to go to work on certain matters where, it is felt, other elements of our society fail. Still, the Constitution does not hand us a blueprint regarding how much liberty and how much welfare should emerge from government action. Instead, this is a matter of procedural interpretation, usually guided both by the democratic process of voter participation and by extensive delegation of authority to experts—for example, departments of the government, government regulators, and license bureaus. Depending on whether a welfare state is more democratic or more republican—meaning, depending on whether law making and law interpretation is carried out more by the people themselves or by various selected political representatives—more or less direct participation of the members of the community in the political process determines what balance will be struck between liberty and well-being as governmental objectives. We might say that the welfare state places a good deal of faith in the wisdom of the electorate and in those the voters choose to represent them.

But now we can ask what we did before in connection with other systems, namely, what standards should be invoked in forging public policy and what standards should voters, especially, invoke as they participate in the political decisionmaking process? Most generally put, the welfare state assumes, alongside democratic theory itself, that the majority (or plurality) is authorized to have a final say in public matters, guided by the needs and wants, whether similar or dissimilar, of the individuals who comprise the whole community. But unlike a pure democracy, the welfare state also accepts the view that sound democracy is impossible without *some* checks. And the individuals involved will know, more or less clearly and precisely, what those checks are—for example, forced labor is prohibited, striking is a human right, the press may speak its mind almost without reservation, people may associate with each other as they choose.

According to familiar welfare state theories, the main *legal* restriction on democratic power is the rights of individuals to a goodly bit of self-expression and self-determination. Welfare for all is pursued by getting the input of all, following the mandate of that input in the most practical way possible. But there is a limit, namely, when such pursuit threatens to thwart, to an unacceptable degree, the personal will and initiative of members of society. Liberty is protected, in turn, by not subjugating individuals to anyone's authority beyond what is required for maintaining a decent, respectable standard of living for all. This may involve some "forced labor" by requiring, for example, that all who are able to contribute some portion of their earnings to the public treasury.

Although such labor as is used for public purposes is extracted often without explicit or even implicit consent of the actual members of a community, advocates of the welfare state argue that it is nonetheless obligatory and may be extracted by the government in order to respect the (positive) right of all citizens to a minimally decent standard of living. In essence, then, a welfare state accepts that individuals have a (negative) right to liberty and a (positive) right to a reasonable standard of living just by being members of the society. The recognition of these rights limits what government can and cannot do, as well as instructs government as to its obligations. The state is *not* to overdo its intrusion upon people's lives. At the same time, it *is* empowered to hold people legally responsible to furnish those in need with essential goods and services just because they are members of the community.

The main difference between the welfare state and socialism concerns the scope of legitimate government intervention in the lives of its citizens. In the welfare state government is restricted in its efforts to direct people's lives toward the pursuit of certain goals, such as economic progress and the security of the people in their health. Not so in a socialist state. In the welfare state even if some wish to use their liberty frivolously, they have the right to do this, but again, not in a socialist state. Moreover, even if some do not earn any wealth by productive effort, thereby failing to express their (Marxian) human nature or neglecting themselves due to incapacity or unwillingness, they are entitled simply as members of the community to some wealth—that is their positive right—although they are not entitled to as much as may be needed for them to live very well. A socialist state would have little patience with such appeals to "positive rights."

## §12 THE WELFARE STATE AND POLLUTION

How can the welfare state approach the problem of pollution? In a welfare state the vehicles of both criminal law and government regulation are available for handling the pollution problem. In other words, in this system, individuals possess rights, the violation of which by way of pollution is a legally actionable offense. Both the criminal and the civil law offer remedies against such violation. The welfare state also engages in the regulation of production, via the political process, which may lead to the establishment of government regulatory agencies. Acceptable levels of pollution may be set and members of the community are required both to observe these levels as they engage in production and to tolerate these levels as they experience the side effects of production.

In a recent ruling by the U.S. Supreme Court it was made clear that various governmental bodies are not fully authorized to impose pollution on the citizens by permitting others to engage in production processes which inevitably pollute the environment. On the other hand, no legal obstacles that would make it illegal to pollute, say, lakes, rivers, or the air have been placed in the paths of various municipal, county, state, and federal boards which issue permits to private and public corporations (especially utility companies) and which themselves (via their own production facilities, e.g., municipal electric companies or federally run power generating plants) produce pollutants.

It is probably fair to say that, from the point of view of the welfare state, the problem of pollution *should* be handled just about the way it *is* handled today in the United States, the United Kingdom, West Germany, Japan, Canada, and other democratic industrial countries. Besides the democratic process, these countries rely also on their basic legal traditions to adjudicate disputes which arise within community life. To the extent that those who pollute and those who are thereby harmed can be identified by the courts, considerable reliance on criminal law is possible. To the extent, however, that those who cause pollution are difficult to identify and the victims are linked rather loosely to the perpetrators, there one must rely mostly on political regulation and some version of a utilitarian cost-benefit approach.

The welfare state has rather extensive powers to place constraints on individual liberty, less extensive than in socialist systems. Whenever some feature of community life is publicly administered, managed, and regulated, it is not possible to introduce considerations of individual rights as the *sole* determinant of public policy. Thus it is rarely a matter of *whether* pollution will be allowed, but rather a question of *how much* of it, *where*, and *under what conditions*. From the perspective of the welfare state, answers call for public policy decisions that depend in part on basic rights, and in part on general goals which express the public interest, including an estimate of the tolerable risks to which people may be exposed.

## §13 A CRITIQUE OF THE WELFARE STATE

The welfare state is often defended on the grounds that it is a buffer against extreme elitism and statism. Nevertheless, it seems that the system is exposed to the charge that the majority can still rule in some cases to the detriment of the interests of minorities and, especially, of individuals. If, for example, the majority of the people in the United States believe in the promise of nuclear power generation, the government would be justified in encouraging the construction of nuclear plants, even if this means acting contrary to the perceived interests of opponents of nuclear power by spending their funds, collected through taxation, to subsidize the nuclear industry (e.g., in the way of limited liability in case of accidents, so insurance costs can be kept low). True, consideration is given in the welfare state to the rights of individuals, but, as in democratic socialism, the consideration is largely procedural, one that permits individuals to take part in the forging of decisions. Once some majority or plurality has won the day, supposed rights to be free from constraints on, and intrusions in, one's liberty by others often are, and, under this theory, often should be, allowed.

Since the welfare state does not limit wealth accumulation in principle but merely taxes the wealthy a bit more—and is perhaps neglectful of the possibility that the wealthy are also better equipped to take advantage of legal loopholes—great discrepancies in economic power are possible within this system. As a result, with politics being much entangled with commerce, the wealthy are in a position to exert considerable influence on political decisionmaking, for example by fielding candidates who are able to wage expensive campaigns. In this way captains of industry can (and do) acquire large shares of political power, placing themselves in a position to guide the system toward a public policy which can (and sometimes does) disregard the interests of those who cannot wield similar power. The implications of all this for dealing with the problem of pollution are not difficult to appreciate. The owners and managers of industry can encourage public policy in such a way that their polluting production processes would be allowed—for example, the appointed regulators would license their plants and issue permits to allow considerable waste emission into lakes, the air, and rivers—while they themselves can afford to live far away and not be harmed by such pollution. Moreover, to wage court fights against such policies is a costly endeavor, well beyond the means of most individual citizens, and even with the welfare state's policy of defending *some* of the rights of individual members of the community through the court system, not *all* the rights of every citizen can be defended in this way. One has only to take an honest look at the living conditions of the citizens of, say, Gary, Indiana, to see how well the welfare state works when it comes to pollution. Many citizens are constantly exposed to air pollution, mainly due to their inability to leave the areas where they reside, while the more affluent have the ability to live in places very little affected by such pollution.

Finally, the welfare state is still not heedful enough of the dignity of the individual. On the one hand it pays only limited respect to negative individual liberty, so that such practices as, say, extensive taxation, conscription, and required (public) education clearly force public policy, as it were, on the backs of individuals who might choose otherwise for themselves or their children. On the other hand, the welfare state also engenders a kind of dependency on the government, in the form of welfare payments, in a considerable number of its citizens. In such a system some minimum standard of living is guaranteed, as a matter of basic (positive) right, to everyone, simply on the basis of state membership and so independently of whether the individual makes the effort to contribute something by his or her own labors. It thus fails to treat adults as adults, but treats them instead as kind of permanent spoiled children— that is, *entitled* to financial support, whether worked for or not. Such treatment, however much some may applaud it, is hardly respectful of those who receive it. Moreover, because the welfare state acts as a kind of proverbial "parent" toward people by imposing upon them policies "for their own good," denying them the liberty to run or not to run risks voluntarily, it again treats adults as children, though in a quite different way from the first.

It is often argued that the welfare state is a kind of halfway house between extreme statism and anarchy, but this is not so. Anarchy is in fact the absence of *any* rules or principles enforced on the members of a human community. In anarchy there is *no government at all*, or so the theory would maintain. The problems with anarchy are not our concern here, but if there is a midway point between anarchy and full statism or totalitarianism, it may well be our next system, capitalism or libertarianism, in which a role for government does exist, but a severely limited role; government exists to protect the (negative) liberty of each citizen, neither more nor less. It is possible that this system can handle the problems of pollution more successfully, when consistently implemented, than any other we have considered thus far.

# V. CAPITALISM

Although this system is mostly discussed in terms of economics, in fact advocates of capitalism as a socioeconomic system have usually tied its features directly to certain specific political and legal principles. Accordingly, capitalism is best described by reference to those of its features that have emerged from the tradition of political philosophy associated with the thought of John Locke, whose views are briefly summarized below.

## §14 THE PRIORITY OF INDIVIDUAL RIGHTS

Essentially, the normative capitalism or libertarianism that gained its classic statement in Locke's works—but has since been worked out in much greater detail and, presumably, cleansed of some of its original flaws—derives the system of justice for human community life from the political principles of natural rights. Specifically, these are the rights of every individual human person to life, liberty, and property. Plainly put, such a system rests on, and, within certain limits, seeks to promote, the ideals of the independence and the freedom of individual persons in their existence, actions, and productivity. No individual may be used against his or her own choice to advance the goals of others. Relatedly, no one may be interfered with unless prior permission is secured, nor may one's labor and produce be used, destroyed, or otherwise controlled by others without permission by the owner, regardless of the importance or nobility of the purpose at hand. These would be the basic political and legal principles of a just society, holds the capitalist, and the proper function of the state or government is to protect the rights of the individual citizen, not to advance the "general welfare" (beyond making it possible for citizens to do so on their own and with each other's voluntary help).

Libertarianism is, then, the socioeconomic arrangement of human communities which aims to preserve, enhance, and protect the ideals mentioned above, primarily because, proponents believe, it is only with such a system in force that it is possible for human beings to both live in dignity and fully pursue their happiness. This view of capitalism is different from another possible approach, one that argues for it on *utilitarian* grounds. This latter defense emphasizes the practical value of capitalism—that is, the system's supposed utility as an effective means for achieving the goals of those partaking in it, regardless of what those goals are. Like the Lockean defense, the utilitarian support involves certain values—even though most of those who advance it like to deemphasize the fact and insist that they are advancing a "value-free" defense. But, unlike the Lockean approach, the utilitarian locates the standard of right and wrong in the *value of the consequences* rather than in *respect for the individual and his or her rights*. In this latter view, the autonomy and independence of individual human beings should be affirmed and protected in a human community, something that requires recognition of private property rights. If there is a legally protected sphere of personal authority, specifiable by reference to the limits of each individual's legitimate autonomy or independence—in Harvard philosopher Robert Nozick's words, *moral space*—then individuals will be at liberty to make choices concerning their lives within those limits, either enjoying the benefits or shouldering the liabilities of their free choices. For example, if John's life is for him to govern and a certain sphere of authority is acknowledged and protected for him, then, were John to choose to be a bum, which leads to his poverty, others should not interfere "for his own good," *or* for the good of others (for example, John's wife) who have *chosen* to associate themselves with John. On the other hand, if John chooses to be a productive person, thereby acquiring various valuable items through his productvity and prudence, he is to be protected from any interference with his use and disposal of these items, provided only that he does not violate the rights of others in the process. In a capitalist system, if a person neglects her health and shelter, then *she and no one else* is to blame, while if she takes care of her health and shelter, then *she and no one else* (unless there is mutual agreement to the contrary) deserves to have the benefits of her labor.

Some people argue that by its own tenets the capitalist or libertarian system must make room for quite a large public sector since in advanced industrial states persons have rights to being provided with numerous goods and services, at least when they cannot provide for these themselves. So-called *positive* rights (e.g., to health care, welfare, education, employment) would, if they exist, require governments to do much more than capitalism might appear to allow. One reason suggested for this is that the individuals who are destitute would not benefit much from just having their right to liberty protected and preserved. It would be meaningless for them to be free from others' intrusion if they couldn't advance on their own; so they must be provided with some initial help by society.

While some destitute people no doubt exist in any society, the issue really is whether this is a political matter at all. People need not be destitute because of any interference by others, so to make it obligatory for others to help them—that is, to regard others' help as a right—would be to impose on others unearned punishment. And though not obligatory, basic human decency and charity would probably cause people to reach out to these destitute folks anyway. If people failed to help, there is no reason to suppose that governments would do any better at the task of securing for the needy what other people refuse to provide.

But the bottom line is that there is no basic right to welfare, since lack of well-being is not a uniquely social problem but rather a problem of living itself. Poverty requires solutions from individuals, by themselves or in voluntary cooperation with each other. The only basic rights that make clear sense are ones specifying limits of social interaction, that is, ones that specify what people in society may *not* do to each other.

## §15 CAPITALISM AND POLLUTION

What is the implication of this for our topic? In plain terms, *capitalism requires that pollution be punishable as a legal offense that violates individual rights*. This may appear to be a rather peculiar thing to say if one regards the United States of America and other Western democracies as capitalist societies. In fact, however, none of these human communities is capitalist in the strict sense of that term, but only in the sense that, more than ever in previous times and places, individual rights, including the right to private property, have gained substantial, though sporadic, legal recognition in them. (Of course, neither is, for example, the Soviet Union a fully socialist society—plenty of low-key capitalist endeavors prevail there and are, indeed, not only legally tolerated but encouraged.) Still, a fledgling capitalist nation like the United States provides some clues as to how a purely capitalist political and economic system would enforce the legal proscription against polluting. For example, in the United States polluters are often sued, under what are called tort or nuisance laws, for harm done to the polluted.[13] And the U.S. Supreme Court has held that when pollution occurs, merely considering the overall public cost of preventing it cannot be construed as an adequate determinant of whether to allow that pollution to continue. In other words, existing law is at least partially committed to resisting pollution regardless of the expense and inconvenience involved to those who pollute, just as the law is largely committed to resisting rape or assault regardless of the expense and inconvenience involved to the system and the perpetrator. (Of course, even in the most principled approach to crime, cost considerations will arise—e.g., the size of the police force and the quality of the equipment used for crime prevention have a lot to do with budgets!)

Regrettably, however, at least viewed from the perspective of libertarianism, most Western democracies treat pollution on an overall cost-benefit basis. For example, whether Lake Erie can be polluted with chemical discharges from the factories and power plants surrounding Buffalo, New York, and Cleveland, Ohio, is mostly a matter of some alleged cost-benefit calculation pertaining to the *overall well-being* of the region's population (including, perhaps, members of future generations).[14] Still, there is evidence that individual property rights are sometimes treated by the courts as inviolate, as they should be, given libertarian theory. Dumping—the act of deliberately or negligently causing the intrusion of harmful wastes upon another's domain—is generally regarded to be a crime in the United States. Pollution, in turn, is a type of dumping, namely, one that occurs in connection with the public realm, as when a chemical firm pours harmful wastes into a public lake or the atmosphere.

Under capitalism any pollution which would most likely lead to harm being done to persons who have not consented to being put at risk of such harm would have to be legally prohibited. As with people who have a contagious disease, so with processes of production which involve pollution, so long as the harmful imposition upon others occurs, without the consent of the victims, the process may not be carried out. This may lead to an increase in the cost of production or to the elimination of some production process, and, in either case, to increased unemployment and related hardship. Still, that would be the consistent way to apply the capitalist-libertarian principle in the legal system. The intentional or negligent violation of individual rights, including the rights of life, liberty, and property, must be legally prohibited. To permit the production to continue on grounds that this will sustain employment would be exactly like permitting the continuation of other crimes on grounds that allowing them creates jobs for others.

More generally, libertarianism rejects in principle the use of cost-benefit analysis as a basis to justify pollution. Even if some region of the country would experience an extensive economic downturn as a result of the prohibition of air or water pollution, for example, that is no reason to allow it. No one has a right to benefit from acts or practices that violate the rights of others. Just as the sexual needs of some potential rapist do not justify raping someone, so the economic needs of some potential polluters do not justify pollution.

An even better analogy might be that of a person with a contagious disease who wishes to carry on his daily activities in public, the members of which would be exposed to harmful germs if he did as he desired. Such a person *would not* be permitted to go on about his activities, according to libertarian thought, although it would be the responsibility of the officials of the legal system to prove that his activities cause the violation of others' rights. (The onus of proving a criminal wrongdoing is on the prosecution, since without such proof untoward and restrictive actions would easily violate individual rights.) Unlike a rapist, who intentionally assaults a particular person to satisfy his needs or desires, the person with a contagious disease may not intend any harmful results to befall members of the public. However, the activities of this person would harm others, or put them at grave risk of serious harm, without their consent. We need not be able to tell who *in particular* will contract the disease before we can justify limiting this person's liberty. The fact that exposure to someone with the disease would harm some indeterminate number of the public, or place them at risk of significant harm, without their consent, suffices to invoke a quarantine against this person. In a similar fashion, although the polluting agent may not intend to harm anyone, and even granting that we are unable to say which individuals will be harmed by the actions of the polluter, the fact that the agent's actions produce pollution suffices to justify prohibition of those activities that produce it (unless the production can be carried out without the polluting side effect).

## §16 THE MORAL SUPERIORITY OF CAPITALISM

Several of the problems facing the previous theories would be manageable by capitalism, although some problems would remain to be solved. First, if the natural rights theory which underlies the libertarian political system has solid foundations in moral theory, and if the moral theory supporting it is itself rationally superior to its competitors, then the system is clearly superior to its alternatives, all considered. Natural rights theory rests, essentially, on the idea that it is possible for us to understand human nature and to derive from this understanding, together with our knowledge of the world in which we live, what would be the proper conditions for human social life. Although much controversy exists concerning these matters, the crux of the libertarian claim— or at least one line of reasoning advanced by libertarians about these matters—is that knowledge of human nature is no more difficult in principle than knowledge about the nature of other things we encounter. That knowledge includes the recognition that persons are the sort of beings that have a moral dimension to their existence, a moral worth or dignity, which, then, must be taken into account in the formulation of human social institutions, including legal systems. We have already mentioned the results of the natural rights theory.

Whether this is ultimately a successful endeavor cannot be fully explored here. But at least the theory avoids the most glaring deficiencies endemic to the other systems we have examined. Unlike fascism, libertarianism does not allocate special powers to an "inspired" leader and, unlike democracy, libertarianism will not allow the interests of the majority to override the rights of the individual. Moreover, while central planning socialism rests on a very dubious metaphysical theory about the gradual but revolutionary development of the human species, with little guidance as to what we should do at present, libertarianism involves a theory about the dignity and worth of human persons here and now and, as we shall see in §17, offers specific guidance regarding current problems calling for public action. The welfare state is, one might say, of two minds about the values it aims to advance, what with liberty and welfare always in potential conflict and with no clear way to resolve that conflict. Capitalism, by contrast, proclaims the ultimate moral significance of the lives of individuals, lives *to be led* by the individuals themselves, and it proposes a social order in which the negative rights of individuals are the primary guidelines for public policy. It does not concern itself with some widely touted values, such as, for example, universal equality, absolute fairness, unbreachable moral duty to lend help where it is needed. It does not reject anyone's efforts, alone or in concert with others, to pursue such values, but it rejects making the general welfare a basis for setting public policy, since that can, and likely will, lead to violations of individual rights. So neither the tyranny of some hero leader nor of some majority threatens individual rights. Within the confines of a libertarian-capitalist system each person would be completely free of others' intrusions or could count on legal sanctions when such intrusions occur. But the rest is up to individuals acting in voluntary groups, establishing uncoerced institutions, or doing whatever is necessary to secure what they value. This may not hold out the promise of some social utopia, where everyone's full satisfaction is guaranteed by government, or even something less ambitious, namely, some guarantee of "reasonable" living conditions for all. But defenders of capitalism would hold such promises to be unfulfillable anyway and offer, instead, what they regard as a plausible vision of a just social order.[15]

## §17 PROBLEMS OF IMPLEMENTATION

How could the libertarian apply his theory in practice? This is of course the crux of the matter for this system. If it is to make good its claim to being the most adequate political theory, all considered (and granting that not everything will be fully satisfactory in it), it must be applicable in the real world, and then in difficult, not only in easy, cases. To show a theory's application to the problem of pollution is by no means easy. Thus it provides an interesting, important test case for assessing capitalism's theoretical mettle. How, precisely—or at least in fairly rigorous outline—could libertarianism's position regarding pollution find expression in a system of law? The following observations are meant to explain, at least partially, how the ideal of a libertarian state might find a home in the real world of law and public policy.

1. Stationary sources of pollution contained within the boundaries of the polluter's private property present no insurmountable problem to libertarianism. Toxic as well as nuclear wastes, for example, can be identified as polluting and if owners of firms dealing with these would act in a proper fashion, they would have to confine their operations to areas where others are left unharmed. Any breach of this requirement would meet extremely severe penalties—that is, the punishment would have to fit the crime. If operations of such firms would be impossible without pollution—that is, without causing emissions that are harmful to others who have not consented to suffer such harm—the operations would have to be shut down. Thus if people are harmed, they would be the ones who contractually gave their informed consent to run the risks associated with pollution. Workplace pollution would raise the issue of

workers' rights, but in a libertarian framework these, too, would be recognized and protected by contract law, including laws regarding fraud and "assumption of risk." Essentially, then, any stationary source of pollution would be dealt with in the way familiar to us in connection with the operations of the free market system of economic and legal affairs—that is, the system of individual private property rights would guide the conduct of members of the society.

Aside from the problematic nature of "rights" of nonexisting (future) persons, which would not be invoked in the libertarian framework since a mere potential, nonexisting person cannot have actual, existing, and binding rights, future owners of private property could manage the problems of contained pollution under contract law—for example, deed covenants running with the land. There would be some problems with abandoned property (which no one consents to take over) and with bankruptcies (where the owner is simply incapable of meeting liabilities). In such cases one could rely, in part, on insurance provisions which may in some cases be legally mandated, given the reasonably anticipated problems with the property in question.

2. Stationary sources placed on or nonstationary sources which move to other property *with* the consent of the owner (whether private person or public entity) seem to present the same contract considerations and difficulties as were mentioned in point 1. For instance, automobiles are nonstationary sources which move from property to property, but which may do so just in case permission of the owners of property has been obtained (perhaps for consideration, perhaps gratis). Chemical wastes dumped on stationary sources might, in turn, seep out and contaminate other places than those on which they had been dumped, so once again arrangements with owners would have to be made to gain permission.

Again, it can be argued that the governments of existing societies, where the problems of pollution are most pronounced, have throughout the last several decades given their implicit (but often quite explicit) permission to have the public's property—lakes, parks, forests, the atmosphere—polluted. To correct this would require some drastic measures, including, first and foremost, the privatization of public properties, where that is possible, and total prohibition where no privatization is possible (recalling the quarantine analogy). To the objection that it may be too late, the libertarian would have to reply that indeed it is better late than never, because to allow current practices to continue is to simply exacerbate the existing pollution problems. As to seepage and similar movements, here the development of the law of trespass and strictures against dumping could again handle the problems. But these fall into our next category of difficulties.

3. Stationary sources placed on or nonstationary sources which move to other property *without* the consent of the owner is the most difficult category. For example, air traffic, factory waste emission, automobile emission on public property (so-called), and so on, are examples of this kind of harmful emissions others would suffer without their consent (ex-

plicit or implicit—that is, by agreeing to suffer them or by acting in ways which imply such agreement). This sort of pollution might be handled, first of all, through what we might call preventive market measures—for example, insurance premiums against the possibility of court suits for liability, or liability bonds. Here there is ample room for reflection but it seems that the earlier mentioned policy of quarantine (see §15) could be employed to handle the most troublesome cases. In brief, where activities issuing in pollution cannot be carried out without injury to third (nonconsenting) parties, such activities have to be prohibited as inherently in violation of the rights of members of the community. When pollution occurs along lines of thresholds, such that only once so much emission has occurred could the emission be actually polluting (i.e., harmful to persons) rather than simply defiling, a system of first come, first served might be instituted, so that those who start the production first would be permitted to continue, while others, who would raise the threshold to a harmful level, would not. This may appear arbitrary, but in fact numerous areas of human life, including especially commerce, make good use of this system, and human ingenuity could well be expended toward making sure that one's firm is not a latecomer.

Certainly a libertarian system would not have the authority to rely on the utilitarian notion, used by many courts today in their refusal to enforce "public nuisance laws," that those harmed by pollution have to "pay" since the benefits of industrial growth outweigh such costs in health and property damage as are caused by pollution. Instead the principle of strict liability would apply: The polluter or others who are bound by contract with the polluter, such as nuclear utilities which may have a pact to share insurance premiums and liability resulting from accident at one member's plant, would be held liable. Benefits not solicited cannot be charged for if one respects the individual's right to choose, as the libertarian system is committed to do.[16]

It might be argued that in some cases protecting the rights of individuals in this strict manner may lead to their not enjoying certain benefits they might have regarded to be even greater than the benefit of not suffering the harm caused by, say, pollution. But this is not relevant. The just treatment of individuals must respect their autonomy and their choice in judging what *they* think is best for themselves, even if and when they are mistaken, so long as this does not involve violating others' rights. Paternalism and libertarianism are indeed incompatible political ideals! The system of rights which grounds the libertarian/capitalist legal framework is sound, if it is, precisely because as a *system* of laws it is the one that is most respectful of individual rights. This general virtue shows equal respect for every human person who embarks on social life, and it is this equal respect for all that justifies the establishment of government for all, even if such a system does not guarantee that everyone will in fact make the most of its provisions. Nor does it guarantee that all values sought by members of human communities would be best secured via such a system—for example, technological progress in outer space travel might be enhanced by not paying heed to the strict liability provisions of the libertarian legal system. In short, the ultimate objective of such a system is a form of justice—not welfare, not progress, not equality of condition, not artistic advancement. The justice at hand pertains to respecting every human person's status as a being with dignity, that is, as a being with the freedom and the responsibility to achieve a morally excellent life in his or her own case.

## VI. CONCLUSION

One must be careful not to expect something of a certain field of inquiry that cannot be produced. For too long the demands placed on the fields of morality and politics have been unjustly severe: Final, irrefutable, timeless answers were sought, and in response to the inevitable failure to produce these a cynicism about the prospects of any workable answers has gained a foothold throughout the intellectual community, as well as among members of the general public. As a result, it is now part of the received opinion of the day that no solid intellectual solution to any of the value-oriented areas of human problems can be reached. The best we can expect is some kind of consensus which vaguely represents the tastes and preferences of a significant number of the concerned population. Yet this "consensus" is a house of cards. Tastes and preferences are so unstable, flexible, and so indeterminable that the only thing to emerge is some kind of arbitrary public policy produced either by bureaucrats or by dictators, official or unofficial.

In morality and politics, and thus in public policy too, there can be some very general answers that are stable enough, ones that apply to human life, so long as there is such an identifiably stable phenomenon as human life. Human life and human community involve certain lasting considerations. And innumerable changing problems that emerge in them can be approached reasonably fruitfully by taking into account some of these considerations. The several political systems we have canvassed in this essay appeal to such basic factors with a view to dealing with one of the more thorny problems of the present epoch of human community life: pollution. Pollution is a relatively recent problem, one that proves to be an important, difficult test for the older political theories considered above: fascism, socialism, the welfare state, and capitalism. We saw that fascism would gauge the justice of the state by reference to the inspired leadership of a hero leader. Pollution problems would be managed differently, depending on the different inspired visions of different hero leaders. Science, economics, and other methods would all be available for use by such a leader, if the leader's intuitions led her or him to approve of these methods. If the leader's intuitions did not include these methods, they would be dispensed with. We saw that socialism would stress the overall well-being of the society as a whole, so that through democratic determination, or the guidance of expert leadership together with a theory of humanity's emancipation, the ultimate objective of producing a human community which satisfies human needs and wants to the highest degree would be the basis of public policy. The problem of pollution would be handled, largely, by appeal to some type of cost-benefit analysis, where the overall benefit to society would be weighed against the burdens that society might have to suffer from engaging in activities that result in pollution. The welfare state, in turn, is designed to balance the widely acknowledged values of individual liberty and well-being, as a matter of governmental, public policy. In such a system each person would be guaranteed some measure of liberty, regardless of overall public benefits that might be lost, as well as some measure of well-being, regardless of the liberty of individuals that might for that purpose have to be sacrificed. Pollution, in turn, would have to be handled by reference to whether these two basic human rights could be secured through producing more or less of it. Capitalism or libertarianism, finally, stresses the ultimate importance of the rights and value of the individual, gauging the acceptability of public policies by their success in protecting individual human rights, even where other values, such as progress in science and technology, might have to be set to one side.

This essay by no means exhausts the treatment of the pollution problem, nor does it enter into great technical detail concerning this quintessentially contemporary problem. These details could only be dealt with in relation to particular problems where charges and countercharges, claims and counterclaims involving harm or injury by way of pollution would be at issue. Nor have we pretended to be able to manage everything smoothly. Nevertheless, it has been argued that the libertarian/ capitalist approach to handling the problems of pollution accords most fully with that prime objective of human community life, namely, human justice. This argument should now serve as a useful starting point to consider some of the more particular problems of pollution as they emerge in the actual, day-to-day affairs of individuals living in community.

## NOTES

I wish to thank Bruce K. Bell and Tom Regan for their valuable help with the preparation of this essay.

1.  *Blakiston's Gould Medical Dictionary*, 4th ed. (New York: McGraw-Hill Book Company, 1979), 1073.
2.  Richard B. Stewart and James F. Krier, *Environmental Law and Policy*, 2d ed. (New York: Bobbs-Merrill, 1978), 3.
3.  *Black's Law Dictionary*, 5th ed. (St. Paul, Minn.: West Publishing Company, 1979), 1043.
4.  Paul Feyerabend, *Science in a Free Society* (London: NLB, 1979).
5.  Robert Heilbroner, *Marxism: For and Against* (New York: W. W. Norton, 1980), 157.
6.  Kenneth J. Arrow, *Social Choice and Individual Values* (New York: John Wiley, 1963, 2d ed.).

7.    Samuel Scheffler, "Natural Rights, Equality, and the Minimal State," *Canadian Journal of Philosophy* (March 1976): 76.
8.    Karl Marx, *Selected Writings* (Oxford, England: Oxford University Press, 1977), 166ff.
9.    *Marxism: For and Against, op. cit.*
10.   *Selected Writings, op. cit.*, 57.
11.   *Ibid.*, 53ff.
12.   For presentations of this view see, e.g., Alan Gewirth, *Reason and Morality* (Chicago: University of Chicago Press, 1979); John Rawls, *A Theory of Justice* (Cambridge, Mass.: Harvard University Press, 1971); and A. I. Melden, *Rights and Persons* (Berkeley: University of California Press, 1979).
13.   See Robert K. Best and James I. Collins, "Legal Issues in Pollution Engendered Torts," *The Cato Journal* (Spring 1982): 102–136.
14.   See Joseph P. Martino, "Inheriting the Earth," *Reason* (November 1982): 30–40, 46.
15.   For the kind of "utopia" promised by libertarians, see Robert Nozick, *Anarchy, State, and Utopia* (New York: Basic Books, 1974), Part III.
16.   For a discussion of the pervasiveness of the violation of individual rights on grounds that people should not benefit without paying, see Tibor R. Machan, "Some Philosophical Underpinnings of National Labor Policy." *Harvard Journal of Law and Public Policy* (Summer 1981): 67–160.

# SUGGESTIONS FOR FURTHER READING

The suggested readings below are arranged according to the six major parts of the essay.

I. Introduction

*Black's Law Dictionary*, 5th ed. (St. Paul, Minn.: West, 1979).
*Blakiston's Gould Medical Dictionary*, 4th ed. (New York: McGraw-Hill, 1979).
Richard B. Stewart and James F. Krier, *Environmental Law and Policy*, 2d ed. (New York: Bobbs-Merrill, 1978).

II. Fascism

Carl Cohen, *Communism, Fascism, and Democracy* (New York: Random House, 1972).
Giovani Gentile, "The Philosophical Basis of Fascism," *Foreign Affairs*, Vol. VI (January 1928), pp. 290–304.
Mario Palmieri, *The Philosophy of Fascism* (Chicago: The Dante Alighieri Society, 1936).

III. Socialism

Marshall I. Goldman, *The Spoils of Progress: Environmental Pollution in the Soviet Union* (Cambridge, Mass.: MIT Press, 1972).
Alec Nove, *The Economics of Feasible Socialism* (London: George Allen and Unwin, 1983).
David E. Powell, "The Social Costs of Modernization: Ecological Problems in the USSR," *World Politics*, Vol. XXII (January 1971), pp. 618–634.

IV.  The Welfare State

Kenneth J. Arrow, *Social Choice and Individual Values*, 2d ed. (New York: John Wiley, 1963).
Alan Gewirth, *Reason and Morality* (Chicago: University of Chicago Press, 1979).
A. I. Melden, *Rights and Persons* (Berkeley: University of California Press, 1977).
Dennis C. Mueller, *Public Choice* (London: Cambridge University Press, 1979).
Mark Sagoff, "Economic Theory and Environmental Law," *Michigan Law Review*, Vol. 79, June 1981.

V.  Capitalism

Milton Friedman, *Capitalism and Freedom* (Chicago: University of Chicago Press, 1962).
Tibor R. Machan, ed., *The Libertarian Reader* (Towota, N.J.: Rowman and Littlefield, 1982).
Ayn Rand, *Capitalism: The Unknown Ideal* (New York: Signet, 1967).
Robert J. Smith, "Privatizing the Environment," *Policy Review*, No. 20, Spring 1982.

VI.  Conclusion

Garrett Hardin and John Baden, eds., *Managing the Commons* (San Francisco: W. H. Freeman, 1977).

# 4

# Ethics and Energy

## K. S. SHRADER-FRECHETTE

## I. INTRODUCTION

### §1 AN HISTORICAL PRECEDENT

In 1825 a self-educated mechanic named George Stephenson was called before a committee of the British House of Commons to defend the steam engine. There was a pressing need at that time for efficient transportation between Manchester and Liverpool, and England was troubled by vociferous debate over the ethics of using a steam-powered railway system between the two cities. As a proponent of travel by rail, Stephenson argued that using the locomotive engines would provide the most economical and convenient moving power that could be employed. They would hasten the progress and prosperity of mankind, he said, and rails would become the great highways of the world.

Stephenson's opponents, who were decidedly in the majority, argued that steam engines were unsafe. Since they admitted the need for efficient travel, however, they argued that the railway, if used at all, should be worked by horses and not by locomotives. (Opposition to the steam engine continued with such vehemence that, as late as 1829, laws [e.g., the Newcastle and Carlisle Railway Act] required that the rails should be worked by horses and not locomotives.) Locomotives, said Stephenson's opponents, would terrify the horses in the neighborhood, so that to travel on horseback or to plow the fields near railways would be dangerous. Moreover, they said, animals would be frightened by the glare of the red-hot chimney, and accidents were certain to occur because of the excessive speed of the engine, which was said to be nine miles an hour. Even better than to have horses work the rails, they said, might be to use an "alternative technology," such as horses drawing barges on canals.[1]

As history proved, Stephenson won out and his opponents lost. And, according to at least one contemporary proponent of nuclear power, the Stephenson case is instructive for the present debate over energy.[2] Just as there was a pressing need for efficient transportation between Manchester and Liverpool in 1825, so now there is a pressing need for energy supplies. And just as there was a debate in 1825 between proponents of "hard" transportation technologies (such as locomotives) and advocates of "soft" technologies (such as horse-drawn barges), so also now there is a debate between proponents of "hard" energy technologies (such as coal, oil, nuclear fission, and the breeder) and advocates of "soft" technologies (such as solar, wind, and geothermal). Most important, just as there were only pseudoethical reasons for halting the progress of the steam engine so, some would say, there are only pseudoethical reasons for halting the "progress" of hard energy technologies such as nuclear fission. (Of course, our judgment as to whether these are merely pseudo-arguments depends on whether we are in favor of the hard technologies or opposed to them.)

Although I believe that the bulk of scientific evidence and ethical reasoning is in favor of the soft technologies, rather than the hard, I also believe that both sides of the energy debate are obscured by a number of faulty arguments. Rather than attempt to provide an overly broad survey of the whole energy scene, here I will present and critically analyze a few key arguments, some used by proponents of soft technology, others, by their opponents. Because of the brevity of this essay, I make no attempt at establishing the general superiority of the soft path over the hard. However, my remarks should facilitate the sort of clarification and insight which is a first step in showing the desirability of the soft path. The primary focus of my analysis will be ethical and methodological, since I believe that the alleged energy crisis really has very little to do with energy. Rather, it is an ethical crisis, and like most things ethical, resolves itself into quarrels about who has the right to do what to whom, on what grounds, at what price, in whose interest, under what definition of welfare, and according to which interpretation of the democratic state. I will begin by giving a brief overview of current and proposed energy strategies and will discuss the distinction between so-called hard and soft energy paths. Second (in Part II), I will present and criticize four arguments used by some proponents of soft energy technologies: (1) the argument from romantic regression, (2) the anarchist argument, (3) the transfer of harm argument, and (4) the zero-risk argument. Third (in Part III), I will present and criticize five arguments used by some proponents of hard energy technologies: (1) the proportionality argument, (2) the normalcy argument, (3) the uncertainty argument, (4) the cost-benefit argument, and (5) the statistical casualties argument. Although not all of the first four arguments are accepted by all proponents of the soft path, just as not all of the last five are accepted by all advocates of the hard path, and although neither set of arguments comprises the total used by either "side," these nine are sufficiently widely used to deserve serious attention. Finally (in Part IV), I will briefly outline how one might justify, in a much lengthier treatment, a choice in favor of the soft path.

There are a number of reasons why, in so short an essay, I will not attempt to argue for a definitive conclusion regarding which energy option is the most ethical. This conclusion is dependent, at least in part, on a number of highly technical scientific and economic factors, some of which are subject to rapid change, such as, for example the cost per kilowatt-hour of nuclear- versus coal-generated electricity. It is also dependent upon a number of complex ethical issues, not all of which can be dealt with here. Instead, my remarks will simply point to a few of the ways in which, in thinking about the ethical assumptions and consequences of energy policy, we go wrong.

## §2 THE CURRENT ENERGY PICTURE FOR THE UNITED STATES

To appreciate the ethical dimensions of various United States energy policies, it is important to understand the current situation in this country. The United States produces a vast amount of energy every year, 31.9 million barrels per day of oil equivalent (or, as it is commonly abbreviated, 31.9 MMBDOE) in 1980, more than any other nation. It is the largest producer of coal, the largest producer of natural gas, the largest producer of electricity from nuclear power, and the third-largest oil producer in the world. Although the United States generates only about 80 percent of the energy it uses, its dependence on foreign nations for that remaining 20 percent is decreasing.[3]

Most official proposals for short-term future United States energy policy embody three goals: (1) minimizing oil imports, (2) relegating solar and unconventional energy sources to a minor role until after the turn of the century, and (3) sustaining growth in energy consumption.[4] These goals are clearly reflected in recent U.S. Department of Energy (DOE) statistics. According to the DOE, the United States used 37.6 MMBDOE in 1980, and is expected to use 43.6 MMBDOE in 1990.[5] In 1980, petroleum products, natural gas, coal, nuclear energy, and solar/renewable sources provided, respectively, 16.9 MMBDOE, 9.7 MMBDOE, 7.3 MMBDOE, 1.3 MMBDOE, 2.4 MMBDOE. Between 1980 and 1990, use of petroleum products is expected to decrease; use of coal is expected to grow by approximately 60 percent, use of nuclear power by approximately 170 percent, and use of solar/renewable sources by only 25 percent.[6]

## §3 "HARD" VERSUS "SOFT" ENERGY TECHNOLOGIES

Because of its three goals of cutting back on oil imports, minimizing solar and unconventional sources, and sustaining growth in energy consumption, the United States is clearly following the hard energy path of coal and nuclear power and minimizing the soft path of solar and renewable resources. According to Amory B. Lovins, a physicist associated with the environmental organization "Friends of the Earth," the hard path is centralized, capital intensive, large scale, complex, and energy intensive, while the soft path is characterized by decentralization, smaller capital investments, small-scale organizational structures, and less complex, labor-intensive technologies.[7] Generally, the term "hard technology," or "high technology," is used to refer to technological developments in advanced societies, while the term "soft," "appropriate," "intermediate," "low," or "alternative technology" is employed to depict developments that are alternatives to those that prevail in advanced societies and modern sectors of underdeveloped nations. Such alternatives are thought by their proponents to be better able to match the needs of all people in a society and to provide a sustainable relationship with the environment.[8]

Lovins' principal criticism of the hard path is that it is economically infeasible. He calculates that extracting low-grade deposits of petroleum and natural gas, building increasingly costly nuclear reactors fueled with increasingly expensive uranium, and making liquid fuel from coal will require a capital intensity per unit of energy that is roughly ten times that of the traditional fossil fuels of the 1970s. Sometime after 1985, says Lovins, this investment expense would mount so rapidly that 75 percent of all investment capital in the United States would be required for the energy industries. Hence, he concludes, there would be no money left to finance other societal needs, and massive political problems would likely follow.[9]

The soft energy path, says Lovins, is able to avoid these economic and political problems by means of a three-step approach: greatly increased technical efficiency in energy use, rapid deployment of soft technologies, and transitional use of fossil fuels. Perhaps the most striking aspect of this path is that decreased use of primary energy (e.g., resources) is postulated with no decrease in the amount of end-use energy (e.g., delivered kilowatts of electrical energy). This is said to come about through thermal insulation, more efficient automobile engines, recovery of usable heat from industrial processes, the "cogeneration" of electricity as a by-product of industrial-process heat, and other innovations.[10]

Interesting as are Lovins' factual and technological claims and the responses of his critics,[11] they will have to be bypassed here. Our interests are in examining several *ethical* arguments, some advanced in support of the soft path, others in support of the hard path. Let us begin with the former.

## II. THE SOFT PATH

### §4 THE ARGUMENT FROM ROMANTIC REGRESSION

The argument from romantic regression[12] proposes that we ought to follow the soft path because hard technologies, in their efficiency, sophistication, and emphasis on consumption, are socially destructive. According to its proponents, "desirable social relations," including "participatory democracy," require that we return to a more primitive level of energy use. As the social critic Ivan Illich puts it: "Participatory democracy demands low energy technology, and free people must travel the road to productive social relations at the speed of a bicycle. . . . People on their feet are more or less equal," but the moment the transportation industry put horsepower behind passengers, it "reduced equality among men, restricted their mobility to a system of industrially defined routes and created time scarcity of unprecedented severity. . . . Everybody's daily radius expands at the expense of being able to drop in on an acquaintance or walk through the park on the way to work. Extremes of privilege are created at the cost of universal enslavement. . . . The speedier the vehicle the larger the subsidy it gets from regressive taxation."[13]

Although all proponents of soft technology do not subscribe to the argument from romantic regression, those who do appeal to a return to the "good old days" when people "split wood not atoms," lived a bucolic and unhurried existence, and were not dependent upon any sources of energy like coal, oil, or nuclear fission. Some of the reasons for advocating such a return are that social relationships were more equitable, people had more leisure time and more freedom because there was no "enforced dependence" on sophisticated power stations or on gas-guzzling machines, and there were more opportunities for the disadvantaged since fewer extremes of privilege were created.[14]

Contemporary as these aspects of the argument from romantic regression sound, their underpinnings are several centuries old. One of the most famous philosophers to present these theories was the French thinker Jean-Jacques Rousseau. In 1755 he published his famous *Discourse on the Origin of Inequality*, in which he claimed that, because of our evolution away from a more primitive state, we humans have become alienated from our natures, preventing us from being our real selves. The most serious feature of modern society, for Rousseau, is the prevalence of an unnatural inequality based on power and wealth, an inequality created because natural needs have been replaced by artificial ones. Modern society, with all its advances, says Rousseau, keeps us from being self-sufficient, as we once were, and it destroys our innate feelings of natural pity.[15]

Apart from whether one agrees with the argument from romantic regression, there are few who are likely to disagree with one of its basic insights: that modern societies, dependent as they are upon sophisticated energy sources and rising gross national products (GNPs), threaten to sever us from what is most human and most desirable in more primitive societies. Anthropologists and biologists are quick to point out that we are physically and genetically suited to life in a primitive tropical savanna where we would have rare contact with larger groups; the current hard-technology society, they claim, "has twisted normal functioning into bizarre reactions" so that we are like gorillas, who are shy, mild, alert, and well-coordinated in the tropical forests of Africa, but who become dangerous and erratic in the zoo of contemporary society.[16] Ecologist Paul Shepard, in *The Tender Carnivore and the Sacred Game*, points out that aboriginal people lived a good life in which only two or three days a week were spent in providing for their sustenance. They spent the remainder of their time in socializing, sleeping, dancing, visiting, being hosts, telling stories, playing with children, and making music. For Shepard, this successful adaptation of humans to the environment broke down 10,000 years ago, with the rise of agriculture.[17]

To accept the thesis that much of modern society, with all its advanced technologies, is dehumanizing is not necessarily to accept the conclusion of the argument from romantic regression. There are a number of reasons why arguing for a return to the past or for primitivism does not provide *sufficient* grounds for accepting soft energy technologies. And, although there may be desirable reasons for choosing the soft path (rather than the hard) it is not clear that an appeal to the virtues of earlier, simpler days provides *necessary* grounds for such a choice. For one thing, the earlier "state of nature" is not something which is known completely as historical fact. As a consequence, proponents of the argument from romantic regression often ignore what appears to be part of that state. Earlier life was often nasty, brutish, and short, and certainly more precarious for the individual than is ours. Proponents of the argument from romantic regression assume that there was nobility, but little savagery, in primitive life. They realize, correctly, that technological development has indeed brought undesirable effects, but they forget that these effects must often "be viewed as the expense of decreasing our vulnerability to nature."[18]

In one sense, we may have been less vulnerable when we were self-sufficient in building our own wood fires, rather than in waiting for electricity to be generated from fission, coal, or oil. In another sense, we are less vulnerable now because we need neither to gather wood, nor to keep the fires going during the night, nor to protect our fuel from downpours. Freedom from such tasks also has provided us with the time and money to develop a culture in which we easily can attend to other needs. The sophisticated educational, communications, and medical networks of today's world would be virtually impossible in a completely soft society. Nevertheless, most of us forget the benefits derived from hard technology in areas such as education and medical care. The jawbone record, for example, reveals that early humans spent many days in unrelieved pain from chronic toothache. During the middle ages, thousands of persons died from pestilence. Perhaps then people did not die of sophisticated cancers, strokes, and heart diseases induced by stress, but they did die, and at an early age, from pneumonia, influenza, and tuberculosis. Infant and early natural mortality were probably astronomically high in early days. Even as late as 1900, more than 13 percent of all American children died before their first birthdays.[19] All this suggests that the proponents of the argument from romantic regression may have their facts wrong if they claim that primitive life was more desirable than that today.

Second, it may also be, as University of Pittsburgh philosopher Nicholas Rescher suggests, that even if people are less happy now than they were in former times, they do not desire to return to earlier days. According to Rescher, people are less happy now because they are victims of their own rising expectations. Introducing the principle of "hedonic discounting," he maintains that people undervalue realized achievements in the light of prior expectations. Having expected more, they do not value what they have.[20] If Rescher is correct, then proponents of the argument from romantic regression may be wrong in assuming that human happiness is significantly worsened by living in a hard-technology society.

Third, apart from whether primitive life was more or less desirable, or whether people were more or less happy than they are now, proponents of the argument from romantic regression likewise appear to err in assuming that technological developments, including hard energy paths, have *caused* societies to be less free or equitable. In making this causal inference, and in assuming that following the soft path will increase societal freedom and equity, they appear to commit the fallacy of false cause. Perhaps it is political systems, not technological advances, that should bear the charge of causing inequity and lack of freedom. If technological society is inequitable, as Illich claims, because only "0.2 percent of the entire United States population can engage in self-chosen air travel more than once a year," while airlines receive a great subsidy "from regressive taxation,"[21] then isn't the problem with distribution and taxation of goods, rather than with the technological advances per se? If so, then perhaps hard technology is merely a convenient scapegoat for those who do not want to bear responsibility for the inequity of the society which their actions have helped to create. Perhaps part of what is wrong with the argument from romantic regression is that its proponents have, as counterculture guru Theodore Roszak puts it, "no sense of sin." They use the argument "to claim a significant kind of innocence"[22] for themselves and to lay guilt on technology.

Of course it is true that, as they are presently employed, many hard technologies do visit inequities on people. Under current regulations, emissions from commercial nuclear reactors clearly violate the rights of various persons to equal protection.[23] Likewise, because of the liability limits set by government in the case of a nuclear catastrophe, countless accident victims are likely to be treated inequitably by virtue of being denied their rights to due process.[24] (These and related points are discussed at greater length in §12 of this essay.) Such inequities, however, are hardly *caused* by fission technology; rather they are caused by the political and regulatory conditions under which nuclear power is used.[25]

Admittedly, because hard energy technologies are more sophisticated, they require control by experts, and such control often is not exercised in the interests of equity. In the nuclear accident at Three Mile

Island, Pennsylvania, for example, Nuclear Regulatory Commission (NRC) officials failed to take account of the rights to equal protection of citizens living near the reactor. By failing to require immediate evacuation and to admit immediately the seriousness of the situation, they placed residents' lives and rights in jeopardy, in an attempt to help the nuclear industry "save face."[26] Such failures, however, would hardly be grounds, unless one were violently anti-intellectual, to condemn the technology. What must be faulted is a populace that needs to become more technically literate and a government that allows *technical* experts to control questions of *ethical* policy. If one were to follow the path of proscribing the use of any technology not capable of being understood by "the man in the street," because then scientific elitists controlling it could more easily employ it in coercive or inequitable ways, then the use of many life-saving medical technologies would have to be proscribed. Surely, however, one would not accept this consequence. Hence one ought not to oppose hard energy technologies solely because their sophistication renders citizens less able to control their use.

Fourth, even if proponents of the argument from romantic regression were correct in alleging that hard technologies themselves promoted or caused a societal situation in which people were less free or were treated unequally, this alone would not prove that use of the technologies was unethical. For one thing, it is not obvious that everyone *needs* to do an equal amount of travel by air, for example, or that everyone *needs* an equal amount of protection from the hazards of hard energy technologies, for example, radiation. Moreover, as Harvard philosopher John Rawls notes, absolute equality of protection is unattainable.[27]

For example, one cannot possibly choose a policy which gives everyone equal *treatment*, with respect to the consequences of low-level radioactive emissions. This is because medical differences among persons, for instance, place some of them at a higher risk. Children, those with allergies, and those with previous medical exposures bear a higher risk than do others when all receive the same treatment. *Equal treatment* (i.e., subjecting all to the same level of risk) is impossible, given one level of exposure but different levels of susceptibility.

Even if it could be had by all, however, it is not clear that there are ethical grounds for claiming that everyone ought to have *equal treatment*, or *the same* distribution of goods or opportunities (e.g., the same protection) as anyone else receives. As legal philosopher Ronald Dworkin observes, there appear to be ethical grounds for claiming only that everyone ought to have *equal concern* or *respect* in the political decision about how goods, treatment, and opportunities are to be distributed.[28] The point is not that anyone's rights may be ignored in the calculations, but that one's interests may be outweighed by another's interests. In the case of monetary policy, for example, government cannot possibly choose an option which gives everyone *equal treatment* with respect to the consequences of inflation. Moreover, even if equal treatment were possible, there may well be morally relevant reasons why *treatment* of two individuals should not be the *same* (*e.g., considerations of merit or need*). In this case, even if the same treatment were possible, genuinely *equal* treatment, for two different individuals, might be quite *different*.

But if equal treatment is impossible, and one's interests may be outweighed by another's interests, then one must choose the policy which gives everyone's *interests* equal (not the *same*) consideration and which provides an equitable basis for deciding when one person's interests are outweighed by another's. But if this is so, then use of nuclear energy, for example, cannot be shown to be unethical merely because its effects do not give persons equal treatment. To show this, one must argue either that there are no morally relevant reasons for different treatment, or that persons' *interests* were not given equal consideration, or that some persons' interests were erroneously judged to be outweighed by the interests of others. All of which is to say that hard technologies cannot be condemned *solely* on the grounds that use of them involves treating people unequally.

## §5 THE ANARCHIST ARGUMENT

In many ways similar to the argument from romantic regression, the anarchist argument fails for many of the same reasons. The argument from romantic regression is that we ought to follow the soft path, because hard technologies force us to leave our primitive pasts in which people were more equal, free, and compassionate. Basically this new argument is that we ought to follow the soft path because hard technologies are centralized, and only completely decentralized societies, so-called anarchist communities,[29] provide desirable political relationships among people. This is because only an anarchist society, "spontaneous and unfettered by authority," is able to provide humankind with relationships that are not "regressive and oppressive,"[30] but instead are diverse, freeing, and egalitarian.

Whether discussed by revolutionaries such as Murray Bookchin,[31] Theodore Roszak,[32] or David Dickson,[33] nearly all versions of the anarchist argument claim that the soft energy path ought to be followed because it is part of a decentralized government and society. For them, the soft path will recreate the Athenian *polis* in which each member of the community will "play his part in all of its many activities."[34]

As with the argument from romantic regression, the anarchist argument rests on an insight which appears fundamentally true. In this case, the insight is that modern society, with its political and industrial centralization, is dehumanizing and oppressive. Although this insight is sound, there are a number of reasons why arguing for decentralized energy technologies, in the name of human freedom and equality, does not provide adequate grounds for accepting the soft energy path. Admittedly there may be good reasons for favoring decentralized technologies, such as onsite solar (e.g., because these technologies do not waste two-thirds of energy resources by converting them to unneeded electricity, or because decentralized systems can match the quality of resources to energy needs). To favor soft technologies in the name of freedom and equality, however, is somewhat questionable. One reason is that, just as the proponents of the argument from romantic regression forget that primitive life was often nasty, brutish, and short, as well as noble, so the proponents of the anarchist argument forget that decentralized societies are often backward, closed, inefficient, provincial, and stultifying, as well as familial. For example, one need only think of some of the closed, small, racist communities in the South. Thus, just as proponents of the argument from romantic regression likely were mistaken in picturing primitive life as more desirable than life today, so also proponents of the anarchist argument might be wrong in picturing the small, self-sufficient, decentralized communities of the past as freer and more egalitarian than today's large, centralized societies.

Second, it is not clear that decentralized energy systems and decentralized political communities provide for any more free or spontaneous relationships among persons than do centralized systems and groups. Although they deliver people from the yoke of centralized control, they force them to bear the burdens of a loss of efficiency. Each does for himself what might more easily be done by a few others. The man who must cut and haul his own firewood for fuel may be free from the oligarchs of centralized utility systems, but he is less free in the sense of being unable to trade his cutting and hauling for a flip of an electricity switch.

Bookchin claims that the position accepted by the proponents of (what I call) the anarchist argument "implies a contempt for efficiency."[35] Such a contempt for efficiency, however, produces diseconomies of time, in the sense that people have fewer hours to do other things because they are busy doing for themselves what might be done more easily in more centralized fashion. These diseconomies of time, in turn, must limit the real freedom of people. They restrict both the quantity and the quality of other pursuits in which persons wish to engage, for example art, music, politics, literature. If proponents of this argument appeal to the classical Greek model of decentralized life in the Athenian *polis*, then they must remember both that these Greeks had slaves to free them from the burdens of being "self-sufficient," and that the fraternal ideals embodied in the political life of Athenian democracy excluded women and slaves. With a substructure of hard-working women and slaves, indeed it was possible for each Athenian male to have the time and the freedom to "play his part" in all of the activities of the *polis*. This leads one to wonder whether it was the decentralized systems, per se, that "freed" people to engage in all the activities of the *polis*, or whether it was unjust political and social institutions (like sexism and slavery) that did so.

Third, it appears likely that many of the practical conditions necessary for attaining the soft-path goals of freedom, self-sufficiency, and equity can only be brought about by some degree of centralized government. Hence decentralization is not necessarily a good in itself. Decentralized political systems make it possible to promote at least four desirable goals: (1) *liberty*, in the sense of a diffusion of power; (2) *flexibility* in realizing local goals; (3) *fraternity*, in the sense of participation with others in small-scale decisionmaking; and (4) *diversity*, in the sense that social policies can be experimental or tailormade to fit the group choosing them. These four advantages, however, are often bought at a great price. From an economic point of view, decentralization frequently does not enable one to take advantage of centralized economies of scale. Decentralized political systems also intensify the "commons" dilemma. For example, each community might prefer higher environmental standards, but none dares take the action to achieve them for fear of losing economic growth to other such communities. Centralized governments, through centralized environmental and energy regulations, however, can help alleviate these commons problems by imposing uniform standards for all. Environmental regulation in the United States clearly shows the benefits of centralization; the federal government has been able to mandate environmental standards which, otherwise, would likely not have been accepted by low-income communities. This is because, as land economists and planners tell us,[36] low-income communities tend to adopt policies which preserve the tax base and which are thereby favorable to industrialization and unfavorable to environmental controls; high-income communities, however, tend to adopt policies which preserve the status of the community, and which are therefore favorable to environmental controls and unfavorable to industrialization. This means that centralized political systems are able to protect poorer communities who might otherwise be victimized by weak environmental legislation. In this sense, centralization enhances their freedom.

A second asset of centralized political systems—which also contributes to the alleged soft-path goals of freedom and equity—is their ability to handle spillovers. Decisions made in one community obviously "spill over" and affect the quality of life in other communities. For example, if one decentralized community polluted the Ohio River in Pittsburgh, then another decentralized community in Cincinnati would bear the spillover effects of pollution. Without a federal authority, these spillovers would create monumental market imperfections. That is, without a federal authority, upstream polluters could avoid the social costs of their damaging the river, while downstream users would have to bear these costs. Since the market takes no account of such social costs, regulations imposed by a centralized government are necessary in order to force people to bear the social costs of actions they impose on others.

A third asset of centralized political systems, and one which also helps provide the necessary conditions for social freedom and equity, is their ability to balance representation. Given decentralized communities obviously bear high costs if they wish to ensure that all sides on given issues are represented effectively. Imbalance in small communities is common, as the existence of the "company town" proves. Centralized governments, however, can often offset this imbalance in representation and set guidelines to prevent authentic local freedom from being coopted, especially by powerful vested interests.

A fourth asset of centralized political systems is that they make possible a necessary "politics of sacrifice."[37] Often control measures requiring material sacrifice must be undertaken, as in the case of siting facilities for toxic wastes. In a purely decentralized community, it is unlikely either that persons would impose this sacrifice on themselves or that they would have the funds and the expertise necessary to accomplish the project in the most desirable way. If "sacrifices" are undertaken by all, on a national basis, however, they can be equalized and implemented by centralized governments better able to face local or short-term opposition.

If it is true that federal economies of scale, taking account of spillovers, balancing representation, and implementing an equitable "politics of sacrifice" are all accomplished more easily by centralized political systems, and that they are all necessary conditions for authentic political freedom and equity, then it may well be that decentralization, alone, is not the best safeguard of freedom and equity. This means that decentralized political systems may be neither desirable in themselves nor desirable as a means for pursuing the goal of *energy* decentralization, via the soft path. If this is so, then while there may be compelling reasons for choosing soft energy technologies, these do not include those given in the anarchist argument.

Like the argument from romantic regression, the anarchist argument appears suspect because it mislocates the causes of human inequity and enslavement. Both arguments seem to blame factors other than humanity for humanity's ills. In blaming either high technology or centralized political systems, both arguments suggest that humans are naturally good, and that all one has to do to "free" this goodness is (according to this argument) to decentralize all centralized energy and political systems or (in the case of the argument from romantic regression) to change the culture to a more primitive one. Whether made by proponents of soft technology, by Marxists, by anarchists such as William Godwin, or by Enlightenment thinkers such as Saint-Pierre, Turgot, or Condorcet, this suggestion faces the same problem. As John Passmore explains, it relies "upon what one can only regard as myths." Man's natural goodness is a myth. "Perfection is no more to be expected from the destruction of existing social institutions than from their extension and their strengthening. The chains which men bear they have imposed upon themselves. . . ."[38] If Passmore is right, then perhaps inequity and slavery are caused not so much by sophisticated technology or by centralized political and energy systems, as by how humans use and respond to those institutions. But if this is so, then both the argument from romantic regression and the anarchist argument fail in a fundamental way. They misidentify the sources of human perfection and imperfection.

## §6 THE TRANSFER OF HARM ARGUMENT

Although he does not subscribe to the problematic anarchist argument and its apparent suggestions about human perfectibility, Amory Lovins provides an excellent example of a much more plausible argument in favor of energy decentralization. Unlike proponents of the anarchist argument, Lovins does not erroneously assume that pursuing the goal of decentralizing the *political* system will provide adequate grounds for justifying the soft technology path of *energy* decentralization. Lovins' argument, in a nutshell, is that centralized energy systems separate the energy output from its side effects and allocate them to different people at opposite ends of the transmission lines.[39] Thus, he would say, Navajo Indians in Arizona bear the inequitable burden of the effects of emissions from coal-fired plants furnishing electricity for Los Angeles, just as residents of New Hampshire bear the inequitable burden of the effects of acid rain caused by Ohio Valley utilities who furnish electricity for Chicago.

More powerful than the anarchist argument, Lovins' reasoning nevertheless has some weaknesses. There is at least one problem with his defining decentralized energy systems as more ethical in their allotment of costs and benefits. This problem is that he assumes such *unequal treatment* of persons in different geographical communities is itself necessarily unethical. As our earlier (§4) discussion revealed, however, there is no right to *equal treatment*, but only a right to *equal consideration of interests* in making the political decision about treatment. This means that Lovins needs to present a more sophisticated ethical argument (and indeed I believe that one can be made). For example, he might show that geographical location is not a morally relevant basis for unequal treatment.[40] Or, he might argue that, in a given situation, persons in different locales did not receive equal consideration in the political decision about handling the spillovers of technology. In other words, since absolute equality of treatment (in all respects) is not necessarily justified, one who argues for decentralized energy systems must show that there are not good reasons for permitting the unequal distribution of effects of centralized systems. It is not sufficient for one to argue merely that unequal distributions exist.

On the practical side, one who accepts Lovins' position on decentralization also needs to answer at least two questions. First, why couldn't those who bear the inequitable costs of centralized energy generation be compensated somehow for their burden? Second, don't even decentralized energy systems have harmful spillover effects on other regions? (For example, suppose that one deforests an area to burn wood there for fuel, and suppose that the effects of the burning are visited only upon those who receive the benefits. Wouldn't this decentralized "system" nevertheless have spillover effects, e.g., in terms of the global problem of the greenhouse effect?) That is, even if one uses an ethically strengthened version of Lovins' argument in favor of decentralized energy systems, one would still need to show that the alleged ill effects (geographical

inequities and spillovers) were truly a consequence of the hard, centralized technology, and not merely the effect of faulty political mechanisms
for regulating the hard technology and distributing its costs and benefits.
It is not unfair to Lovins to point out that he has not shown this.

## §7 THE ZERO-RISK ARGUMENT

One of the most common justifications for the soft path, especially in the
popular literature, is the zero-risk argument. Proponents of this argument claim that because hard-energy technologies, like nuclear power,
do not have zero risks and, in fact, are very dangerous, the soft path
should be followed. In other words, proponents of the zero-risk argument rely on the mere assertion that a given technology is dangerous as
sufficient grounds for condemning it.

In one popular book, for example, a well-known advocate of the soft
path, United States Senator Mike Gravel, argues that hard path technologies, such as nuclear fission, are wrong because they will cause an increase in cancer.[41]

The reason why the zero-risk argument is so powerful (despite its
flaws, which I will address) is that the risk statistics for hard technologies are quite high. In the case of nuclear power, for example, United
States government documents indicate that, were a core melt and resultant release of radiation to occur, property damage alone could run as
high as $17 billion; in addition, 45,000 immediate deaths, 100,000 cases
of cancer, and contamination of an area the size of Pennsylvania could
occur.[42] Moreover, on the basis of estimates given by current nuclear advocates, such as Norman Rasmussen, it is easy to show that even these
conservative data predict that a Three-Mile Island type of accident
could occur in the United States as often as once every other year.[43] Likewise, on the basis of currently accepted government risk probabilities,
the chance that a core melt will occur, sometime in the thirty-year lifetime of one of the 151 reactors now operating or under construction in
the United States, is approximately one in four.[44] Simply citing such
alarming statistics provides a powerful emotive appeal to abandon hard
technologies such as nuclear fission.

The main problem with many soft-path appeals to the zero-risk argument is *not* that they are wrong in their *factual claims* about hard energy
technologies, but that they do not go far enough and present real *ethical*
analysis. Proponents of the zero-risk argument simply make the tacit assumption that, if a risk is large enough or alarming enough, then this
alone provides a sufficient reason for not accepting it. This assumption,
however, is obviously false, since the absence of zero risk, in varied areas
of life, is rarely thought to provide grounds for rejecting the source of the
risk. If some statistics are to be believed, then the annual risk of death
for a person doing an average amount of driving is greater, by a factor of
200, than is the risk of death for a person living near a nuclear reactor.[45]
Moreover, as risk theorist Chauncey Starr points out, every judgment

about the acceptability of a given risk is a function of the *benefit* awareness regarding that risk.[46] For example, one might take even a serious risk if the benefits are great enough, perhaps in terms of time or money.

Numerous other factors, in addition to mere magnitude, determine the acceptability of a risk: whether it is assumed voluntarily or imposed involuntarily; whether the effects are immediate or delayed; whether there are or are not alternatives to accepting the risk; whether the degree of risk is known or uncertain; whether exposure to it is essential to one's well being or merely a luxury; whether it is encountered occupationally or nonoccupationally; whether it is an ordinary hazard or (like cancer) a "dread" one; whether it affects everyone or only sensitive people; whether the factor causing the risk will be used as intended or is likely to be misused; and whether the risk and its effects are reversible or irreversible.[47] Hence, to argue simply that a given technology ought not to be accepted, because the normal pollution it causes will induce a given number of deaths, is incomplete and inconclusive. One also needs to address ethical issues such as whether consent was given to the risk, whether it is distributed equitably among all, whether it is compensated, and whether the benefits outweigh the risks. In other words, one needs to ask not only what the risk is but also whether the risk is worth the benefits it will bring.

Every time a vaccine is approved for mass dosage, policymakers rightly assent to the thesis that the benefits (of large numbers of people being protected against a given disease) outweigh the risks (of certain susceptible people dying as a consequence of immunization). Now admittedly one often can choose whether or not to be inoculated and one cannot choose whether or not to receive radioactive emissions from nuclear power plants. Despite this disanalogy, the vaccination case clearly shows that even nonzero risks sometimes ought to be accepted.

Moreover, to the extent that proponents of soft paths argue for them under the assumption that soft energy technologies are risk-free, to that degree they are in error. One can easily show, for example, that a given number of fatalities, especially in the construction industry, are likely to occur for every given number of kilowatt-hours of solar electricity which is generated.[48] It is not just production of solar energy which has risks, however. There is no activity which is completely risk-free in all respects. Moreover, one cannot reduce one risk without, at the same time, increasing another. For example, one could reduce pesticide-induced carcinogens by prohibiting all forms of pest control except biological ones. But this lowering of the *health* risk to workers and consumers would increase the *financial* risk to the farmer, since most biological controls are currently more expensive to implement, if protection from pests is desired at the same level as that achieved by chemicals.

Recent government regulation of the meat industry illustrates the same points about the nonexistence of zero risk and the unavoidability of risk transfers. When the United States Occupational Safety and Health Administration ordered the meat industry to place guardrails between animals and the people who slaughtered them, it sought to reduce the risk of accidents. What it ignored, however, was that this alleged risk *diminution* was really a risk *displacement*. Although the guardrails *reduced accidents*, the Food and Drug Administration showed that they also *increased* the risk of disease to the workers because the guardrails harbored germs.[49]

What all these considerations come down to is that the zero-risk argument, in itself, is incomplete and needs to be supplemented with arguments about the *ethical desirability* of particular risk displacements. Arguments about the desirability of risk displacement must focus not just on mere magnitudes of fatalities and injuries, but also on violations of justice and on discussion of the limits of one's rights. This means that environmentalists ought not simply to present "horror stories" about allegedly high risks in the areas of energy technology, pesticide use, or meat preparation. If they wish an effective argument, they ought to show, on ethical grounds, why one risk is more or less desirable than another, or why one risk is a better or worse tradeoff for another. If they erroneously assume, either that there are zero risks, or that risks are unacceptable merely because they are nonzero, then we are likely to have public policy which neither reduces risks nor addresses the relevant ethical considerations for assessing risks.

## III.  THE HARD PATH

### §8  SOME ARGUMENTS IN FAVOR OF THE HARD PATH

Failure to engage in as complex an ethical analysis as is needed is not simply an error into which some proponents of the soft path fall. The same sorts of incompleteness characterize many hard-path arguments, especially those I wish to discuss, namely (1) the proportionality argument, (2) the normalcy argument, (3) the uncertainty argument, (4) the cost-benefit argument, and (5) the statistical-casualties argument. Although far from exhausting the support offered for the hard path, these arguments are instructive because they illustrate some of the ethical problems with this energy strategy.

### §9  THE PROPORTIONALITY ARGUMENT

One very common argument used even by sophisticated proponents of hard energy technology is (what I call) "the proportionality argument." This is that (1) because the ethical value of risk avoidance is proportional to the risk (defined as probability of fatality), and (2) because the risk associated with nearly all hard energy technologies is lower than that associated with other risks which society chooses to accept, (3) therefore hard energy technologies, such as liquified natural gas and nuclear fission, are ethically defensible or of a "cost" acceptable to society.[50] Proponents of the proportionality argument often claim, for example, that automobiles cause more deaths than do nuclear power plants. Therefore, they argue, if society accepts automobiles, it ought to accept the plants.[51] In making this argument, its proponents fall prey to at least three questionable assumptions: (a) that "risk" is adequately defined as "probability of fatality"; (b) that the value of risk avoidance is independent of any variable (such as benefits) except probability of fatality, and (c) that there is a linear relationship between societal risk and the ethical value of risk avoidance, or the cost of that risk. Since assumptions a and b seem to me to be obviously implausible, I would like to focus on assumption (c), which proposes an ethical criterion for the acceptability of all risks, but especially those posed by hard energy technologies.

In accepting assumption (c), proponents of the proportionality argument maintain that policy should be made on the basis that risks with a higher probability of fatality are less acceptable, ethically, than those with a lower one.[52] They claim that it is "inconsistent" for the public both to tolerate 50,000 automobile deaths per year and to be alarmed at generating electricity through nuclear fission.[53] Nuclear advocate Maxey, for example, says that those who view nuclear risks as more dangerous than other, more probable, risks have "pathological fear" and "near clinical paranoia." If the public only understood that hard technology catastrophes have low probabilities, claim advocates like Maxey, then the public would not fear hard-technology risks more than other "accepted" risks having a higher probability of fatality.[54]

Because they make assumption (c), proponents of the proportionality argument do not view the observed societal aversion to the low-probability, catastrophic risks of hard technology (e.g., nuclear core melt risk) as evidence against them. Rather, they claim that the public makes incorrect value judgments as to the unacceptability of the hard technology *because* they are ignorant of the fact that hard technologies have quite low probabilities of causing fatalities.

In using assumption (c) of the proportionality argument, proponents of hard technology do not so much defend their views as they attack the persons who oppose hard technologies and claim that they are ignorant and/or needlessly fearful. Apart from the fact that personal attacks have no place in a logical argument, proponents of the proportionality argument are very likely factually wrong in assuming that opponents of hard energy technologies hold their beliefs because they are ignorant about the real risks involved. Recent research regarding nuclear power indicates, for example, that both proponents and opponents of nuclear power have the same perception of the *magnitude* of the *risks* involved. Psychometric data indicates that they merely disagree on the benefits alleged to come from use of this technology.[55] But if disagreement over the acceptability of a hard technology, like nuclear fission, is not a function of one's knowledge of risk probabilities, then proponents of the proportionality argument err when they claim or imply that the public views hard technology risks nonlinearly (i.e., with more aversion than they should, given the probabilities involved) *because* they are ignorant.

Even if the risk probabilities were low, which may not be true (see §7), it would still be reasonable to claim that certain hazards of hard technologies were less acceptable than other hazards having a higher probability of causing fatalities. Many other ethically relevant features, such as the *distribution* of the risk, its tradeoff with benefits, or whether it is compensated, voluntarily accepted, and fully understood, could equally well explain why it is reasonable, both to claim that the value of risk avoidance is not proportional to the probability of the risk and to oppose certain hard energy technologies.

The main problem with the proportionality argument, therefore, is that it rests on an implausible assumption, one that makes the ethical acceptability of a risk a function *solely* of mathematical/scientific/technological considerations, namely, probability of fatality. This means that its proponents underestimate the richness and complexity of the value component in deciding between soft and hard technologies. What is worse, in misunderstanding this value component, proponents of the argument erroneously dismiss the objections of their opponents (e.g., that nuclear risks are neither compensated nor adequately insured) merely as the product of someone who is technically illiterate or inconsistent in rating various probabilities.

## §10 THE NORMALCY ARGUMENT

Much the same sort of problem occurs with the normalcy argument. In using this mode of reasoning, proponents of hard energy technologies argue that, so long as the levels of hazard (pollution, cancer, genetic disorder) caused by hard technologies are of the same, or a lower, order of magnitude as those "normally" present, then these hazards are acceptable. If someone objects to their (normalcy) argument, then they simply claim, either that people are ignorant of the *real* level of normal hazards, or that they "inconsistently" value lower-magnitude technological hazards as worse than higher-magnitude "natural" hazards. On this view, a person cannot consistently choose, for example, to live in Denver, Colorado (which has very high background levels of radiation), and, at the same time, decide that current levels of emissions from nuclear reactors are unacceptable. This is because, they say, one is exposed to *more* radiation by living in Denver than by living near a nuclear plant governed by current emission standards. Other "natural hazards" frequently mentioned by proponents of the normalcy argument include automobile accidents, dam failures, and fires.

Part of what is wrong with this reasoning is that it appeals to the proportionality argument and thereby assumes that risk probabilities *alone* constitute sufficient grounds for judging whether a risk is acceptable, apart from whether the risk is insured, voluntarily chosen, completely understood, and so on. The other problem with the normalcy argument

is its assumption that, because something is "normal," it is morally acceptable and provides a criterion for the moral acceptability of other things.

Nobel prize winner Hans Bethe gives one of the clearest examples of
the normalcy argument in a recent article in *Scientific American*. He
claims that hard energy technologies, like nuclear power, have lower
risks than do other activities accepted by society and, therefore, that the
nuclear risks ought to be accepted.[56] In other words, he says, although a
nuclear accident could cause 5,000 cancer deaths and 3,000 cases of
genetic damage, nuclear power should be accepted because "the small
increases in these diseases would not be detected" and would be "insignificant compared to the eight million injuries caused annually by other
accidents."[57]

What Bethe has done here is to *define* an effect of a hard technology
(viz., having a lower probability of causing accidental fatalities than
other "normal" activities) as ethically acceptable, rather than to argue
*why* this particular effect ought to be judged acceptable. In failing to
realize that (1) "a given risk is lower than another already accepted
risk," is not equivalent to (2) "the second risk *ought to be* accepted,"
Bethe has *assumed* what he ought to prove and has therefore begged the
question of the acceptability of nuclear power. Bethe has *defined* the
question of the acceptability of a technology as involving only questions
of risk levels. In so doing, he does not realize that many other factors affect the acceptability of a technology. Some of these factors include the
alleged benefits of taking given risks. Others include whether the costs
and benefits of the technology are equally distributed among all members of society. Still other relevant issues concern whether victims of
technological accidents are likely to be compensated for their losses. By
law, nuclear catastrophe victims are prohibited from receiving more
than 3 percent compensation for their property losses, because of the
Price-Anderson Act (see §12.)

Also, in making a given "normal" probability of risk a criterion for
what level of risk is acceptable, proponents of the normalcy argument
make consistency both a necessary and a sufficient condition of sound
moral judgment. This surely cannot be right, since if society acts immorally in accepting "normal" risk A, for example, a given level of automobile accidents, then its decision to accept risk B, because it is of a similar or lower magnitude than A, cannot be called moral. Yet, by virtue of
their appeal to consistency, proponents of the normalcy argument would
have to say that acceptance of risk B is moral. On the other hand, as was
already pointed out, if society acts morally in accepting risk A, then its
decision to accept risk B, which is of a lesser magnitude than risk A, cannot be called *moral* purely on the grounds of the magnitude of the risk.
This is because, for example, there might be insufficient reasons for taking risk B, or because B's burden might be distributed inequitably, or
because it might be involuntarily imposed. For instance, if society acts
morally in accepting the risks of commercial air travel, then its decision
to accept the risks of using unpasteurized milk, a risk that is smaller than

the airplane risk, cannot be called moral purely because of the risk
levels. As this case shows, there may be insufficient reasons for accepting
the smaller (milk) risk, but sufficient reasons for accepting the larger
(airplane) risk.

Moreover, because proponents of the normalcy argument define an
ethical notion, that is, acceptable risk, in terms of a nonethical (sometimes called a "naturalistic") one, that is, society's past choices regarding
risks, they commit "the naturalistic fallacy." This fallacy consists in the
failure to recognize that *ethical* statements are different in kind from
*nonethical* ones. It is committed whenever one attempts to define ethical
characteristics (e.g., what is morally desirable) in nonethical terms
(e.g., what people actually desire). Such a procedure is erroneous
because it ignores the differences between science and moral philosophy.
A social-scientific account of what people *do* (e.g., when they behave as
racists) is never, in itself, sufficient grounds for a philosophical account
of what they *ought to do*. This is because people could do other than
they have done, and because their doing something does not make it
*right* to do it. Also, if the naturalistic fallacy were ignored, then one
would have to say that something was right *simply* because, as a matter
of fact, it was what was accepted by society at the time. This means that
racism, infanticide, and sexism, for example, would have been "right."
And, of course, they are not. But if they are not, then societal "choices"
do not tell us what is ethical. And if societal choices do not tell us what is
ethical, then both the naturalistic fallacy and the normalcy argument
are unsound.[58]

## §11 THE UNCERTAINTY ARGUMENT

Another argument often used by proponents of hard technology is that,
because we do not know that a certain energy technology is cost-
effective, dangerous, harmful, or impossible to implement within desirable standards of human health, therefore we should assume that the
technology is cost-effective, harmless, and so on, until proved otherwise.
Again, the paradigm case of hard energy technology, nuclear fission,
provides a framework within which numerous appeals to the uncertainty
argument have been made. United States policy, favoring generation of
electricity by means of nuclear fission, has always been based on the
argument that, even though the costs, the methods, and the hazards of
waste disposal are uncertain, one can assume that radioactive waste disposal is cost-effective, possible, and safe. A similar situation holds for the
case of decommissioning nuclear reactors; although no one knows the
costs and hazards of decommissioning, United States policymakers
assume that it will be cost-effective and possible. One government document, in particular, admits that there is great uncertainty regarding (1)
the magnitude of the radioactive impact of nuclear waste disposal facilities on human life; (2) the long-term costs of waste storage; and (3) how
much radiation will be released to the environment; and, consequently,

how much ground, air, and water will be contaminated as a result. Nevertheless, continues the document, "the large uncertainties in the environmental, health, and injury figures do not alter the conclusion that these costs are small . . . None of these shortcomings, however, invalidates the major conclusions and findings of the study . . . [that] direct environmental impacts . . . are essentially absent in the nuclear fuel cycles."[59]

The official United States government position of assuming that this hard energy technology is safe and cost-effective, even though there is extensive uncertainty regarding it, is curious since, in the case of numerous *soft* technologies, such uncertainties are often used as grounds for concluding that they are *not* safe and *not* cost effective. One recent United States document, for example, concluded that because of "relative [to other energy technologies] costs," new and/or unconventional soft energy technologies, such as solar and geothermal, will not be used extensively until at least 1995.[60] If radioactive waste management (for high-level wastes and transuranics) must continue indefinitely,[61] and if the costs of nuclear waste storage are *unknown*, however, how is it that, relative to nuclear fission, soft energy technologies are said to be *more* costly?

Use of uncertainty to dismiss soft technologies and to affirm hard technologies is all the more puzzling since the U.S. Office of Technology Assessment determined that it would be cost effective for solar energy to supply over 40 percent of total United States energy demand by the mid-1980s, provided that government regulations and subsidies to hard technologies did not continue to put solar systems at a disadvantage. Moreover, by the 1990s, says the same report, solar energy even can be economically competitive with other forms of electricity supplied to industrial facilities.[62]

If, indeed, hard and soft technologies have been treated differently, despite basic uncertainties in our knowledge of both, perhaps one reason for this differential treatment is that government subsidies to hard technologies, which total well over $10 billion per year,[63] are not included in the calculated "cost" of generating electricity by means of hard technologies, even though this cost is borne by taxpayers. Although government subsidies are also ignored in the cost calculations for soft energy, and although these subsidies have been only a tiny fraction of those given to hard technologies,[64] their omission is significant since, in the eyes of the U.S. Office of Technology Assessment, it is government subsidies that play the crucial role in determining whether soft technologies are said to be cost-effective.[65]

Whether or not uncertainties have been treated inconsistently, depending on whether they concern soft or hard technologies, any attempt to draw a conclusion about cost-effectiveness, when basic cost parameters are unknown, is highly suspect. Such attempts commit a logical fallacy, *the appeal to ignorance*. The fallacy consists of assuming that, because we are ignorant of something or have no proof that it is *not* the case, therefore it is the case. Because they have no proof that hard technologies are not safe and not cost-effective, proponents of the uncertainty argument commit the appeal to ignorance by assuming that they are safe and are cost-effective. Obviously the absence of proof that something is not safe does not mean that it is safe. It could be that no data are available one way or the other, or that the requisite studies have not been done, or that they have been done but the results suppresed. In the case of nuclear fission, there have been many appeals to ignorance, both because of inadequate data and because of attempts to *avoid collecting* evidence about the technology's harmfulness and to *suppress* data regarding its hazards. Hence, in many cases, the alleged uncertainty about nuclear fission is really a carefully orchestrated cover-up of its problems. Moreover, even were there no cover-ups, it would still be illogical to conclude, on the basis of ignorance, that nuclear power is safe or cost-effective.

One of the most famous cover-ups of the dangers of nuclear fission occurred when the government suppressed the results of the Brookhaven Report. During the suppression, the government's public statements contradicted the report's conclusion that a nuclear accident would be of catastrophic environmental proportions. After twenty years of denying the very conclusions drawn by the report it had sponsored, the government was forced to release the Brookhaven findings under the Freedom of Information Act. (The same sort of cover-up had already occurred with respect to the hazards of military uses of nuclear fission. For a decade after Hiroshima, the United States tested nuclear weapons and kept the public in ignorance of the crucial environmental consequences of that testing. It was not until the mid-fifties that the independent scientific community began to agitate for the release of government data on fallout. Led by scientist-activist Linus Pauling, many scientists appealed for a halt to nuclear testing.)[66]

Numerous other data indicate that the United States government has either suppressed or ignored data about the hazards of commercial nuclear fission. It has given repeated permission, not only for site preparation and construction activities prior to any public hearing or construction permit for a nuclear plant, but also before required environmental impact statements have been filed.[67]

Government policymakers have ignored the costs of radioactive waste storage, and then erroneously concluded that the 1980 annual operating and maintenance costs for one 1,000-megawatt coal plant were $5,400,000 as compared to $5,200,000 for a nuclear plant of the same size. If, in the calculations of nuclear costs, one includes government monies actually budgeted and spent annually for commercial nuclear waste management, and if one prorates these monies among commercial nuclear reactors, then the annual costs of waste management, per 1,000-megawatt reactor, can be shown to be anywhere from $3,800,000 to $1,900,000.[68] Both these figures are considerably more than the $200,000 annual cost differential which (the government says) exists between nuclear and coal plants.

There is additional evidence that the government ignores or suppresses the hazards of nuclear energy. It is well known that United States regulatory agencies will finance only speakers who are proponents of fission, that they have "punished" employees who have attempted to promote nuclear safety, and that they have censored government reports critical of atomic energy.[69] There are grounds, then, for believing not only that hard-path proponents are wrong to use the uncertainty argument, but also that some of them have attempted to portray situations *known* to be quite serious as *uncertain*.

## §12 THE COST-BENEFIT ARGUMENT

A major reason why energy choices are not made as rationally as they might be is that proponents of hard-path technologies often use an incomplete argument to support the alleged low costs of hard energy options. I call this "the cost-benefit argument." It consists of the claim that the most desirable energy policy can be determined solely by aggregating (summing) the costs and benefits of alternative energy strategies according to the classical economic method known as cost-benefit analysis. The problem with this argument is that cost-benefit analysis contains a number of unacceptable ethical and methodological presuppositions. When the cost-benefit argument is used to determine energy choices, these presuppositions often skew the conclusions in favor of hard-path technologies, such as nuclear fission or coal. But since these presuppositions are unacceptable, cost-benefit defenses of hard technologies are too. That is what I hope to show in what follows.

Although all the key presuppositions of cost-benefit analysis cannot be discussed here,[70] I am able to highlight a few problems with perhaps the most important of these presuppositions, one that figures heavily in many cases in which proponents of the hard path use the cost-benefit argument. I call this central presupposition "the aggregation assumption"; its employment constitutes what economist Ezra Mishan refers to as "the fallacy of aggregation."[71]

To understand what is meant by the aggregation assumption, recall that, according to classical cost-benefit analysis, an action (e.g., using nuclear fission to generate electricity) is desirable if it results in an excess of benefits over costs. To determine whether the benefits outweigh the costs of an action, all its effects are expressed in monetary terms (e.g., the costs of radiation-induced cancers, the benefits of avoiding use of fossil fuels) and calculated according to prices determined by the market. (This presupposes that gains and losses, for all individuals in all situations, can be assigned a monetary value or computed numerically; this is, of course, quite difficult, if not impossible, to accomplish.)

The aggregation assumption is that it is acceptable to perform an action (e.g., using fission to generate electricity), allegedly to improve the community well-being, even though distributional effects are ignored. An example will make this assumption clear. Suppose that a given action (e.g., supplying 10 percent of the nation's electricity needs by using liquefied natural gas instead of oil) made a given set of individuals "better off" by a total of $10 million, while another set of individuals was made worse off by $1 million. Even though the first set of persons would receive the benefits of this action, while the second set would bear the cost, according to classical cost-benefit analysis, this would be a desirable action because it would produce an excess gain of $9 million for the community as a whole. In other words, classical cost-benefit analysis sanctions actions that produce excess gains over losses, apart from how those gains and losses are distributed among various persons. This is why economists charge that a likely consequence of accepting the aggregation assumption (and the cost-benefit argument) is not only that distributional inequities will occur and will be sanctioned, but also that those in the community who are made worse off will be found primarily among lower-income groups.[72] This is probably also why social scientists have cautioned that the use of quantitative economic criteria ought not to be assumed to lead to greater equity and evenhandedness in policy. Because use of the cost-benefit argument allows policymakers to ignore evaluation of distributional effects, this means that use of the argument is likely to "reflect the dominant ideological orientations of the most powerful and articulate groups affected by the phenomena measured."[73] Obviously lower-income groups, being generally less powerful politically, are less able to protest the costs forced on them by the power brokers of society.

If these charges against cost-benefit analysis and the aggregation assumption are true, as I think they are, this is significant for energy policymaking and for technology assessment generally. This is because cost-benefit analyses are the bases through which economics is routinely made "the final test of public policy."[74]

To see how the cost-benefit argument, with its central aggregation assumption, has been used by hard path proponents, consider the so-called Inhaber Report, a comparative analysis of the relative merits of major hard and soft-path energy options. It was completed in 1978 for the Canadian Atomic Energy Control Board.[75] In his report, Inhaber concluded that the total risk or cost to humans was greater for the soft technologies, such as solar power, than for the hard technologies, such as nuclear fission. Although this conclusion has been condemned because it is based on numerous factual inaccuracies,[76] it is also suspect because Inhaber used the cost-benefit argument to establish this point, and the cost-benefit techniques allowed him to ignore a number of key ethical problems, many of which are a consequence of the aggregation assumption. Clearly one energy technology could have a smaller magnitude of risk than another, but if that risk were grossly inequitably distributed, then the overall social cost of the technology might be greater, particularly if those who bore that cost did not receive the benefit of the energy produced.

In the soft- versus hard-path case, the issue of Inhaber's ignoring the distribution of costs is important for several reasons. First, radioactive wastes will be lethal for hundreds of thousands of years, and many of their costs will be borne by future generations rather than by those of us who benefit from nuclear-generated electricity. Second, hard-path energy technologies (like nuclear power) are centralized, which means that their pollution *costs* are borne primarily by those who live near the facilities, while their energy *benefits* are received by those living far away. In the case of nuclear fission generation of electricity, those living within a fifty-mile radius of a reactor bear a cancer and genetic damage risk which is up to fifty times greater than that borne by the general United States public.[77] This same set of persons living near a reactor also bears an extraordinary financial and medical risk (from catastrophic accidents) which is not borne by the rest of the population. This is because under current law (the Price-Anderson Act), designed to keep utilities from going bankrupt, coverage for property damages, in the event of a major nuclear accident, is limited. In the case of the accident which (the United States government says) could cause $17 *billion* in property damage, homeowners together could collect a total of only $560 *million*, or approximately 3 percent of their property losses. The remaining 97 percent of the losses are, by law, uninsurable and incapable of being recovered.[78] Third, soft-path technologies (like onsite solar) are largely decentralized, which means that, in large part, the same set of persons bears the costs as receives the benefits of the energy.

What is disturbing about the Inhaber study is not only that distributional costs were ignored, but also that Inhaber seems not to see that his use of the cost-benefit argument presents great methodological difficulties with potentially serious effects on both public policy and human well-being. In response to Inhaber's conclusions, those living near nuclear plants could obviously respond: "Yes the technology is cost-effective, but *for whom?*" Most importantly, if the *complete* costs, either of using nuclear fission, or coal, or some other technology, are not *known*, then proponents of the hard path ought not to claim that their chosen energy technologies are more cost-effective than those of soft-path advocates. Since the United States is currently following the hard path, use of the cost-benefit argument thus means that this methodology will contribute to a bias toward the status quo in our energy policy. In a world that is short on fossil fuels and forethought, such a bias could be disastrous.

From an ethical point of view, Inhaber and many other hard path proponents are committing themselves to a very questionable philosophical stance. By virtue of their using the cost-benefit argument, they are clearly following a *utilitarian*, rather than an *egalitarian*, ethic. In other words, they appear to be guided by the utilitarian principle of maximizing the greatest amount of good for the greatest number of people, rather than by the egalitarian principle of guaranteeing equal justice for all.

According to the *utilitarian* account of moral obligation, the sole basic standard of right and wrong action is the "principle of utility." This principle posits, as the moral goal of all human actions, the greatest possible balance of good over bad for mankind as a whole.[79] Principles of individual rights and equal justice are recognized only to the extent that doing so will lead to the greatest good. As a consequence, following a utilitarian ethic can lead to individual violations of principles of equal treatment and of justice, at the same time that the good is maximized for humankind as a whole.[80] For example, a utilitarian would have to accept as right the action of framing and executing an innocent man, if his death would prevent serious riots which would take the lives of many persons.[81] Those who follow (what I have called) an *egalitarian* ethic, however, would not have to accept as right the execution of this innocent man. For them, the moral good is not maximizing the good for all mankind but achievement of "equality in the assignment of basic rights and duties," apart from the totality of good achieved by equality.[82]

If Inhaber's use of the cost-benefit argument means that he ignores the fact that some persons bear higher health risks and financial risks because of hard energy paths, then his analysis is not egalitarian but utilitarian. Even if one assumes that the technological and economic benefits, arising from ignoring the inequality of risk distributions, lead to the greatest good for the greatest number, Inhaber is wrong in ignoring this inequity. The difficulty with this and with any utilitarian stance is that it allows, in principle, disenfranchising minorities of their rights in order to serve the good of the majority. But if minorities may be deprived of rights on utilitarian grounds, then the very concepts of equal justice and of individual and inalienable rights become meaningless. Even utilitarians recognize this fact; moral philosopher J. J. C. Smart admits: "It is not difficult to show that utilitarianism could, in certain exceptional circumstances, have some very horrible consequences."[83] Such horrible consequences, say utilitarians, are "the lesser of two evils (in terms of human happiness and misery)."[84] That is, they claim that more human suffering might be caused by following principles of equity than by attempting to maximize the good of all people. They also maintain that the right to equal protection and to equality of treatment is not absolute; to believe otherwise, say utilitarians, would delay "social improvement."[85] This suggests that utilitarians would justify inequitable distributions of the costs and benefits of various energy technologies by claiming that *good reasons* (e.g., "the economy," "energy demand") justify ignoring such inequities. This brings us to the issue of what constitutes *good reasons*, either for allowing, or for omitting consideration of, inequitable distributions of technological and environmental costs and benefits.

Harvard philosopher John Rawls says that inequities ought to be allowed only if there is reason to believe that the practice involving the inequity will work for the advantage of everyone.[86] If we discount unethical or purely political motives, then it seems reasonable to assume that Inhaber and other proponents of the cost-benefit argument probably believe that permitting or ignoring inequitable distributions of technological and environmental costs and benefits will work for the advantage of everyone. Given the tendencies of many persons to discount safety risks on the grounds that "the economy needs" the hard energy technology,[87] or that certain pollution-control standards are not cost-effective and beneficial to industry (and therefore to our national well-being),[88] Inhaber and other proponents of the cost-benefit argument and utilitarian approaches would likely justify distributive inequalities as "required for the promotion of equality in the long run." They likely would hold this position since almost any other defense would be open to the charge that it was using some humans as mere means, rather than treating them as ends in themselves.[89]

The basic problem with using this "equality in the long run" argument to justify current distributive inequalities is that it contains a highly questionable factual premise, namely, that promoting technology, economic expansion, and increased production *will* lead to greater equality of treatment among persons in the long term. This premise is doubtful since, although technology and economic expansion have brought an absolute increase in the United States standard of living in the last thirty-five years, the relative shares of United States wealth held by various percentages of the population have not changed. Even in a political (as opposed to economic) sense, it is not clear that technological and economic growth has promoted equal treatment, because there is a close relationship between wealth and the ability to utilize equal opportunities.[90] This is why, as economist Mishan puts it, the poor rarely share in the growth of real wealth; they are "isolated from economic growth."[91]

Technological expansion (with its concomitant neglect of the distributive inequities in technological costs and benefits) ordinarily does not help to create a more egalitarian society because technology generally eliminates jobs; it does not create them. In the last thirty years, virtually all new jobs in the United States have been the consequence of an expansion of the service sector of the economy rather than the result of technological expansion or economic growth.[92] Even in the cases when technological growth has brought increased employment, this has often been at the expense of the poor, who usually live near technological facilities presenting a health hazard and who cannot afford to move away. It is well known that the poor bear a disproportionate burden from air pollution and that various adverse environmental and technological impacts often are imposed unequally on the poor, while the rich receive the bulk of the benefits.[93]

All this suggests that it is erroneous to ignore uncompensated distributive inequities, on the grounds that this neglect will help everyone. With few exceptions, distributive inequities are likely to continue to harm those who already bear many of society's burdens, people who, because of their poverty, are usually in a position of virtual helplessness. Their helplessness, however, is the key to showing that, although some discrimination is unavoidable, good reasons usually do not support utilitarian discrimination against victims of unequal environmental impacts. This is because one has a moral obligation to protect the utterly helpless. Absolute helplessness demands absolute protection.[94]

## §13 THE STATISTICAL-CASUALTIES ARGUMENT

Another way in which proponents defend hard energy paths is through acceptance of (what I call) "the statistical-casualties argument." In using this argument, advocates of hard energy technologies claim that they should be accepted because they are safe, in that "no one has ever been killed" as a consequence of United States commercial nuclear reactor operation.[95] Proponents of the statistical-casualties argument are able to make this extraordinary assertion, about no one having been killed or injured, because of a highly questionable assumption underlying their argument. This is that *statistical casualties caused* by nuclear fission do not count as *persons killed* by the United States commercial nuclear program.

In the absence of a serious reactor accident, namely, one causing immediate deaths, one is able only to speak of the "statistical casualties" caused by normal operation of the nuclear fuel cycle. Calculations of the number of "statistical casualties" are made by using a "dose-response curve," according to which scientists estimate that for a given radiation dose, a given number of deaths or injuries occurs. According to the standard dose-response curve, the one used by the pronuclear U.S. Nuclear Regulatory Commission, for example, a *dose* of one rad of radiation induces a carcinogenic *response* of 0.0002 cases of cancer per year.[96] (Of course, there are also, for example, mutagenic (causing genetic deficiencies) and teratogenic (causing birth defects) responses associated with this same dose; hence the carcinogenic effects do not represent the total response induced by this dose.)

Although *which* cancers are caused by given doses of radiation cannot be determined, scientists do know that every bit of radiation exposure causes an increased risk of various radiation-related diseases and fatalities. For a number of reasons, however, no identifiable persons can be said, with certainty, to have been killed by radiation from the normal operation of the nuclear fuel cycle. This is because 25 percent of the United States population will contract cancer, for example, apart from reactor hazards, and because there are many carcinogens, in addition to radiation. Moreover, many cancers only appear years after radiation exposure. Hence it is difficult, if not impossible, in the case of cancer fatalities, to distinguish reactor-related deaths from non–reactor-related ones. Because of this difficulty, hard-path proponents repeatedly claim that "no one has been killed" as a consequence of the United States commercial nuclear reactor program.

The difficulty of proving that (on the basis of statistical casualties calculated by means of the standard dose–response curve) radiation has caused a *particular person* to die or to contract cancer is illustrated by recent attempts of veterans to claim benefits because of radiation injuries received in the 1950s. As has recently come to light, hundreds of thousands of United States soldiers were exposed to high levels of radiation because of their participation in atomic bomb testing during the 1950s. For example, on August 31, 1957, troops were marched "to within 300 yards of ground zero" soon after the "Smoky" atomic blast. Although the U.S. Department of Energy has found records of 900 overexposed individuals involved in tests dating from 1951 to 1962, benefits have been granted only to ten men of the many "who claimed their disabilities were the result of radiation exposure received during the U.S. nuclear weapons tests."[97] Because of the problems caused by radiation-related injuries and the possible violations of servicemen's rights, the House Commerce Subcommittee on Health and Environment held three days of hearings in January 1978 to hear testimony by servicemen.[98] According to Orville Kelly, United States Navy commander of Eniwetok Atoll during weapons tests in the 1950s, between 200 and 400 thousand soldiers there were exposed to high levels of radiation. Since radiation was not monitored, and not everyone either had or wore a dosimeter, the government claims that it has proof of only 900 overexposures. Kelly, a leukemia victim who died recently, was denied benefits for himself, his wife, and his four children because the Veterans' Administration said that he could not prove that his cancer was caused by radiation received during the weapons tests. Kelly was within five miles of ground zero during twenty-three nuclear tests and was exposed to fallout.[99]

The case of servicemen irradiated several decades ago illustrates some of the problems with using the statistical-casualties argument to defend hard energy technologies such as nuclear fission. If this argument is accepted, with its assumption that *statistical casualties* do not represent *persons killed* by nuclear generation of electricity, then many people who deserve to be compensated for their injuries will not be. They will not be able to prove that their cancers and other ailments were caused by normal operation of the nuclear fuel cycle. *In principle* there is no way to prove whether or not radiation from a particular plant has caused a cancer. And, if the Energy Research and Development Administration is correct, then a total of 30,530 deaths in the next 100 years will be caused by legally allowable emissions of only four of the numerous isotopes (tritium, krypton-85, iodine-129, and plutonium-239) released from commercial nuclear fuel cycles during normal operation.[100] This means, provided that the statistical-casualties argument is accepted, more than 30,000 deaths neither will be attributed to commercial use of atomic energy nor will be compensated because of the difficulty of proving that they were caused by nuclear power. Continued adherence to this argument therefore will force government and the courts to employ an *argumentum ad ignoratiam*, an argument from ignorance. They will have to conclude that neither an accident nor normal nuclear emissions caused a particular cancer whenever the victim is unable to prove this causality. Besides being a logical fallacy, such an argument from ignorance places a double burden on citizens. First, because use of the statistical-casualties argument limits the opportunities of radiation victims to obtain due process and equal protection under the law, it also places the utility industry's interests above those of consumers. Second, because of the very acceptance of this argument, it is impossible, *in principle*, to adjudicate radiation-injury claims involving equal justice under law.

Admittedly, use of the statistical-casualties argument has some important benefits. It lessens utility costs for nuclear generation of electricity, since radiation victims cannot sustain their due-process claims for compensation. This, in turn, might enable customers to pay lower prices for the energy they use. Both these assets (lowering utility costs and consumer prices) may well contribute to the industrial and economic health of the country and therefore to the well-being of United States citizens. The price paid for this alleged well-being, however, is very great: (1) accepting a utilitarian ethic for distributing the costs and benefits of energy generation and consumption (see §12, where the utilitarian framework is discussed); (2) sanctioning the possible violation of citizens' rights to equal protection from radiation hazards and to due process, in the event that they attempt to seek compensation for radiation-related injuries; and (3) placing the financial responsibility for the harm caused by hard-path technologies upon the shoulders of those victimized rather than upon the shoulders of those who caused it. From an ethical point of view, these consequences of the statistical-casualties argument throw great doubt on the advisability of using the argument to promote hard energy technologies.

The problems with the statistical-casualties argument are not only *ethical*, however. A major difficulty with it is purely *factual*. It is simply incorrect to assume, as do many hard-path proponents (see note 95), that because one cannot *prove* that a *particular* cancer fatality was caused by radiation from the nuclear fuel cycle, therefore no fatalities are attributable to nuclear power. The existence of the dose-response curve, already discussed, belies this point (see note 96), as does the government prediction that more than 30,000 deaths will occur as a consequence of normal operation of commercial nuclear fuel cycles (see the previous note). Most importantly, virtually all reliable scientific and professional associations, including the Federal Radiation Council and the International Commission on Radiation Protection, maintain that there is no *safe* dose of radiation, that is, no such thing as a radiation threshold below which there is no deleterious biological effect.[101] If this is true, then it is impossible that there *not* be some casualties from normal operation of the nuclear fuel cycle.[102]

## IV.  TOWARD A SOUND ENERGY POLICY

Where does all the criticism of arguments used by soft-path proponents (§4–7) and advocates of the hard path (§9–13) leave us? Obviously, since these represent only nine out of a multitude of considerations which are central to the energy debate, no clear position regarding the most ethically desirable energy option has emerged. To attain such a position, one needs to examine the logical, methodological, factual, and ethical underpinnings of many arguments put forth by a number of energy spokespersons.

Were all these arguments marshalled and analyzed in detail, I believe that they could be used to show the overall superiority of the soft path, although this is too massive a task to be accomplished here. One way to do this would be to use them to establish each of the points listed below. Taken collectively, these nine points provide a broad "energy argument," a convincing case in favor of the soft path.

1. The U.S. Office of Technology Assessment is correct in asserting that the soft path is capable of supplying, cost effectively, 40 percent of all United States energy needs by 1985.[103]

2. The authors of the Harvard Business School study *Energy Future* are correct in asserting that conservation can enable the United States to avoid any increased use of hard path energy technologies until the soft path is able to supply, cost effectively, the remaining 60 percent of all United States energy needs.[104]

3. Achievement of a zero-risk energy technology is impossible, and therefore the most desirable energy option is that which (all other things being equal) is least costly/risky, with respect to its total medical, economic, legal, and political effects, and that which is most equitable in its distribution of costs and benefits.

4. Although there are differences among the various hard and soft energy technologies, with respect to levels of various types of risks, over the long term, the hard energy path is more risky, with respect to ethical, medical, economic, legal, and political effects than is the soft energy path; moreover, there aren't any good reasons for tolerating the higher risks of hard technologies.

5. All soft-path energy technologies distribute their costs and benefits more equitably, with respect to both *time* (so as to discriminate less against future generations) and *geography* (so as to discriminate less against those who receive negative impacts from energy facilities from which they receive no benefits), as well as with respect to *social class* (since the poor often bear the environmental risks of centralized energy technologies); moreover, there are no good reasons for tolerating the greater inequities of hard technologies.

6. Both because of utilitarian principles and because of principles of distributive justice, the short-term advantages of employing hard energy technologies do not offset the long-term disadvantages mentioned in point 4.

7. With respect to one particular hard-path option, nuclear fission, the actual harms caused are not as fully measurable and therefore not as adequately compensable as are those caused by the soft path technology; therefore, these harms are more onerous than those of the soft path.

8. Even were nuclear harms more compensable than those caused by the soft path, this would not justify use of nuclear fission because such compensation would amount to too extensive a recourse to utilitarian principles condoning rights violations in circumstances where the public's well-being was allegedly served.

9. Therefore, because the soft path is more equitable and less risky/costly than the hard path, and because there is no compelling

reason for accepting the less equitable, more risky/costly hard path, especially when alternatives are available, the soft path is the most desirable energy option.

By examining various arguments in favor of the hard path and the soft path, I have evaluated some of the numerous subarguments relevant to several of the nine points in this larger "energy argument." For example, the cost-benefit argument, the normalcy argument, the proportionality argument, and the zero-risk argument are four of the many subarguments whose analysis is crucial to establishing point 3 in the above list. Likewise the statistical-casualties argument is important in establishing point 4, while the anarchist argument and the argument from romantic regression are two of the many subarguments relevant to establishing point 5.

Owing to the breadth and complexity of these points, it is clear that there are no easy ways to establish what I call the "energy argument." It can be done, however, by means of many slow steps, some of which were taken in this essay. If my conclusions are correct, then they indicate that there are flaws in some of the arguments used by some of the advocates of both the hard and the soft paths. If this is true, then the student of energy ethics cannot take the easy route of following some famous guru, whether it be Lovins of the soft path or Bethe of the hard path. The moral is that there is no substitute for philosophical analysis and no alternative to critical thinking. The energy world has not yet found a philosopher king, and so we each must take up that work.

## NOTES

1. This account of the controversy over the steam engine is taken from Fred Hoyle and Geoffrey Hoyle, *Commonsense in Nuclear Energy* (San Francisco: W, H. Freeman, 1980), 77–85 (hereafter cited as: Hoyle, *Nuclear*).
2. Hoyle, *Nuclear*, 77.
3. U.S. Department of Energy, *Secretary's Annual Report to Congress*, vol. 1: Posture Statement, Outlook, and Program Review, DOE/S-0010 (81) (Washington, D.C.: U.S. Government Printing Office, 1981), p. 1–6 (hereafter cited as: DOE, 1981).
4. A. B. Lovins, *Soft Energy Paths* (New York: Harper & Row, 1977), 26, makes the same point (hereafter cited as: Lovins, SEP).
5. DOE, 1981, pp. 1–4, 1–8, and 1–9.
6. DOE, 1981, pp. 1–4, 1–8, and 1–9.
7. "Energy Strategy: The Road not Taken?" *Foreign Affairs* 55 (1977): 65–96.
8. Although the soft path may be thought to refer only to scientific and technological developments, its proponents believe that it refers to a whole society. Such a broader characterization makes it clear that many proponents of soft energy believe that major social change is required if resource-related as well as other problems are to be solved. Despite the differences among all those who advocate soft-energy societies, proponents of the soft path tend to see soft-energy societies as ecologically sound; requiring only a small energy input; having low pollution; using reversible materials and

energy sources; being functional for all time; having a craft industry and a low degree of specialization; being organized into communal units with a village emphasis; being integrated with nature, having democratic politics and a no-growth, steady-state economy; being labor-intensive and decentralized; characterized by diverse solutions to technical and social problems, by emphasizing the "quality," rather than the quantity, of its products, and by work being undertaken primarily for satisfaction; comprised of small, self-sufficient units; and as integrating science and technology with the culture and enabling scientific and technological work to be performed by all.

Likewise, despite the difference among all those who are proponents of the hard path, advocates of the soft path tend to see hard-energy societies, on the other hand, as ecologically unsound; requiring a large energy input; having high levels of pollution; using nonreversible materials and energy sources; being functional for only a limited time; having mass-production industries and a high degree of specialization; being organized into the nuclear family with a city emphasis; being alienated from nature; having consensus politics and a growth-oriented economy; being capital intensive and centralized; characterized by singular solutions to technical and social problems, by emphasizing the "quantity" rather than the quality of its products, and by work being undertaken primarily for income; comprised of small units totally dependent upon others; and as having a science and technology which are performed by an elite and which are alienated from the culture. C. R. Humphrey and F. R. Buttel, *Environment, Energy, and Society* (Belmont, Calif.: Wadsworth, 1982), 188–189 (hereafter cited as: EES).

9.    Lovins, SEP, 28–31.

10.   Lovins emphasizes that soft energy technologies can be matched in scale and quality to end-use needs more easily than can hard energy sources. The large-scale, hard path, centralized forms of energy production contain significant diseconomies of scale and tend to produce energy whose quality exceeds that required for most end uses. Perhaps the best example of this is devoting electricity to home space heating. This is wasteful, says Lovins, because the laws of physics require that a power station change three units of fuel into two units of waste heat and one unit of electricity. The costly process of upgrading the fuel is all for nought, since changing a room temperature by *tens* of degrees does not require a nuclear reaction temperature, for example, of *trillions* of degrees. Using electricity for space heating is as inefficient as using a chainsaw to cut butter, says Lovins. SEP, 40.

11.   Lovins' critics have usually made one of two possible responses. Proponents of the hard path have said that soft technology is too costly or technically infeasible. See, for example, C. B. Yulish, *Soft vs. Hard Energy Paths: 10 Critical Essays on Amory Lovins' "Energy Strategy: The Road Not Taken"* (New York: Charles Yulish Associates, 1977), and Energy Information Administration, U.S. Department of Energy, *1981 Annual Report to Congress*, DOE/EIA-0173 (81/3, vol. 3, (Washington, D.C: U.S. Government Printing Office, 1981), p. 86. A second line of opposition, coming not from proponents of the hard path but from radical critics, is that the soft path is unlikely to occur in an advanced capitalist society. This is because private profit and large-scale capital wield enormous power and are unlikely to invest in soft path technologies which will lower their profits. In other words, proponents of the radical critique maintain that Lovins' views presuppose that the U.S. economic system is more malleable than it is. See, for example, P. Bereano, "Alternative Technology: Is Less More?" *Science for the People* (September–October, 1976): 6–9, 34–35; C. Garman and K. Alper, "Alternative Technology: Not a Revolutionary Strategy," *Science for the People* (September–October, 1976): 14–17.

12.   The term "romantic regression" is taken from K. Keniston, "Toward a More Human Society," in H. K. Girvetz (ed.), *Contemporary Moral Issues* (Belmont, Calif.: Wadsworth, 1974), 400–401.

13.   Ivan Illich, *Energy and Equity* (New York: Harper and Row, 1974), 12, 16–17 (hereafter cited as: Illich, EE).

14.   Illich, EE, pp. 16–17.

15.   Jean-Jacques Rousseau, *The First and Second Discourses*, ed. R. D. Masters, trans. J. R. Masters (New York: St. Martin's Press, 1964), 78–181.

16.   H. H. Iltis, O. L. Loucks, and P. Andrews, *Criteria for an Optimum Human Environment*, in R. T. Roelofs, J. N. Crowley, and D. L. Hardesty, eds., *Environment and Society* (Englewood Cliffs, N.J.: Prentice-Hall, 1974), 92–93.

17.   These points are discussed in D. H. Strong and E. S. Rosenfield, "Ethics or Expediency" in K. S. Shrader-Frechette, *Environmental Ethics* (Pacific Grove, Calif.: Boxwood Press, 1981), 8.

18.   W. Lowrance, *Of Acceptable Risk* (Los Altos, Calif.: William Kaufmann, 1976), 3 (hereafter cited as: Lowrance, *Risk*).

19.   Lowrance, *Risk*, 5.

20.   *Unpopular Essays on Technological Progress* (Pittsburgh: University of Pittsburgh Press, 1980), 3–22, esp. p. 12 (hereafter cited as: *Essays*).

21.   Illich, EE, 17.

22.   Theodore Roszak, *Person/Planet* (New York: Doubleday, 1978), 89 (hereafter cited as: Roszak, PP).

23.   See K. S. Shrader-Frechette, *Nuclear Power and Public Policy*, 2d ed. (Boston: D. Reidel, 1983), Chap. 2 (hereafter cited as: *Nuclear Power*).

24.   See Shrader-Frechette, *Nuclear Power*, Chap. 4.

25.   Of course, it could well be that, if one were careful, either to avoid such inequities or to compensate for them, then it would be uneconomical to employ nuclear fission to generate electricity.

26.   For accounts of these problems at Three-Mile Island, see Shrader-Frechette, *Nuclear Power*, Chap. 4.

27.   John Rawls, *A Theory of Justice* (Cambridge, Mass.: Harvard University Press, 1971), 7, 74, 78 (hereafter cited as: Rawls, *Justice*).

28.   *Taking Rights Seriously* (Cambridge, Mass.: Harvard University Press, 1977), 273.

29.   Murray Bookchin, "Ecology and Revolutionary Thought," in R. T. Roelofs, J. N. Crowley, and D. L. Hardesty, eds., *Environment and Society* (Englewood Cliffs, N.J.: Prentice-Hall, 1974), 191 (hereafter cited as: Bookchin, Revolutionary).

30.   Bookchin, Revolutionary, 191.

31.   Murray Bookchin, *Post-Scarcity Anarchism* (Berkeley: Ramparts Press, 1971).

32.   Roszak, *PP*.

33.   David Dickson, *The Politics of Alternative Technology* (New York: Universe Books, 1974).

34.   Bookchin, Revolutionary, 191.

35.   Revolutionary, 193.

36.   See, for example, K. E. Eklund, "A Social Access Explanation for Community Land-Use Evaluation," *Land Economics* 53, no. 1 (February 1977): 80.

37.   This is the term used by R. B. Stewart, "Paradoxes of Liberty, Integrity, and Fraternity," in K. S. Shrader-Frechette, *Environmental Ethics* (Pacific Grove, Calif.: Boxwood Press, 1981), 142: Stewart also lists the same four desirable effects of decentralization as have been discussed here.

38.   John Passmore, *The Perfectibility of Man* (London: Duckworth, 1970), 189.

39.   SEP, 153–157.

40. In "Environmental Impact Analysis, Technology Assessment, and the Problem of Geographical Equity," forthcoming in *Research in Philosophy and Technology*, I argue for this point.

41. M. Cravel, "Who Is the Critical Mass?" in Richard Munson, ed., *Countdown to a Nuclear Moratorium* (Washington, D.C.: Environmental Action Foundation, 1976), 173.

42. "Theoretical Possibilities and Consequences of Major Accidents in Large Nuclear Power Plants," U.S. Atomic Energy Commission Report WASH-740 (Washington, D.C.: Government Printing Office, 157); and R. J. Mulvihill, D. R. Arnold, C. E. Bloomquist, and B. Epstein, "Analysis of United States Power Reactor Accident Probability," WASH-740 update, PRCR-695, (Los Angeles: Planning Research Corporation, 1965).

43. Norman Rasmussen, author of the famous "Rasmussen Report" (which assessed the safety of United States nuclear power plants), said that he calculated the Three-Mile Island accident to have a probability of from one in 250 to one in 25,000 per reactor-year ("Methods of Hazard Analysis," in *The Three-Mile Island Nuclear Accident*, ed. T. H. Moss and D. L. Sills (New York: New York Academy of Sciences, 1981), 29. For the 151 reactors now operating or under construction, the one in 250 figure comes down to an annual probability of 46%. $P = (1-P$ (no annual TMI-type accident in the U.S.) $= 1 - (1 - (\frac{1}{250}))^{151} = 1 - (0.996)^{151} = 1 - 0.545 = .455 = 46\%$.

44. $P = 1 - P$ (no core melt in any of the 151 reactors over a 30-year lifetime) $= 1 - (1 - 1/17000)^{4530} = 0.239$ or approximately 24%. The probability of a core melt, per reactor-year, is 1 in 17,000 and is taken from the key United States study of nuclear safety, the "Rasmussen Report," i.e., United States Nuclear Regulatory Commission, *Reactor Safety Study—An Assessment of Accident Risks in U.S. Commercial Nuclear Power Plants*, Report No. (NUREG-75/014) WASH-1400, (Washington, D.C.: U.S. Government Printing Office, 1975), 157ff. For a discussion and criticism of this study, see Shrader-Frechette, *Nuclear Power*, 73ff.

45. B. L. Cohen and I. S. Lee, "A Catalog of Risks," *Health Physics* 36, no. 6 (June 1979): 720.

46. "Social Benefit versus Technological Risk," *Science* 165, no. 3899 (September 19, 1969): 1236.

47. William W. Lowrance, *Of Acceptable Risk* (Los Altos, Calif.: William Kaufmann, 1976), 87.

48. Herbert Inhaber, "Risk with Energy from Conventional and Nonconventional Sources," *Science*, 203 no. 4382 (February 23, 1979): 718–723, calculates the risks of using solar energy. Although his is perhaps the most famous study of solar risks, as compared to those from conventional energy sources, it should be noted that his analysis has been widely repudiated as biased because it underestimates conventional energy risks and overestimates solar risks. In this regard, see John P. Holdren, Kirk R. Smith, and Gregory Morris, "Energy: Calculating the Risks (II)," *Science* 204, no. 4393: 564–568, and K. S. Shrader-Frechette, "Adams, Inhaber, and Risk-Benefit Analysis," *Research in Philosophy and Technology* 3 (1980): 343–365.

49. This example is taken from A. Wildavsky, "No Risk Is the Highest Risk of All," *American Scientist* 67, no. 1 (January–February 1979): 33.

50. For examples of this argument, see L. Lave, "Panel: Perception of Risk," Mitre Corporation, *Risk Assessment and Governmental Decision Making* (McLean, Va.: The Mitre Corporation, 1979), 541; and C. Starr and C. Whipple, "Risks of Risk Decisions," *Science* 208, no. 4448 (1980): 1116.

51. See notes 52 and 53 in this essay.

52. See, for example, B. Cohen and F. Lee, "A Catalog of Risks," *Health Physics* 36, no. 6 (June 1979): 720.

53. See, for example, D. Okrent, "Panel: Use of Risk Assessment . . .," in Mitre Corporation, *op. cit.* (note 50), p. 663 and D. Bazelon, "Risk and Responsibility," *Science* 205, no. 4403 (1979): 278.

54. See, for example, Cohen and Lee, *op. cit.* (note 52), p. 707, and M. Maxey, "Managing Low-Level Radioactive Wastes," in J. Watson, ed., *Low Level Radioactive Waste Management* (Williamsburg, Va.: Health Physics Society, 1979), 410, 417.

55. B. Fischhoff, P. Slovic, and S. Lichtenstein, "Facts and Fears," in R. Schwing and W. Albers, eds., *Societal Risk Assessment* (New York: Plenum, 1980), 181–216, and R. Otway, "Risk Assessment and the Social Response to Nuclear Power," *Journal of the British Nuclear Engineering Society* 16, no. 4 (1977): 327–333.

56. H. A. Bethe, "The Necessity of Fission Power," *Scientific American* 234, no. 1 (January 1976): 27.

57. Bethe, *op. cit.* (note 56), 26.

58. For further discussion of the naturalistic fallacy, see G. E. Moore, *Principia Ethica* (Cambridge, England: Cambridge University Press, 1951), esp. pp. 23–24, 39–40, 60; W. K. Frankena, "The Naturalistic Fallacy," *Mind* 48, no. 192 (October 1939): 467, and Shrader-Frechette, *Nuclear Power*, 135ff.

59. U.S. Atomic Energy Commission, *Comparative Risk–Cost-Benefit Study of Alternative Sources of Electrical Energy* (WASH-1224) (Washington, D.C.: U.S. Government Printing Office, 1974), 1–22 through 1–24; see also pp. 5–29 through 5–31, 5–43, and 5–48 through 5–50.

60. Energy Information Administration, United States Department of Energy, *1981 Annual Report to Congress* DOE/EIA-0173 (81)/3, vol. 3 (Washington, D.C.: U.S. Government Printing Office, 1981), 86.

61. J. M. Deutsch and the Interagency Review Group on Nuclear Waste Management, *Report to the President* (TID-2817), (Springfield, Va.: National Technical Information Service, October 1978), iii.

62. U.S. Office of Technology Assessment, *Application of Solar Technology to Today's Energy Needs*, 2 vols. (Washington, D.C.: U.S. Government Printing Office, September 1978), vol. 1, pp. 3, 18, 21 (this volume hereafter cited as OTA, Solar).

63. Lovins, SEP, 19.

64. Shrader-Frechette, *Nuclear Power*, gives data on relative United States government expenditures and omissions in these areas.

65. OTA, Solar, 3, 7, 24–25, 74–99.

66. For discussion of the cover-up of these hazards of military and commercial uses of nuclear fission, see Shrader-Frechette, *Nuclear Power*, 85–86, and Barry Commoner, *The Closing Circle* (New York: Bantam, 1971), 197.

67. See Shrader-Frechette, *Nuclear Power*, 86.

68. See Shrader-Frechette, *Nuclear Power*, 57–58.

69. See Shrader-Frechette, *Nuclear Power*, 86.

70. For a lengthy treatment of cost-benefit analysis, see Ezra Mishan, *Cost-Benefit Analysis* (New York: Praeger, 1976) (hereafter cited as: CBA); and Mishan, *Welfare Economics* (New York: Random House, 1969). For a discussion of many of the philosophical presuppositions of cost-benefit analysis, see Sidney Hook, ed., *Human Values and Economic Policy* (New York: New York University Press, 1967), and K. S. Shrader-Frechette, "Technology Assessment as Applied Philosophy of Science," *Science, Technology, and Human Values* 6, no. 33 (Fall 1980): 33–50.

71. CBA, 407.

72. Mishan, CBA, 393, makes a similar point.

73. A. D. Biderman, "Social Indicators and Goals," in R. A. Bauer, ed., *Social Indicators* (Cambridge, Mass.: The MIT Press, 1966), 131–132.

74. J. K. Galbraith, *The New Industrial State* (Boston: Houghton Mifflin, 1967), 408.

75. Herbert Inhaber, "Risk with Energy from Conventional and Nonconventional Sources," *Science* 203, no. 4382 (February 23, 1979): 718–723.

76. See, for example, J. P. Holdren, K. R. Smith, Gregory Morris, "Energy: Calculating the Risks (II)," *Science* 204, no. 4393 (1979): 564 (hereafter cited as: Energy).

77. AEC, WASH-1224, p. 4–16.

78. For further discussion of accident consequences, the Price-Anderson Act, liability limits, and the philosophical implications of these policies, see Shrader-Frechette, *Nuclear Power*, esp. Chap. 4.

79. For discussion of the principle of utility and the utilitarian framework for ethics, see John Stuart Mill, *Utilitarianism, Liberty, and Representative Government* (New York: E. P. Dutton, 1910), esp. pp. 6–24 (hereafter cited as: *Utilitarianism*). See Jeremy Bentham, *The Utilitarians: An Introduction to the Principles of Morals and Legislation* (Garden City, N.Y.: Doubleday, 1961), esp. pp. 17–22. See also J. J. C. Smart, "An Outline of a System of Utilitarian Ethics," in *Utilitarianism: For and Against*, ed. J. J. C. Smart and B. Williams (Cambridge, England: Cambridge University Press, 1973) 3–74 (hereafter cited as: *Utilitarianism*).

80. Smart, *Utilitarianism*, 69–71.

81. Smart, *Utilitarianism*, 69–70.

82. John Rawls, *Justice*, 42–43; Charles Fried, *Right and Wrong* (Cambridge, Mass.: Harvard University Press, 1978), 116–117, 126–127; and Alan Donagan, *The Theory of Morality* (Chicago: University of Chicago Press, 1977), 221–239.

83. Smart, *Utilitarianism*, 69.

84. Smart, *Utilitarianism*, 72.

85. Mill, *Utilitarianism*, 58–59.

86. Rawls, *Justice*, 60ff.

87. See Hans Bethe, "The Necessity of Fission Power," *Scientific American* 234, no. 1 (January 1976): 26ff., who makes such an argument.

88. This argument is made by assessors in the employ of the Nuclear Regulatory Commission; see Shrader-Frechette, *Nuclear Power*, 29.

89. W. K. Frankena, "The Concept of Social Justice," in R. B. Brandt, ed., *Social Justice* (Englewood Cliffs, N.J.: Prentice-Hall, 1962), 10, 14, offers this argument as a sound (and apparently the only) basis for justifying inequalities and differences in treatment among persons.

90. See J. P. Plamenetz, "Equality of Opportunity," in W. T. Blackstone, ed., *The Concept of Equality* (Minneapolis: Burgess, 1969), 88.

91. E. J. Mishan, *21 Popular Economic Fallacies* (New York: Praeger, 1969), 235 (hereafter cited as: *Fallacies*).

92. See R. Grossman and G. Daneker, *Jobs and Energy* (Washington, D.C.: Environmentalists for Full Employment, 1977), 1–2, and Mishan, *Fallacies*, 237.

93. Virginia Brodine, "A Special Burden," *Environment* 13, no. 2 (March 1971): 24. D. N. Dane, "Bad Air for Children," *Environment* 18, no. 9 (November 1976): 26–34; and A. M. Freeman, "Income Distribution and Environmental Quality," in A. C. Enthoven and A. M. Freeman, eds., *Pollution, Resources, and the Environment* (New York: W. W. Norton, 1973), 101 (hereafter cited as: Freeman, IDEQ; and Enthoven and Freeman, PRE). See also A. V. Kneese, "Economics and the Quality of the Environment," in Enthoven and Freeman, PRE, 74–79 (hereafter cited as: Kneese, EQE); A. M. Freeman, R. H. Haveman, A. V. Kneese, *The Economics of Environmental Policy* (New York: John Wiley, 1973), 143 (hereafter cited as: Freeman, Haveman, and Kneese, EEP); and, for example,

Jane Stein, "Water for the Wealthy,"*Environment* 19, no. 4 (May 1977): 6–14. The point is documented well by Freeman, who argues that distribution of environmental pollution is a consequence "of the broader distribution forces at work in the economic system." Although there are minor exceptions to this rule, says Freeman, the poor bear a disproportionate burden of environmental hazards, and pollution is not "the great leveler," since the wealthy have "the means to protect themselves" from environmental insults. Even though the issue of who benefits most from pollution controls is complex (Freeman, IDEQ, 101–104; Freeman, Haveman, Kneese, EEP, 144–145; Kneese, EQE, 78–80), Freeman, Haveman, Kneese, and other economists (see EEP, 143–144) conclude: "on balance, that the improvement would be pro poor." In any case, there are several means whereby the costs of pollution control can be shifted from the poor and middle class to members of higher income groups (see Freeman, IDEQ, 104–105; and Freeman, Haveman, and Kneese, EEP, 145–148).

94.   Hans Jonas, "Philosophical Reflections on Experimenting with Human Subjects," in K. J. Struhl and P. R. Struhl, eds., *Ethics in Perspective* (New York: Random House, 1975), 242–253.

95.   See, for example, Fred Hoyle and Geoffrey Hoyle, *Commonsense in Nuclear Energy* (San Francisco: W. H. Freeman, 1980), 29, who say: "for the civil nuclear industry there has been no clear-cut evidence of any . . . death or injury, which means that . . . the best estimate for the future number of injuries and fatalities is zero."

96.   U.S. Atomic Energy Commission, *Comparative Risk–Cost–Benefit Study of Alternative Sources of Electrical Energy* (WASH-1224) (Washington, D.C.: U.S. Government Printing Office, December 1974), p. 3–95. According to the *Code of Federal Regulations*, 10, Part 20 (Washington, D.C.: U.S. Government Printing Office, 1978), 184, one "rad" of radiation is "a measure of the dose of any ionizing radiation to body tissues in terms of the energy absorbed per unit mass of the tissue."

97.   M. Korchmar, "Radiation Hearings Uncover Dust," *Critical Mass Journal* 3, no. 12 (March 1978): 5 (hereafter cited as: Radiation). See also R. Kraus, "Environmental Carcinogenesis: Regulation on the Frontiers of Science," *Environmental Law* 7, no. 1 (Fall 1976): 83–135.

98.   Subcommittee on Health and Environment of the Committee on Interstate and Foreign Commerce, United States House of Representatives, Effect of Radiation on Human Health, vol. 1, Serial No. 95–179, Hearings, 95th Congress (Washington, D.C.: U.S. Government Printing Office, 1979). See also Committee on Veterans' Affairs, United States Senate, *Veterans' Claims for Disabilities from Nuclear Weapons Testing*, Hearings, 96th Congress (Washington, D.C.: U.S. Government Printing Office, 1979). For discussion of weapons tests in Utah in the fifties, see Joint Hearing Before the Subcommittee on Oversight and Investigations of the Committee on Interstate and Foreign Commerce, House of Representatives, and the Health and Science Subcommittee of the Labor and Human Resources Committee and the Committee on the Judiciary, United States Senate, *Health Effects of Low-Level Radiation*, Serial No. 96–41, 96th Congress (Washington, D.C.: U.S. Government Printing Office, 1979). See also Korchmar, Radiation, p. 5.

99.   Facts regarding the Orville Kelly case came from a personal conversation with him in my home on August 17, 1978. For information regarding other servicemen who were denied benefits, see the references cited in note 98.

100.  Energy Research and Development Administration, *Final Environmental Impact Statement: Waste Management Operations, Idaho National Engineering Laboratory* ERDA-1536 (Springfield, Va.: National Technical Information Service, 1977), pp. III–103 and III–104.

101. ICRP standards are given in J. P. Holdren, "Hazards of the Nuclear Fuel Cycle," *The Bulletin of the Atomic Scientists* 30, no. 8 (October 1974): 16, and confirmed in J. Gofman and A. Tamplin, "Nuclear Power, Technology, and Environmental Law," *Environmental Law* 12, no. 2 (Winter 1971): 59–63, and O. Hansen, "Development and Application of Radiation Protection Standards," *Idaho International Law Review* 12, no. 1 (Fall 1975): 1–32.
102. Apart from the problems associated with the statistical casualties argument, it is simply false to assert that nuclear fission has killed no one. Military reactors in the United States have killed persons. (See Combustion Engineering, Inc., *SL-1 Annual Operating Report* (Idaho Falls, Idaho: Combustion Engineering, Inc., Nuclear Division, June 15, 1961), (END-1009, Contract AT (10-1)-967, (IDQ-19024) for an account of the famous Idaho accident). Also, citizens in other countries have been killed by accidents in the nuclear fuel cycle. See Z. A. Medvedev, *Nuclear Disaster in the Urals*, trans. George Saunders (New York: Norton, 1979) for an account of the famous accidents at Kasli in 1957 (p. 185), in the Urals in 1958 (p. 191), and at Kystym in 1958 (p. 188). All of these accidents caused a number of injuries; the second and third were the most serious and involved explosions. In the disaster in the Urals, several hundred people were killed, more than 1,000 square kilometers were contaminated (and will remain a danger zone for scores of years), and thousands of persons were evacuated and hospitalized. This particular accident, perhaps the best-known Russian nuclear catastrophe, was caused when buried wastes from nuclear power plants exploded. Medvedev, an exiled Soviet scientist, has been confirmed in his accounts of these incidents both by other members of the scientific community and by official United States documents obtained under the Freedom of Information Act. Many of these once-secret United States intelligence documents are reproduced in his book, *Nuclear Disaster in the Urals*.
103. See OTA, Solar (note 62).
104. See Robert Stobaugh and Daniel Yergin, eds., *Energy Future: Report of the Energy Project at Harvard Business School* (New York: Random House, 1979).

# SUGGESTIONS FOR FURTHER READING

The works that are most relevant to the several arguments and issues discussed in the preceding essay are cited in the accompanying notes. Among these, the following are of general interest, are accessible to the educated reader, and are likely to be available in most college or university libraries.

I. Introduction

§§1–3 A. B. Lovins, *Soft Energy Paths* (New York: Harper & Row, 1977).

II. The Soft Path

§4 Ivan Illich, *Energy and Equity* (New York: Harper & Row, 1974).
Theodore Roszak, *Person/Planet* (New York: Doubleday, 1978).
§§5–6 David Dickson, *The Politics of Alternative Technology* (New York: Universe Books, 1974).
§7 William W. Lowrance, *Of Acceptable Risk* (Los Altos: William Kaufmann, 1976).

K. S. Shrader-Frechette, *Nuclear Power and Public Policy* (Boston: D. Reidel, 1980).

### III. The Hard Path

§§8–10 C. Starr and C. Whipple, "Risks of Risk Decisions," *Science* 208, no. 4448 (1980): 1116.
§11 U.S. Department of Energy, *1981 Annual Report to Congress*, DOE/EIA-0173(81)/3 (Washington, D.C.: U.S. Government Printing Office, 1981).
§§12–13 J. J. C. Smart and B. Williams, eds., *Utilitarianism: For and Against* (Cambridge England: Cambridge University Press, 1973).

### IV. Towards a Sound Energy Policy

U.S. Office of Technology Assessment, *Application of Solar Technology to Today's Energy Needs*, 2 vols. (Washington, D.C.: U.S. Government Printing Office, 1978).
John Rawls, *A Theory of Justice* (Cambridge, Mass.: Harvard University Press, 1971).
Ronald Dworkin, *Taking Rights Seriously* (Cambridge, Mass.: Harvard University Press, 1977).
K. S. Shrader-Frechette, *Environmental Ethics* (Pacific Grove, Calif.: Boxwood, 1981).
W. K. Frankena, "The Naturalistic Fallacy," *Mind* 48, no. 192 (October 1939).
R. Stobaugh and Daniel Yergin, eds., *Energy Future* (New York: Random House, 1979).

5

# Ethics and Economics in Environmental Law

## MARK SAGOFF

‹›

### I. BACKGROUND

"To assert that there is a pollution problem or an environmental problem," William Baxter writes, "is to assert, at least implicitly, that one or more resources is not being used so as to maximize human satisfactions." Baxter, a professor of law at Stanford University, now serves as assistant attorney general of the United States in charge of the Antitrust Division of the Justice Department. He believes that "environmental problems are economics problems, and better insight can be gained by the application of economic analysis."[1]

From an economic point of view such as Baxter's, environmental problems are *problems* because they represent the failure of markets to allocate resources to those who value them most, which is to say, to those who are willing to pay the most for them. On this view, when we face an "environmental problem," the government may intervene to make markets function efficiently, and thus solve the problem. "Efficiency," Richard Posner writes, "means exploiting economic resources in such a way that human satisfaction measured by aggregate consumer willingness to pay for goods and services is maximized." Posner, a law professor at the University of Chicago, is now a federal circuit court judge. He believes that resources ought to be allocated in ways that maximize social wealth, that is, the total or aggregate amount that consumers would be willing to pay for them. Posner adds that resources have the greatest *value* when they are employed in this way. "Value too is defined by willingness to pay."[2]

Not all policy analysts or even all economists believe, of course, that efficiency, understood as optimal consumer satisfaction, ought to be the goal of environmental policy. Not all agree, in other words, with the slogan that "more is better, insofar as the 'more' consists in items that people want to buy."[3] Those who believe that environmental regulation should aim, primarily, to maximize the aggregate of goods and services for which people are willing to pay, however, often treat this view not as an abstraction of economic theory but as a kind of common sense. Larry Ruff, for example, who served as director of research at the Environmental Protection Agency before becoming a program officer at the Ford Foundation, takes this "commonsense" approach to pollution. "We are going to make little real progress in solving the problem of pollution," he writes, "until we recognize it for what, primarily, it is: an economic problem which must be understood in economic terms."[4] Ruff advises that pollution be reduced (or raised) to "optimal" levels, which is to say, levels at which any increase in environmental protection "would cost more than it is worth," while any decrease would "reduce benefits more than it would save in costs."[5]

## §1 THE PRESIDENT ACTS

On February 19, 1981, President Reagan acted to bring economic "common sense" in the form of cost-benefit analysis into regulatory policymaking. In Executive Order 12,291,[6] published in the *Federal Register* that day, he required all executive departments and agencies, insofar as the law permitted, to support every new major regulation with a cost-benefit analysis establishing that the benefits of the regulation to society outweigh its social costs. The order directs the Office of Management and Budget (OMB) to review every such regulation on the basis of the adequacy of the cost-benefit analysis supporting it. This departs from tradition. Historically, regulations have been reviewed not by the OMB but by the courts on the basis of the relation of the regulation to authorizing legislation (e.g., the Endangered Species Act), not to cost-benefit analysis.

The significance of the presidential order can be understood in the context of the important distinction between *cost-benefit analysis* and *cost-effectiveness analysis*. Cost-benefit analysis serves to determine the *ends* of regulatory policy, for example, the levels of pollution that *should be* permitted or the amount of wilderness that *should be* preserved. Cost-effectiveness analysis looks only for the most economical or thrifty *means* for achieving a particular goal that has been determined independently. As one commentator puts the thought: "*Cost-benefit analysis* . . . is used by the decisionmaker to establish societal goals . . ., whereas *cost-effectiveness analysis* only compares alternative means for achieving 'given' goals."[7]

The economists who, in the 1940s and 1950s, developed cost-benefit analysis thought that public investments should return a profit to society as a whole just as private investments, if they are sound, return a profit to the corporation or firm that makes them. They applied this principle, quite reasonably, to projects in which the government invested a great deal of taxpayer money, notably to build dams and to irrigate farms. These economists compared the capital and other costs of building a large water project with the market value of the benefits that were expected to result. The market values (the prices goods and services cost when they are traded) were comparatively easy to measure: The price of labor, cement, land, and the like were known; the dollar value of irrigation, hydroelectric power, and flood control could be estimated. The Flood Control Act of 1939 called for an economic comparison of the pluses and minuses of each major water project. It permitted the government to finance a project only when "the benefits to whomsoever they accrue (are) in excess of the costs."[8]

An economist who analyzes the costs and benefits of a project to society as a whole asks basically the same sorts of questions as an accountant might ask who analyzes the costs and benefits of an investment decision for a particular firm. The economist, however, must take into account all the effects of the project on the whole society—both the value of the goods and services the project will produce and the loss of the resources it will consume and that might have been used in other ways. E. J. Mishan, an economist at the London School of Economics and author of basic texts on cost-benefit analysis, puts the point this way:

> Instead of asking whether the owners of the enterprise will become better off by the firm's engaging in one activity rather than another, the economist asks whether society as a whole will become better off by undertaking this project rather than not undertaking it, or by undertaking instead any of a number of alternative projects.[9]

During the Depression, Congress passed a good deal of legislation to make business, once again, America's business. Since the purpose of these laws tended to be economic—to increase productivity and social wealth—cost-benefit analysis played a major role in political decision-making. The environmental and civil rights legislation of the 1960s and 1970s, however, greatly changed this situation. Congress passed these laws—as it had much earlier approved of child labor legislation—primarily not for economic but for ethical reasons. In the case of environmental legislation, Congress responded to the shame many Americans felt at the deteriorating quality of the natural environment. It enacted laws intended to clean up the air and water and not necessarily to achieve "optimal" levels of pollution as determined by willingness to pay. Similarly, Congress acted to make the environment in the workplace *safe* without worrying very much whether, at the same time, it made the workplace *productive*.

The difference between an *ethical* and an *economic* basis for public policy might be approached, at least intuitively, by means of examples. In the nineteenth century, many immigrant parents sent their small children to toil for long hours in dark, satanic textile mills, where many of them died. Many adults, too, worked ten and twelve hours a day under horrible conditions for pitiful wages. All too many impoverished women had to choose between the sweatshops and prostitution. These adult workers (and the parents of the children) voluntarily contracted with employers; the free market functioned; one might even argue that these arrangements were efficient. Whether they were efficient or cost beneficial or not, however, is quite beside the point. Congress eliminated them on quite other grounds, namely, that no decent, self-respecting society tolerates these conditions whether free markets create them or not.

Congress, at least in the past, seems to have adopted something of the same ethical attitude with respect to the destruction of the wilderness, the despoliation of scenic landscapes, the pollution of water and air. Congress apparently has taken the view that a self-respecting and dignified society, on ethical and aesthetic grounds, does not trade a magnificent natural heritage for a bowl of consumer porridge, even if the porridge has a higher market value than the heritage. The policy decisions of the past with respect to the workplace and the environment, moreover, have strongly affected the prices individuals are now willing to pay for environmental safety and beauty and cleanliness; the law has had an educative effect; it has changed expectations. Thus, when economists now measure willingness to pay, for example for safety in the workplace, what they measure is not "raw" consumer or worker preferences, but preferences molded and transformed by fifty years of progressive, ideological legislation. Imagine what the market data would look like if it were taken from *unregulated* markets, in which child labor was permitted and in which people could work twelve hours a day for less than minimum wages. Imagine the depressing circumstances that would then be considered optimal and efficient!

In the 1960s and 1970s, moved by the popularity of environmental issues, Congress enacted many environmental laws that are frankly aspirational and leave little room for cost-benefit analysis. Consider, for example, the Federal Water Pollution Control Act Amendments of 1972, which require all industries to install, by 1977, the "best practicable (pollution) control technology currently available." By 1983, industries must install the "best available technology economically achievable."[10] What is economically *achievable*, of course, is not the same as what is economically *efficient*. The Endangered Species Act of 1973, to take another example, contains provisions which, if consistently applied, could bring the economy to a screeching halt.[11] The Clean Air Act Amendments of 1977 contain provisions nearly as draconian, for example, those that prohibit significant deterioration of air quality in areas that already meet or exceed national standards.[12] Finally, the Occupational Safety and Health Act of 1970 sets *feasibility*, not *efficiency*, as the criterion for environmental safety in the workplace. The statute instructs the secretary of labor to set with respect to exposure to toxic substances the standard

> which most adequately assures, to the extent feasible . . . that no employee will suffer material impairment of health or functional capacity

even if such employee has regular exposure to the hazard . . . for the period of his working life.[13]

The political atmosphere changed again, however, in the 1980s when the recession focused attention on our need, as a nation, to increase the production and consumption of goods and services. President Reagan, during his first month in office, issued the executive order I have already mentioned. A fundamental ideological conflict arises between the cost-benefit approach of the President, on the one hand, and the ethical concerns expressed in legislation, on the other. Conflicts of this sort may produce bloody confrontations, fighting in the streets, political arrests, repression, and even civil war in some nations. In our country, however, this kind of crisis leads usually to two different results. First, it leads to the development of new college and (if the conflict is fundamental enough) graduate level courses, such as Environmental Ethics, for which this essay provides reading. Second, the conflict may be played out in fascinating cases litigated, until all interest is exhausted, in the courts.

## §2 THE COURTS RESPOND

The Constitution, plainly, does not require cost-benefit analysis. Therefore, the courts, in general, uphold laws as legitimate if they are properly enacted whether or not they pass a cost-benefit test. For example, in *Hill* v. *TVA*, the case that involved the snail darter and the Tellico Dam, the Sixth Circuit Court specifically rejected an interest-balancing or cost-benefit test for applying the Endangered Species Act. The court said: "Economic exigencies . . . do not grant courts a license to rewrite a statute."[14] The court implicitly distinguished the ethical or ideological motives that citizens might express through the political process, on the one hand, from the interests and preferences they reveal as consumers, entering and exiting from markets, on the other.[15] The court concluded that "the welfare of an endangered species may weigh more heavily on the public conscience, as expressed by the final will of Congress, than the writeoff of those millions of dollars already expended on Tellico."[16]

The Occupational Safety and Health Act, which responded to a shameful history of labor conditions involving sweatshops and company towns, expressed the commitment of the American public to make the workplace safe. It entitled each worker, insofar as feasible, to a hazard-free environment. Since an absolutely risk-free workplace is impossible, however, the responsibility fell upon the Occupational Safety and Health Administration, and, derivitively, upon the courts, to balance the commitment expressed in the law, on the one hand, with our interest in economic productivity, on the other. How should this "balancing" be done?

In two cases, one involving a revised regulatory standard for benzene,[17] the other, cotton dust,[18] lawyers for industry argued that the courts should strike down any health or safety standard unless (1) it responds to a significant risk and (2) it involves compliance costs reasonably related to the likely benefits of the regulation as measured in cost-benefit terms. In the *Benzene* case, a plurality of the Supreme Court, in a decision deeply divided along several lines, agreed with industry that a regulation must be justified by a significant health risk. In *Cotton Dust*, however, where the industry conceded the significance of the risk, the Court (as in *Hill* v. *TVA*) upheld the regulation as an expression of public values, even though it arguably would not pass a cost-benefit test.[19]

The *Cotton Dust* case put the Reagan administration on notice that, if it were to achieve the kind of economic accountability it sought in the regulatory agencies, it would have to change the law. The administration moved quickly to do this: It put the substance of the executive order before Congress as the Regulatory Reform Act of 1981.[20] The bill, in the Senate version, provides the president with very broad powers of "executive oversight"; for example, it authorizes him to screen all major regulatory actions in order to "ensure" that these actions satisfy a detailed cost-benefit test the president would also have to approve. This authority would be vested in the OMB, which in effect, then, may review environmental and workplace standards on cost-benefit grounds.[21] The power of the OMB would extend, under the bill, not only to executive but also to the so-called independent agencies, for example, the Federal Reserve Board, the Federal Communications Commission, the U.S. Consumer Product Safety Commission, the Federal Election Commission, and the Nuclear Regulatory Commission.

The Senate passed the bill by a huge majority. (No one, in an election year, can vote against "regulatory reform.") The measure would have passed in the House (in a somewhat weaker version)[22] early in October 1982, but for the press of other business and timely filibustering by Representative John Dingell before the Rules Committee. It remains to be seen (as of this writing) whether Congress will back away from its role of interpreting the public conscience and of expressing public values, especially about the environment, and act instead to promote the efficiency of the economy and to maximize the satisfaction of preferences that consumers reveal in markets.

Citizens look to legislatures, particularly to Congress, to define and to pursue public values, which is to say, the goals or ethical convictions that characterize us as a community—aspirations, one might say, that *make* us a nation and not merely a market. Congress responded to this expectation most forcefully during the New Deal and, again, during the 1960s and 1970s, when it passed the basic statutory or public law that regulates markets in order to achieve community ends—for example, a safer workplace or a cleaner environment. This experiment with public law balances or complements the efforts of the courts to enforce private or common law among us, the rules or rights, in other words, that protect us as individuals from each other, provide security, and promote exchange.

Since the New Deal, the Supreme Court has interpreted constitutional law in ways that further protect the individual against the government and its goals and purposes; the Court has extended the rights of personhood and privacy. At the same time, however, Congress, respecting those rights and limits, has worked through legislation to develop the common values and aspirations that give us a sense of ourselves as a community and not merely as a market; values, then, we pursue not as individuals but as a nation. I believe that Congress should continue at this task: It should not abandon public values, including environmental values, which Americans defend and for which, as citizens, they give reasons. Congress should recognize—as many policy analysts do not—that Americans do regard themselves as citizens, as members of a community defining and seeking shared aspirations, and not merely as consumers, as individuals in a market competing for scarce resources. Accordingly, I believe that Congress should reinforce its basic commitment to environmental law, not, of course, to make markets more efficient, but to build our sense of community to balance much the Supreme Court has done to enhance our sense of individuality and privacy. I shall defend this general view in the pages that follow.

In the next part of this essay (Part II), I consider a conceptual problem that afflicts those who use cost-benefit analysis as a guide in making public policy. This problem will introduce the important issues policymakers confront when they deal with environmental policy exclusively in economic as distinct from political terms. In Part III, I discuss one of the legal problems that beset economic analysis in the context of land use policy. I shall consider there the "takings" problem, so-called because the Fifth Amendment to the Constitution says: "nor shall private property be taken for public use, without just compensation." Then, relying on the distinction between cost-benefit analysis and cost-effectiveness analysis, in Part IV I shall discuss proposals to use economic or market incentives to encourage pollution abatement.

In Part V of this essay, I describe some of the problems policy analysts confront when they try to include public values in cost-benefit analysis, for example, when they provide what are called "shadow" market prices for the aesthetic or moral commitments that concern us as a political community if not as self-interested individuals. Some analysts set such "prices" by asking citizens how much they would be willing to pay, for example, for the knowledge that the nation preserves species, makes the workplace safe, or whatever. I offer criticisms of this technique that suggest additional ways in which cost-benefit analysis fails as an approach to environmental policy and law. These criticisms, I hope, will help justify my view that Congress has, until now, at any rate, taken essentially the right course in defining environmental objectives not on economic but on ethical, ideological, and political grounds.

## II. A PROBLEM FOR COST-BENEFIT ANALYSIS

Economists and policy analysts who agree with the approach taken by Posner and Baxter (many, of course, do not) confront a formidable problem in supporting "efficiency," "wealth maximization," or "consumer satisfaction" as the primary goal of public policy or as a criterion for assessing our values as a society. I do not refer now to the technical problems that may be involved in determining "shadow" prices—that is, hypothetical prices—for environmental goods and services (like clean air and water) that are not, in fact, marketed. Nor do I refer now to the political obstacles Congress has placed before the application of cost-benefit analysis by refusing (at least as of this writing) to endorse it on a wholesale basis. Nor do I refer, finally, to the moral objection that *not* all our preferences should be treated equally, since those caused by manipulation, such as advertising, are not as autonomously chosen, and therefore, are not as deserving of societal respect, as those that represent a person's more considered values. These "more considered" values, as I think, include those public concerns the individual would defend or give reasons for in political argument no matter what he or she rushed out to buy for him or herself. I shall discuss these concerns as we proceed. Here, the problem I wish to consider is a *conceptual* one; it is a problem that involves the way we understand the notion of willingness to pay insofar as it may be used as a basis for public decisionmaking.

The notion of "willingness to pay" is importantly ambiguous. It may refer (1) to what one is willing to *give* in exchange for what one does not now own or over which one has no right. It may refer (2) to the amount one would *take* in exchange for what one already owns or for some right one has to its use. You can apply the concept of willingness to pay in either sense (1) or (2); you can apply the concept, in other words, once you have already determined whether you are dealing with buyers or sellers of a resource. Policy analysts who use the willingness-to-pay concept, however, do not decide beforehand whether they are determining "bid" or "ask" prices; in other words, they leave ambiguous the question whether the resource is bought or sold. They presume, indeed, that whoever would bid the most should own the thing in question—and thus they use the willingness-to-pay criterion to establish rights of ownership to the nation's natural resources.

In the following pages, I shall argue that Americans, as citizens, possess the resources in question and that the government holds them as a public trust and not as a consignee or as an auctioneer. Accordingly, it is for Americans as sellers to set prices—not for a market. Yet many policy analysts, including William Baxter, believe that resources should be transferred as they would be in an auction, where there are no buyers and sellers, but only bidders. Baxter measures "human satisfaction" by the amount a person would bid or pay for something. Then he writes: "If any resource can be shifted from a first deployment to a second, and it would yield a greater amount of satisfaction in the second, then it should be so shifted."[23]

## §3 THE "BID-ASKED" PROBLEM

The problem put succinctly is this. The prices we would demand if we were to sell things we own often are not in the same "ballpark" as the prices we would offer to obtain them. We ask a lot more than we bid. This is especially true when an individual thinks some moral, aesthetic, sentimental, or political value is at stake. Examples may be found in any newspaper account of neighborhood residents who refuse to sell their homes to the redevelopment authority even when they are offered inflated prices. They would not have paid those prices to move into the neighborhood. Why, then, does it take the police, followed by the bulldozers, to move them out?

During the high tide of planned urban development in the 1950s and 1960s, many homeowners argued, as they were displaced, that eventually people would see that high-rise buildings, not working-class neighborhoods, are slums. The "gentrification" movement of the 1970s and 1980s, in which upwardly mobile people "restore" hideous slums turning them into glorious heritage, vindicates this prediction. How tastes change! The homeowners argued they had a right to their houses. They were being forced out, said they, so that the moguls of capitalism could make more money.[24] They believed that the culture of their tenements was better in itself than the crazy world of glass and concrete with which planners would replace it. They did not prefer to be bought out. This refusal may be irrational; it may be principled as well.

The commitment these homeowners made to their neighborhoods helps us to understand, by analogy, why many Americans (a majority, if opinion polls are to be believed)[25] are committed to protect the natural environment. They say price is no object when it comes to preserving what they have long taken pride in.[26] Many Americans contend, moreover, that a simpler way of life is better, in itself, than the life of consumption some may seem to prefer instead. This simpler life—or the possibility of it—requires us to live more in harmony with nature, and is therefore disturbed when, for example, a beautiful mountainside is marred by a resort complex or spoiled by strip mining for the coal it contains.[27]

Individuals who believe that the law gives them a right, for example, to clean air and water will demand much more to give up that presumptive right than they might pay to acquire it. Many reasons explain this disparity between prices we bid and ask for the same things. The first reason may lie in *hysteresis*, that is, the sense that things we lose are more valuable to us than things we never gain. As the Scottish philosopher David Hume (1711–1776) described it: "Men generally fix their attentions more on what they are possess'd of, than on what they never enjoyed: For this reason, it would be greater cruelty to dispossess a man of any thing than not to give it him."[28] Since Colonial times, Americans have possessed a magnificent natural heritage and we have taken clean air and water for granted. Thus hysteresis, not to mention hysteria, becomes a factor when we are dispossessed of what we have so long enjoyed.

Second, individuals simply resent being asked to pay for what they believe they already own or have a right to. One turns to the law not to a market to keep what one has. The "protection" racket aside, people do not pay criminals, for example, not to attack them or break into their homes. Similarly, environmentalists are unwilling to pay polluters not to pollute, though they are eager to sue them and send them to jail if they do. To be sure, one could buy off a corporation to keep it from strip mining a wilderness just as one could bribe an intruder not to break into one's home. As a matter of principle, however, one may regard that possibility as extortion. One pays "protection" money of that sort only to the Mob.

Third, people are more constrained by their budget in buying things than in selling them. Analysts, moreover, may ask people how much they are willing to pay for hundreds of environmental benefits; thus, people must divide a little disposable income hundreds of ways. Ask a person what he or she would demand to relinquish any *one* of those benefits, however, and the sky is the limit. The reason that asking prices so much exceed bidding prices may be a simple one: A person's ability to receive so much exceeds his or her ability to pay.

Anyone can draw the moral of these observations. Many economists propose to establish an "optimal" allocation of certain environmental resources by determining how much potential users would pay for them. Willingness to pay, however, may be measured in relation to prices either asked or bid. These are not the same. To decide whether to rely on the bid or the asked price, one must first decide who owns the resource, or, if it is unowned, who has a right to its use. One must decide, for example, if Americans purchase clean air as consumers or whether, as citizens, they sell it. This question cannot be answered by appealing simply to the notion of willingness to pay. To answer it, we must think about the reasons —political, historical, cultural, ethical—that give Americans status as either the buyers or, more likely, the sellers of resources for which no market exists, for example, clean air and wilderness.

Our legal and political history points decisively to the view that Americans may keep environmental resources and need not bid for them. The government, then, would hold these resources in public trust and not as ordinary property of which it may dispose, as it will, to the highest bidder. (The government does dispose of some property this way, of course, for example, old army bases it no longer wants.) In the Clean Air and Clean Water acts, Congress has affirmed the historical right of Americans to an environment they can be proud of as a nation, including clean air and water, wilderness preservation, and so on. In these laws, the environmental movement won a political victory which has generally been upheld by the courts; this victory is not to be taken away by analysts who have their own technical conception of what sound regulatory policy is.

Analysts, therefore, should not ask how much we would be willing to pay to purchase environmental "benefits" but how much we would ask in exchange for them. They should recognize the difference, in other words, between a market (in which buyers must pay the asking price) and an auction (in which the highest price bid takes the item in question). Congress, representing public opinion, reflects the unwillingness of the majority to trade the beauty and authenticity of our natural environment for increased consumer goods and services. The willingness-to-pay criterion, interpreted in terms of what we would pay to acquire what is construed as not ours to begin with, becomes irrelevant when citizens are seen to be owners of a heritage they share rather than buyers of resources for which they must compete.

A proponent of the "willingness-to-pay" criterion for environmental policy, however, might take a hard line at this point. He or she may concede that, as a matter of historical and legal interpretation, citizens have often been viewed as owners, not buyers, of "fragile" resources such as clean water and air. Still, the fact that history and law favor this view does not show that we should accept it. "Values" are not the same as, and do not follow from, "facts," even historical and legal facts. Instead, what we value as a society may be revealed by what individual consumers will pay for now and in the future—not by what might have happened in the past. If so, then we should regard all those who compete for the use of unowned resources as having exactly the same status, namely, that of buyers. And we should then set up markets in those resources; we should auction them to whoever bids the most.

This reply deserves our attention. How would such an auction allocate environmental resources? I shall answer this question by considering the likely effect of the efficiency norm as it may be applied in regulating the use of land, particularly, agricultural land. I shall then argue that the market approach, if adopted on a wholesale basis, holds a monstrous promise of making good things bad. Yet, as I shall argue later in this essay, market incentives—for example, auctioning "rights to pollute"—to achieve independently selected environmental goals remain untouched by any of the criticisms I have made. Then, I shall consider whether market strategies for achieving our national objectives, as opposed to determining them in the first place, provide cost-effective means for meeting the goals we set politically for the natural environment.

## III. EFFICIENCY AND THE USE OF THE LAND

The goal of efficiency, at least as it is usually understood, conflicts with many of the objectives dear to environmentalists. A distribution of resources is said to be efficient if it allots commodities to those who value them most. Those who value them most, in the view we have discussed, are those who, as buyers, are willing to pay the most for them. The individuals, or, more plausibly, the corporations who pay the most for land expect to get a large return on their investment. They may be real estate developers. They subdivide. They replace comparatively unprofitable farms, swamps, and woodlands with money-making gas stations, quick-eat places, furniture outlets, shopping centers, and condominiums.

## §4 THE EXAMPLE OF AGRICULTURAL LAND

Is an efficient distribution of resources a good one? The citizens of Anne Arundel County, Maryland, may not think so. Anne Arundel County has maintained much of its rural character in spite of the fact that it lies within commuting distance of the District of Columbia. Its citizens prize the quiet and beauty of their environment. Their conception of the good life and of what gives value to life requires them to protect the pastoral and agrarian tradition they love. They feel threatened every time Presidential Realty or the Grace Corporation buys a farm and puts up a billboard saying: "Coming Soon . . ."

An acre of land in Anne Arundel County, if it is planted in corn, may be sold for about $2,000. It can bring as much as $100,000, however, if it can be planted in garden apartments. This includes land set aside for a sauna, tennis courts, swimming pool, and garage. When individuals compete for the use of a resource they own in common—when they fish the same lake, for example—they often overexploit the resources they seek, each one reasoning that his effort to conserve will be wasted, since the next person will simply take whatever of the common stock he leaves. There is no "problem of the commons," however, when you are dealing with New Age Realty. The developer subdivides; your apartment number is printed on your deckchair, locker, and parking space.

The people of Anne Arundel County moved there, or many of them did, in order to flee the "burbs." Now more people, seeking a little peace from advertising and from automobiles, want to join them. They saw the ads and drove out. They want the seclusion others have. They desire a little room—a few trees, at least—between themselves and the Joneses. After a few years, as a result, there may be little to choose between Anne Arundel County and its congested neighbor, Prince George's County. Thus the will of the consumer would triumph again.

What should the citizens of Anne Arundel County do? Must they sit idly by while commercial ventures destroy the things they believe in, the things that give value to their lives? If efficiency is our guide, the answer is yes. The only measure that makes sense in this view is willingness to pay. The citizens of Anne Arundel County might as well forget their moral, aesthetic, and ideological convictions, then, unless they can back them up with money.

The residents of Anne Arundel County may look for ways to outbid the corporations in order to preserve the environment they cherish. They could pay $1,000 per bushel for corn to make that crop as profitable as garden apartments. Butter and sugar corn is good; however, it is not *that* good. The citizens may also try to buy the farms to preserve them. That would be expensive. When the county buys development rights to one acre the next acre becomes even more attractive to developers. (Is it the open space nearby, perhaps, that makes a subdivision sell? Are the developers really selling the open space, then, without paying for it?) The cost of the development rights may run to hundreds of millions. The State of Maryland could not foot the bill.

The citizens of the county have one more strategy to try. They might zone for agricultural use the land they wish to save. This would throw the problem to the courts. Judges would observe that the proposed zoning ordinance does not pay compensation to the landowners who might otherwise have sold their property, at high prices, to developers. The judges would then have to determine whether the ordinance is a legitimate exercise of the police power or an illegitimate, because uncompensated, exercise of eminent domain.

Let us suppose that the judges who decide this matter are convinced that efficiency is the proper goal of public policy and of the soundness of their decisions insofar as these decisions affect public policy. They would think it significant that land within commuting distance of Washington, D.C., is good as gold if it is developed for modern commercial and residential use. Land that may only be farmed, however, commands a much lower price. These judges, moreover, may be suspicious of the power of voting majorities to impose their conception of the good life on recalcitrant minorities. They may conclude, then, that the proposed zoning ordinance is an unjust "taking" of the property rights some farmers might otherwise sell, for huge amounts, to subdividers. They might decide that a free market, not a zoning board or an elected assembly, is the legitimate indicator of the popular will.

And what would be the result of this decision? Mondo Condo. High-Rise Heaven. Bungalow Bonanza. Gala opening . . . move fast . . . 'cause they won't last. Wet bar. Adult game room. Class action. Luxury package. The *blitz* is on.


## §5 TWO APPROACHES TO ZONING

Suppose the citizens of Anne Arundel County do pass a zoning ordinance restricting commercial and residential development of agricultural and other open lands. This ordinance may greatly decrease the value of the property farmers might otherwise have sold to subdividers. Ought the farmers who want to sell their land to developers bear this loss? Should they be compensated, instead, by a program that buys development rights from them or pays them some part of the lost market value of their land?

Bruce Ackerman, a professor at the Columbia Law School, in a book on the "takings" issue, described two ways in which judges may approach this question. "The only trouble," he writes, "is that these two forms of legal thought—forms that I shall associate with the Scientific Policymaker, on the one hand, and the Ordinary Observer, on the other —suggest very different ways of resolving legal perplexities."[29] Indeed they do. The Ordinary Observer, as we shall see, agrees with the general practice of the courts, which is to balance a variety of moral, economic, and political considerations in arriving at decisions in particular cases. The Scientific Policymaker, on the contrary, would derive a decision in every case from a universal principle or from a comprehensive theory.

An ordinary observer (to continue with Ackerman's terminology) takes the view that legal terms, such as *property, taking,* and *harm*, have plain meanings in ordinary language and that "legal language cannot be understood unless its roots in the ordinary talk of non-lawyers are constantly kept in mind."[30] A judge who is an ordinary observer will ask whether the county took title or physical possession of the land or whether it simply regulated its use. The judge will ask whether the prohibited use of the land threatened to do harm or whether the regulation is intended not to prevent harm but to provide a good. He or she will inquire whether a few individuals are singled out to bear the cost or whether the ordinance places the burden equitably on a large nonsuspect class of individuals. (Judges suspect illegal discrimination when a law imposes costs on a racial, religious, or political minority, e.g., blacks and people who voted for a losing candidate. A class of individuals is not "suspect" in this way if the people in it are identified by some quality relevant to the legitimate purposes of law, e.g., landowners and fishermen.)

If the judge is an "Ordinary Observer," he or she will ask whether the farmers received a fair hearing. Is their loss very large? Can they still make some reasonable return on their land? Questions such as these reveal judicial notice of ordinary concepts about property and ordinary concerns about justice.[31] A judge who asks these questions may rely on legal history and precedent and upon a sense of how our institutions function generally in order better to apply these concepts and to understand these concerns.

In contrast, someone who is a "scientist" about the language of the law "conceives the distinctive constituents of legal discourse to be a set of technical concepts whose meanings are set in relation to one another by clear definitions without continuing reliance upon the way similar-sounding concepts are deployed in non-legal talk."[32] The scientist would understand the legal term *property* to refer to different bundles of rights various people sometimes have to the same things. The scientist may then conclude that "whenever the law removes *any* user right formerly resident in one bundle and places it in another," a *taking* has occurred.[33]

The problem for the "scientist" then lies in giving a sharp technical sense to the concept of "just compensation." Ackerman describes this as the mission of the scientific *policymaker* who understands "the legal system to contain, in addition to rules, a relatively small number of general principles describing the abstract ideals which a legal system is designed to further." Ackerman adds: "It is this statement of principle, presumed by the policymaker to form a self-consistent whole, which I shall call a Comprehensive View."[34] The policymaker *defines* a "perfectly functioning set of legal institutions" as "one which always generates a decision that best furthers the Comprehensive View guiding the legal system."[35]

It is easy to think of examples of comprehensive views. In a monarchy, political decisions are supposed to further the interests of the monarch; in a theocracy, God. I suppose that the Nazis had a few principles in their comprehensive view in relation to which they attempted to justify the most hideous decisions in history. These examples, which are the first which come to mind, may convince us to reject scientific policymaking as scary. Ackerman notes that given the wide variety of possible comprehensive views, a judge's choice of one as legally binding must be limited in a very constraining fashion. "Yet what are these limits?" Ackerman asks. He replies that despite the importance of this question, he will not attempt to answer it.[36] Instead he treats two comprehensive views which he finds in present legal culture and which indicate the direction of contemporary legal thought.

## §6 THE DANGER OF A "COMPREHENSIVE VIEW"

Ackerman (with some apology) labels the two comprehensive views he discusses *Kantian* and *utilitarian*. He deals only briefly with the Kantian approach, which like many commentators, he assimilates with the "protection of individual rights even when large coalitions . . . wish to abridge them."[37] Thus, Ackerman reads Kant's categorical imperative to require, in the phrase made popular by Ronald Dworkin, an Oxford professor of jurisprudence and leading political theorist, that individual rights act as "trumps" over social interest.

I believe that there is a distinctively Kantian perspective on environmental law, but this perspective, as I think, is not one that simply emphasizes the importance of rights or entitlements. (A rule-utilitarian might take rights seriously, construing them as principles that will maximize utility if consistently applied.) The point of the categorical imperative, as I understand it, is to guarantee the individual freedom of each person to act as a legislator, that is, to "universalize" his or her judgment by urging it not merely as an individual but as a member of the community. Thus, a Kantian state would take seriously not just the rights of individuals but their opinions as well; it would weigh these opinions fairly or equally, which is to say on their merits, in the policymaking process, in which those individuals would themselves participate. The question of a "Kantian" approach to public policy, however, demands full consideration on its own terms, so I shall not pursue the matter here.

Let us turn to the "utilitarian" comprehensive view specifically as it applies to the *takings* clause of the Fifth Amendment. Here the question arises why compensation should *ever* be paid—if indeed we may assume that social utility is furthered when the state takes land to build a school, armory, or something like that. In the "utilitarian" view the reason cannot be that the Constitution demands compensation in certain clear cases, for, while "the methods of Scientific Policymaking seem familiar, . . . the harsh fact is that they bear very little relationship to the rules that are presently applied by the judges in the name of the Constitution."[38] Someone may argue, of course, that these rules—or the Constitution itself—can be given a utilitarian justification. One may give freedom of speech a "utilitarian" explanation, for example, by talking in terms of a "market for ideas."[39] (Why would we give proven bores, then, the right to talk?) The problem, however, is that the "utilitarian" policymaker must give an "efficiency" rationale for following constitutional requirements—and thus he or she might give a similar justification for *abandoning* them.

It seems to me that the "scientific policymaker" with his or her "comprehensive view" is scary whether he or she is a Moral Majoritarian, a party-line communist, a Moslem revolutionary theocrat, or the kind of utilitarian technocrat Ackerman describes. All of these true believers are in possession of comprehensive views ultimately so vague and indeterminate in their application that they can easily be used to justify whatever action the policymaker likes. The policymaker could regard anyone who disagrees, of course, as not being a true Christian, Moslem, Marxist, or Utilitarian, and thus as needing reeducation. These doctrinaire approaches to public policy regard all the ordinary conceptions of political justice—individual rights, due process, the separation of powers, the avoidance of suspect classifications—as either incidental results of the Comprehensive View or as so much eyewash. People years ago described authoritarianism in government as "tyranny." That word is not too old fashioned to describe "scientific" policymaking today.

We have before us now good reason to reject the efficiency norm as a basis for environmental policy and, more generally, as means for determining what our collective goals should be and the way our laws ought to be read. Those who would introduce this norm as a "Comprehensive" or "Scientific" view of policymaking risk making a shambles of our shared environment and a joke of our political life.

## §7   TWO OBJECTIONS

The criticisms I have raised against the efficiency norm in environmental policy might occasion two objections. First, someone might point out that among our cherished political ideals, freedom remains the most important. If this is a free society, moreover, then the government cannot tell you what to do with your property, but you may do with it as you please, as long as you do no harm to anyone else. The farmers in Anne Arundel County, then, have a right to sell their land to developers, if the ideal of freedom is to be respected. The Ordinary Observer, who would restrict this right to achieve "collective" or "public" ends, violates historical or cultural ideals—in this instance, freedom. It is the "Scientific Policymaker," who relies on the principle of the free market, that abides by that ideal.

Second, someone might object that, while public values and shared aspirations are well and good, they are not cheap. We must balance these laudable goals with other legitimate interests, for example housing, mining, timbering, and the like. This takes us back to some form of rational or scientific policymaking, indeed, it takes us back to efficiency, cost-benefit analysis, and the concept of willingness to pay.

The first objection assumes that every individual, if he commits no tort, that is, no harm for which the injured party is entitled to compensation, has a right to develop his property as he pleases, without regard to the larger goals or purposes of the community. This assumption might have some weight if people when they buy property have any reason to make it, but they do not. Settled legal doctrine has held for nearly a century that environmental statutes and ordinances, if they are arrived at openly and fairly and single out no individual or "suspect" class, may serve legitimate public ends. The freedom we have as citizens to pursue these ends through the political process balances and is perfectly consistent with our freedom as individuals to pursue our private interests by acquiring and disposing of goods. These freedoms conflict in specific circumstances; we have courts of law and well-entrenched conceptions of due process and equal justice by which to adjudicate those conflicts.

The Supreme Court, in a recent case, decided whether compensation must be paid to landowners who were prevented, by open space zoning, from developing intensively property they owned along a ridge overlooking San Francisco Bay. The Court, as might have been expected, held unanimously that the landowners were not entitled to payment. It reiterated the point that zoning to protect open space lies well within the police power and serves public purposes "which have long been recognized as legitimate."[40]

The second objection, which centers on the inevitability of cost-benefit analysis, confuses a consequence of a political decision with a condition. Let me explain. Those who support the cost-benefit approach believe that the doctrine of willingness to pay is not the outcome of public debate and political decisions; they argue, indeed, that willingness to pay should be a determining factor in those decisions. The reverse, however, is true. Our collective willingness to pay, whether as buyers or sellers, for a public good like education, environmental quality, or defense results from public decisionmaking; it is not a datum that enters or can affect it.

Occupational safety and health, for example, constitutes a public value insofar as it reflects on society as a whole and is something we collectively are ashamed of or take pride in. How much are we willing to pay for it? Plainly, society is willing to pay enough to limit to ten parts per million (ppm) benzene exposure in the workplace. The government set that limit long ago; it is generally accepted; no one has made a serious attempt to weaken it. Attempts to strengthen it, moreover, have failed after much litigation and debate. We can infer, then, that at the present time we are willing to pay to set the benzene standard at ten but not, say, at one ppm.

Similarly, we are willing to pay a lot for clean water and air. How do we know this? We know it because the Clean Water and Clean Air acts remain popular and are reauthorized or continued even though everyone understands that they involve tremendous social costs. Why does the citizenry overwhelmingly support these laws? Why, in other words, is it

willing to pay for them? The reason is not *itself* willingness to pay. The reason that people are willing to pay for clean air, let me repeat, is not that they are willing to pay for clean air. No; the reasons are aesthetic, ethical, cultural, historical, economic, and ideological; these reasons are discussed, on their merits, in the legislative history of the relevant laws. The one "value" that is not and need not be discussed is our willingness to pay for clean water and air, for this, of course, is precisely what the discussion is supposed to determine. Willingness to pay, in other words, is *not* a value or a *definition* of value or a *reason* to value anything. It is rather *the response we have to make*, collectively and individually, in order to acquire or to keep many of the things we do value *after* determining how much we value them. To find out what we are willing to pay for, then, we have to determine what we value, not the other way round.

Public officials debate and decide in public forums our societal priorities; as an automatic consequence, then, they decide as our representatives what we are willing to pay for. It is specious to suppose that willingness to pay is itself a value that can enter this discussion; it is the outcome of that discussion. There are people who believe, nevertheless, that willingness to pay is the reason that we are willing to pay, for example, for clean water and air. They also believe, perhaps, that the dormitive principle is the reason that opium puts you to sleep.

# IV.  COST-EFFECTIVENESS

Economists who are critical of the willingness-to-pay approach to public policy—there are many, of course—may contend, nevertheless, that market incentives offer *cost-effective* mechanisms by which environmental goals, once chosen, can be achieved. This recommendation appeals to common sense. Once we choose a target—cleaner air, for instance—why not choose a cost-effective means to hit it? Why not save time, trouble, and money?

## §8 MARKET STRATEGIES FOR ABATING POLLUTION

The most efficient way to achieve a given standard of air or water quality, in principle, may be a system of marketable air or water emission rights (rights to emit pollutants). The argument or rationale is clear. Bruce Yandle, professor of economics at Clemson University in South Carolina, puts it this way:

> Such a market would make it possible both to hold air emissions to a desired level and to allocate them to those who produced the greatest economic benefits to society. . . . Second, having to pay for air emission rights would make the value of air quality obvious to both buyers and sellers, thus leading to conservation and an efficient use of pollution control devices. . . . After all, by reducing emissions . . ., a firm could generate a saleable emission right. . . . Air quality would be maintained or even improved, efficiency enhanced, and social conflict reduced.[41]

A nationwide system of marketable pollution rights, however, confronts a major problem. Rights travel depending on who purchases them, but we want to control where pollution goes. We want to keep it from concentrating in any one area. Congress, moreover, sets higher air quality standards for some places (e.g., Yosemite) than for others (e.g., Los Angeles). The "costs" of a particular amount of pollution may vary, in addition, not only by place but also by time of day, altitude, season, wind direction, the proximity of pollutants with synergistic effects (for example, vanadium serves as a catalyst in producing acid rain), and so on. Thus, pollution rights would not be easily transferable. The government might sell them only for particular places or times. I shall return to this suggestion presently.

Under a system of marketable pollution rights, the government sets a limit on the total amount of pollution it will allow in an area and allows polluters to bid competitively for rights to some part of that total amount. Under a scheme of emissions taxes or charges, however, the government does not limit the amount of pollution but charges a tax or a fee for each additional unit. These charges could be made to reflect the differential costs of emissions, for example, by place, time, wind direction, and the like, as well as by amount. These charges could be combined, as is expedient, with areawide trading options (the "offset" concept), plant-wide trading options (the "bubble" concept), and temporal trading options (the "banking" concept). These schemes allow polluters to decrease discharges in one area or at one time or place in order to "offset" an increase at some other. Many stratagems such as these have been suggested to provide market incentives to make polluters reduce pollution.

If the government adopted a tax or a charge scheme for controlling emissions, it would face a formidable problem in determining how much to charge in order to achieve the air or water quality standards it sets. Fees could be determined arbitrarily and then adjusted on a trial-and-error basis, but industries are quickly "locked into" the control technologies they install, and thus they cannot easily adjust to rising and falling prices. The government may also have to assess fees in relation to the costs polluters could pay to abate pollution—and this is difficult. Accordingly, a limited auction system, rather than an effluent tax scheme, may be the most cost-effective strategy we can hope for. The economic literature fully and, I think, brilliantly discusses the relevant issues, to which I cannot do justice here. I shall limit myself to two general comments here, and list some of the best articles in the notes.[42]

First, those who advocate market incentives or strategies to reduce pollution do not, therefore, recommend that we rely on cost-benefit analysis to establish "optimal" levels of pollution. Rather, they propose cost-effective methods for meeting the standards we set politically or on ideological grounds. Thus, those who advocate a system of emission charges, for example, do not depend in any way upon an economic conception of our priorities; they need not refer to the conceptions of efficiency I have criticized in Parts II and III and shall criticize further in

Part V. The economists I have read are completely aware of this. They point out, in addition, that reducing pollution and improving environmental quality, for example air quality, while causally related, are logically different things. One does not necessarily produce a marginal unit of improved air quality by eliminating a marginal unit of a particular pollutant. The synergistic effects of pollutants are too complex to allow a simple one-to-one relationship between reducing emissions and improving air quality. Thus, cost-benefit or efficiency arguments about environmental quality lack any clear conceptual relationship with market incentives for controlling air or water pollution. None of the arguments I make in this essay against the efficiency norm in environmental policy, then, would apply to market incentives as means to achieve environmental goals in cost-effective ways.

Second, in spite of arguments that favor a market in transferable pollution rights, if only on a local and experimental basis, both Congress and the EPA have resisted it. In recent years, many public officials have come to regard economists as Scientific Policymakers of the sort I described and criticized earlier (§5–§6). Many of these officials have a tendency to think of Scientific Policymakers (a healthy tendency, I will say) as fascists. They think of economists, at best, as lobbyists for efficiency, a sort of special interest group, who would substitute cost-benefit analysis for the deeper political judgment of these officials themselves and, as a result, possibly put them out of their jobs. So there is a lot of hostility. This hostility does not stop at condemning "optimality" or "efficiency" as policy goals but spills over to affect anything that economists might recommend. This includes effluent taxes and marketable pollution rights—matters that have no conceptual connection with efficiency or with cost-benefit analysis.

The hostility politicians have directed against economists, while completely unfair, may seem understandable. Some economists who accept a view like Baxter's or Posner's (see I) have promoted a theory of public policy that would replace the citizen with the consumer—a theory, in other words, that conceives of us not as a nation united together in pursuing common ideals and aspirations but as individuals in a market competing for scarce resources. This theoretical approach (which has been largely adopted by the Reagan administration) would use economic analysis rather than the political process to determine the values we stand for as a nation and the extent to which we stand for those values. The idea that *all* economists are bent on replacing Constitutional processes with cost-benefit analysis, and thus replacing ethical with economic judgment, is of course, a misperception. In the following pages, I shall describe the extent of this misperception. I shall also explain how it has prevented public officials from properly assessing policies many economists recommend to meet politically set environmental objectives in cost-effective, that is, in money-saving ways. These recommendations, as we shall see, have nothing to do with a market ideology, efficiency, cost-benefit analysis, willingness to pay, or Scientific Policymaking. They are just thrifty and effective stratagems for meeting our national goals for the natural environment.

## §9 AN IMPORTANT SURVEY

In *What Price Incentives? Economists and the Environment*, Steven Kelman, a professor at the Kennedy School of Public Administration, describes a survey he conducted among public officials and others responsible for making national policy for the environment. The survey, conducted in 1978, found that very few participants in the policymaking process could speak knowledgeably about *cost-effectiveness* as an argument for effluent charges or taxes. Instead, most officials—whether they supported these market incentives or opposed them—associated cost-effectiveness arguments with the function of the "free market" and with efficiency arguments in general. They hardly saw the difference between cost-effectiveness and cost-benefit arguments.

The few policymakers who supported economic incentives, such as effluent taxes, to abate pollution did so because they saw this as a way to leave environmental policy to the market. The many who opposed these incentives, as a rule, also did so because they, too, confused these methods with an overall market approach to environmental quality. Many, including Karl Braithwaite and Leon Billings, two prominent Congressional committee staffers, used the survey as an occasion to exercise themselves against economists, who think "you get an automatic correctiveness by drawing in more market forces. They love the market, and they want to adjust the equation slightly for externalities so that the market can go ahead and run."[43]

Environmentalists responded to Kelman's survey also by directing invective against what they took to be the economic point of view. One asked: "How do you figure out a tax for contaminating my wife's milk?" Another said: "I'm not really fond of economists' tendency to be technocrats." The general spirit of the survey response can be judged by Kelman's brief interview with Leon Billings:

> Billings began by stating that "there is a basic philosophical difference between regulatory people and economists. Economists don't care whether you achieve a reduction of pollution. They don't really care, but we really do care. The economic approach is inequitable, because it permits a choice on the part of the polluter whether to spend on pollution control or on other things." Billings went on to say that the problem with economists was that "they worship things economic." Billings stated that he had "heard" the [cost-effectiveness] argument and added that "it may or may not be valid." He was not able to explain it. Instead, he used the question to express distaste for economists, whom he regarded as "zealots."[44]

Kelman summarizes the concerns expressed in the survey in four arguments. "Using economic incentives in environmental policy," he writes, "means bringing environmental quality into a system of markets and prices of which it previously has not been a part." Chiefly for that reason, the use of incentives (1) implies "indifference towards the motives of polluters . . ."; (2) "fails to make a statement stigmatizing polluting behavior"; (3) devalues by attaching a price to what one may consider "above" a market; and (4) may "produce a situation where wealthier people choose to pay the charge . . . while poorer people, to avoid the charge, are the ones to change their behavior."[45] Kelman observes that this last criticism, which concerns equality or justice, does not apply specifically to the use of effluent charges in environmental policy.[46]

## §10  A DEFENSE OF INCENTIVES

The problem, however, seems to be that none of these objections applies to the use of market incentives to achieve mandated environmental objectives in cost-effective ways. To see this, one must always keep in mind the distinction between *efficiency* and *cost-effectiveness*. In order to achieve an *efficient* level of pollution control, we would start with the discharges or sources that are the cheapest to clean up or to abate; we would then proceed until the cost of controlling the next unit of pollution equals the benefit, also measured in economic terms, of controlling it. The "marginal" cost of pollution abatement, we could then say, equals the "marginal" benefit. A *cost-effective* strategy also starts with the cheapest discharges to control but continues until an environmental standard is reached that may be set independently. Thus, it provides an economical means of reaching an objective but does not determine what that objective should be.

If we seek efficiency in setting environmental standards, then, I believe, we bring environmental quality into a system of markets and prices in which (I agree with Kelman) it does not belong. The Clean Air Act, the Water Pollution Control Act, and other laws avoid efficiency: They set standards on the basis of our self-perception and pride as a political community, not on the basis of our wants as self-interested consumers. This is as it should be. We need not abandon the pride we take in these standards, however, even if we allow ourselves to achieve them by cost-effective means. Nothing will be gained, certainly not environmental quality, by wasting money; we need not feel guilty, then, about achieving ideological objectives in the least costly ways.

One way to achieve cost-effectiveness in pollution abatement might be to establish a market in pollution "rights" such as I described in §8. Because of the problem I mentioned there, namely, our interest in achieving different standards at different places, such a market would have to be zoned into regions within which rights could be purchased or exchanged. We would probably still require some political oversight—for dangerous levels of effluent could develop in small areas within a larger region. At these levels, however, polluters would probably be restrained by common law, that is, by suits individuals could bring against them for damage pollution may cause to property and to health.

Under a regional system, each polluter will be required to purchase rights to discharge effluents in every area that those effluents affect. The polluter would then decide whether it is cheaper to purchase a right or to abate pollution. If the latter, the polluter may sell the right it owns to another polluter who cannot as cheaply control its discharges. Markets in each area would then reach a competitive equilibrium, which is to say, each right to discharge pollution would be owned by the polluter willing to pay the most for it; presumably, that polluter would otherwise have to pay the most to control its discharges. The number of pollution rights, of course, remains fixed; the government limits the pollution allowed in order to meet the regional standards it has set. Accordingly, such a regional or zoned market scheme could achieve these standards in the least costly ways.

Not all economists believe that the goals of environmental policy should be based on cost-benefit analysis; not all are lobbyists for efficiency or for Scientific Policymaking. Many or most are sensible to the fact that Americans have strong convictions about environmental quality as citizens—convictions we do not reveal in markets, where we simply buy the best and cheapest goods we can, but in the political process and in public opinion polls. Many economists share Kelman's distaste, indeed, for what he calls "the larger context of economic theory," which, if taken seriously, might substitute its own technocratic values (consumer satisfaction, wealth maximization) for the nobler and deeper aspirations with which we have traditionally associated ourselves as a society. Economists who agree with Kelman about the "larger context" have offered helpful and incisive analyses of particular policy problems. They have attempted not to usurp the power of political representatives to determine the goals of our nation; they have suggested, however, useful ways of meeting those goals. I include environmental objectives. The recommendations these economists make ought not to be rejected because economists are "technocrats" who see everything in terms of "a system of markets and prices." Many of these recommendations, on the contrary, show us how we can reach more of our national objectives by meeting each of them in less costly ways.

## V. ON "PRICING" FRAGILE VALUES

Throughout this essay, I have contrasted the values we reveal as individuals competing, as we do, in markets and the values we express as citizens in public opinion polls and through political action. Values of the first sort—those that characterize the self-interested consumer—have only the individual as their subject: They express *my* wants and needs. Values of the second sort—community-regarding or impersonal values— reflect my view not of my own interest but of the public interest; they express what I think is good not for me but for the community. These values are mine insofar as I regard myself as *one of us.*

I said in the last section that many or most economists recognize this distinction. Many would refrain, then, from identifying a market as an ideal instrument for policymaking—because markets are structured for us to make choices as self-interested individuals and not as community-regarding citizens. These economists would allow the political process to express our shared or community aspirations, for example, with respect to the environment. Then they suggest effective means for meeting those aspirations.

Some analysts and economists, however, believe that cost-benefit analysis can take the values, arguments, and convictions of citizens into account. These Scientific Policymakers treat these convictions (really, all opinions other than their own) not as ideas deserving a hearing, not, then, as views to be judged on the basis of the reasons that might be given for them in debate, but as wants or interests that should be priced. They try to figure out, therefore, how much citizens would be willing to pay for their beliefs and in this way, they evaluate them, according to their special conception of what value is. The primary technique they use is to ask citizens how much they are willing to pay for the satisfaction of knowing that the government has acted consistently with some principle, for example, to preserve wilderness. These analysts then suppose that they have an adequate "shadow" or hypothetical market estimate of the worth of what they call "fragile" values or "intangible" wants.

In the following pages I wish to exercise myself against this strategy. I believe that the political process, for all its flaws, provides a better forum for discussing and determining public values than can be found in the hypothetical markets some economists suggest for the purpose. I think it is better that we think about our values and argue them on their merits rather than that we try to price them "at the margin" instead.

## §11 CONSUMER DOLLARS AND CITIZEN "SATISFACTIONS"

Consider the following example. Recently, Interior Secretary James Watt has promised to give concessionaires a greater role in managing our national parks. These entrepreneurs know how to *sell* a park, to turn an unprofitable wilderness area into a money-making congeries of gas stations, golf courses, condominiums, bars, motels, restaurants, gift shops, and discos. The MCA corporation, producer of Muzak, already manages much of Yosemite National Park, and only strong legal constraints, now perhaps to be lifted, have prevented it from integrating that area into its entertainment and amusement empire.[47] One could speculate that wildlife in our national parks, then, might be replaced by actors disguised as various Disney characters. Surely consumers—especially those with children—would be willing to pay more to experience Bambi than to see an ordinary deer. Tourists from every state come to view Bugs Bunny and Donald Duck at Disneyland; why not at Sequoia National Park? Why are we wasting money on preservation when we could make money by basing our wilderness policy on Loony Toons instead?

The problem, as many people point out, is this. Markets reveal our consumer interests, but they often fail to reveal our countervailing views and concerns as citizens. To be sure, I would visit a national park only if I found a warm bed and a cold beer (and maybe Bambi) waiting for me: I'm soft and decadent. The Loony Toons experience, then, is probably what I would pay for as a consumer. Yet, as an American, I believe that the nation owes more to wilderness than to turn it into an amusement park; I believe in preservation. Accordingly, the things I pay for in markets do not necessarily or even usually represent the values I want my representatives to protect in legislation.

Many economists recognize this "schizophrenia" between the consumer and the citizen. They recognize that no market puts a price on the protection of an endangered species, for example, or on the pride we take in *not* exploiting a wilderness. Many of us are concerned with the fate of the whales—and this has nothing to do with maximizing the sustained yield of blubber. Most of us recognize that concerns of this sort properly belong in the political process: Our legislatures are supposed to deal with our ideological or community-regarding values. Yet there are some technocrats, as I mentioned, who believe that matters such as these —matters in which we determine our character, indeed, our identity as a nation—can be brought into cost-benefit thinking. They would then establish a surrogate or hypothetical market for these "soft variables" or "intangible benefits" by asking individuals how much they are willing to pay, for example, to know (or at least to think) that the wilderness is preserved.

I have made a number of criticisms of cost-benefit analysis already (see Parts II and III); I should like to add two criticisms of this particular use of it. First, this use allows economists to justify virtually any policy *or its opposite*, since it is easy enough to find "fragile values," "intangibles," and "moralisms" to support almost any position. Aaron Wildavsky, professor of political science at the University of California, Berkeley, once made the point that the "new economics," in which citizen opinion serves as a "fudge" or "finagle" factor, has become a kind of storytelling. "If the old economics will not let you have what you know is right, it follows that a new economics is evidently needed. The term *new economics of environmental resources* is used to designate an emerging trend and permits economists to avoid direct confrontation with political problems by bringing in aesthetic factors to make economic analysis come out 'right.'"[48]

Because the "shadow" pricing of "intangibles" functions as a large, indeed, inexhaustible, fudge factor, economists who engage in it are able to support, on what then seem "scientific" grounds, environmental causes that might otherwise have failed a cost-benefit test. It is to be emphasized in this respect that cost-benefit analysis, thus expanded, could serve the goals of environmentalism at least as much as it would work against them. During the 1960s and 1970s, indeed, economic arguments proved to be a mainstay of the environmental movement; environmentalists were the first to espouse them. Only recently has the tide turned. The environmental movement, which has long had powerful friends among economists, now fears it has enemies as well.

Second, the use of cost-benefit analysis to measure our political or ideological convictions rests on what philosophers call a category-mistake. This is a mistake one makes in describing an object in terms that do not appropriately apply to it, as when one says that the square root of two is blue. It is nonsense to test the worth of an ideal or a principle by asking what people are willing to pay for it. As well try to establish the truth of a theorem by asking what it is worth, in economic terms, to mathematicians. Nobody asks economists how much they are willing to pay for their view that cost-benefit analysis should form the basis of regulatory policy. No, the views of economists are supposed to be judged on their merits, not priced at the margin. Why shouldn't this courtesy extend to contrary opinions as well?

I have now attempted to describe some of the conceptual and moral shortcomings of cost-benefit analysis as it may be used to establish our goals as a society. I have argued that we cannot determine our goals as a society by determining how much people are willing to pay individually for this policy or that. (How much are technocrats willing to pay, as individuals, for their cherished value of efficiency?) We must determine collectively, through responsible argument and debate, what we believe in and, therefore, what we are willing to pay for as a society. What is crucial is the reasons or arguments citizens may give to convince other citizens that we together should attempt certain goals or to pursue certain aspirations. The appropriateness or merit of those aspirations and goals are no more to be determined by cost-benefit analysis than are the truths of mathematics or the reasonableness of competing economic theories.

## §12 MARKETS ARE NOT THE MEASURE OF ALL THINGS

The Reagan administration has called for cost-benefit analysis to justify every major regulation put forward by any federal department or agency. How bad is that? At one level, it is not too bad: It may be viewed as a sort of jobs bill ("make work") for economists. All it does is to add another level to bureaucracy, another level of paperwork, forcing competing sides on a policy question to state their arguments in terms of "willingness to pay." This slows things down in the agencies considerably, but they are pretty much frozen anyway. The executive order I described merely furthers the administration's general goal of substituting regulatory relief for regulatory reform.

At another level, the insistence on cost-benefit analysis requires policymakers to use a formula rather than their heads and this demeans them as it demeans us as citizens. It prevents us from achieving a certain kind of self-determination that a democracy is supposed to provide; it prevents us from deciding who we are not just what we want. Let me explain.

Economists who use cost-benefit analysis to ascertain the price of "fragile values," especially, community-regarding beliefs or opinions, include in their concept of economic efficiency not only values for which markets exist but even values for which no market exists and none is appropriate. For example, if Jack and Jill want to marry, a world in which they do marry, *ceteris paribus*, is more efficient in this sense than one in which they do not. Were Jill to marry John, this could count as an externality to Jack, even though this "externality" has nothing to do with a market. Economists who widen the concept of an externality to include *anything* that is unpriced employ their ingenuity by inventing surrogate markets. They may ask, therefore, how much you are willing to pay for a wilderness policy in which you have no marketable interest as a consumer but of which you approve for moral or aesthetic reasons. This is supposed to measure the value of something, perhaps the policy, perhaps the approval, perhaps the reasons. It is easy for economists who go this route to argue that anything that is a moral or an aesthetic failure is a market failure as well.

Cost-benefit analysis becomes a ludicrous exercise when it extends the concept of a market failure, in this way, to include mistakes, shortcomings, and idiocies of all kinds. We do not use markets to determine the number of planets. Why should we devise markets, then, to establish whether an environmental policy makes cultural, aesthetic, or moral sense? People have ideas; they have beliefs they can defend; they have arguments to offer concerning the right and wrong way to treat wilderness, wildlife, rivers, and lakes. How can surrogate markets, however ingenious, determine whether these beliefs are true or whether these arguments are sound? Markets provide a forum for the exchange of commodities not the exchange of ideas. To use market analysis is not to find a neutral way to choose among values but to insist upon efficiency, that is, a particular value. It is to respect only one set of opinions—those put forward by certain economists—and to provide a shadow price to all the rest.

It is a mistake to turn the management of our national parks over to hucksters. It is not, however, an economic mistake. It is another kind of mistake. It is a moral failure, an aesthetic failure, a cultural failure, but it is not a market failure. There is simply no relevant market to have failed. As well suppose that we could correct Secretary Watt's spelling mistakes as his aesthetic and moral mistakes by applying cost-benefit analysis. As well suppose that by devising surrogate markets we could correct his errors in arithemetic or improve his tennis. There is a right and a wrong way to spell, to add figures, or to stroke a backhand, and it has nothing to do with pricing costs and benefits. Similarly, there is a right and a wrong way to manage the national parks. The right thing to do is to preserve our incredible heritage as an aesthetic and natural monument; the wrong thing to do is to make it a big drive-in for Winnebagos. This has nothing to do with what turns a social profit or maximizes wealth or satisfies aggregate consumer demand. It has to do with our history, culture, and self-perception as a nation.

More fundamentally, it has to do with our *identity* as Americans and as persons. The technocratic economist has his or her own view of what we are, that is, what lies in our essential nature. Economic theory describes us all as self-interested individualists intent on maximizing the satisfaction of our personal preferences. For these economists, there is nothing more to *being* a person and certainly nothing more to *being* an American than that. They have your number. They know what you are. They describe you as "irrational" if you act in any other way. Then they help you achieve your true identity, that is, to realize your potential as what you are, namely, a consumer. They help you get the things you are willing to pay for, that is, whatever items you happen to want to buy.

Now, many of us have a very different view of what we are essentially as persons and as citizens. First, as persons, we do not think that we are essentially consumers; we insist on loyalty and love of a kind that markets demean and for which they are inappropriate. We also cherish characteristics like courage and intelligence and warmth and imaginativeness and a score of other traits that no one can sell or buy. We want to live in a society in which these traits flourish and in which people can realize themselves by realizing them. This has nothing to do with efficiency or with willingness to pay.

As Americans, moreover, we share and strive to be worthy of an identity—of a national character—before we consider our interests or our wants. This is not the identity certain technocrats prescribe; we do not see ourselves as a nation of consumers. Rather, we see ourselves as a nation called upon, in part, to appreciate and to preserve a fabulous natural heritage and to pass it on reasonably undisturbed to future generations. This is not a question of what we *want*; it is not exactly a question of what we *believe in*; it is a statement of what we *are*. Perhaps we should be different: Perhaps we should be consumers, self-interested maximizers, competitors for scarce resources within markets. But this must be argued, not simply accepted on an economist's say so. Why should we accept that image of ourselves? Why can't we strive for a more edifying and more humane conception of what we are as persons and as a nation?

When we argue against the technocratic thinking that seems to have swept the present administration, we need not, though we may, rest our objections on the environmental degradation likely to result. We should also object to *our* degradation as persons and as a nation. We will object as long as we regard ourselves as something other than bundles of preferences in search of a perfect market. We will fight off cost-benefit analysis as long as we think we have something to say about our national policy as citizens and not merely something to pay as consumers. The political rights we have under the Constitution, however, allow this objection—this disgust—to be forcefully expressed. Citizens in a participatory democracy such as ours have no one to blame, every four years, but themselves.

At the same time, the ire we may feel should not blind us to the many advantages of economic analysis when it is used to help us achieve our

goals in effective and thrifty ways—for we have had enough of throwing money away just for the symbolic value of doing so. Thus, if scrubbers, for example, are not a cost-effective way of reducing air pollution, we should be willing to spend less, for example, by burning cleaner coal. We should let the economist help us so that we can achieve more of the goals for which, after all, we must pay.

## VI. CONCLUSION

In this essay, I have argued that cost-benefit analysis does not provide an acceptable criterion for setting environmental policy and law. It may reflect at the collective level some of the desires and preferences that motivate us as individuals, but that is not necessarily what we want our collective or political choices to express. Rather, we have values or commitments as citizens that often contradict the preferences or interests we would pursue as individuals. Cost-benefit analysis either ignores these values (as it should, whereupon it can be ignored) or it ridicules and distorts them by according them a "shadow" or imaginary market price (as it should not, whereupon we must expose its deficiencies rather than ignore them).

These values we cherish as citizens express not just what we want collectively but what we think we are: We use them to reveal to ourselves and to others what we stand for and how we perceive ourselves as a nation. These values are not merely chosen; rather they constitute and identify we who choose. To be sure, we can constitute ourselves not as a national political community but as a market—but this is what we would never do. To think of ourselves in market terms—to think we are ruled by cost-benefit analysis and not by law—is to degrade ourselves and to abandon our particular character and history and future as a nation. To say this, however, is to speak as with a voice from a wilderness. Wilderness, rivers, estuaries, bays, forests, and farms have voices: They express our shared values and transmit them. They speak to us and for us. And when the wilderness disappears, voices from it disappear as well.

## NOTES

1. William Baxter, *People or Penguins: The Case for Optimal Pollution* (New York: Columbia University Press, 1974), 17.
2. Richard Posner, *Economic Analysis of Law* (Boston: Little Brown, 1972), 4. Economic texts on environmental quality generally adopt this criterion of value. For example, E. J. Mishan, *Cost-Benefit Analysis* (New York: Praeger, 1976), 24. ("In economics, in 'normative' or allocative economics at least, the worth of a thing to a person is determined simply by what a person is willing to pay for it.") See also A. Freeman, III, et al., *The Eco-*

*nomics of Environmental Policy* (New York: John Wiley, 1973), 23. ("In principle, the ultimate measure of environmental quality is the value people place on these . . . services or their willingness to pay.")

3.    Arthur Okun, *Equality and Efficiency: The Big Tradeoff* (Washington, D.C.: Brookings Institution, 1975), 2.

4.    Larry Ruff, "The Economic Common Sense of Pollution," in *Microeconomics: Selected Readings* (2nd ed. E. Mansfield ed. 1975), 498.

5.    *Ibid*, 500–1.

6.    46 Federal Register 13,193 (1981). The order carries the title "Federal Regulation." For a discussion of the separation of powers questions raised by the order, see M. Rosenberg, "Beyond the Limits of Executive Power: Presidential Control of Agency Rulemaking Under Executive Order 12,291," *Michigan Law Review* 80 (1981) and "Symposium: Cost-Benefit Analysis and Agency Decision-Making: An Analysis of Executive Order No. 12,291" *Arizona Law Review* 23 (1981).

7.    M. Baram, "Cost-Benefit Analysis: An Inadequate Basis for Health, Safety, and Environmental Regulatory Decisionmaking," *Ecology Law Quarterly* 8 (1980):473.

8.    For a discussion of the history of cost-benefit analysis in the Flood Control Act of 1939 and subsequent legislation, see Peter Steiner, "Public Expenditure Budgeting," in *The Economics of Public Finance*, Alan Blinder, et al., eds. (Washington, D.C.: Brookings Institution, 1974), esp. pp. 331ff.

9.    E. J. Mishan, *Elements of Cost-Benefit Analysis* (London: Allen and Unwin, 1971), 13.

10.    33 U.S.C. §1311(b)(1)(A) (1976).

11.    Public Law No. 93-205, 87 Stat. 844 (codified at 16 U.S.C. §§1531–1543). I have argued for this thesis in M. Sagoff, "On the Preservation of Species," *Columbia Journal of Environmental Law* 33 (Fall 1980):33–67.

12.    42 U.S.C. §7472 (Supp. II 1978).

13.    29 U.S.C. §655(b)(5) (1976).

14.    549 F. 2d 1064 at 1074 (6th Cir. 1977), affid. 547 U.S. 153 (1978) (quoting *West Virginia Div. of Isaak Walton League, Inc.* v. *Butts*, 522 F. 2d 945, 955 (4th Cir. 1975)).

15.    For a discussion of the "exit" and "voice" options in the expression of values, see S. O. Hirschman, *Exit, Voice, and Loyalty* (Cambridge, Mass.: Harvard University Press, 1970), and S. O. Hirschman, *Shifting Involvements: Private Interest and Public Action* (Princeton, N.J.: Princeton University Press, 1982).

16.    549 F. 2d 1074 (6th Cir. 1977). The Supreme Court, in reviewing this case, affirmed that Congress may enact legislation to serve purposes other than that of correcting market failure or making benefits exceed costs. *TVA* v. *Hill*, 437 U.S. 153, 187–88 (1978).

17.    Industrial Union Dept., *AFL–CIO* v. *American Petroleum Inst.* 448 U.S. 607 (1980).

18.    *American Textile Mfgrs. Inst.* v. *Donovan*, 101 S. Ct. 2478 (1981).

19.    For a study of these issues, at an advanced and technical level, see Richard Stewart and Cass Sunstein, "Public Programs and Private Rights," *Harvard Law Review* 95 (6) (1982):1193–1322.

20.    Senate Bill No. 1080, 97th Congress.

21.    §624.

22.    H. R. 745, 97th Congress.

23.    Baxter, *People or Penguins*, 27.

24.    In a television interview a resident of the North End of Boston, refusing to move from her home, said spontaneously: "We are not among those who, spawned from nothing, have become unseemly rich." The remark seems worth recording.

25. See U. S. Council on Environmental Quality, *Public Opinion on Natural Environmental Issues* (1980).

26. A plurality of respondents to a major Resources for the Future poll thought that environmental protection is too important to *consider* costs. *Ibid.*, 3.

27. For discussion of this example, see Ronald Dworkin, "Liberalism," in *Public and Private Morality*, Stuart Hampshire, ed. (Cambridge, England: Cambridge University Press, 1978), 141.

28. David Hume, *A Treatise of Human Nature* bk. 3, pt. 2, sec. 1. In L. A. Selby-Bigge (ed.), (Oxford: Oxford University Press, 1978), 482. For discussion of hysteresis see Russell Hardin, *Collective Action* (Baltimore: Resources for the Future, 1982), 82.

29. Bruce Ackerman, *Private Property and the Constitution* (New Haven: Yale University Press, 1977), 9.

30. *Ibid.*, 10.

31. For discussion, see E. F. Roberts, "The Right to a Decent Environment: $E = MC^2$: Environment Equals Man Times the Courts Redoubling Their Efforts," *Cornell Law Review* 55 (May 1970). See also Fred Bosselman, et al., *The Taking Issue* (Washington, D.C.: U.S. Government Printing Office, 1976).

32. *Private Property*, 10–11.

33. *Ibid.*, 28.

34. *Ibid.*, 11.

35. *Ibid.*, 34: italics removed.

36. *Ibid.*, 41.

37. *Ibid.*, 78.

38. *Ibid.*, 34.

39. Frank Michelman argues that utilitarian satisfactions, when they become this speculative or general, deteriorate into "useless mush." See his "Norms and Normality in the Economic Theory of Law," *Minnesota Law Review*, 62 (1978), esp. 1037.

40. *Agins* v. *City of Tibouron* 14 ERC 1555 at 1558 (1980).

41. Bruce Yandle, "The Emerging Market in Air Pollution Rights," *Regulation*, Vol. 2, No. 4 (July/August 1978):21–29.

42. See Clifford S. Russell, "What Can We Get from Effluent Charges?" *Policy Analysis* 5 (Spring 1979):155–180; "Technology-Based Emission and Effluent Standards and the Achievement of Ambient Environment Objectives," *Yale Law Journal* 91 (1982):792–813; Susan Rose-Ackerman, "Effluent Charges: A Critique," *Canadian Journal of Economics* 6 (1973): 513–528; Laurens Rhinelander, "The Bubble Concept: A Pragmatic Approach to Regulation Under the Clean Air Act," *Virginia Journal of Natural Resources Law* 1 (1981):177–215; and many others.

43. Quoted by Steven Kelman, *What Price Incentives? Economists and the Environment* (Boston: Auburn House, 1981), 103.

44. *Ibid.*, 102–103.

45. *Ibid.*, 27–28.

46. *Ibid.*, 28.

47. See J. Sax, *Mountains Without Handrails* (Michigan: University of Michigan Press, 1980), 73–75.

48. A. Wildavsky, "Aesthetic Power or the Triumph of the Sensitive Minority over the Vulgar Mass," reprinted in *Pollution and Public Policy: A Book of Readings*, ed. P. Paulsen and R. Denhardt, pp. 36–47, see esp. p. 38 (1973). The article was originally published in *Daedalus*, vol. 96 (1967): 1115–1128.

# SUGGESTIONS FOR FURTHER READING

Further readings are mentioned below in connection with the section (§) of the essay to which they are pertinent.

§1.   For the distinction between cost-benefit and cost-effectiveness analysis, see Michael Baram, "Cost-Benefit Analysis: An Inadequate Basis for Health, Safety, and Environmental Regulatory Decisionmaking," *Ecology Law Quartery* 8 (1980). For discussion of Executive Order 12,291, see "Symposium: Cost Benefit Analysis and Agency Rulemaking: An Analysis of Executive Order 12, 291," *Arizona Law Review* 23 (1981). Resources for the Future, an organization in Washington that supports economic research into environmental issues, has issued a series of books detailing the cost-benefit approach to public policy. See, for example, A. Freeman, R. Haveman, and A. Kneese, *The Economics of Environmental Policy* (Baltimore, Md.: RFF and Johns Hopkins, 1973).

§2.   Those wishing to see how the arguments developed here affect occupational safety and health should read Mark MacCarthy, "A Review of Some Normative and Conceptual Issues in Occupational Safety and Health," *Boston College Environmental Affairs Law Review* 9 (1981–82). Anyone wanting to compare New Deal regulation with regulation today should see Bruce Ackerman and William Hassler, *Clean Coal/Dirty Air* (New Haven: Yale University Press, 1981), and Ellis Hawley, *The New Deal and the Problem of Monopoly* (Princeton, N.J.: Princeton University Press, 1966), pts. I, II.

§3.   Basic essays concerning the "bid-asked" problem include: Duncan Kennedy, "Cost-Benefit Analysis of Entitlement Problems: A Critique," *Stanford Law Review* 33 (1981); G. Edwin Baker, "The Ideology of the Economic Analysis of Law," *Philosophy & Public Affairs* 5 (1975); and Mark Kelman, "Consumption Theory, Production Theory, and Ideology in the Case Theorem," *Southern California Law Review* 52 (1979).

§§4,5.   Good studies of the "takings" question, just compensation, and environmental zoning include: Bruce Ackerman, ed., *Economic Foundations of Property Law* (Boston: Little, Brown, 1975); Fred Bosselman et al., *The Taking Issue* (Washington, D.C.: U.S. Government Printing Office, 1971); and Fred Bosselman and David Callies, *The Quiet Revolution in Land Use Control* (Washington, D.C.: U.S. Government Printing Office, 1973).

§§6,7.   Theodore Lowi criticizes liberal political theory on the grounds that it advocates "policy without law" and thus rests on a comprehensive view of policymaking not found in the Constitution. See his *The End of Liberalism* (New York: Norton, 1979, 1969), esp. pp. 92–126, 298–313. On the same subject, see Kenneth Culp Davis, *Discretionary Justice: A Preliminary Inquiry* (Baton Rouge: LSU Press, 1969); J. Skelly Wright, "Beyond Discretionary Justice," *Yale Law Journal* 81 (1972); and Louis Jaffe, "The Illusion of the Ideal Administration," *Harvard Law Review* 86 (1973).

§§8,9,10.   For a survey of the literature and a defense of the conclusion that "A zoned pollution rights scheme should replace the current technology-based emission and effluent standards," see Note 42, "Technology-Based Emission and Effluent Standards and the Achievement of Ambient Environmental Objectives," *Yale Law Journal* 91 (1982).

§§11,12.   These arguments are developed further, with extensive citations to the literature, in Mark Sagoff, "Economic Theory and Environmental Law," *Michigan Law Review* 79 (1981), and "We Have Met the Enemy and He Is Us *or* Conflict and Contradiction in Environmental Law," *Environmental Law* 12 (1982).

6

# Troubled Waters: Global Justice and Ocean Resources

## ROBERT L. SIMON

## I. THE SEA AROUND US

### §1 INTRODUCTION

Vast areas of the earth are rich in mineral deposits and other natural resources but lie outside the boundaries of sovereign states. For example, the value of resources believed to lie locked in the Antarctic continent is thought to be enormous. Equally valuable minerals may be discovered someday in accessible regions of outer space. Of special interest today, valuable nodules of manganese, copper, nickel, and cobalt lie in the deep sea bed. Already, mining consortiums are developing the technology and making the plans for extracting these mineral treasures. In a world where resources may grow increasingly scarce, the value of the mineral nodules of the ocean floor is potentially huge. The resources that may someday be extracted can be of enormous significance for us all. Not only will an increased supply help hold down world prices, thereby lowering the costs of our own purchases; in addition, as other sources of supply run dry, these new resources may become vital links in the technological chain that supports our standard of living. Perhaps most important, revenues from deep sea mining may be a significant element in an emerging New International Economic Order designed to focus upon and help improve the economic status of developing Third World nations.

It is important to keep in mind the magnitude of both the resources at stake and the technological problems which have to be overcome to actually get them. By some estimates, vast areas of the Pacific floor are covered by manganese nodules. This includes not only the continental shelves, with depths of more than 200 meters, but also the ocean deep, with depths of over 1,000 meters. Clearly, the pressure caused by tons of water above the ocean floor is tremendous.

The technology that mining companies develop for undersea operations is of crucial importance. According to one proposal a mining machine will crawl along the sea floor. It will rake up nodules and bottom material using a rakelike scoop. Then a conveyor will carry the nodules through a high-pressure spray which will flush off clay and other useless material. Nodules will then be crushed and sent through a special buffer-type machine which will pump them at a planned rate to a mining ship on the surface.[1] The costs of planning and operating such complicated operations, as well as that of designing and building the necessary technology, are very great.

Beyond these obvious technological challenges looms a less obvious but no less real political one. In the absence of a stable political framework, developers may not be willing to make the long-term commitment necessary for deep sea mining. According to some estimates, it may take mining companies up to twenty years to recoup their initial investment in setting up just one mining operation at a particular site.[2] Without reasonable assurances of political stability for decades to come, few banks or lending agencies are likely to make the huge investments that are required.

Moreover, deep sea mining may be of serious ecological concern. Will changes in the deep sea environment alter delicate balances which enable forms of ocean life to survive? Does potential danger to species which inhabit the ocean threaten vital ecological chains on which we all depend? Is the ocean floor a wilderness of intrinsic value that should be preserved untouched by human hands or technology? Is it permissible for mining companies or even international agencies to extract treasures from the ocean floor without adequate concern for ecological considerations? Who should have the responsibility of deciding when adequate ecological safeguards are in place? Although these questions address important ecological concerns, they clearly touch on fundamental issues of international politics as well.

There is wide disagreement among the nations of the world about who should control deep sea resources and over who should profit from their extraction. As we will see, debates about natural resources lying outside national boundaries raise fundamental questions of global justice and equity.

## §2  GLOBAL JUSTICE AND THE LAW OF THE SEA: SOME QUESTIONS

What principles of justice apply to the acquisition and distribution of natural resources which lie outside national boundaries? At least two views are worth considering. According to the first, the deep sea bed is a "commons" in a *strong* sense. In this interpretation, every person on the globe is an equal owner of all the resources to be found in the deep sea bed and is entitled to an equitable share of the benefits that deep sea mining might produce. Such a view is endorsed by the vast majority of the nations of the world who since at least 1973 have been participating in the United Nations Conference on the Law of the Sea and who signed the Law of the Sea Treaty in December 1982.[3]

In the second view, the deep sea bed is a commons only in a *weak* sense, according to which only those who actually appropriate the resources found there are entitled to the resulting benefits.[4] This second interpretation of the idea of the commons seems to be that of the Reagan administration, which has refused to sign the Law of the Sea Treaty that emerged from long years of negotiations among the nations of the world.

The dispute over rights to resources in the deep sea bed is part of a broader dispute over the obligations of the more affluent developed nations to the developing states of the Third World. The developing nations have been arguing in the United Nations and other forums for the institution of a New International Economic Order, which would redistribute wealth from the affluent developed nations to the Third World. In view of the severe deprivation and suffering that are endemic to many developing nations, their claims warrant the most serious consideration. Using as yet unappropriated natural resources for the relief of the worst-off peoples of the globe may be a reasonable first step toward the creation of what many would regard as a more equitable world order. Thus, the question of who should own the resources of the deep sea bed impinges directly on what may be the central moral issue of our time: how to address the problems of starvation, deprivation, and underdevelopment that blight the lives of countless millions throughout the globe.

The Law of the Sea Treaty, which emerged from the United Nations Law of the Sea Conference, at least purports to deal with issues of global justice. While it does not address ecological concerns in depth, Treaty advocates claim that it views the deep sea bed as "the common heritage of mankind" in the strong sense: Every person is an equal owner and development is to benefit all humanity. Whether the actual provisions of the Treaty are in accord with this strong sense of "common ownership" is a point that will be discussed in §14.

The United States has refused to sign the Treaty. Some proponents of the American position argue that the deep sea bed is a commons only in the weak sense of being available to anyone who can actually develop it, while others, such as *New York Times* columnist William Safire, have referred to the Treaty as a "sellout," arguing not only that it violates rights of the developers but also that it harms American national interests without making any compensating contribution to global equity to balance the scales.[5] Other critics of the Treaty raise political doubts about whether the West would have adequate voice in the international arrangements for development which the Treaty would create and over whether unfriendly groups, such as the Palestine Liberation Organization (PLO), might share in the benefits. Should the United States have joined the majority of other nations and signed the Treaty? Is there a principled basis for our rejection of the Treaty or does rejection signify only a desire for profit even at the expense of global justice?

This paper explores the issue of what principles of justice apply to the acquisition and distribution of resources, such as those lying in the deep sea bed, which are found outside national boundaries. In Parts II, III and IV of this paper, we will examine the concept of global justice, consider arguments that "justice" has no application to international affairs, and then go on to investigate whether the deep sea bed is a universal common, and, if so, whether in the strong or weak sense. Finally, in Part V, we will assess the United States government's rejection of the Law of the Sea Treaty in light of our overall discussion.

## II. JUSTICE AND INTERNATIONAL AFFAIRS

### §3 SOCIAL JUSTICE AND GLOBAL JUSTICE

In his widely discussed monumental work, A *Theory of Justice*, John Rawls of Harvard University writes:

> Justice is the first virtue of social institutions as truth is of systems of thought. . . . Each person possesses an inviolability founded on justice that even the welfare of society as a whole cannot override. For this reason justice denies that the loss of freedom for some is made right by a greater good shared by others. . . . Therefore, . . . the rights secured by justice are not subject to political bargaining or the calculus of social interests.[6]

Rawls correctly identifies *social* justice with the proper acknowledgment of rights and duties within society. Social justice assigns people what they are due, not what it is in the overall social interest to give them. For example, in the context of the grading system in American universities, justice requires giving students the grades they deserve or have earned, even though on some particular occasion, more overall happiness might be achieved if a student is shown mercy and given a better grade than is warranted by the quality of the work the student has done.

Often, proponents of different ideological positions will appeal to competing conceptions of justice. However, in appealing to conceptions of *justice* rather than some other moral value, their concern is with what is owed to persons as a matter of right, fairness, or entitlement as opposed to what it is in the public interest to grant or what considerations of kindness or charity might incline us to provide. Thus, people with different conceptions of social justice can agree with Rawls when he maintains that "justice is the first virtue of social institutions."

However, this point of agreement contains two assumptions which need to be questioned before we consider who may justly control undersea resources. First, it might be assumed, although not necessarily by Rawls, that justice is a virtue only of social institutions, in which case questions of justice can arise *only within* particular societies. Second, it might be assumed that the only moral agents of concern from the perspective of justice are *individual persons*.

Both assumptions pose problems given our interest in global justice. If justice applies only within and not between societies, or if only individuals and not states or corporations can act justly or unjustly, then the issues of just acquisition and distribution of unowned natural resources cannot arise.

Persons who accept the view called *political realism* deny that moral considerations, including those of justice, can or should apply beyond the bounds of particular societies. Political realism should be distinguished from general skepticism about morality. The skeptic denies that any moral principles or judgments can be known or warranted. The political realist, however, does not deny and may even insist on the validity of moral principles within particular societies. The realist maintains only that morality has no legitimate application in international relations. If the realist is correct, our inquiry into global justice and natural resources is pointless, for there is and can be no such thing as global justice. We need to begin, then, by considering the case for political realism itself.

## §4  THE CHALLENGE OF REALISM

Although so-called realism in international affairs often is associated with contemporary figures such as the late Hans Morganthau, a distinguished political scientist, it has a long history. Indeed, perhaps the classic example of the effect of realist assumptions on policy is from the writings of the ancient Greek historian, Thucydides.

In his *History of the Peloponnesian War*, Thucydides describes the "Melian dialogue" between the generals of imperial Athens and the leaders of Melos, an isolated island colony of Sparta. The Athenians sought fealty from Melos. When the Melians refused to submit, "the Athenians put them to it by wasting of their lands."[7] In Thucydides's account of the dialogue between the two sides, the Athenian generals put moral considerations to the side. The reality according to the generals is, "They that have . . . power exact as much as they can, and the weak yield to such conditions as they can get."[8] The Melians refuse to surrender until forced to yield by force of arms. Afterward, Thucydides writes, "the Athenians . . . slew all the men of military age, made slaves of the women and children; and inhabited the place with a colony" of their own.[9]

Perhaps the barbarous treatment of the Melians by the Athenians is sufficient to discredit political realism. We condemn the behavior of the Athenians, which we could not coherently do if moral considerations had no application to international affairs.

While this sort of quick response to political realism is not without force, a defender of realism doubtless would object that we have begged the question by assuming that the condemnation of the Athenians is actually coherent. Accordingly, while we cannot undertake an exhaustive analysis of realism here, it will prove useful to investigate the major presuppositions of realism in some depth in order to assure ourselves that the central question has not been begged.

## §5 CAN NATIONS ACT?

If moral judgments can be made in international affairs, to whom do such judgments apply? It might be thought that moral judgments can apply only to individual persons. Hence, one might conclude that since international affairs involve relationships among nations, not persons, moral judgments simply are inapplicable at the international level.

However, this argument is dubious for at least two reasons. First of all, even if nations are not moral agents, it does not follow that morality does not apply in international affairs. The officials who run national governments and the leaders of nations are individual persons. There is no more reason to think their conduct in international affairs is immune to moral evaluation than there is to think their conduct in domestic affairs is immune to moral scrutiny. Accordingly, to the extent that the behavior of nations is nothing over and above the behavior of individual persons, the argument that there are no moral agents in international affairs fails.

Moreover, there are good reasons for viewing nations as moral agents in a collective sense. This does not mean that nations are something over and above the people and practices that constitute them. It does imply that it is intelligible to attribute behavior to a collective in cases where it cannot be broken down and attributed to individual constituents.

For example, if a sports fan claims that the basketball team played poorly, he may not mean that any specifiable individuals played poorly. Instead, it is quite common to hear fans explain, "All the individual players played decent individual games, but they just didn't mesh as a team." Such fans need not be committed to the questionable metaphysical view that a team is more than the players who make it up. Rather, such fans may be viewing the individuals who make up the team not from the perspective of individual performance, but of team success. From that perspective, the claim about the team may be justified, even if the person who asserts it is unable to explain it in terms of individual performance. It is not that the team is "more" than its members. Rather, it is that the criteria for assessing *team* performance may be logically independent of those for assessing *individual* performance.

Just as we may refer to teams as agents, we also may refer to other organized collectives, such as clubs, corporations, and even nations as agents. Thus, claims such as "Britain acted decisively during the Falkland crisis" seem intelligible and coherent. Such a statement need not entail that any specifiable Britons acted decisively as individuals let alone that each and every Briton acted decisively. Rather, it is Britons in their official roles as leaders who made institutions work in such a way that decisive *collective* action took place. We have seen that evaluating the performance of the basketball team may require judgment from a perspective different from that for evaluation of individual performance. Similarly, we may evaluate from the point of view of collective national institutions, national interests, and national aspirations as well as from the point of view of the individual person.

Indeed, some of the most prominent of the realists, such as Hans Morganthau, have argued that the postulate "Nations act to secure their perceived self interest" is invaluable in explaining and predicting the behavior of states.[10] But if we can make intelligible claims about nations acting in pursuit of their interests, we surely can also make intelligible claims about their behavior in other respects as well. In particular, moral judgments about the behavior of nations seem no less coherent than prudential judgments about the efficiency of their pursuit of self-interest.

Accordingly, if, as the realists themselves acknowledge, it is plausible to think that nations can be treated as agents for the purpose of making *prudential* judgments about how efficiently they pursue national interests, it is equally plausible to think they can be thought of as *moral* agents also. If the latter claim is somehow especially implausible or incoherent, the realist has not yet told us why. Accordingly, unless the political realists present some special argument for their view, we may continue to make moral judgments about the behavior of nations and other collective entities in international affairs.

## §6 THE HOBBESIAN ARGUMENT

What may well be the classic attempt to defend the political realist's view is based upon the philosophy of Thomas Hobbes. In his book *Leviathan* (1651), Hobbes describes what life would be like in the absence of a powerful political authority. In such a "state of nature," egoistic humans of approximately equal power would compete for relatively scarce resources. Such a state of nature would be a war of all against all in which life would be "nasty, brutish and short." In such circumstance, no one would have any reason to behave morally. Persons would reason that helping others would only expose them to aggression, since provision of such help would simply disadvantage the agent relative to those who would stab him in the back for personal gain.

The assumption here is that no one is required to behave morally when moral behavior carries with it grave risks to the agent. Just as a weak swimmer is not morally *required* to leap into a stormy sea to save a drowning child, so it can be argued that we have no obligation to be moral when others would simply take advantage of our conformity to the moral rules in order to do us in. Accordingly, Hobbes concludes that right and wrong, justice and injustice, have no place in the absence of a strong sovereign who can enforce common norms of behavior, which apply fairly to everyone, protecting those who obey by punishing those who do not.

What has this to do with international affairs? Political realists tend to argue, as Hobbes himself suggested, that the international arena *is* a

Hobbesian state of nature. There is no sovereign or world government powerful enough to compel nations to obey common norms or protect those who do conform. Moreover, nations compete with each other for scarce resources, military supremacy, and ideological superiority. What is such a highly competitive world, dominated by entities which at least tend to act only in their perceived national interests, except a potential war of all against all?

Realists can maintain then, that in a world where no nation can count on any other nation acting morally toward it, any nation would be taking an enormous risk by acting morally itself. Since obligations to act morally have application only when there is reason to believe others will tend to act morally as well—for otherwise morality would *require* agents to take grave risks and so be far too demanding—such obligations have no place in international relations.

What are the implications of this Hobbesian argument for formulation of policy toward development of resources found outside national boundaries? It implies that the technologically advanced nations which are able to exploit such resources operate under *no moral contraints whatsoever* to other nations. For example, if they exploit the deep sea bed without sharing benefits with the less developed nations, no injustice *would* be done because none *could* be done. "Injustice," in the Hobbesian view, is not a concept which is even applicable to international relations. But is this Hobbesian argument itself defensible?

The Hobbesian argument contains two kinds of premises. First, there are premises claiming that in fact international affairs is characterized by certain features. For example, we are told that there is resource scarcity, that there is no sovereign and hence no law, and that nations resemble individual egoists in a war of all against all. Second, there are attempts to draw implications about the role or lack of role of morality from the premises about the specified features of international affairs. Thus, we are told that *since* moral behavior by nations is enormously risky, it follows that moral obligations have no place in relations among states. Each kind of premise of the Hobbesian argument is open to serious question.

Consider the Hobbesian claim that the international arena resembles an unrestricted free-for-all of equals, each of whom stands in opposition to all the others. Unfortunately for the realist, it can be argued plausibly that the picture of the world of international relations as a huge free-for-all is vastly overdrawn.[11] For example, nation states are *not* all equal in terms of resources and power. Some are far more powerful than others and so are at less risk than are weaker, less developed states. Thus, it would be far less risky for the United States to donate one percent of its gross national product (GNP) to the World Health Organization than it would be for Bangladesh to perform the same action. In addition, states do not always operate as isolated agents but form alliances and other kinds of relationships with other states. Although self-interest may be the original motivation for such behavior, other kinds of ties develop as well. For example, in view of the close relationship between the United States and Britain, it would have been morally difficult for the United States to side with Argentina against Britain in the 1982 war over the Falkland Islands.

It is inaccurate, then, to describe international affairs as strictly analogous to a Hobbesian war of all against all. Indeed, some rules or norms are generally acknowledged in relations among nations—there are even rules of war which nations are expected to follow when they are at war with one another—although such rules may not have the same binding character as the laws of a well-ordered domestic society. For example, nations tend to give weight to treaties they have signed and to common codes of behavior subscribed to by all. Iran's seizure of the United States embassy and its staff in 1979 was so shocking precisely because it violated a well-known norm requiring respect for diplomatic personnel that has been observed by virtually all other nations even under extreme conditions of provocation.

Perhaps most important, just as individuals in Hobbes's state of nature are led by their common reason to conclude that they will do better collectively under a sovereign than without one, so too do nations have reasons for concluding that all will do better within a rule-governed framework than without one. The Nuclear Test Ban Treaty and the Salt I agreement constitute examples, in the area of arms control, of countries deciding that their interests are better served by conformity to an agreed-upon set of rules than through dog eat dog competition. As we will see, similar considerations may apply to the exploitation of undeveloped natural resources.

So far it has been argued that the Hobbesian defense of political realism is inaccurate in picturing international relations as a "state of nature." Perhaps even more important, the Hobbesian position is mistaken in what it thinks follows from the picture of international relations as a state of nature, even assuming the accuracy of such a characterization. It does seem true that in a Hobbesian state of nature, you, as an individual, would not be morally required to provide so much aid to your less fortunate neighbors that they might become a threat to your own welfare. However, less stringent obligations might still apply. If, during a hike through the Hobbesian state of nature, you come upon a stranger drowning in quicksand, it is by no means clear that you are morally permitted to walk on by without even trying to help, especially if little risk to your own safety is involved. Similarly, it is doubtful if the mere existence of a Hobbesian state of nature would entitle persons to rape, torture, and mutilate the weak simply for their own momentary pleasure.

Along similar lines, one could argue that even if international relations do resemble the Hobbesian state of nature, the strong (i.e., the affluent and powerful nations) have an obligation to help the weak (i.e., the developing nations) at least so long as no significant risk to themselves is involved. The greater the power and resources of a state, the less risk it is likely to run in providing aid to others and hence the greater the range of moral obligations it might be expected to meet.[12]

What our discussion suggests, then, is not that morality is totally inapplicable to international relations, even when international relations are (perhaps implausibly) viewed as a state of nature. Rather, it suggests that moral principles do apply. In particular, the morality of international relations may be the same morality that applies to individuals under conditions of (1) unusual risk and (2) lack of grounds for belief in reciprocal compliance by others. Under conditions where (1) and (2) hold, conformity to the same moral rules which apply within a well-ordered domestic society may require too much of the agent. But while this may excuse agents from conformity to *those* rules, at least when genuine risk is actually involved, it does not follow that no moral rules apply.

Accordingly, the political realist's appeal to Hobbes is not a good reason for concluding that principles of justice are inapplicable to international affairs. The account of international affairs as a Hobbesian state of nature *and* the account of what follows from such a postulate are each open to serious objection. Of course, we have not examined all the possible arguments for political realism. However, the Hobbesian argument has been particularly influential so perhaps our discussion at least shifts the burden of proof back to the realists. As we have seen, we do make moral judgments about international relations and have not been given good reason for thinking these judgments are any less intelligible or defensible than similar judgments about behavior within particular states. Accordingly, we have good reasons for believing that our inquiry into principles of global justice is appropriate and cannot be ruled out a priori by the political realists. Let us ask then what principles of justice *ought* to govern the acquisition and distribution of resources found in the deep sea bed and in other territories lying outside the boundaries of sovereign states.

## III.   GLOBAL JUSTICE AND NATURAL RESOURCES

### §7  THE MAJOR OPTIONS

Two opposing principles compete for our informed support in this area. The first has its roots in John Locke's *Second Treatise of Government* (1690), a work whose principles underlie much of our own Constitution.[13] In this work, Locke argues that the earth and its fruits have been given to mankind in common. But they are ours "in common" only in the weak sense explained in §2. Individuals or groups may acquire property legitimately by removing it from the universal common through their own labor or by justly acquiring it from those who have already done so. In this view, which will be referred to as *Global Libertarianism*, unappropriated natural resources lying outside national boundaries belong to no one in their original state but can be appropriated by anyone who can discover and extract them.

Distinct from and opposed to Global Libertarianism is a view which will be called *Resource Egalitarianism*. In this view, the earth and its fruits—at least those lying outside national boundaries—are a common in the strong sense (see §2). As understood by representatives of many Third World nations, and by many individuals in the more developed nations as well, resources found in the deep sea bed are part of the "common heritage of mankind." This means that resources in the deep sea bed actually belong to everyone and may be exploited only for the benefit of mankind as a whole, regardless of who does the actual exploration and extraction.

Clearly, these two approaches have very different implications for policy. For example, Global Libertarianism justifies the right to develop resources exclusively for private profit. Resource Egalitarianism does not. Which view is the most defensible? That is the central question which will be explored in the remainder of Part III. Let us begin with an examination of Global Libertarianism.

## §8  GLOBAL LIBERTARIANISM

Libertarianism, as understood here, is the political philosophy which holds that it is morally forbidden to interfere with personal liberty.[14] Coercion may be used to protect the liberty of an innocent person against interference, but is otherwise prohibited. Other goals such as equality, the elimination of poverty, or the pursuit of excellence may be achieved through voluntary cooperation but, according to libertarianism, no one may be coerced into contributing to the pursuit of such ends, however desirable they may be in themselves. Libertarians equate the inviolability of the individual with noninterference with individual liberty.

For libertarians, the liberty to appropriate and exchange property is particularly fundamental. If individuals could not appropriate unowned material, or exchange what they own with others on a voluntary basis, their ability to implement their own goals would be enormously constrained. But how is property to be appropriated in the first place? This issue is crucial to our central concern which involves the appropriation of previously unowned resources lying outside national borders. Here, many libertarians rely heavily on the principles of appropriation developed and defended by John Locke.

*1. Lockean Labor.*   According to Locke, as long as we are in a state of nature, particular agents can appropriate resources through their labor. Locke maintains of the individual in the state of nature that

> The labor of his body and the work of his hands, we may say, are properly his. Whatsoever then he removes out of the state that nature has provided . . . he has mixed his labor with and joined to it something that is his own, and thereby makes it his property.[15]

It may be objected that if the resources appropriated are very rare, others might be deprived of their own chances at appropriation. By the time they go there, all the resources already would have been appropriated. Surely, just getting there first, perhaps only through good luck, does not entitle one to exhaust a scarce resource. Locke was not insensitive to this point and so modified his theory of property acquisition by the addition of a proviso.

> For this labor being the unquestionable property of the labourer, no man but he can have a right to what that is once joined to, *at least where there is enough and as good left in common to others.*[16]

According to this proviso (the so-called Lockean proviso), individuals can appropriate goods from the storehouse of nature only so long as similar opportunities for appropriation remain for others. As Locke argues,

> Nobody could think himself injured by the drinking of another man . . . who had a whole river of the same water left him to quench his thirst; and the case of land and water, where there is enough for both, is perfectly the same.[17]

This approach to the acquisition of previously unowned resources surely has enormous intuitive appeal. What can be more obvious than that if I plant corn, tend it, and care for it, and you merely watch me work without providing aid, then the ears of corn which grow are mine and not yours. I'm *entitled* to them and you are not because I and not you earned them through work. What could be more clear and obvious?

Similarly, suppose entrepreneurs develop the technology to extract minerals from the deep sea bed, and then actually mine the mineral deposits found there. Why don't they too come to own the fruits of their labor? Why should anyone who has not done the work necessary to extract the minerals have any claim of ownership upon them? Why don't the rules which Locke argues should apply in the state of nature apply in international relations which at least resemble a state of nature in some important respects? (But see §6 as well.)

While such a view clearly has attractions, upon examination it turns out to face serious difficulties. Let us consider some of the major difficulties with Locke's account of appropriation, with special emphasis on their significance for international affairs.

Locke, as we have seen, assumes that laborers legitimately control their bodies and the labor they perform with their bodies. They come to *own* previously unowned external objects by mixing what they do control, the labor of their bodies, with other objects. But as Robert Nozick, a present-day proponent of a Lockean approach, asks, why don't the workers simply lose their labor rather than gain new property? To borrow an example from Nozick, if you grow a tomato, squeeze tomato juice from it, and mix the juice with the Atlantic Ocean, you lose your juice rather than gain the Atlantic.[18] Why isn't this so in other cases? Is the connection between labor and ownership as tight as the Lockean account assumes?

Unfortunately for the Lockean account, there is no simple and obviously correct response to this question. This and related difficulties with the Lockean account of just acquisition raise extensive problems which require a more exhaustive treatment than would be appropriate here.[19] For now, let us consider the special difficulties which arise when the account is applied to the appropriation of natural resources in the international arena.

First, the Lockean paradigm of the individual worker mixing labor with nature's bounty so as to produce some usable good does not resemble closely the exploitation of resources in the deep sea bed, Antarctica, or outer space. In such cases, extraction of valuable resources will be carried out by huge corporations and consortiums, not individual workers. The "owners" presumably will be the stockholders, not those who perform the actual mining or invent the technology which makes it possible. Even if it is granted that individual workers on the Lockean paradigm have absolute control over what they produce, it is not obvious that distant stockholders have the same entitlement. No doubt the stockholders are entitled to a fair return on investment but that is not the same thing as absolute ownership and control.

It is worth noting also that in the international context, it is not always clear just what has actually been appropriated by labor. Suppose, for example, that a mining company is extracting manganese nodules from the deep sea bed. It has been estimated that in order to recoup its initial investment, the company may need to mine an individual site for nearly twenty years. What does such a company own after the first year of extraction? Suppose we concede its ownership over what it has extracted already. But why, on the Lockean account, would it be wrong for a rival company to extract valuable minerals from the same site during the next year? Since the remaining minerals have not yet been mixed with the first company's labor, it cannot base a claim to them on the Lockean theory of appropriation. But if a company's access to a site was not accorded protection for a sufficient period, why would it invest in such a site in the first place?

It is far from clear that general and abstract principles such as those found in Locke's theory provide a defensible and determinate solution to such a problem. There may be a need for actual negotiations among nations so as to establish a mutually acceptable framework through which the kind of stability required for investment can be secured. But then the applicable rules of appropriation would be those which emerged from the negotiations, not the Lockean principles themselves, although the former may well reflect the influence of the latter in important ways.

However, even if we acknowledge that it is Locke's principles rather than those that might result from international negotiations that should apply, a strong case still can be made against allowing *unrestrained* private exploitation of the deep sea bed. Remember that Locke himself acknowledges that appropriation through one's labor is permissible only when *as much* and *as good* is left over for others. Where scarce resources are at stake, this Lockean proviso is *not* satisfied. By extracting valuable resources, the miners are leaving less for others. Moreover, since they presumably will extract resources from the most accessible sites first, what is left over will be harder and more expensive to acquire than what was extracted earlier. Accordingly, a strong case can be made that unrestricted private exploitation of the deep sea bed is impermissible, even on Lockean grounds, because of the violations of the Lockean proviso it would entail.

*2. Revising the Lockean proviso.*   Libertarians might object that the problem is not with the Lockean theory of acquisition through labor but rather lies in the Lockean proviso which restricts the application of that theory too rigidly. A revised Lockean proviso might allow original acquisition when no other parties are disadvantaged by it. Thus, you have no grounds for complaint if I grow crops on my farm since you are made no worse off by my productive labor.

Is this revised Lockean proviso satisfied where extraction of scarce resources is at issue? Critics might object that if such resources are exploited only for the benefit of a relatively few developers, others *are* disadvantaged since they will be left without adequate resources for their own future needs. If you use a large share of such resources, there is little left for me. What is left is harder to acquire than what was already taken so I must use more of my assets than you did in the extraction process. So I am disadvantaged relative to you and even the revised Lockean proviso remains unsatisfied.

This point applies not only to *presently existing people* who will be disadvantaged by extraction of resources by others; it also has special force when applied to *future generations*. If major resource deposits are exploited by the present generation, what will be left for those who come after us?

Of course, the Libertarian can make a number of replies. For one thing, he can amend the Lockean theory by addition of what has come to be called a *just savings principle* which prohibits developers from exhausting important resources. Or the Libertarian can take another tack and argue that as present resources are exhausted, new technologies will become available which use resources the potential of which the present generation does not yet even appreciate.[20]

However, neither of these replies seems to fit harmoniously within a Libertarian framework. The idea of a just savings principle implies that we might have positive obligations to save resources for others, even at the price of our own liberty to appropriate and consume. While some Libertarians might agree that such concern is admirable, they hardly can regard it as *obligatory* without compromising libertarianism's exclusive emphasis on negative liberty from outside interference. Similarly, the (perhaps overly optimistic) proposal that resources are virtually inexhaustible does not deny that we would come to have positive obligations to others if future scarcity was a probable outcome of present policies.

Accordingly, if Global Libertarianism is not to collapse into a more egalitarian outlook, the Libertarian will have to have second thoughts about the revised Lockean proviso (and the just savings principle). According to the revised proviso, the deep sea bed can be mined only if extraction and development of resources does not disadvantage others. Should the Libertarian accept such a restriction?

The Libertarian might argue that the revised proviso is too restrictive. It forbids those acts which disadvantage others. But surely it often is permissible to perform acts which have the result of making some people worse off than they otherwise would be. For example, teachers may give better grades to some students than others, baseball managers may pick only the best players for their teams, owners of businesses may charge lower prices than their competitors, and athletes may try to defeat their opponents. In any competition, successful agents disadvantage unsuccessful ones. Indeed, the very point of a Lockean theory of appropriation is to reward the successful.

The Libertarian argument, then, is that if we are permitted to act only if we do not disadvantage anyone, our goals, plans, and opportunities would be at the mercy of others. If I have worse grades than you, for example, I could argue that you should not be permitted to apply to law school, since by applying you would be reducing my chances for admission. Indeed, the Libertarian may argue, the very point of *individual rights* is to create a sphere of inviolability surrounding each person which even the welfare of the majority cannot normally override. There would be no freedom of speech, for example, if individuals could be silenced any time their views might disadvantage the targets of their criticism. Similarly, the Libertarian can argue that if the individual's ability to appropriate and exchange property is curtailed by the revised Lockean proviso, the individual's control of his or her life is unduly restricted.

This rejoinder by the Libertarian is not without force but, as we will see, it may not be wholly satisfactory either. For one thing, it may be necessary, as we will see in §9, to set limits on the liberty to appropriate property if the equal rights of all are to be respected. This and related objections will be explored in §9 where the response of the Resource Egalitarian to Libertarianism will be explored.

For now, we can conclude that both the Libertarian emphasis on the integrity and liberty of the individual and the critics' insistence that there must be some restriction on appropriation of resources each has a point. Without the former, the individual becomes merely another resource. Without the latter, those who first find valuable but scarce resources may exhaust the supply leaving nothing for the rest of humanity, whatever its plight. Accordingly, let us now consider whether the developing nations' strong interpretation of the "common heritage of mankind" is more defensible than the principles of the Libertarian.

## §9 RESOURCE EGALITARIANISM

Resource Egalitarianism is the view that as yet unappropriated natural resources lying outside the boundaries of nations are the common heritage of mankind in the strong distributive sense. That is, everyone has an equal right to benefit from the extraction and development of the resources in question. Although all arguments for this view cannot be considered here, two in particular deserve consideration. The first emphasizes the moral arbitrariness of the factors that place some individuals, corporations, or nations in a better position than others to exploit such resources. The second maintains that considered from an impartial and disinterested perspective, it is the position of the Resource Egalitarian rather than the Libertarian that is most warranted.

Before turning to consideration of these arguments, it is worth emphasizing the Resource Egalitarianism makes a relatively modest claim. It does not hold that all persons ought to end up with equal incomes or wealth, let alone that each person has a right to an equally satisfying life or to the means which make such a life possible. Rather, it asserts the claim only that every person has an equal prima facie right to benefit from the exploitation of resources found outside national boundaries. Let us consider this claim of the Resource Egalitarian.

First, the claim is one of equality. Everyone's claim is equal in strength. However, if we think of such a right as prima facie, it does not follow that, in actuality, everyone will have a claim to an exactly equal share of the benefits of exploitation of resources. To say a claim of right is prima facie is to say the claim can be modified by competing moral considerations. A prima facie rights claim becomes an unqualified claim of right only when there are no overriding moral considerations that conflict with it. Accordingly, *if* Resource Egalitarians believe that special contribution requires special reward, they might acknowledge that developers of undersea resources should receive a special profit, and so should benefit more from exploitation of resources than others. However, any Resource Egalitarian will deny that the developer comes to own, in the sense of exclusively controlling, such resources or that others may be denied an equitable share of the benefits of development.

Resource Egalitarianism, then, emphatically denies the basic claim of Global Libertarianism. This is because the Resource Egalitarian not only allows but may require interference with the liberty of developers in order to ensure a fair and equitable distribution of the benefits of development of natural resources. Since liberty is inviolable for the Libertarian, including liberty to appropriate unclaimed goods, and since the Resource Egalitarian denies that original appropriation entitles the appropriator to absolute control over what is appropriated, the two positions are in conflict. What can be said in defense of Resource Egalitarianism?

*1. The Appeal to the Geologic Lottery.*   The case for Resource Egalitarianism can be defended by appeal to the moral arbitrariness of the initial distribution of resources around the globe. In order to better understand this argument, let us first consider the analogous claim concerning the talents and abilities of individual persons.

Some philosophers have argued that whether or not an individual possesses unusual skills and abilities depends upon a combination of the genetic lottery and the initial distribution of favorable home environments, factors for which individuals themselves are not responsible. People do not pick either their genes or their parents. Therefore, the philosophers in question conclude that individuals do not deserve their allotment of natural capacities. Since individuals do not deserve their capacities, talents, and abilities, they do not deserve the benefits that flow from such unmerited gifts either. As one influential writer on the subject has maintained, even

> the assertion that a man deserves the superior character that enables him to make the effort to cultivate his abilities is especially problematic: for his character depends in large part upon fortunate family and social circumstances for which he can claim no credit.[21]

Since it is a matter of luck who winds up with favorable or unfavorable characteristics in the genetic-environmental lottery, claims based on such characteristics are not fundamental elements of a defensible conception of social justice.

Charles Beitz, author of an important study of the nature of global justice, argues that an even stronger but logically parallel argument can be made concerning rights to natural resources. As Beitz explains, "The fact that someone happens to be located advantageously with respect to natural resources does not provide a reason why he or she should be entitled to exclude others from the benefits that might be derived from them."[22] The geologic lottery determining the distribution of natural resources is at least as arbitrary as the genetic-environmental lottery determining the allocation of individual capacities. Neither can be the basis of moral claims of deserving the goods which flow from the initial allocation.

Therefore, Beitz concludes, an adequate account of global justice must include a resource-redistribution principle.[23] While Beitz does not argue for a specific version of such a principle, the general direction it would take is quite clear. Resources are not to be viewed as the private assets of any particular person, group, or even nation. Rather, they are to be developed in such a way as "would give each society a fair chance to develop just political institutions and an economy capable of satisfying its members' basic needs." Underlying this approach is the fundamental premise that "each person has an equal prima facie claim to a share of the total available resources. . . ."[24]

The argument based on the geologic lottery does seem stronger than the parallel argument about individual talents and capacities. Capacities, talents, and abilities are so attached to persons that they cannot be treated as part of a "common pool" without violating personal integrity. If an individual is to be respected as a moral agent, he must be seen as a person who exercises his choices and decisions through use of his abilities and talents. To constrain an individual from developing talents and capacities is to limit his ability to implement his will. To regard those capacities and talents as part of the common heritage of mankind, to be developed and utilized only if others benefit, comes dangerously close to reducing each individual to a thing or to a tool to be used only for the benefit of others. However, "unlike talents, resources are not naturally attached to persons. . . . Thus, while we might feel that the possession of talents confers a right to control and benefit from their use, we feel differently about resources."[25]

The first thing to note about this argument is that even if successful, it makes a negative rather than positive point. That is, it shows, at most, that claims to natural resources cannot be based on accidents of the geologic lottery, not that everyone has a prima facie claim to benefit from the exploitation of such resources. Strictly speaking, the denial that a certain justification of claims by individuals or states to special rights does not prove that no other justification is available. Indeed, as we have seen (in §8), the Lockean argument for control of resources is not based on their geographic proximity but on the labor expended in their extraction.

The immediate retort, of course, is that one can't work on what isn't there. If one's land contains no oil deposits in the first place, all the labor in the world won't extract an ounce of oil. So it is just luck which determines who has the opportunity to invest labor in natural resources in the first place. And claims of justice cannot be based on luck.

This point is well worth our further consideration. In assessing it, the distinction between *potential* resources and *actual* resources will prove useful. A resource is potential for a given group if it could be used by them, given adequate technology for extraction and utilization. It becomes actual for a given group if it in fact is accessible to them and they have the technology to make use of it. Thus, oil buried in the off-shore continental shelf was only a potential resource for the United States of the early twentieth centry but is an actual resource for us now.

The implication of this is that while the distribution of potential resources will be a function of the morally arbitrary geologic lottery, the distribution of actual resources need not be. Individuals, groups, or nations may invent or develop the technology needed to turn a potential into an actual resource. Thus, some may take better advantage of the potential resources available to them than do others. It is not at all clear, in such cases, that the resources actually available are simply a result of contingencies for which no one is responsible.[26] For example, not only can human action affect the actual resources available to us, good judgment about the likelihood of potential resouces being turned into actual ones can contribute to effective development in other ways. A country which lacks natural resources within its own territory might do well economically by effective use of its human capital. In fact, there is no correlation between the share of natural resources available to a state and its economic status. Thus, Japan, which lacks substantial resources, has done far better than many relatively resource-rich states, such as Nigeria or Mexico.

It is at best unclear, then, that redistributive concerns about natural resouces can or should be dealt with separately from broader global distributive issues. Resources actually available can depend on individual action and social policy. Moreover, from the point of view of the individual, the political, economic, or social circumstances into which the individual is born is no more a matter of personal choice or responsibility than the share of potential resources lying within the sphere of authority of the state. Yet these circumstances can have a far greater impact upon the individual's fortunes than natural resorces alone.

It can be argued that the whole social-economic system of the state should be viewed as a global resource, in just the way Beitz recommends we view natural resources. The trouble with this is the difficulty of assimilating at least some of the factors which contribute to the success of a social-economic system, such as human intelligence, choice, values, and talents, to the model of a morally arbitrary lottery. As we noted above, such factors are integrally related to the nature of persons as moral agents. To view them as mere accidents rather than as *acts* persons perform or *qualities* they develop through their own personal effort reduces persons to mere resources for the production of overall good. If the Global Egalitarian presses this kind of argument, he will face many of the same difficulties which arise in connection with appeal to the genetic lottery of personal talents and abilities.

It cannot simply be assumed, then, that the *actual* resources available to a person, group, or society must be the result of a morally arbitrary geologic lottery. Moreover, if the force of the appeal to a geologic lottery is unclear where resources lying *within* national boundaries is at issue, it appears especially weak where relatively inaccessible resources lying *outside* national boundaries are of concern. Where extraction of resources from the deep sea bed, Antarctica, or eventually even outer space is concerned, it is precisely such qualities as inventiveness, initiative, technological discovery, and social policy—precisely the sorts of things for which *persons* are responsible—that are likely to be crucial. If the lottery argument is problematic, it is especially so where natural resources lying outside the territory of states is at issue.

However, we should not be too quick to conclude that the lottery argument fails completely. A proponent of the argument might concede that individuals do make a contribution to the exploitation of natural resources, and in some contexts turn potential into actual resources. However, he might add that people have vastly *unequal opportunities* to make such contributions. A child born into a relatively affluent middle class family in America, because of factors for which she is not responsible, such as the high level of educational institutions and scientific research in her society, may have opportunities to pursue a scientific career which are unavailable to a child born into a family of farmers in Chad barely living at the subsistence level. The second youngster may have as much innate ability as the first, and might have developed the same personal characteristics given a reasonable diet and health care. But those are just not available. Neither is the opportunity for an advanced education.

In a world of vastly unequal opportunities, where some are born into relative affluence and others into a subsistence economy or worse, to view natural resources as the exclusive property of those who exploit them perpetuates and extends the initial inequalities. It is as if, to use a well-known analogy, one runner starts a 200-meter race 100 meters ahead of his opponent and then wins the race. Moreover, in the next generation's race, his children would start even further ahead than his opponent's children, since the advantages of victory would be passed from generation to generation. Is this even remotely fair or just?

Note that the argument has shifted from one based on a geologic lottery to one based on the good fortune of being born into favorable social and economic circumstances. Adherents of this argument might concede that if everyone had an equal or at least not enormously disadvantageous starting point, due weight should be given to initiative, inventiveness, and other important virtues of persons who successfully develop nature's bounty. But since that condition is *not* satisfied, natural resources, particularly those lying outside the domain of particular nations, should be viewed as the common heritage of mankind in the strong sense, and developed for the benefit of all.[27]

This argument may not be entirely convincing to the Libertarians. They can retort that although opportunities are grossly unequal at the global level, those with the more favorable chances may be entitled to their advantageous starting point. That is, their inherited advantages may have been earned by their ancestors who in turn were entitled to pass them on to their descendants.

A full discussion of this Libertarian defense would take us into a complex tangle of issues involving equal opportunity and rights of inheritance. Were the original advantages really earned? Were they acquired at best through good luck or at worst by exploitation of others? These fundamental questions have no obvious answer. For our purposes, however, let us concede to the Libertarian both that the original advantages were earned—or at least that they were not unjustly acquired—and that benefits may be passed on to heirs. We can then concentrate on what may be central to present concerns; namely, whether there is any direct and fundamental moral basis for the claims of all people to a share of as yet unappropriated natural resources. That basis, if there is one, is most likely to be found after we have explored the idea of basic moral rights.

2. *Impartiality and Rights.* As we have seen, Libertarians hold that individuals have only *negative* rights to liberty from interference. Many other thinkers maintain that, on the contrary, individuals also have *positive* rights to at least the minimal necessities which are prerequisites for a distinctively human kind of life.[28] Negative rights are those which obligate others only to leave the rights bearer alone. Thus, the right to free speech is negative if all it requires is that speakers not be interfered with under appropriate conditions. Positive rights require others to do more than refrain from interfering. They may require provision of some actual good or service. For example, the right to life is construed as a *positive* right if it requires not only that we refrain from killing the rights

bearer but also that we provide him with basic necessities when he is unable to do so for himself.

Although the whole question of rights is a complex one, it is important to see the main outlines of the case that all persons possess basic positive rights. To do so requires that we examine the second argument mentioned in the first paragraph of §9, the one that stresses impartiality. This is our next order of business.

In *A Theory of Justice*, John Rawls has suggested that we think of principles of justice as those that would be accepted unanimously by rational, self-interested agents in a hypothetical position of impartial choice. In this conception, the principles of justice are those we would want to govern the distribution of benefits and burdens if we were rational and, though self-interested, did not allow calculations of personal gain or partisanship to affect our choice. To ensure impartiality, Rawls asks us in effect to consider what principles we would accept if we were behind a "veil of ignorance." This veil denies us knowledge of our own personal characteristics, the characteristics of our society, our own personal values, and even knowledge of the age in which we live. Presumably, in the global interpretation of Rawls's theory, it denies us knowledge of which state we inhabit in the actual world.[29]

The specific question of concern here, then, is what principles for appropriation of resources we might adopt if we were in ignorance of whether we lived in a more affluent, technologically developed society or a less affluent, technologically underdeveloped society. Of course, it is difficult if not impossible to *deduce* or *prove* what we would adopt, or even whether different persons would choose the same principles. Much depends on just which assumptions we make about what people want, their willingness to take risks, and their knowledge of the distribution of resources throughout the world.

But while a proof cannot be presented, some considerations which seem reasonable ought to receive due weight. In particular, there seem to be certain eventualities we might want to protect ourselves against.

First, we surely would want to ensure ourselves, as best we could, against the evils of grossly inadequate diet, health care, and educational opportunities. Without these the quality of our life, and indeed life itself, would be severely threatened. Second, we also would want opportunities to secure our personal goals through our acts, choices, and use of our abilities. This would include the opportunity to develop our capacities and use them to secure our ends. We would not want to be viewed as a mere resource, a means to be used only for the benefit of others. Finally, as consumers of the services of others and as recipients of their actions, we would want to be able to influence their performances by our own praise or blame, or through use of some system of financial incentives, such as constituted by the free market. Thus, if we prefer serious movies to low-budget horror films, or if we prefer the reverse, we would want to be at liberty to influence the production of more of the kind of movies we like, through expressions of either praise or blame, or through the pocketbook by our patronage. Accordingly, our basic goals from a position of impartial choice would include insurance against serious deprivation, opportunity to develop and exercise our capacities in pursuit of our goals, and freedom to defend our goals and influence those of others. These concerns are so fundamental that we would want them protected by a system of fundamental rights and entitlements. If such concerns were left to mere charity, it would be up to others whether or not they were protected. From behind the veil, we would not only have no way of knowing how efficient charity might be, we surely would not want to make such matters of fundamental concern contingent on the unreliable benevolence of others. Rather, we would want to assert our *entitlements* to the good in question. Such entitlements or rights would include not only the personal freedom properly valued by the Libertarian but also positive claims to a safety net or welfare floor which would protect us from severe deprivation.[30]

This constraint on what justice requires has important implications for our central question regarding the distribution of benefits that accrue from deep sea mining, as we will shortly see in §11. First, however, there is an important objection that is likely to be raised by the Libertarian which deserves our attention.

## §10  THE COHERENCE OF LIBERTARIANISM

The Libertarian surely would want to reject positive rights of the kind argued for in §9 on the grounds that their enforcement would require interference with personal liberty. For example, taxes which might be required to support a safety net would interfere with the personal liberty to dispose of one's income as one wishes.

But this point should not be accepted too hastily. Consider why the Libertarian values negative rights in the first place. It must be because human agency, which is protected by negative rights, is considered of supreme value. Human agents are viewed as ends in themselves, free to act according to their own purposes. The Libertarians reject positive rights precisely because they fear that the positive obligations such rights would generate would lead to the exploitation of the individual for the benefit of others. Individuals are reduced to means for the production of social welfare and no longer are regarded as ultimate ends.

But if human agency is a supreme value, isn't it logically suspect to refuse to protect the conditions under which it can develop? If we are concerned to protect X from being coerced by Y in order to protect X's capacity to direct his own life as he sees fit, shouldn't we equally be concerned by the fact that Y is malnourished and Z has no educational opportunities? Malnutrition, inadequate health care, and lack of educational and employment opportunities can so limit the paths open to us that our moral agency amounts to no more than a philosophical abstraction with no actual significance. Reflection on this point may lead us to question whether Libertarianism, which assigns absolute weight to negative liberty and no weight to positive rights, even though each may be essential to our status as moral agents, is either logically or morally coherent.

Our doubts on this score may become even deeper when we consider that full enforcement of the negative rights valued so highly by Libertarians carries with it the imposition of positive obligations on others.[31] For example, if your negative right to be free from coercion is to be protected by the state, I have the positive obligation to pay taxes to support the police and judicial system. Since the Libertarian must recognize positive obligations in *some* areas anyway, and since the development of moral agency requires positive as well as negative support, the exclusive Libertarian emphasis on negative rights does seem vulnerable to the charge that it is theoretically untenable.

This is not to deny the value of the Libertarian emphasis on personal liberty. However, what has been suggested here is not that the value of liberty should be questioned but that we should not tolerate severe deprivation. The insistence that *some* constraints be placed on the liberty of property owners or developers to satisfy the positive rights of others is far from a rejection of individual freedom. Such constraints imply neither that liberty is worthless nor that it may be limited by any factor less significant than the basic and fundamental rights of others.

## IV. GLOBAL JUSTICE AND UNAPPROPRIATED RESOURCES

### §11 TOWARD A PLURALISTIC SYNTHESIS

What are the implications of this discussion of global justice for the appropriation of resources lying outside national boundaries, and in particular those found in the deep sea bed? Perhaps the most defensible conclusion to draw is that both the Global Libertarian and the Resource Egalitarian have contributed important insights which need to be taken into account, although neither is entirely correct. The Libertarian is quite right to suggest that individuals may appropriate and exchange property in pursuit of personal goals. Any too-restrictive policy in this area is open to the charge of reducing persons to the status of resources to be efficiently utilized for the benefit of others.[32] Persons are entitled to a sufficient degree of freedom to enable them to live their own lives and develop their capacities and talents as they choose. But on the other hand, the Resource Egalitarian, even if his appeal to the geologic lottery is misguided, is quite right to argue for the creation of a global welfare floor or safety net. Indeed, the argument for such a conclusion need not be based on exceedingly controversial premises about the immorality of inheritance or the unearned character of the wealth of the developed states. Rather, it can be based on direct appeal to positive human rights founded on considerations of impartiality and respect for persons as moral agents, values which as we have seen have their roots in elements of the Libertarian philosophy itself.

Accordingly, a defensible policy on appropriation and exploitation of natural resources would combine elements of both Global Libertarianism and Resource Egalitarianism. It would allow for *limited ownership rights* for the developers, but it would also *require* them to pay the equivalent of a tax for the benefit of the globally disadvantaged. Personal profit and the creation of a global safety net would each be allowed for.

## §12  TOO MUCH FOR TOO FEW?

At this point, representatives of the mining companies and others concerned with the exploitation of the deep sea bed, Antarctica, and outer space might argue as follows. The principles you propose, they might acknowledge, are fine in themselves. But why shouldn't they apply generally? Why impose a special burden on those who take the significant risks inherent in developing resources found in relatively inaccessible areas? Why shouldn't the movie star, professional athlete, physician, business executive, and even your friendly neighborhood philosophy professor also be required to contribute?

While the burden of supporting positive rights on a global scale surely should be fairly shared, there are special reasons for thinking that an international agreement concerning sea bed mining is a good place to begin. For one thing, since the resources in question, like those which someday may be found in Antarctica or outer space, lie outside national boundaries, they have not yet fallen under the sphere of authority or control of particular individuals, corporations, or states. Therefore, an international agreement concerning such resources would not run head-on into preexisting claims. No one has yet had a chance to stake such claims in the first place. Thus, the "rules" of the "acquisition game" would not be changed right in the middle of play.

Second, extraction of resources from the deep sea bed, unlike contractual arrangements, say, between a professor and a university, arguably require international cooperation if only in the form of noninterference by nations not involved directly in the mining.[33] Since some of the benefits of the mining would be due to the cooperation of other nations, it seems reasonable, on grounds of reciprocity, to propose that some of the benefits be used for purposes of global economic development. The developer of resources in the deep sea bed, in short, is in a position which differs in morally relevant ways from that of the ordinary businessman or woman, the assembly line worker, the professional athlete, or the professor.

A further consideration involves the need for cooperative international procedures in an increasingly dangerous world. As resources grow scarcer, or as nations search for new kinds of resources, international competition for minerals is likely to grow more and more intense. It is important to develop an international framework for cooperative development so that conflicts endemic to our species will not flare up over the deep sea bed, Antarctica, or minerals found in outer space. We now have the opportunity to use mining of the deep sea bed to develop a model framework for international agreement on rights to natural resources, one which could serve as a guide for development in other areas as well. Concern for world peace as well as global justice supports the creation of such model procedures.

However, it does not follow that we should accept the view that the ocean floor is "the common heritage of mankind" in the strong sense without amendment. Rather, in the light of our discussion, a pluralistic approach is wanted. While the best manner of synthesizing Libertarian and Egalitarian values surely is difficult to discern—indeed there may be no single correct weighting but rather a number of equally acceptable ones—perhaps the following represents a useful guideline.

From Global Libertarianism we can accept the principle that those persons or organizations which contribute to the discovery, development, and extraction of actual resources are entitled to an appropriate economic return which in large part may be dictated by the market forces of supply and demand. Violation of this principle shows a lack of respect for persons as moral agents by divorcing their actions from the very goals for which such acts might reasonably be carried out. However, it does not follow that producers are entitled to *all* the profits of their work. Rather, the equivalent of an international tax on profits may provide revenue to be used to support the positive rights of the globally deprived and disadvantaged. Just as a domestic tax can be used to support the welfare of others, so too can an international tax support the requirements of global justice. In this way, the central insights of both Global Libertarianism and Resource Egalitarianism can be given significant weight.

This is at best a sketch of principles that might govern the just exploitation of resources found outside national boundaries. Moreover, it leaves many central issues untouched. For example, attention has not been paid to the ecological problems raised by extensive development of the deep sea bed. While the attempt to combine questions of justice and ecological ethics into an overall theory goes far beyond the scope of this paper, it is important to realize that the issues of justice we have been pursuing are not the only ones at stake.

## V. GLOBAL JUSTICE AND THE LAW OF THE SEA: SOME ANSWERS

### §13 THE LAW OF THE SEA TREATY

Our discussion so far provides a basis for assessing the United States government's position on the Law of the Sea Treaty. As was noted in §2, in 1982 the United States refused to sign the Treaty after at least ten years of negotiations and in spite of support for it by a large majority of other nations. The Treaty contains provisions safeguarding the freedom of the seas, regulates scientific research on the oceans, and assigns maritime nations control of the mineral resources lying off their shores. The Treaty also calls for international regulation and control of deep sea mining. It is these latter provisions that were objected to by President Reagan and the United States government. Let us consider these provisions in more detail.

The Treaty maintains that the high seas, those areas of the ocean outside a 200-mile offshore limit, are the common heritage of mankind in the sense that ownership resides in humanity as a whole rather than in private interests. Proponents of the Treaty claim the Treaty acknowledges and respects common ownership in the strong sense characterized earlier (§2); as we will see, however, the provisions of the Treaty fail to guarantee the right of all persons to an equitable share of benefits that accrue from mining of the deep sea bed. The Treaty contains provisions for establishment of an international authority to regulate mining of the deep sea bed. Any private company or other organization desiring to mine the deep sea bed is required to apply to the international authority for a permit. The authority is to grant permits when certain conditions are satisfied, including the following:

1. The company must secure the sponsorship of one of the states that is party to the Treaty.
2. The company must propose two mining sites, one for itself and the second for the use either of a developing nation or of the commercial arm of the international authority, called the Enterprise.
3. The company must pay the international authority a portion of the mining profits, to be contributed either to the authority's operating funds or directly to developing nations.
4. The company must sell its mining technology at a fair price either to the Enterprise or to the developing nation mining the second site.

In addition, the Treaty incorporates a commodity ceiling which limits the amount of minerals that may be mined from the deep sea bed during any particular fiscal period. This limit is designed to protect those nations which already mine such minerals on land from a sudden fall in prices due to increased supply.

This Law of the Sea Treaty seems to have at least three important virtues. First, and perhaps most important, the Treaty represents an attempt by the nations of the world to work out a mutually acceptable framework for cooperative development of the deep sea bed. As such, it can be viewed as a model for international agreements which can discourage the kind of competition which can lead to enmity and war. It takes international relations a step further from a Hobbesian war of all against all toward something approaching the rule of law within domestic societies.

Second, the Treaty calls for directing funds and technology which would otherwise be under the control of the more affluent and developed nations to the states of the Third World. Hence, it at least seems to contribute to the formation of a global safety net which, as we have seen in §9, is reasonably viewed as a requirement of global justice.

Finally, the Treaty does not seem to use the developers of resources as mere means for the benefit of the globally disadvantaged. For example, while technology must be transferred to the international sea bed authority, the transfer must be for a fair and reasonable price. Hence, producers and developers are not treated as mere means to be utilized for the benefit of the disadvantaged, but are regarded as moral agents entitled to pursue their own goals and concerns, although within constraints set by both the negative *and* positive rights of others.

## §14 A CRITIQUE OF THE TREATY

Despite its apparent virtues, the Treaty may also contain significant flaws. Let us consider first the claim that the Treaty, by transferring some of the benefits which accrue from deep sea mining to developing countries, contributes to the formation of the kind of global safety net required to safeguard positive rights to minimal well-being. On this view. the Treaty embodies the principle that the deep sea bed is the common heritage of mankind in the strong sense. But is this really the case?

If the deep sea bed is part of the common heritage of mankind in the strong sense, then every individual has a claim, not only to "ownership" in some abstract sense but to actually benefit from its development. This claim is a claim of *individuals*. However, the Treaty calls for the transfer of benefits to developing *nations* or *states*. Ideally, the states would use the resources transferred for the benefit of their citizens. But in the real world, this hardly can be taken for granted, especially when the sorry record of many developing nations in the area of human rights is taken into consideration.

In fact, so far as the provisions of the Treaty are concerned, states may use the funds in question for *any* purpose they regard as important. Such purposes might include purchase of military equipment or the suppression of internal dissent as well as expenditures on economic development or on relieving the plight of the most seriously deprived. Such wide discretion as to how the funds obtained from deep sea mining may be used is not consonant with the view that the Treaty is an instrument of global justice. In this respect at least, the Treaty fails to ensure respect for the individual rights of those who are not themselves involved in deep sea mining but who, as individuals, have fundamental entitlements to a share of the benefits.

The interests and rights of such persons also may be adversely affected by the implementation of a commodity ceiling. The justification for such a ceiling is that it protects those nations which mine minerals on land from a sudden drop in price that might be caused by a sharp increase in supply, brought about by deep sea mining.

However, the economic effect of such a commodity ceiling is to keep prices *higher* than they might otherwise be. This point has special force when one realizes that many of the world's poorer nations are commodity *importers* who will have to pay the higher prices perhaps at significant cost to their own prospects for economic growth. One need only consider the damage caused to many developing nations by the policies of the Organization of Petroleum Exporting Countries (OPEC) to see the force of this point. Thus, it should be remembered that the Treaty favors those states already in the commodity export business, including such developed nations as Canada, over those who might gain from the lower prices which deep sea mining might ultimately generate. It is far from clear that such an initial bias is compatible with principles of global justice.

The Treaty also may fail to respect the rights of those who contribute to the development of the deep sea bed. Recall that the Treaty requires direct transfer of technology to the international sea bed authority (along with "fair" compensation for the owners). According to American critics of the Treaty, this is one of its most objectionable features.

> One of America's greatest assets is its capacity for innovation and invention and its ability to produce advanced technology. It is understandable, therefore, that a Treaty would be unacceptable to many Americans if it required the United States or, more particularly private companies, to transfer that asset in a forced sale to the Enterprise or to developing countries.[34]

Some may view this as just a selfish rationalization designed to protect a competitive technological advantage, but whatever the motive for the American position, there do seem to be several points in its favor.

First, it is far from clear that appropriation of new technology can be justified by appeal to the environment-genetic lottery argument (see §9). Invention does reflect such morally significant qualities of persons and organizations as perseverance, intelligence, dedication, judgment, and initiative. It seems to be a virtual paradigm of the kind of thing for which humans can be responsible and for which they deserve praise and reward. Unlike the oil deposit which happens to be in one's backyard, it is not the result of luck or contingency.

Second, unlike exploitation of resources, invention of technology does not exhaust a finite pie leaving little for others. Accordingly, it is doubtful if appropriation might be justified by application of a Lockean proviso (see §8).

One might object that inventors have been favored by luck, for example by being born into technologically advanced societies that can provide necessary educational advantages, so that the environment-genetic lottery argument does apply. Perhaps this point has some force, in spite of the doubts expressed in §9. However, one can reasonably question whether it justifies so strong a step as required transfer of technology, especially in light of our earlier claim that the recipient states are not required to use such benefits for just goals.

However, it follows from our earlier discussion in §8 and §9 that those who profit from the use of advanced technology do have obligations to support the positive rights of others. It is therefore plausible to think that the inventors and owners of the technology used in deep sea mining, as well as the miners themselves, should pay some form of global tax to be used for the benefit of the world's disadvantaged peoples. But requiring actual transfer of technology seems too strong. Appropriation, unlike a tax, takes what one has created without consent and does seem to violate the owner's integrity as a moral agent.

It appears, then, that the Treaty is at best a flawed instrument for achieving global distributive justice. Such a conclusion supports the view of such supporters of the United States rejection of the Treaty as William Safire who argue, as we have seen in §2, that the Treaty does not contribute to global equity. Although such a view may be over-stated, it does seem doubtful in view of its flaws that acceptance of the Treaty is a *requirement* of global justice.

Nevertheless, it is unclear that the Treaty should simply have been re-jected. After all, its implementation might not only make some contribu-tion to a global safety net but also would serve as an example of interna-tional cooperation in the area of resource development—an area where the dangers of excess competition, including war, are all too obvious. Insofar as official American criticism of the Treaty remains restricted to assertion of unrestrained Libertarian principles, such a policy seems not only philosophically unjustified but to be an expression of economic self-interest alone. This hardly puts the United States in a morally defensible position from the perspective of global justice, which, as we have seen, does not support an unrestrained form of Global Libertarianism. Thus, while the United States's rejection of the Law of the Sea Treaty was not indefensible, one cannot help but wonder whether a less than fully ade-quate Treaty was rejected for the wrong reasons.

## §15 RECOMMENDATIONS FOR THE FUTURE

A revised Law of the Sea Treaty that met the criticisms raised above would not only incorporate features required by global justice, its adop-tion would arguably be in the best interests of the United States and the mining companies themselves. Without some Treaty, American mining companies may be hobbled by their inability to secure loans covering the extended period of time required for development of a mining site. Many analysts believe "that banks will not lend the estimated $1.5 bil-lion needed to develop an undersea mine, since (lack of a ratified) Treaty would make title to ownership uncertain."[35] Ironically, American oppo-sition to the Treaty, based in part upon moral beliefs concerning the en-titlements of the developers, could, if continued against even a revised Treaty, handicap the developers who may find themselves unable to ac-tually mine sites because of a lack of stability that only a Treaty signed by the United States could remedy.

Despite the fact that the Treaty is a flawed instrument for achieving global justice, it does not follow that the United States should rest content with having rejected it. After all, even if the Treaty is less than ideal, it at least incorporates values of international cooperation and some concern for the plight of the developing nations. Critics may maintain, with some plausibility, that the flaws do not justify "a course of isolation and obstruction . . . creating the impression that America wants the benefits of the sea law while refusing even a single concession to a global consensus."[36] It is important to see, then, that the choices available to us include more than just simple acceptance or rejection of a less than satisfactory Treaty.

Rather, in the future, the United States could argue for a moral position which synthesizes the insights of the Global Libertarians with those of the Resource Egalitarians. For example, the United States could propose that the Treaty be revised so that a reasonable share of the profits from deep sea mining go either to relief agencies or to global institutions such as the World Bank, which have a special concern for stimulating economic growth. Alternatively, funds may go only or at least disproportionately to those developing nations which have the best records of respect for fundamental individual rights and for directing funds toward relief of deprivation and economic development. Incentives might be devised to ensure that revenues are not used for internal repression or military agression. As it is, the Treaty's failure to require that developing nations use the funds they receive for purposes of relief and development removes much of the punch from the safety net argument used by supporters of the Treaty.

The United States, then, should return to the negotiating table with additional provisions designed to ensure that the benefits of deep sea mining which would accrue to the developing nations be used in morally permissible ways. If a more acceptable Treaty cannot be reached and the United States does decide to "go it alone" in deep sea mining, a share of the profits should be subject to a special "global" tax. The revenues obtained from this special tax would then be spent in one of a number of ways, including those described in the preceding paragraph, designed to implement a global safety net. Such a policy would place the United States publicly on record as supporting the use of resources found in the universal commons—territory lying outside the boundaries of sovereign states—to help eliminate gross deprivation and poverty which so dominates the lives of literally hundreds of millions of persons throughout the world.

## VI. REVIEW

### §16 SUMMING UP THE ISSUES

We have seen that the deep sea bed, and other areas lying outside national boundaries, can be regarded as the common heritage of mankind in either of two senses. In the weak sense, such territories and the resources they contain belong to *no one* until they are appropriated by just means. In the strong sense, they belong to *everyone* and are to be developed for the benefit of the human race as a whole.

Our discussion suggests that neither perspective is totally correct. The Libertarian correctly emphasizes the importance of the development and exercise of capacities by individuals in pursuit of their goals and rightly denies that persons should be used merely as means for the betterment of the disadvantaged. The Egalitarian argues correctly that individuals have rights, not only to liberties but to the basic means of a minimally decent existence, such as a decent diet, adequate health care and educational facilities. It has been suggested that although there is no reason in theory why these obligations to support a global safety net should fall especially on those who mine the deep sea bed, the appropriation of resources from the universal common is an appropriate starting point for institutionalization of global obligations of distributive justice.

As we also have seen, the existence of the state system complicates application of these conclusions. In particular, distribution of the benefits of resource exploitation among states does not imply just distribution among individuals. At worst, repressive states may use such resources to commit injustice. If only for this reason, ratification of the Law of the Sea Treaty by the United States was not morally required.

However, rejection of the Treaty carries with it significant moral costs. Principal among these is the failure to institutionalize cooperative practices for the development of resources lying outside national boundaries. International competition always is dangerous. Without a cooperative framework in place, powerful nations may be tempted to appropriate minerals found in new areas for themselves and to exclude the less powerful from access or benefits of development. If resources are scarce, the excluded nations may find ways, including terrorism on the high seas, to retaliate. In an age when nuclear weapons are becoming increasingly available, and other terrible weapons, including bacteriological ones, are all too accessible, institutionalization of cooperative practices should be given a priority of a high order.

Even if the Law of the Sea Treaty, in its present form, is a far from ideal means for implementing obligations of global justice, those obligations remain in force even after rejection of the Treaty. Accordingly, it is not enough for the United States simply to reject the Treaty and go it alone in deep sea mining. Even if the position of the Reagan administration has a basis in considerations of equity (since the Treaty may incorporate only the rhetoric but not the spirit of the "strong" interpretation of the commons), rather than on pure economic self-interest or unrestrained Global Libertarianism, the go-it-alone policy is not our best alternative, even from the point of view of national interest. Instead, the United States should either propose a more defensible version of the Treaty or announce that it will withhold a "global justice" tax from the profits of its own undersea mining companies, as outlined in §15.

Mining of the deep sea bed provides us with an opportunity to develop cooperative institutions for development of resources lying outside national boundaries. Without such a model, competition for resources will most likely extend not only to the ocean depths but to Antarctica and eventually outer space. Even if the United States goes it alone, success will be achieved only at great practical and moral cost. We will have isolated ourselves from the majority of nations of the world. More important, we will have failed to respect the moral rights of their disproportionately poverty-stricken populations.

This does not mean we should uncritically accept the political excesses of the developing states, some of which are extremely corrupt and virtually none of which are democratic. It does mean, however, that we should make serious efforts to meet our moral obligations. What is so troubling about American rejection of the Law of the Sea Treaty, which after all may have been justified, is the tone of American pronouncements which seem to place highest priority on Global Libertarianism and American economic interests. On the contrary, our discussion indicates that global justice cannot be reduced to unrestrained libertarianism or replaced by considerations of national self-interest alone. Americans, in short, need to think far more deeply about the issues raised by the prospect of deep sea mining and by resources found in the global commons.

## NOTES

I would like to thank Tom Regan for his encouragement and for his acute editorial suggestions. I am also grateful to the Rockefeller Foundation, the National Humanities Center, and Hamilton College for their support.

1. For discussion of recent technological mining, see C. E. Gregory, *A Concise History of Mining* (New York: Pergamon Press, 1980).

2. Elliot Richardson, former United States Ambassador to the Law of the Sea Conference, in a speech at Duke University, Spring 1982.

3. Useful commentary on the Law of the Sea Conference and the draft treaty which emerged from it includes Frederick Arnold, "Toward a Principled Approach to the Distribution of Global Wealth: An Impartial Solution to the Dispute over Seabed Manganese Nodules," *San Diego Law Review*, vol. 17, no. 3 (1980): 557–589, and Patricia Minola, "Moon Treaty and the Law of the Sea," *San Diego Law Review*, vol. 18, no. 3 (1981): 455–471. A less scholarly summary and favorable review of the Conference's work is provided by Marie Eduarda Gonclaves in her article, "Who Owns the Oceans?" *UNESCO COURIER*, vol. 30 (1977): 4–8. An exchange between James Malone, special presidential representative to the Third U.N. Conference on the Law of the Sea, who defends the American rejection of the draft treaty, and a proponent of the treaty, Ambassador Engo, from the United Republic of Cameroon, is found in the *Journal of Contemporary Studies*, vol. V, no. 2 (1982): 81–104.

4. That such a view is at least the proper starting point for global negotiations is suggested by Robert A. Goldwin in his paper, "Locke and the Law of the Sea," *Commentary*, vol. 71, no. 6 (1981): 46–50.

5. William Safire, "Son of 'Sea Law Sellout,'" *The New York Times*, May 3, 1982, p. 25.

6. John Rawls, *A Theory of Justice* (Cambridge, Mass.: Harvard University Press, 1971), 3–4.

7. Richard Slatter, ed., *Hobbes' Thucydides* (New Brunswick, N.J.: Rutgers University Press, 1975), 377–385, quoted by Michael Walzer in *Just and Unjust Wars* (New York: Basic Books, 1977), 5.

8. *Ibid.*

9. *Ibid.*

10. Hans Morganthau, *Politics Among Nations* (New York: Alfred A. Knopf, 1978) especially pp. 5–10.

11. See Charles Beitz, *Political Theory and International Relations* (Princeton, N.J.: Princeton University Press, 1979) particularly pp. 27–66, for such an argument.

12. This point is suggested by Beitz, *ibid.*, 41–42.

13. Locke's *Second Treatise* is available in a wide variety of editions.

14. Robert Nozick's *Anarchy, State and Utopia* (New York: Basic Books, 1974) is a widely discussed contemporary defense of libertarianism.

15. John Locke, *Second Treatise of Government* (1690), Chap. V, sec. 27.

16. *Ibid.*, V, 27.

17. *Ibid.*, V, 20.

18. Nozick, *op. cit.*, 175. For a treatment of appropriation to which I am heavily indebted, see Lawrence Becker, *Property Rights: Philosophic Foundations* (London: Routledge and Kegan Paul, 1977), Chaps. 3 and 4.

19. For a fuller account, see Becker, *op. cit.*, Chaps. 3 and 4.

20. For an interesting although highly controversial critique of the view that we face increasing shortage of vital natural resources, see Julian L. Simon, *The Ultimate Resource* (Princeton, N.J.: Princeton University Press, 1981).

21. Rawls, *op. cit.*, 104.

22. Beitz, *op. cit.*, 138.

23. *Ibid.*, 141.

24. *Ibid.*, 141.

25. *Ibid.*, 139.

26. This recapitulates my argument in "Global Justice and the Authority of States," forthcoming in *The Monist*.

27. In any case, not everyone who benefits from the policies of resource-rich nations or from the ingenuity of their scientists deserves to so benefit. Most are "bystanders" who profit fortuitously from the efforts of others. For discussion, see Brian Barry, "Humanity and Justice in Global Perspective" and David A. J. Richards, "International Distributive Justice" in J. Roland Pennock and John W. Chapman, eds., *Ethics, Economics and the Law, Nomos XXIV* (New York: New York University Press, 1982).

28. For discussion of positive and negative rights in the context of international affairs, see Henry Shue, *Basic Rights* (Princeton, N.J.: Princeton University Press, 1980), particularly pp. 35–40.

29. The basic model here of course is the veil of ignorance developed by Rawls in *A Theory of Justice*. For application to world affairs, see Beitz and Richards, *op. cit.* For criticism of the application of Rawls's theory to international affairs, see Simon, "Global Justice and the Authority of States," *op. cit.*

30. Rawls argues that we could go further and ensure, consistent with respect for basic liberties, that the disadvantaged be made as well off as possible. However, such a thesis rests on a number of controversial assumptions and hence is open to stronger objection than the more minimal assertion that we should support a basic welfare floor.

31. This point is made by Shue, *op. cit.*, 35–40.

32. The claim here is not that imposition of positive obligations of *any* kind reduces persons to resources but only that requiring inordinate sacrifice or especially heavy burdens does so. In a world where suffering is endemic among millions, it surely is admirable to assume especially heavy obligations to help but it is not in my view morally required that we do so. But for a view which suggests that at least under present conditions morality is

highly demanding, see Norman Care's "Career Choice" forthcoming in
*Ethics*. For an argument defending recognition of achievement as a requirement of respect for persons, see Robert L. Simon, "An Indirect
Defense of the Merit Principle," *The Philosophical Forum*, vol. X, no. 2–4
(1978–1979).

33.     It may be argued in response that few developing nations actually have the
military power to disrupt mining operations so that their cooperation is unnecessary for mining success. However, even if this point is true, developing nations can contribute to an international climate discouraging to
economic investment in other ways. For example, they can argue in international forums against exploitation of resources by the West, contributing
to a climate of political hostility and tension which puts other investments,
which such countries can affect, at risk.

34.     See Malone, *op. cit.*, 88.

35.     *The New York Times*, Sunday, September 26, 1982, p. E9.

36.     *Ibid.*, Friday, December 17, 1982, p. A38.

# SUGGESTIONS FOR FURTHER READING

For further examination of the topics discussed in this essay, readers are encouraged
to consult the sources cited in the footnotes as well as those that follow.

§2.    For important historical discussions of international law and the status
of the sea, discussions from which the present debate has evolved, see Hugo
Grotius, *De Juri Belli ac Pacis libri tres* (1625) translated by F. W. Kelsey (Ox-
ford: Clarendon Press, 1925) and Emer de Vattel, *The Law of Nations or the
Principles of Natural Law* (1758) translated by Charles G. Fenwick (New York:
Oceana Publications, 1964). Historical and contemporary treatments of private
property are included in a useful anthology edited by Virginia Held, *Property,
Profits and Economic Justice* (Belmont, Calif.: Wadsworth, 1980).

§5.    For discussion of the moral status of collectives, such as the state, see Joel
Feinberg, "Collective Responsibility," *The Journal of Philosophy*, Vol LXV, No. 7
(1968), and Virginia Held, "Can a Random Collection of Individuals Be Morally
Responsible?" *The Journal of Philosophy*, Vol. LXVII, No. 14 (1970). Hedley
Bull defends the institution of the state in international affairs against those who
take an individualist perspective in his essay, "The State's Positive Role in World
Affairs," *Daedalus*, Vol. 108, No. 4 (1979).

§7.    For an excellent general discussion of different perspectives of the
responsibilities of the affluent towards the deprived groups in international affairs, see Onora O'Neil's "The Moral Perplexities of Famine Relief," in Tom
Regan, ed., *Matters of Life and Death: New Introductory Essays in Moral Philosophy* (New York: Random House, 1980).

§8.    Robert Nozick's *Anarchy, State and Utopia* cited in the footnotes is a
widely discussed account of one version of libertarianism. Critical responses to
Nozick's position are found in Jeffrey Paul, ed., *Reading Nozick* (Totowa, N.J.:
Rowman and Littlefield, 1981).

§9.    The literature devoted to discussion of Rawls's *A Theory of Justice* is
extensive. Some of the more important critical reactions are found in Norman
Daniels, ed., *Reading Rawls* (New York: Basic Books), which also contains a
useful bibliography. For criticism of the idea that the genetic-environmental lot-

tery undermines the grounds of individual claims of desert, see George Sher, "Effort, Ability and Personal Desert," *Philosophy & Public Affairs*, Vol. 8, No. 4 (1979). For a general discussion of positive and negative rights, see Norman E. Bowie and Robert L. Simon, *The Individual and the Political Order* (Englewood Cliffs, N.J.: Prentice-Hall, 1977), Chapter Three.

§14.　For a discussion of the idea that international justice must work at the level of states and not individuals, see Robert W. Tucker, *The Inequality of Nations* (New York: Basic Books, 1977).

# 7

# For the Sake of Future Generations

## ANNETTE BAIER

## I. INTRODUCTION

Moral philosophers have only quite recently worried over the question of what we are morally obliged to do, or not to do, for the sake of persons who will live after we are dead. Classical moral traditions give us little help with this question. Though ordinary common sense moralities have usually regarded waste as immoral, and have recognized a vague general obligation to leave our camping places as clean as we found them, such popular moral beliefs are not specific about exactly what our duties to future people are, nor about the ground of such obligations—whether for example their basis lies in the rights of our successors to a fair share in what we might squander, to a camping site no dirtier than that enjoyed by their predecessors. We do not find most older moral theorists addressing the questions of what is due to future persons, why it is due, nor how any such moral dues link up with what is due to those persons whose lives overlap with our own.

## §1 SEEING INTO THE FUTURE

Several explanations might be offered for this recent emergence of the question of obligations to future persons. The increase in our ability or sense of our ability to foresee the long-term effects of our policies might be thought to explain it. As long as persons could not see how their actions affected later generations, they could not be expected to feel any obligation to bring about good rather than bad effects. Our recently won confidence that we do control the fate of future persons brings with it a moral burden, responsibility for what we knowingly do. As long as our ancestors did not know what they did to us, and could not reasonably be expected to have known it, they cannot be blamed for any ill effects they produced, nor praised for any good effects. We, rightly or wrongly, feel we can estimate the effects of our policies, we think we know just how our great-great-grandchildren's teeth will be set on edge by the sour grapes we eat.

My use of this biblical metaphor shows that this hypothesis to explain the lack of classical discussions of our topic cannot be quite correct—people have always believed they could foresee *some* long-term cross-generational effects of actions, and have engaged at least in praise of ancestors for their lasting mighty works, if not so often in condemnation of ancestors for their less welcome legacies.

> Let us now praise famous men, and our fathers that begat us. The Lord has wrought great glory by them through his great power, from the beginning. . . Their bodies are buried in peace, but their name liveth for ever more. (Ecclesiasticus 44)

It has been a normal human wish that future generations will not curse their predecessors, but rise up and call them blessed. This repeated wish, however, has not been accompanied by any clear doctrine about just how much it is reasonable to expect from previous generations, about just what we must avoid doing, to avoid meriting the curses of our successors, nor about the ground for such intergenerational obligations. There has always been a willingness to pass moral judgment on past persons for meritorious or wrongful actions of theirs, some of these actions by which we are affected, but the exact link between the recognized merit or demerit of those actions, and their foreseeable consequences for us, has not been so clear. Maybe the "great glory" for which ancestors were praised were glories of piety, exemplary obedience to a divine law, rather than glorious world building for later persons. Indeed the preacher who invited us to praise ancestors cited them as "giving counsel by their understanding and declaring prophecies." (*Ibid.*) They bequeathed to us their counsel and prophecies, not any more mundane bequest.

## §2 LAWS AND CONSEQUENCES

Consequentialist moral theories see the moral status of actions to depend on their good or bad effects. But as long as doing the right thing is equated with doing what one believes God requires, one does not need to know about the long-term consequences of one's actions to discern right and wrong. One can leave it to God to see to it that our doing the right thing does some good to someone or something, at some time or other. The immorality of, say, willful waste, will be thought to lie not in its causal link with woeful want, but in divine prohibition of wasteful policies. A belief in divine goodwill toward human beings will lead the believer to expect that there is *some* link between the content of the divinely ordained moral law and human welfare, but not a link we need to discern in order to know what is right. Then it would make sense to praise past persons for their great acts, from which we do in fact benefit, without thereby praising them *for* benefiting us. We might praise them because they did what was right or virtuous, and praise God that the consequences of their virtuous action for us are beneficial rather than harmful. For a non-consequentialist moral theory, it is possible that there are duties whose discharge does benefit future generations, yet which are not duties *to* those future generations. They might be the beneficiaries of our obligations, without being either those to whom the obligations are owed, or those for whose sake the obligatory action must be done. "Against thee only have I sinned," said David to God, not thereby denying that his sinful action (arranging the death of his ladylove's husband, Haaman) harmed another human, nor even that God prohibits such acts *because* they harm other humans. If our duties are to God and His law, our moral task would not be to fathom God's reasons, but to obey, trusting in the goodness of the will whose word is law. For such a religious non-consequentialist, it might be wrong to squander resources, poison air and water, and the like, not because future generations would thereby suffer (although this consequence of wrongful action is foreseen) but simply because God and His moral law forbids it. Future persons could condemn us for such wrongful action, action which in fact hurt them, but would do so not because it hurt them but because it was wrong, contrary to God's will and so to the moral law.

## §3  FROM RELIGIOUS ETHICS TO SECULAR ETHICS

One does not need to equate morality with the revealed content of God's will or God's law in order to be a non-consequentialist in moral theory. The great German philosopher Immanuel Kant (1724–1804) believed that human reason could discern the moral law, and that we need know neither about God's will nor about the actual long-run consequences of individual right and wrong acts in order to recognize this law. Just as it is in the power of human reason, in its scientific employment, to discern regularities or laws which hold good in physical nature, so reason in its practical employment can recognize law—indeed can *make* law to govern human behavior. The moral lawmaker, Kant claimed, was the individual acting as if setting an example all other persons would follow. For us to know what acts to perform, what example to try to set, theoretical predictive reason often has to help practical legislative reason, in order to work out what would be involved if everyone followed a particular example. But once we are satisfied that we can will that everyone follow our example of, say, ceasing to make nuclear weapons, then we have established that policy as morally right, and are not to consider as morally relevant the *actual* consequences of this policy in the real world where others may not and often do not all follow our example. The right thing to do must be seen to have acceptable consequences *were everyone to do likewise*, but may not have good consequences when done only by some. "Let justice be done, though the earth perish," or, in this case, although the just person or just nation perishes.[1]

This complex moral theory of Kant's both gives our power to envisage consequences of various policies an important role to play in moral reasoning, yet does not identify the right action with that which will in the actual state of things have the best consequences. Kant still needs and keeps a divine power in the background of morality, a power who is to see to it that the discrepancy between ideal and real world consequences is somehow compensated for, some day, so that obedience to the moral law does not, *in the end*, prove destructive to those who do what is right or to the world they would will into being. Kant's is a nonconsequentialist moral theory where the test of moral rightness is the rational acceptability of hypothetical *universal* conformity to a policy, and of the consequences over time of such conformity. We are to do the act which we can will as universal law in "a system of nature," that is, in an ongoing world with interaction and feedback.

This ethical theory holds out some promise of applicability to the question of our duty to future persons, since any practice like dumping toxic wastes where they will poison soil, air, or water seems forbidden by Kant's test—we cannot conceive of a system of nature in which all humans regularly do this, yet survive as a species. It is not a coherently universalizable practice. Some, such as the contemporary Australian philosopher John Passmore,[2] have seen Kant's ethics as addressing the question of our obligations to future persons, and there is no doubt that Kant's test of moral rightness can easily be applied to condemn many current practices, and also that the very form of his *test* for rightness (Can I will this as a law in a system of nature?) forces us to think about the long-term implications of policies. But, as far as I know, Kant did not himself actually draw out the consequences of his theory for this issue. He did make some claims about our *motivation*—he believed that we cannot help but care to some degree about future persons and the sort of life they will have—but he did not spell out what our duty to such persons is, or even if there are any special duties we owe them. To find out whether we do wrong if we refuse to help our contemporaries when they are in need, Kant's test forces us to consider what our world would be like, over time, if such refusal were the universal rule; so to discern our duty to anybody, we must in a sense think of everybody, future persons included, according to Kant's test. Future persons therefore come into his theory implicitly, but not as ones whose interests give rise to any *special* problems about duties on our part. Future persons themselves, and the foreseeable consequences of our actions for them, come into Kant's theory only indirectly. His theory is usable only by moral agents capable of seeing the long-run implications of policies for whole systems, natural and social, and he believed that we moral agents do in fact care about the future of the human world, but he did not spell out any particular obligations we have or, for that matter, which we fail to have, to future persons.

## §4   MODERN MORAL THEORIES AND THE PERSON-AFFECTING PRINCIPLE

Post-Kantian moral theories, both utilitarian and some *rights* theories, have focused attention very strongly on the *effects* of right and wrong actions on the good of human persons, often making this the decisive test of their rightness or wrongness. They see human moral agents, not some supervising God,[3] as responsible for the foreseeable effects of their actions. Modern moral theorists, while agreed on seeing morality as promoting our human good, disagree over what precise effect on human (and perhaps animal) good determines the moral rightness of an action: Utilitarians see the crucial thing to be the effect of an action or policy on people's *happiness*, others emphasize the effect on *interests*, while those who hold a theory of rights (either rights arising from a hypothetical agreement, or so-called natural rights) see the crucial question to be the effect of an action on people as rights' holders.

The violation of a right is, of course, a special sort of effect on a person and on his or her good. It cannot be equated with making that person unhappier, or less able to get what she in fact wants. If I don't want to vote, then the violation of my right to vote by the removal of my name from electoral rolls will not hurt me—it may not even be noticed by me. Nevertheless someone else on my behalf might correctly protest the violation of my right, and correctly say that my position is worsened by this inability to do what in fact I have no wish to do. I might even myself protest, and insist on my rights, then never exercise them. Once we see ourselves as right holders, the violation of our rights becomes an injury, even if it makes no *other* difference to our lives. The violation of my rights affects my position among right holders, even if that position is not very important to my particular goals in life. I shall return to this question of the relation between what affects our happiness and what affects our interests and our position among persons in §10. For the moment I want merely to draw attention to the agreement between most utilitarians and most of those who hold a rights theory that the moral wrongness of an act consists in some sort of bad effect it has on people.

The principle which they agree upon (but which religious moralists, or even Kantians, need not accept) has been called the *Person-Affecting Principle*, which says *that for any action to be wrong, it must affect some person or persons (usually other than the agent) for the worse*. This is a minimal requirement of wrongness—the principle does not say that all acts which have any bad effects on others are wrong, but only that, if an action has *no* bad effect on anyone, it cannot be really wrong.

Versions of this principle, sometimes called the principle of *No Wrongs without Victims*, were used by the nineteenth-century English social philosopher John Stuart Mill (1806–1873) and by many reformers since then, to distinguish "real" wrongs from those traditionally frowned-upon actions which seem in fact to have no victims, to do no harm to any (nonconsenting) person. The principle seems to sort moral prohibitions into those soundly based on the requirements of human good, and mere taboos and expressions of culturally fostered distaste or disgust. It was used by the framers of Britain's controversial Wolfenden Report to distinguish "moralistic" bad legislation, which created "victimless crimes," from those parts of the criminal law which protect persons from becoming, in a variety of ways, the victims of other persons.

The *Person-Affecting Principle* directs us always to think of the consequences of our actions for other people, when making a moral decision. It is natural, if one finds the principle plausible, to think of consequences for future people as well as for our contemporaries, and to see a moral agent's responsibility as extending to the foreseeable effects of our actions on future and distant as well as present and close persons. I suggest, then, that one reason why it is only recently that the question of our duty to future persons has been discussed is that it is relatively recently that ethical theory has seen the responsibility for consequences to fall on human agents, and only recently that the Person-Affecting Principle has come to seem acceptable. It took so long for the question of our duty to future persons to come to our attention because it took so long for ethics to free itself from theology, and to make morality concerned primarily and directly with the human good. It took the same long time for us to accept the related, sometimes frightening fact that, if we do not consider the consequences of our policies for future people, no one will—that neither gods nor hidden hands will arrange things for us so that doing anything we for any reason believe to be right will in fact advance the human good not only now but also indefinitely into the future. This increasing secularization of moral theory, and with it the increasing acceptability of the Person-Affecting Principle, along with our increasing ability to trace consequences and our increasing power to perform acts with dramatically great foreseeable consequences for future persons, has forced this moral issue on our attention.

Paradoxically enough, however, that same Person-Affecting Principle which seems to direct us to think about future persons has been invoked by some recent thinkers to reveal a problem in the very idea that future people could possibly be our victims. I turn next to that worry.

## II. THE FUTURITY PROBLEM

### §5 OUR KNOWLEDGE OF FUTURE PEOPLE

There are several features of future people, in relation to us, which can make the idea that we have duties to them seem problematic. I shall consider their *unknowability*, their *indeterminacy*, and their *contingency*.

We do not know much about all those children who will be born during the next seven months, although their genetic makeup is now quite fixed and determinate. For people further in the future, not only *do* we not know details about them, those details are not yet fixed, so are unknowable. Such lack of knowledge, especially when due to the not-yet-determinate status of future people, does, I think, rule out our having to them one kind of duty which we can have to our contemporaries. For example, some people now living are accustomed to a particular diet, and *could* not easily adapt to a different one. There would be no point in shipping canned pork and beans off to avert a famine in a Muslim country—the people could not eat it. We know, or can find out, this sort of special need, when we are considering the effects of our policies on our contemporaries, but we cannot know this sort of fact about distant future people. Since they are not yet determinate people, their special requirements are as yet unknowable. *Some* wrongs we can do to our contemporaries, those harmings which depend upon their special needs, we cannot knowingly do to future persons. Their indeterminacy protects us against the charge of doing them that sort of wrong.

But such wrongs, although real, are only one sort of wrong we can do people, and there are plenty other wrongs which do not depend upon the victims' special needs, but on their common human nature. However little we know about future people, however much about them is not yet fixed, as long as they are human people they can be expected to need air, water, some fruits of the earth to eat. They will be vulnerable to poisons, just as we are, and we can, it seems, affect the availability to them of the unpoisoned air, water, soil, undestroyed naturally self-renewing or self-cleansing basic physical resources, which we as a species need. By the Person-Affecting Principle then, as far as we have seen, there can be wrongs to future persons despite their indeterminacy and our ignorance of their special needs. The principle will not itself tell us how bad the effects of our action must be for future persons to have been wronged, but it allows room for the idea that we really can wrong future persons. So far so good.

There is, however, the third characteristic of future persons to consider, namely their *contingency*. Not merely is their identity now indeterminate, but what will eventually fix it are a host of causal factors including the actions and inactions of their predecessors. It is *this* fact, the *contingency of future people on their predecessors*, which generates what has come to be seen as the worst philosophical "problem of futurity,"[4] one which might seem to cancel all duties we may have thought we had to future persons. I turn to that problem.

## §6 THE ONTOLOGICAL PRECARIOUSNESS OF PERSONS

A thing is ontologically precarious, precarious in its very being, to the extent that its coming into being is dependent on other things. To appreciate just how precarious we all are, or were, we need merely think of the many possible things our parents might have done which would have led to our own nonbeing, to our total absence from the human scene. Not merely do deliberate parental actions of family planning determine which children come to exist, but all sorts of outside factors determining the precise time of conception also play their role—such things as owl hootings or train whistles which wake potential parents in the night. The English philosopher Derek Parfit, who has in the last ten years in a number of influential papers[5] explored this problem thoroughly, asks how many of us could truly claim that we would have existed even if railways had never been invented. A recent electricity blackout in the city of New York was followed nine months later by a significantly increased number of births. As times goes on, the number of descendants of these "blackout babies" will probably become larger and larger, so that factors such as trains and blackouts come to figure in causal ancestry of a larger and larger proportion of the population.

Philosophers have long been aware of this radical contingency of particular existent things on earlier happenings, of the reverberating effects of seemingly trivial events, given a long enough time. In metaphysical discussions of causal determinism, and in theological discussions of divine predestination, the implications of this dependency of future on past realities have often been explored, and moral philosophers have often worried about the implications of this interrelatedness of things for our free will and moral responsibility for what we do or fail to do. Recently the implications for our responsibility for and to future people have been drawn out by Parfit and others.

## §7 WANTING THE PAST TO HAVE BEEN DIFFERENT

If anyone's existence would have been prevented by so many thinkable changes in earlier history, it seems to follow that there are severe constraints on seriously judging that it would have been better if some earlier event, no matter how bad it may seem, had not occurred. In particular, one must consider the likelihood that, had it not occurred, one would not have existed at all to do any judging.

I am inclined to judge that the potato famine in Ireland and food shortages in Scotland in the nineteenth century were bad things, and that it would have been better if those in charge of agricultural policy in Britain had made different decisions which would have averted those hard times. Then I reflect that my great-grandparents left Britain for New Zealand because of those very hard times. Had they not done so, they would not have met one another, married, had the children they did. Had the famine been averted, their great-grandchildren, if any, would have been *other* possible people, and I would not have existed. So do I *sincerely* judge that it would have been better had the past been different, had those persons who, as things actually turned out, did have me as a great-grandchild had a less difficult life, had not been faced with famine? I will sincerely make this judgment only if I can sincerely say that it would have been better, all things considered, that I not have existed. (Alternative interpretations of this judgment are examined below, in §9.) So it is not easy as one might have thought to judge that it would have been better for the past to have been other than it was. Even to wish that one's own parents had been richer, or more fortunate, or healthier than they were in youth becomes hard, since any change in their lives before the time of one's own conception probably would have brought with it one's own nonexistence.

## §8  THE NO OBLIGATION ARGUMENT

Let us now see how this presumed fact, the extreme ontological precariousness of persons (and indeed of all other particular things), and the consequent difficulty of wanting the past to have been different, can be made to yield the conclusion that we have no obligations to future persons. We need to add, to what I shall call the *precariousness* premise (P), a version of the Person-Affecting Principle which I will call the *victim* premise (V), which says that a person has not been wronged by another unless he has been made worse off by the other's act, unless, that is, he is thereby the other's victim. Now we can construct a simple argument from P and V, to give us the conclusion C that nothing which we do can wrong future persons, unless what we do is so bad that future persons wish they had never been born. To spell it out more fully:

V.  We do not wrong a person by our current action or policy unless it would have been better for that person had we not acted that way.

P.  For any actual future person F, the outcome had we not done what we are doing would (in all likelihood) have been that F not exist at all, rather than that F exist and be better off.

∴ C.  Unless it would have been better for F not to exist at all, we are (in all likelihood) not wronging F by what we are doing.

This argument, if it works, works whatever our actions are—however wasteful, depleting, or polluting. As long as future persons are not so affected by our actions that they can make a charge of "wrongful existence"[6] against us, they have no complaint against us, since they cannot claim to have been wronged by what we did. The only wrong, it seems, that we can do future persons is to allow them to exist in an intolerable world. As long as that world is tolerable enough for them not to regret existing, they are not wronged by our world-spoiling activities. No future person will be able to say to us (or to our ghosts), "If you had acted rightly, *I* would have had a better life."

This is a very troubling argument. What troubles most of us about it is that the conclusion seems at odds with our moral intuitions on this matter. For, once the issue has been raised, most of us do feel that we would be wronging our successors by unrestrainedly depleting and polluting the earth even if that did not render their lives intolerable. We may be unclear exactly what we must, in decency, do for the sake of future person (I take up this problem in Part III), but most of us do feel not only that it is wrong to pollute and deplete, but also that it is "future people," in some sense of that phrase, who are the ones who are wronged if we act wrongly in this regard. The contemporary American political philosopher Thomas Schwartz, when he propounded an early version of our argument above, concluded not that we were free to do what we liked, as far as the consequences for the world future people will live in goes, but rather that *we owe it to one another*, to our *contemporaries* who do happen to care about humanity's future, to restrain our earth-ravaging activities. If Schwartz is right we will have sinned only against our contemporaries, if we poison the wells of the future; we will not have sinned against the persons who suffer the poisoning.

Now although it is good to have our conviction that we are not morally free to pollute the earth endorsed and given some basis, despite the troublesome argument we are examining, I think that we still are apt to feel that Schwartz's proposed basis for our obligations is not the right one. Many of us also care about the future of various precious artworks, or other nonsentient things. If we have a duty to preserve such things, it is a duty to our fellow art lovers, not to the artworks themselves. It seems wrong to put our concern for our successors in the same moral boat as our concern for the future of anything else which happens at present to have a place in our affections. Surely it must be in some sense for future persons' sakes, not just for our own sakes, that we consider what sort of existence for them our actions entail? If Schwartz is right, then if we could make ourselves or let ourselves cease to feel concerned about the future of our human communities, then we would be rid not only of a sense of obligation not to pollute but also of the obligation itself. If it is only that "those who would like our distant descendants to enjoy a clean commodious well stocked world just may owe it to their like-minded contemporaries to contribute to these goals,"[7] then if we all cultivate indifference, cease to care, we can come to owe nothing to anyone in this regard. Can this be right? For whose sake, and for whose good, ought we conserve scarce resources and refrain from putting delayed-action poisons in our common wells—if, that is, we do have a duty to conserve and not to poison? To help us see if it can be said to be for the sake of future persons, despite the troubling argument, we need first to have a closer look at the conclusion C, and the qualification in that conclusion. When would a person judge that it would have been better, for her *own* sake, that she not have been born?

## §9  BETTER FOR ONE NOT TO HAVE BEEN BORN

We have already seen in §7 how one can become committed to the judgment that it would have been better if one had not been born. One is committed to this if one seriously judges that some event such as a famine (without whose occurrence one would not have been born) was a bad thing, better averted. But such a judgment (if we ever really do make it) is made from an attempted God's-eye view, so to speak, one that takes into account *all* those who are involved. It is not made from one's own self-concerned standpoint, since one might make it although

one's own life was pleasant enough, or was until one starts being obsessed
with what went into one's own "prehistory," the human cost of one's own
existence. To make the issues clearer, we need to distinguish two "objective" judgments from two subjective judgments. The former are judgments about the comparative value of alternative "world histories,"
made from no particular person's point of view, while the latter are
judgments about a particular life history, made from the point of view of
the one whose life it is.

$O_1$  All things considered, the world history (after some chosen fixed
point) where F comes to exist is, given the causal chains which
produced F, and the nature of F's life, worse than alternative
world histories in which F does not exist.

$O_2$  The world history containing F's life is, because of F's own dread-
fully intolerable life, *thereby* a worse world history than alternative world histories in which F's existence is prevented.

We could only make this second objective judgment if we (or F)
could make one of two more subjective judgments, ones made from F's
own point of view:

$S_1$  For F's own sake, or from her own self-concerned point of view,
the sooner her life ends the better.

$S_2$  For F's own sake, or from her own self-concerned point of view, it
would have been better if her life had never started.

The qualification in C, the conclusion of the No Obligation Argument, seems to refer only to those cases where the judgment $O_2$ could be
made, and this in turn requires us to make either $S_1$ or $S_2$. Which of them
does $O_2$ presuppose?

I think that $S_2$ is what is needed to support $O_2$. $S_1$ is the judgment
made by most suicides, but a person need not be driven to suicide in
order to judge $S_2$ and to have a valid claim of wrongful existence against
someone. There are powerful forces, religious, instinctive, and altruistic, which may prevent even desperately unhappy people from ending
their own lives even when they judge $S_2$. Nor is it true that one need
judge $S_2$ in order to judge $S_1$. One's life can *become* intolerable enough to
make one judge $S_1$, although long stretches of it were good and one
would not judge $S_2$. For one to judge $S_2$, one's life would have had to be
continuously intolerable, or some bits so bad that they clearly outweighed the good bits, when weighed not from a momentary but from a
"life's-eye" point of view. One does not need to suppose that a suicide's
life was as bad as that, bad enough to support $S_2$, in order to understand
how suicide can look the best option. But it is just this very strong judgment, $S_2$, which F would need to make to charge her predecessors with
wronging her by allowing her to exist at all.

The conclusion, C, of the No Obligation Argument then, presupposes that S₂ makes sense, that it is conceivable that a person could be wronged by having been allowed to come into existence at all. Persons who judge S₂ are victims of previous events or actions in a sense which is *wider*, or different, than that in which our contemporaries are victims of our assault or neglect. In the latter case, we can say that the victim's *life* is worse than it would have been without the assault or neglect. But the victims of earlier events who are driven to S₂ judgments about their own lives are not complaining that they don't have lives better in this or that respect, they are complaining that they are, and ever were, alive at all, given their life prospects. This means that we must interpret premise V in a fairly wide way, to include this sort of victim, if V is to be even *compatible* with giving any sense to C, the conclusion which is supposed to follow from V and P. The argument itself requires us to recognize that not all victims of policies are victims because their *lives* would have been better in some respect if someone had done something different, rather some people are victims because they are alive—period. This fact will become important in the following sections when I try to diagnose the fault of the No Obligation Argument.

## §10 VARIETIES OF VICTIMS, VARIETIES OF ILLS

So far we have seen that there can be victims of events and policies, those who judge S₂, whose claim is not that their lives would have been better had those events not occurred. Earlier, in §4, we said that one can be affected for good or ill by a policy or action in a variety of ways. One's rights may be violated, even when one might not need to exercise those rights to further the interests one in fact has. Similarly, one's interests can be injured, say by loss of a job opportunity, or a pension scheme, even when one would not have wanted that job and does not yet care about one's old age. Normally what advances one's interests *does* help one get what one wants, and getting what one wants does make one happy, but one's interests can be injured without that affecting one's getting what one wanted, and one's wants can be frustrated, although getting what one wanted would not have made one happy. Misery, frustration, injury to one's interests, violation or denial of rights, all unfavorably affect a person's good but can do so in different ways. The good of a person is complex since persons are and usually see themselves as bearers of rights, possessors of interests, as well as goal-directed and sentient. To act for the sake of some person or group is to act to advance any of these components of their good. The good of persons, seen prospectively, includes more than what will in fact give them happiness, since they may not be aware of some of their interests, so not be unhappy at their nonadvancement, and they may neither know nor care about some violations of their rights. One needs not only to be fully self-conscious but also to have what today we call a "raised consciousness" for one's feeling of happiness to reflect the level to which one's rights and interests as well as one's purposes and tastes are respected.

As I am using the term "interests,"[8] we have an interest in the obtaining *conditions*, or *states of affairs*, such as our own good health, our prosperity, peace in our time, liberty, where these conditions are favorable for our success in satisfying a whole range of particular desires we have and expect to have in the future. The sort of things a parent or godparent wishes for a child are general goods of this sort, conditions which will enable the child to acquire and cultivate ambitions, desires, and tastes which can in those conditions be satisfied, and give pleasure when satisfied. Although it might occasionally turn out that these conditions are *not* needed or even favorable for the satisfaction of the actual desires the child comes to have, as a general rule the furthering of one's interests *does* increase the extent to which one's desires get satisfied, just as normally getting what one desired does give one the pleasure one expected it would. In acting in the interests of a person, we are trying to increase their *prospects* of satisfying their desires, and so, normally, of being happy with the outcome.

As a person grows from childhood to adulthood, and tastes and concerns become formed, these very general interests, shared with almost all persons, become specified in ways which often limit the number of other persons with whom we share them. An interest in peace in our time will become associated with an interst in the success of the political party whose plan for peace one judges the best one. One will have an interest not only in health but in the maintenance of a specific health insurance scheme, not just in prosperity but in the wise policies of certain banks and corporations, not just in liberty but in the removal of some specific threats to liberty. However specific one's interests become, they usually are still specifications of interests most people have, interests in livelihood, health, peace, in a decent community which provides scope for public participation and for private friendships, for satisfying work and for the enjoyment both of nature and of a rich, varied, and historically conscious cultural tradition.

Among the interests we share with others are interests we have only because we are cooperating with others in some project. Membership in a nation gives us this sort of interest in the nation's affairs, and gives each of us an interest in the protection of our individual roles as citizens and taxpayers. As a member of the taxpaying public my interests are injured by the tax fraud of my fellows as well as by misuse of public funds by officials. Here my interest is the same as that of any other honest taxpayer, an interest in not being ripped off. Yet this interest I share with many others can clash with more private interests I may have, if for example my employer is among those guilty of tax fraud and my job depends on his illgotten "savings." My interest as a member of the taxpaying public and my interest as an employee of this employer may be in conflict with one another. Often we need to refer to the *roles* we play, roles relating us to others and to schemes of cooperation, to specify the variety of our interests, and many of the duties and rights we have, and wrongs done to us, also depend upon these social roles. I have duties as a daughter, family member, department member, teacher, university employee, and citizen, and I have rights as all of these, as well as a member of a particular professional association, health insurance scheme, and so on. Since in most of these roles my rights and interests coincide with those of some others, I will protest any violation of rights, and wrongful injury of interests, even if I foresee that my own goals will not be frustrated by those wrongs. For example I will protest *as* university teacher, if tenure guarantees are broken, even if I am about to retire and so will not be hurt myself.

Let us now try to apply these points about the complexity of a person's good, its inclusion of *interests* to be protected or furthered as well as desires to be satisfied and pleasures to be enjoyed, to the case of future people. Because interests are *always* future-oriented, and because we can know what they are, at least at a general level, without having much if any information about what particular tastes and desires a person has, it seems to me that future persons' *interests* can be determinate even when the persons themselves are not yet determinate, even when the *whole* of what will count as their good is not yet fixed. Of course, in being sure that, whoever they are, they will *have* an interest in clean air, we are also usually assuming that they will *want* to breathe, and be *pained* by inability to do so—some assumptions about their sensitivities and their desires will be included in our claims about their interests. A person whose interest in good health is badly injured will most probably also have frustration and pain, as "ills" which accompany the ill of ill health. We may even feel we know what *particular* desires a future person will have because of grave ill health—for example, in extreme cases the desire to end life. So in concentrating on the *interests* of future people in what follows, I shall not be supposing that in injuring interests we are not usually also frustrating and hurting. I shall, however, be relying on the *possibility* that an injury to a person's interest can (and sometimes should) be averted, although that does *not* bring that person a better life, more satisfaction and less frustration, more pleasure and less pain. Interests are important, and injury to interests is important, *whether or not* averting the injury in fact leads to less frustration and less pain for the one whose interest it is.

Future people, once actual, will come to have specific interests as well as general ones, and will have particular desires and sensitivities, as well as interests, which will need to be taken into account by anyone *then* concerned with their good. We now *cannot* consider their good "all things considered," because all the relevant things are not yet determinate. But we *can* consider some vital dimensions of what will be their good, and do so when we consider those of their interests which are general enough, or, even though specific, predictable enough, to be already fixed. (One specific interest we can be fairly sure that people a few generations after us will have is an interest in the advancement of knowledge of methods of *detoxifying* all the resources we are currently poisoning. This is not an interest people in the past have needed to have.)

What we now need to consider is whether the fact that our acts help to *determine* both the identity of future persons and some of the specific interests they will have means that *those* acts cannot at the same time damage interests of those persons. The No Obligation Argument seems to allow us to injure only one of the interests a future person might have, a rather complex interest, namely the interest in not existing at all if other vital interests, such as health, are to be very badly served. This is a conditional interest—an interest in not existing unless other unconditional interests can be tolerably well served. The No Obligation Argument in effect claims that unless a future person has *this* exceptional interest injured by us, she is not wronged by us by those policies of ours which "select" her for existence. Is it possible, contrary to what the argument claims, for us to wrong a person by injuring an interest she has even though she comes to *be* a person with that interest only because of the very actions which also injure that interest? Can that person say *both* "If you had acted differently, *my interests* would have been better served," *and* also "Had you acted differently, I would not have been one of those who exist and have such interests"? I shall try to show that such a complaint makes sense.

## §11  SELECTING POPULATIONS BY OUR ACTS

Before looking at future people, let us consider present people, and sketch analogous ways in which our actions can injure their interests, perhaps violate their rights. Take a case such as a teacher who writes a course description. It is surely primarily for the sake of the students who will be in the course that such descriptions are written, with whatever care is taken. Yet *who* precisely they turn out to be depends to some degree on the course description itself, if it is an elective course. The description, and the care taken in writing it, both is for the sake of the students, and also helps to select which students are those for whose sake a course plan is produced. The teacher's actions help to fix the class population. Similar sorts of cases arise with immigration policy—the ways in which a nation encourages or discourages immigrants help to determine who comes, but once in a country an immigrant might complain, "You didn't warn me about the high unemployment. Had you done so, I probably wouldn't have come." (Note that it need *not* be claimed that they regret being there for them to have a complaint.) Have we injured and perhaps wronged the class members who suffer once in the badly described course, the immigrants who come with inadequate advance warning of conditions, even if, once in the class or nation, they do not on balance regret being there?

It is important to see that a version of the No Obligation Argument can be used to give a negative answer here too. To any complainer we can say, "If you wouldn't have been in the relevant population (class member, immigrant) had we done what you say we should have done, then you are not a wronged member of that population. You would not have been a *better-off* class member or immigrant, had we acted as you think we should have, *you* would not have been a member of that population *at all*. So you have no complaint as class member, as immigrant." Must they then reformulate their complaint, and say that it was the population of those *considering* joining the class or nation, not those actually joining it, whose interests are injured by the poor descriptions and plans? Such wider populations certainly are affected, but it would seem counterintuitive to say that when a teacher designs a course and makes the design known in a course description she is fulfilling a duty only to the wider group of all those who might consider joining, not also to the narrower group who actually join. Any class member (or immigrant) whose complaint is responded to by these moves would, if she had her wits about her, say, "I *as class member* (immigrant) as well as a potential class member have been wronged by the bad advance description. You owe it to all those deciding whether to join, and in particular to those who *do* so decide, to have an adequate plan and to give adequate advance notice of it. Had you done the right thing, I would not have *been* a class member, but you didn't, and I am, and I, like all other members, have been wronged by you."

It seems to me that this response is right. The interests of ours which can be injured include those dependent on the act which does the injury, in this case the act which helped make one a class member. This may sound paradoxical, but the paradox disappears once we are clear about what interests are, and how we can possess them in virtue of roles we fill and come to fill. Sometimes we come to fill a particular role, giving rise to an interest, because of the very act of another person which injures our interest once we are in that role.

Of course the extent of the analogy between this case and the case of future persons is limited. *They* do not *decide* to become actual persons, it is "decided" for them. But we can find, among injuries to present persons, cases of nonvoluntary as well as voluntary membership in some group where the act of determining membership also injures the interests of the members, as members. An annexation of a territory subjects the inhabitants to a new rule, makes them members of a new "population," and may simultaneously make them second-class subjects, a disadvantaged minority. After the second world war, Transylvanians who had been Hungarians became subjects of Rumania, and could complain (as many of them did) that the very act which made them Rumanians also injured their interests as Rumanians. Adopted children sometimes feel that the very fact that they are adopted gives them a lower place in their adoptive parents' affections than those who are the parents' "own" children in the biological sense. The very act which made the adopted children members of their new family, some feel, injured them *as* members of that family. (They may feel this without believing that it would have been better had they never been adopted, without feeling that they are, all things considered, injured by the act of adoption.) Could future persons, as our successors, be injured by us although the injuring act selected them *as* our successors? Well, so far we can say that the fact that they didn't *choose* that status does not rule that out. Nevertheless the fact that our acts determine who will exist, and so do not *shift* them from one "population" into another, but determines their very availability for *any* population, must not be glossed over.

This fact certainly limits the analogy between our relation to future people and our relation to students in our elective courses, to our adopted children, and to members of our annexed territories. We do not by any act literally *select* from a host of already determinate possible people the ones who will become actual, as would-be adoptive parents might survey the row of orphaned babies in a nursery, picking out the one to become their child. If there *are* fully determinate possible people, we cannot distinguish them as such. All we can do is consider similar descriptions of them such as "the next child I shall have," or "my future eldest great-great-grandchild," or "the first future person who may actually formulate a complaint beginning, 'Those Americans who had any say over policy in the 1980s are to blame for. . . .'" Although each of these titles is designed to pick out one and only one person, we have little idea what that person will be like, or what their total good will consist in. To discern injuries to people we know, we consider them, fully determinate people about whose good-all-things-considered we may have opinions, people whose full range of characteristics enables them to fit many descriptions and fill many bills, then we emphasize the role relevant to the injury we discern: "He was injured *as a parent*," or "*as an employee.*" With actual people we do not know, we usually know more of the roles and bills they fill than simply the one relevant to the injury, so that although we do not know much about, say, those who are starving in the Sahara, we can say *something* about who it is whose interests in health and nourishment are so injured. With future people, there may be nothing yet fixed and known about them except the general interests we need to consider to try to avoid injuring them. All there is, yet, are those interests, not yet the actual people whose interests they will be, whose good those interests will help comprise. So we should not pretend that our relation to future persons is not significantly different from our relation to already existent persons, nor pretend that making them existent is simply moving them from the "population" of possible people into the more exclusive population of actual people. Any responses we make to the No Obligation Argument should avoid that confusion.

Nevertheless we ought also not forget that any act which injures an actual person's long-term interests is one which looks ahead to the not-yet-fixed *older person* the injured one might become. If I now lose my retirement pension rights, I am injured, even though, as far as I know, the older person of retirement age is not yet fixed in her needs or wants. There are many possible future me's. I may become rich enough not to need any pension, or become a beachcomber and not want one, or I may not live long enough to reach retirement age. All these uncertainties for the future are always there, and my interests lie in being somehow prepared for any of them. My interests are injured if I today lose my pension rights, even if I come into an unexpected inheritance or drop dead tomorrow. We must steer clear, then, not only of blurring the difference between future not-yet-actual people and actual people, but also of exaggerating it, of treating the interests it is wrong to injure as always the interests of people with determinate sets of concerns, wants, tastes. Only the dead are *fully* determinate, and the very finality, fixedness, of the nature of their wants and the character of their lives severely limits the interests they can have.

## §12 PAST, PRESENT, AND FUTURE PERSONS

Although a past person cannot any longer suffer, nor want anything, some interests and rights of past people can still be protected or neglected. If I tell malicious lies about some dead persons, their interests in having and keeping a good name is injured. I can do things for the sake of past persons, although they neither know nor feel the effects of what I do. Once we are dead, the range of things which it is possible for others to do for our sake, or to do us ill, shrinks. But we may still, for the dead person's sake, protect his reputation, do what he wanted or would have wanted (especially with his estate), and we may even do things like putting flowers on his grave, thinking that to have some link with what pleased or would have pleased him. (If we put flowers on the grave of someone who hated flowers, it certainly is not done for that one's sake.) The very finished fixed character of the past person's life history puts him beyond most of the harms present and future persons can suffer—he cannot be hurt or frustrated, nor has he any longer many of the interests and rights living persons have. He is safe from much but not all ill.

Future persons too seem safe from being harmed by us in certain ways in which we may harm our contemporaries. We cannot deny them their marital rights, nor any contractual rights, nor libel them, nor take an unfairly large share of a good to which they too have *contributors'* rights. (But we *may* take, for ourselves, too large a share of what earlier people "bequeathed" to an indefinite run of future generations, or ruin a "bequest" which could have been enjoyed much longer but for our spoiling activities.) Just as there are many harms and wrongs we *cannot* do past people, so there are many harms and wrongs we *cannot* do future people.

Future people will, whoever they turn out to be, have a good, but only some components of that good are yet fixed. Must we say the same of the interests which help comprise that good, that they *will be* their interests, but are not yet their interests? We have seen how some interests, like that in not being spoken ill of, last longer than does the person whose interest it is. I have argued that some interests preexist the person whose interests they are. Common predictable human interests, such as the availability of unpoisoned soil as a resource, seem to depend in no way upon that combination of specific interests, concerns, wants, tastes that comprise the concrete *individuality* of persons, which possible people lack, and which future people do not yet have. Whoever becomes actual will have such common interests and we know they will, so I see nothing wrong in saying that those already existent interests are now *theirs*. We do not need to know exactly who "they" are to recognize the reality of their common human interests. Whomever we allow to become actual, those ones have the interests all people have and we can also see what specific form some of those interests will take, since it depends on our policies. Of the interests people claim as their interests, some were predictable before the person's conception or birth, others come into being only because of particular unpredictable facts about them and choices they make. It is the interests which are fixed and predictable in advance which we can say preexist the person of whose good they form a part, and usually it is other less predictable and more specific interests of theirs, such as the success of a particular book they wrote, which last once they are dead. People cast shadows in the form of interests both before them and after them.

We can, then, speak of acting *for the sake of* a person not merely when we act to promote that one's all-things-considered good, as an actual living person, or act to prevent injuries to their *individual* and perhaps eccentric interests, but also when we protect the general interests they have, *in advance of their existence*, or do things for them *after they are dead*. We can even prevent a person's existence, for that person's sake, when we think that, if she were born, she would judge S2. The concept of a person's sake is the most flexible and so the best concept for us to use to cover all the ways in which what we do can be *better for* a person. If, contrary to what the No Obligation Argument concluded, there *are* things we can do which are better for future persons, in addition to preventing their coming to exist to judge S2, then they will be things we do *for their sake*.

## §13 THE NO OBLIGATION ARGUMENT REJECTED

We can now see what is wrong with the No Obligation Argument. The Victim Premise, V, did not spell out all the ways in which a person can be a victim, and only if some of those ways, especially ways of injuring interests, are neglected or denied does the conclusion C really follow from V and P. To see this we should expand V, mentioning all the ways we have distinguished in which something can be worse or better for a person's sake.

The revised version, $V_r$, will read

$V_r$   We do not wrong a person by our action or policy unless it would have been better, for that person's sake, not to have acted that way because our present actions bring

(1) more suffering than the person would have had, had we acted differently;

or (2) more frustration than the person would have had, had we acted differently;

or (3) greater injury to the person's interests than would have occurred had we acted differently, where such interests include the interest in not existing at all, if other interests are to be very badly injured;

or (4) greater violation of the person's rights than would have occurred had we acted differently.

What do we get when we add the original Precariousness Premise to $V_r$? I think we need first to add a premise we can derive from the preceding account of the nature and variety of our interests, namely

I   Among the interests of a person which can be injured are interests which are fixed before the identity of those whose interests they are is fixed, and includes interests which a given person comes to possess only because of the very act which injures those interests.

When we add I to P and $V_r$, I think we can get a revised conclusion, $C_r$, which is very different from the No Obligation conclusion.

$C_r$ Therefore the wrongs we can do a future person are usually restricted to injuries to interests fixed before the identity of future persons are fixed (and to such frustration and pain as is consequent upon the injury to such interests), and cannot include injury to interests not yet fixed or frustration of wants and concerns not yet fixed or hurts to sensibilities not yet fixed.

$C_r$ is very different from C since it not merely allows the wrong of "wrongful existence," now included as injury of an already fixed conditional interest of all persons, but it also allows those *injuries to other already fixed interests* where the act which does the injury at the same time helps settle who it is whose interest it is.

We have avoided the No Obligation conclusion, C, by allowing the concept of an effect on a person to include "*effect*" *on interests*, including interests which come to be possessed only because of the "affecting" act. Parfit regards such interpretations of the Person-Affecting Principle as a "cheat," and himself avoids the No Obligation conclusion by renouncing the Person-Affecting Principle in favor of a vaguer principle which says, "It is bad if those who live are worse off than those who might have lived,"[9] a principle explicitly allowing comparisons between *different* possible people, not just comparisons of the possible fates of people of fixed identity. I think that once we come to see what sort of things interests are, and how indirectly injury to them is linked to worsening of the determinate life history of a person, then it is no "cheat" to allow the Person-Affecting Principle to include effect on interests, including those of the future people whose very existence to possess interests is due to the act which perhaps adversely affects those interests. So although no future person may be able to say to our ghosts, "If you had acted differently and rightly, I would have had a better life," plenty to the future people might well be able to say, "Interests which are, as it turns out, *my* interests, have been injured by what you did, and would have been less injured had you acted differently."

All we have done, so far, is to try to show that there is no good reason to think that the only wrongful injury we can do future people is to inflict "wrongful existence" upon them. We can now admit other injuries to their interests, other things we can, perhaps wrongfully, fail to do *for their sakes*. But which of these other injuries to the interests of future persons *should count as wrongs?* That is a question we have yet to consider, and different moral theories will give different answers. All would agree that our duties to future people are what can in reason be demanded of us for their sake, that wrongs to future people are neglectings of these duties, but there is no agreed way of determining *what* it is reasonable to demand of any of us for others', including our successors', sakes. In what follows I shall rely largely on widely shared intuitions rather than upon any (of necessity controversial) moral theory. To *really establish* the content of our duties and obligations would take a lot more space, a lot more thought, and knowledge of what happens when communities try to practice and pass on such versions of our obligations.

## III.  THE CONTENT OF OUR OBLIGATIONS

### §14 POPULATION CONTROL

One of the obvious ways in which future person F will be affected by previous generations' policies is in the size of F's generation. Utilitarians believe that we should maximize happiness. If it is the total amount of it which is to be maximized, then they must recommend that we increase the world's population, even when that brings a lowered standard of living. As long as the larger population is composed of persons who, despite the overcrowding, do not regret existing, then the total amount of human happiness can be greater in the world with the lower quality of life than in the less crowded world with a higher quality of life. This conclusion, which most people find repugnant, can be avoided by making what is to be maximized average, not total, happiness. It can also be avoided by rejecting the utilitarian claim that wrong acts are those which fail to maximize happiness. The position defended so far in this paper is not utilitarian, and allows us to say that a person F may be wronged, because that one's interests are injured, where such injury can occur both by making that one a member of a grossly under-populated world, and by making him or her a member of an over-crowded world. At this juncture, it is overpopulation and not underpopulation which is the ill we are most likely to inflict on our successors—unless, of course, our weapons policy leads to the death of the majority, and problems of underpopulation for the survivors.

In an earlier article on this topic, written before the recent discussion of the Futurity Problem we have just tried to solve, I said "Our duty to future persons is to see to it that there are not too many of them."[10] Suppose that F is a member of a much too large generation, living in a very overcrowded and famine-threatened world but not wishing he had not been born. If he makes a complaint of the form "There are too many of us. Our forefathers did too much fathering. They should not have allowed so many of us to exist," then he will, if he accepts the precariousness premise, have to allow that, had his forefathers acted as he believes they should have, he might not be there to commend them for their population control policies. But if what we have said above is correct, he *can* in consistency say "I do not regret my existence, but my interests are injured by the size of the population of which I am a member, a population which should have been controlled in size by earlier generations. I realize that if they had done what they should have I probably would not have existed at all. As it is, I do exist, with the same interests in suitable population size as every other member actual and possible of my or any generation, and this interest was injured by the policies of previous people." There is nothing incoherent in this charge, as we now can see. If F were pressed on the question "Do you *really wish* that your predecessors had done what they ought, and so deprived you of your unregretted existence?" F may reasonably say "What I on balance wish or do not wish is not decisive as to whether or not my interests have been injured."

It would seem, then, that among the obligations we can plausibly be claimed to have to future generations, especially those in the near future, is the obligation to adopt policies designed to limit population growth. Such policies will of course have to weigh the rights and interests of present people against those of future people, and so avoid unnecessary coercion, and recognize the interest most people have in reproduction, an interest which should ground some reproductive rights. One of the most urgent tasks of applied moral philosophy is to work out just what are properly construed as a person's reproduction rights, just what population control measures are compatible with recognition of such rights.[11]

## §15 FAIR SHARES: ANOTHER PROBLEM

Since the sorts of things we can and should do for the sake of future generations are limited to safeguarding already fixed interests of theirs which, like the interest in reproduction, are mostly common human interests and rights, one might expect that among these is the right to a fair share of whatever no one has a special title to, or a fair share of what they have as good a title to as do we. Do we have duties of *distributive justice* to future generations? Should first come be first served?

Here we encounter another problem. We cannot judge whether or not we have taken more than our fair share of some cake unless we know how many others there are who want a piece. This is a problem whether the "cake" is the earth's supply of fossil fuels, or some humanly created benefit "bequeathed" by some earlier benefactor to successors.

In the village of Lindos, on the Greek island of Rhodes, is a fountain, with a water system, designed and built in the sixth century B.C. by the local "philosopher" Cleovolus, and still functioning well. Suppose that recent use of some chemical as a fertilizer in the water catchment area will not only overtax the system's natural filter capacity but eventually lead to the clogging, cracking, and eventual destruction of the conduits in the system. Suppose that the prediction is that, unless the fertilizer use is regulated, the water system will be irreversibly destroyed in 200 years. Does that mean that, unless something is done, twenty-third-century inhabitants of Lindos will be done out of their rightful inheritance from Cleovolus? If a regulation were introduced which, if observed indefinitely, would postpone the system's predicted demise by another 200 years, or even another 1,000 years, would that be enough? For how long must we preserve, and with how many others must we share, for distributive justice to have been done?

When we turn from the Lindos water supply to questions of world supply of essential human resources, this problem is magnified. We simply do not and cannot know what size the population of the earth will be in 200 years, since we do not know and cannot control, although our policies may influence, the policies of the previous generation, those living say 180 years from now, and they are the ones who will have the greatest say about that. Nor do we know how long the human race will continue, how many generations it is for whose sake we should be regulating our own policies. How can we work out what our share of the earth's exhaustible resources is, if we cannot know and have no power to decide how many we are, in the end, sharing those resources with? (Of course there is one way in which we can control that, namely by arranging that we be the last generation, easily enough done if we use our stockpiles of nuclear weapons. I assume that we rule out this theoretical option—that we do not deliberately make ourselves the last generation.[12])

Our *power* to determine how many more people there will be is shared with all the future people, so is small, and our *knowledge* of how many more people there will be seems just as unimpressive. How then can we act for the sake of distributive justice to future persons, ignorant as we must be about how many of them there will be?

Faced with this daunting vision of an endless procession of faceless successors, all clamoring for our consideration, we might well be led to moral despair. Is it not a hopeless task to try to give them all their due, when, for all we know, there are indefinitely many of them, with indefinitely diverse needs, wants, and abilities? Surely we must somehow narrow the moral task, if it is to be a manageable one. The eighteenth century Scottish philosopher David Hume (1711–1776), speaking of human beneficence, said, "It is wisely ordained by nature that private connections should commonly prevail over universal views and considerations, accept a duty to invest for a future we will not live to see, leaving it to the experts to argue over the details of that investment portfolio.

What of our sacrifice compared to that to be made by future people? If, as must be assumed for the earlier claims about dependable returns on investment to be true, the national wealth steadily increases, then future people will be better off than we are anyway, so can afford more easily than we can now to set their own world in order. Two things need to be said about this. First, unless we continue doing some investing, at a cost of foregone present consumption, the assumed growth will not take place. Secondly, this sort of comparison of how much better off the "beneficiaries" are, compared to their "benefactors," can be made to our moral disadvantage as beneficiaries as well as to our advantage as benefactors. If it is *unfair* to expect us, poorer than they will be, to invest on their behalf, it was unfair that our predecessors, poorer than we are, sacrificed on *our* behalf. We could take a tough line and say "The more fools they. We won't repeat their foolishness. From now on, save for yourself." But this would be hypocrisy or foolishness on our part. Unless from our predecessors we had inherited not only an advancing technology and a growing economy, but also some unpoisoned land, air and water, it would not have done us much good. Unless we pass these on to our successors, at whatever sacrifice is needed to do so, it will not do them much good to have their projected greater wealth.

This is an obvious point, and one which does not depend upon the intricacies of controversial economic theories. Even economists who argue for a relatively high social discount rate, that is for relatively small public investment in long-term projects, make an exception for those "public goods" which, if lost, are impossible or extremely difficult to regain. Concluding an article arguing for a relatively high social discount rate, the American economist William J. Baumol writes, "However this does not mean that the future should in every respect be left to the mercy of the free market. There are important externalities and investments of the public goods variety which cry for special attention. If we poison our soil so that never again will it be the same, if we destroy the Grand Canyon and turn it into a hydroelectric plant . . . all the wealth and resources of future generations will not suffice to restore them."[17]

Where we are in doubt whether a certain change for the worse is or is not irreversible, it would seem the prudent thing to suppose the worst. Few of us happily incur the risk of cancer (from, say, cigarette smoking) on the grounds that by the time we fall victim to the disease a cure may have been found for it. Similarly with responsible thinking on behalf of future people—we should not *count* on their finding ways to detoxify what we are poisoning. The sacrifice required of us to stop the poisoning seems much less than the burden placed on them if we bet wrong on their ability to undo what we are doing.

What we have considered in this section is whether there is any good reason to endorse our natural tendency to let the more distant future count for less than the close future, supposing each to be equally real. We

otherwise our affections and actions would be dissipated and lost, for want of a proper limited object."[13] Even if we should have a view to more than "private connections," Hume is surely right that our moral concerns, including our concerns for justice, need a limited object if they are not to be dissipated and lost, or worse still, if our moral will is not to be paralyzed by the hopelessly large scope of our moral task. To take, as our moral burden, putting the world to rights for the indefinite future is to all but guarantee that we will *do* very little. If we not merely can but do have obligations of justice to future generations, we must find a way of limiting those obligations.

## §16 DISCOUNTING FOR DISTANCE IN TIME

Hume drew attention to our natural tendency to give preference to that which and those who are "close" to us, over those who are more distant, whether that distance is in blood relationship, in space, in time, or even in political opinion. Even within our own lives we tend to treat the present and near future as counting for more than our own more distant future—we postpone unpleasantness, as if pain next year is not as bad as pain tomorrow, let alone pain today. Of course, on reflection, we would agree with Hume that distant future ills are "never the less real for being remote"[14] and that this holds good for all varieties of remoteness. The suffering of strangers is as real as that of our loved ones, that of strangers half a world or half a century away as real as that of our neighbors. Our unreflective attitudes, however, do give preference to what is close to us, in all these senses of "close." What is out of sight tends to be out of mind.

If we could morally endorse this natural tendency, then our obligations to future people would shrink dramatically. We could concentrate on our own descendents and, among those, concentrate more on those closer in time to us. While accepting a duty to be our brother's and perhaps our nephew's keeper, we would accept less responsibility for the welfare of grandnephews, and perhaps none at all for the friends and contemporaries of great grandnephews. Or, even if we did accept some responsibility for non-kin, we would weaken it as those generations get remoter in time from us. We do apparently endorse some version of this preference for those close to us. We would be shocked, for example, if a mother refused to give to her own child any special attention above and beyond what she thought due from her to all the world's children. Why do we think it not merely natural but best for each to recognize special duties to close relatives? Presumably for the reason Hume gave, that this ensures better chances of care for each than each would have if everyone cultivated an impartial benevolence to everyone, so to no one in particular. Division of the moral labor is the more efficient way to get the moral work done, and kinship is an obvious and easy way to apportion the child care labor. Other ways have been tried, for example in kibbutzim, but it is not yet clear if the gains exceeded the costs. The important thing for our purposes is that there always are costs—kinship as a way of allocating responsibility for others has its costs, and so does any alternative method. To direct people to take responsibility for what is "nearest" them at least reduces the "transport" costs of getting the assistance from the giver to the receiver.

But we do not on reflection endorse all versions of preferential treatment for what is close. When this takes the form of "living for the present," of giving priority to today's over tomorrow's pleasures, we give only qualified endorsement. We encourage people to make prudent provision for their own future, to think ahead. If such prudence is a virtue of individuals, it surely is also of nations and other collectives. As the English economist Sir Roy Harrod said, pure time preference is "a polite expression for rapacity."[15] Those who are charged with responsibility for the community's welfare must think ahead, and should make prudent provision of some sort for the presumably indefinite future of the community, just as a wise person makes provision for a personal future of unknown but limited duration. In this case, however, we encounter a complication. Whereas it costs more of our present resources to, say, feed the starving in Bangladesh than to feed the same number of starving in our own country, it costs much less of our present resources to feed that same number fifty years hence, provided we can profitably invest that lesser amount and let it yield an increase proportional to the time it is invested. Whereas there are "transport costs" of caring for the spatially distant, there seem, as long as productivity is increasing, to be transport *benefits* when the resources are "transported" through time. So a little, when invested, goes a long way, and goes a longer way the longer it is invested. Just as when I now, in my fifties, want to provide from my current resources for my own life from now on into my sixties, seventies, and eighties, I need to invest less for my eighties than for my seventies, and less for my seventies than my sixties, and keep most of all for my (present) fifties, so, even if we wanted to be as evenhanded with future generations as I wish to be with my older self we would need to sacrifice less of current resources for those who are more distant in time from now than for those who are closer, to yield the same returns for all.

How much less? Economists do not agree about what this "social discount rate" is, nor even on what factors should determine it.[16] In the individual case it is fairly clear that the "time discount" rate should be determined by the projected rate of return on investment. This in turn will depend upon tax considerations, the future of the economy, the risks involved in the particular investment made. For public decisionmakerers, however, investment decisions are made by the ones who *control* tax and monetary policies, whose decisions influence the state of the economy, the risk of foreign wars or other disturbances, and so on. So we get considerable disagreement about how governments should make long-term investment decisions, how they should measure the opportunity costs of postponing the receiving of a benefit, that is, of long-term investment. Whatever we may come to agree on about what we should be *aiming* to

do for future generations, economists will disagree about how best to set about fulfilling those aims.

What should we be aiming at? On the individual level it is fairly clear that a person who lives to be eighty will regret *not* having saved earlier, and may also regret having sacrificed too much earlier, may come to realize that her individual time discount rate was too low. Indeed, taking into account the chances that one will not live into one's eighties, it may be quite sensible to sacrifice very little now for the sake of one's eighty-year-old self—not only will a little have gone a long way by then, but that amount may accrue to one's heirs rather than to oneself. If one's investment decisions are purely self-interested, one might sensibly discount very heavily for futurity. But public bodies, if they represent an ongoing public interest, need not be concerned with the chances that the society not survive to reap the returns on long run investment. (There are no actuarial tables for nations.) They must assume that their other decisions, in foreign policy and environmental policy, will not lead to the death of the nation they represent, so must assume that the returns of long-term investments will be in fact received. The only question they need worry about is the complex question of opportunity costs, if it is assumed that they *should* think ahead for all future generations.

Should they? Should we, in our capacity as citizens? Or is there an argument parallel to that which leads us to recognize special duties to close relatives which would lead us to suppose that it is better if, at each time, a government *restricts* its responsibility to a few generations ahead, rather than trying to plan for all time? Is neglect of the interests of distant future generations benign neglect, just as my "neglecting" your children, and your "neglecting" of mine, may be benign neglect in a society which recognizes parental duties?

To think clearly about such moral matters we have to consider what (if any) sacrifice is involved in the various alternatives and what each sacrifice yields to others. If it is indeed true that we can with a tiny sacrifice now confer considerable benefits on distant future people, that would itself be a good reason to accept the duty to make that small sacrifice. If, however, an unreasonable sacrifice is demanded of us, both absolutely or compared with what is being demanded of others, we might well see reason to recognize a moral right not to make such a sacrifice. Have others made long-term investments from which we benefit, as future people would benefit from any we made on their behalf? It seems that the answer is "yes." Past generations *have* "saved," have invested in parks, water reservoirs, waste disposal systems, and so on, designed to outlast the investors, and from which we benefit. The degree of sacrifice needed by the present generation to make parallel investments in disposal of new forms of waste, in maintenance of water supply systems, and so on, seems no greater than past persons have already fairly steadily made for people future to them. So, unless the degree of sacrifice demanded of us turns out to be disproportionately great, we should

have found no reasons to do so. At most there may be arguments for a certain division of labor between generations, as the best means to see to it that all are well served, but even these arguments do not apply to public goods, especially to those goods which no individual, nor any one generation, can supply for themselves, but where dependency on earlier people is unavoidable, and where there is danger of irreversibility. One of the goods we enjoy is that tradition of receiving benefits from past persons and contributing to the maintenance and provision of such public goods for future people. To destroy that tradition might well be itself irreversible. All the economic rationality we bequeath to future people would not itself suffice to restore lost trust in such a cross generational cooperative scheme.

## §17 BETTER WAYS TO DETERMINE OUR OBLIGATIONS

Discounting for futurity is not the right way to get a definite limited content to our obligations to future people. Nor can we work out what those duties are by trying to see what is their fair share of some divisible shareable good to which each person has a right, perhaps a contributor's right. For one thing, we cannot be sure that future people *will* contribute, and even if we assume that they will, we do not know how *many* of them there are or what their contribution is, or therefore what their fair share is. We know neither the size of the cake nor the number of those who deserve a piece. What then *are* we obliged to do for future people? What duties do we have if not duties of distributive justice?

From what has already been argued, it seems reasonable to say that our duties are to avoid endangering future persons' vital interests by reckless action now, by creating, or failing to try to remove, clear dangers to those interests. This sort of consideration for people's interests is not dependent on our knowing exactly how many people there are who are threatened. I think I have a duty to remove dangerous objects like broken glass from the sidewalk in front of my house, even though I do not know how many people are endangered. I will *want* to do it,[18] for the sake of myself, my family, and my friends, and I have an obligation[19] to do it for them and for any strangers. Since *what* I should do is not affected by how many people are endangered, my ignorance of numbers is no obstacle to my knowing what my duty is.

There are many dangers which seem to face us and our successors which are dangers *however* many people we all are, and where what should be done is the same however many we are. Radiation will affect us, however thinly or densely we are spread over the affected area. A poisoned river or lake is useless to those living near it, whether they be few or many. Of course, if there are *other* rivers and lakes, to which people may move and "use up," then numbers will count. Numbers count when the good is one which is both divisible and consumed. In recent times more and more of our activities *have* "consumed" the goods used in those activities. Cleovolus's water system was not "used up" by its use over the centuries, but will be "used up," at a faster or a slower rate, if the water flowing into it is contaminated with conduit-clogging chemicals. Whereas agriculture practiced in some ways does not "use up" the land or the water supply, practiced in some modern intensive ways with pesticides and chemical fertilizers it does. Some of our policies are ensuring that more and more problems *become* ones where numbers count. Once the numbers count, we do need estimates of numbers to determine both our "fair share" of burdens and benefits and to determine exactly what dangers face us. In those cases we must simply do the best we can to estimate numbers. But there are still many dangers which face us where *what* is endangered is not (yet) a supply of to-be-consumed goods, but a source or "mother" of potentially endless such supplies—seas, forests, rivers, soil, atmosphere. Our obligations then are clearest, since not dependent on fallible estimates of numbers. They are obligations not to arrange the future death of the goose that lays the variety of eggs we and future people can be reliably expected to need and want.

The seventeenth century English philosopher John Locke (1632–1704), to whom the Founding Fathers of this nation looked for a formulation of the moral and political principles on which the nation was founded, said that among our duties to others in a prepolitical "state of nature" was to leave "enough and as good" of whatever one used of those resources of the earth to which mankind has a "common title." We are in a state of nature toward distant persons, even to our own distant descendants, since no one political order can be known to forge ties of common citizenship between us and them. There are grave problems about knowing how much of the divisible and exhaustible goods are "enough" for future people, but to know what counts as leaving "as good" an earth as we enjoyed is not as difficult. Our obligations to future people, then, can reasonably be seen to include everything this general obligation entails, the passing on of unruined self-renewing sources of the satisfiers of basic human needs and wants, the providers of human enjoyment. These self-renewing sources include not just physical ones like seas, forests, and land, but cultural ones such as art and science (and products of it such as Cleovolus's water system), social institutions including ones which help us to take responsibility for the consequences of our policy for future people, and moral ideas themselves. To people in the near future, those in the generations whose size and fate we more directly control, we owe in addition responsible planning, planning aimed at seeing not merely that they inherit basic resources "as good" as ours, but also the means to get "enough" of the divisible exhaustible goods we know they will need. To enable them to get enough, control of population size as well as of size of our depletion of nature's resources is needed.

Our obligations to future people, then, do vary depending on whether they are close enough in time to us for their *particular* needs and abilities to be foreseeable, and for us to have control over how many of them there will be, what opportunities they will have, what supply problems they will face. To people in the *next* few generations we have extra obligations, obligations over and above those owed to all future people. To all future people, however distant and unknowable in numbers, special abilities, special opportunities, special needs, we are obligated not knowingly to injure the common human interests they like all of us have —interests in a good earth and in a good tradition guiding us in living well on it without destroying its hospitability to human life.

A good tradition is one conscious of its roots in the past and of its influence on the future. From past thinkers we have inherited the basis for that scientific knowledge which has enabled us to create, for future people, both great opportunities and great dangers. It seems fitting that to this bequest we add some attempt at an understanding of the moral issues that we face, and that they too will face, issues requiring us to clarify our ideas about our moral relations to past and to future people. Such attempts will build on the moral ideas and practices we have inherited, but we have seen how much more work still needs to be done before we can "give counsel by our understanding." Not only should our population, our agricultural, industrial, and defense policies be ones we would praise or at least not condemn if we could change places with our descendants, but our thinking about these policies also ought to set a good example. Even if such thinking by philosophers and reflective people fails to have the effect on current public policy which some of us hope for, it can nevertheless do useful work in getting the right discussions launched, the right questions posed. Even if future people, looking back at us, can say no better than "Well, at least they *worried* about what they were doing to the world we were to inherit," that worry may itself be a fitting legacy.

## NOTES

Several friends and colleagues have helped me during the writing of this essay by their helpful suggestions and criticisms of earlier drafts. In particular I am indebted to David Gauthier and to Alan Meltzer for help with §16, although of course its faults are all my own. From Tom Regan I have had much help in simplifying and clarifying the argument of the paper. I am aware of some of its oversimplifications, and some of its evasions of hard and important questions.

1. Actually Kant seems to mean that we should not discontinue the administration of justice, such as punishing wrongdoers, even if the world is perishing, not that our just acts themselves may lead to that perishing of the world. However, nothing in his account guarantees that unilateral just acts, especially punitive ones, will not destroy the world.

2. For a discussion of the implications of Kant's philosophy for our duty to future generations see John Passmore's *Man's Responsibility for Nature: Ecological Problems and Western Traditions* (New York: Scribner's, 1974), Chap. 4. Passmore's quotes Kant's statement, in the *Idea of a Universal History*, eighth thesis, that "human nature is such that it cannot be indifferent even to the most remote epoch which may eventually affect our species, so long as this epoch may be expected with certainty."

3. See Jerome Schneewind, "The Divine Corporation and the History of Ethics," in *Philosophy and History*, Richard Rorty, Quentin Skinner, and

Jerome Schneewind, eds. (Cambridge, England: Cambridge University Press), for a discussion of the effect on ethical theory of loss of faith in a divine world manager.

4.    See "The Futurity Problem," Gregory Kavka, in *Obligations to Future Generations*, Richard Sikora and Brian Barry, eds. (Philadelphia, Pa.: Temple University Press, 1978), 180–203, and "The Paradox of Future Individuals," *Philosophy and Public Affairs*, vol. 11, no. 2 (Spring 1982): 93–112.

5.    See Derek Parfit, "On Doing the Best for Our Children," in *Ethics and Population*, Michael Bayles, ed. (Cambridge, Mass.: Schenkman Publishing Co., 1976), "Future Generations: Further Problems," *Philosophy and Public Affairs*, vol. 11, no. 2 (Spring 1983): 113–172, "Energy Policy and the Further Future: The Identity Problem," in *Energy and the Future*, Douglas MacLean and Peter Brown, eds. (Totowa, N.J.: Rowman and Littlefield, 1983): 166–179.

6.    "Wrongful life" is recognized in some legal jurisdictions as a tort—that is, a harm for which one may sue for damages. The California Appellate Court, in *Curlender* v. *BioScience Laboratories*, allowed a wrongful life cause of action on behalf of an infant born with Tay-Sachs disease after the parents had been falsely assured that they were not carriers of the recessive genes. See Maxine A. Sonnenberg's "A Preference for Non-Existence: Wrongful Life and a Proposed Tort of Genetic Malpractice," *California Law Review* (January 1982): 477–510. In such legal cases a problem parallel to that expressed in the No Obligation Argument is whether a case for legal action exists when the plaintiff has in any way benefited from the defendant's act. The proper application of the so-called Benefit Rule in such cases is an issue which raises in law the same problems as the No Obligation Argument in ethics, but philosophers have not yet appealed much to the legal literature for help in getting a solution to it. In the case of *Berman* v. *Allen*, the New Jersey courts rejected the wrongful life claim on behalf of a child with Down's syndrome, partly on the grounds that life even with a major physical handicap is better than no life.

7.    Thomas Schwartz, "Obligations to Posterity," in *Ethics and Population*, ed. Bayles (*op. cit.*, note 5): 13.

8.    See Joel Feinberg's discussion of interests in "Harm and Self Interest," and in "The Rights of Animals and Unborn Generations," in Joel Feinberg, *Rights, Justice and the Bounds of Liberty*, (Princeton: Princeton University Press, 1980). I follow Feinberg in seeing interests as "somehow compounded out of" goals and wants (p. 166), but not to be identified with them. Feinberg's definition is: "A person has an interest in Y when he has a stake in Y, that is, when he stands to gain or lose depending on the condition or outcome of Y" (p. 45). Feinberg, however, does not want to speak, as I shall in §§11 and 12, of an interest existing before its possessor does.

9.    Parfit formulates this principle in "Energy Policy and the Further Future: The Identity Problem," MacLean and Brown, *op. cit.*, 171. He called solutions similar to mine a "cheat" in "Doing the Best for Our Children," Bayles, *op. cit.*, 103 and 111.

10.    "The Rights of Past and Future People" in *Responsibilities to Future Generations*, Ernest Partridge, ed. (Buffalo, N.Y.: Prometheus Press, 1980): 181.

11.    See Mary Ann Warren's helpful discussion of this in "Future Generations," in *And Justice for All*, Tom Regan and Donald VanDeVeer, eds. (Totowa, N.J.: Rowman and Littlefield, 1982), 139–168.

12.    I discuss this in "The Rights of Past and Future People." See Note 10.

13.    David Hume, *Enquiries*, Selby Bigge and Nidditch, eds., 229n.

14.    *Ibid.*, 535.

15. Sir Roy Harrod, *Towards a Dynamic Economics* (London, England: Macmillan, 1948):40.

16. See, for example, Stephen A. Marglin, "The Social Rate of Discount and the Optimal Rate of Investment," *Quarterly Journal of Economics*, vol. LXXVII, no. 1, Feb. 1963, 95–111; and William J. Baumol, "On the Social Rate of Discount," *The American Economic Review*, vol. LVIII, no. 4, Sept. 1968, 788–802.

17. Baumol, *op. cit.*, 801.

18. For a discussion of whether we can be got to *want* to do things for future people, see Norman Care, "Future Generations, Public Policy, and the Motivation Problem," *Environmental Ethics*, Fall 1982, 195–213.

19. In this paper I have discussed mainly the way we can injure others, and some bad ways of selecting which injuries to others to treat as morally allowable. I have *not* said much about the sound basis on which we *should* select which injuries to others are moral wrongs. I incline to a theory which is neither Utilitarian nor Natural Rights, nor Contractarian, but resembles the last in holding, with Hume, that a morality deserving of respect must be a trans-generational cooperative scheme of rights and obligations from which each participant can, over a normal lifetime, expect at least that he/she is "a gainer, on balancing the account" (*Treatise*, 497). This requires, at the least, that one not have been "duped," at best, "infinite advantages." It is extremely difficult, however, to judge whether a particular person in a particular scheme *is* a gainer thereby, difficult even to answer the question "gainer compared with what?" Even when we have answered that question, and perhaps found our own morality failing to pass this test, found that it does make some people dupes of others, it is very difficult to know if any proposed change would really be an improvement by the same criteria. To have any well-based opinion about that one would need knowledge or imagination of the range of viable options, and knowledge of the fate of societies which tried them.

## SUGGESTIONS FOR FURTHER READING

For a more detailed understanding of Parfit's position see the articles referred to in note 5. For a range of approaches to the topic of obligations to future people see the anthologies *Obligations to Future Generations*, Richard Sikora and Brian Barry, eds. (Philadelphia, Pa.: Temple University Press, 1978); *Responsibilities to Future Generations*, Ernest Partridge, ed. (Buffalo, N.Y.: Prometheus Press, 1980); and *Ethics and Problems of the 21st Century*, Kenneth Goodpaster and K. M. Sayre, eds. (Notre Dame: University of Notre Dame Press, 1979).

For a discussion of interests see Joel Feinberg in the article referred to in note 8 (this is also to be found in *Philosophy and Environmental Crisis*, William T. Blackstone, ed. (Athens: University of Georgia Press, 1974) and also to his "Harm and Self Interest," in *Rights, Justice, and the Bounds of Liberty* (Princeton: Princeton University Press, 1980). For a wider discussion of the human good see Georg von Wright, *Varieties of Goodness* (New York: Humanities Press, 1963).

For discussions of discounting for futurity see Richard and Val Routley, "Nuclear Power—Some Ethical and Social Dimensions," in *And Justice for All*, Tom Regan and Donald VanDeVeer, eds., 139–168 (Totowa, N.J.: Rowman and Littlefield, 1982); Mary B. Williams, "Discounting Versus Maximum Sustainable Yield," *Obligations to Future Generations*, Richard Sikora and Brian Barry, eds., 169–179

(Philadelphia, Pa.: Temple University Press, 1978); and Derek Parfit, "Energy Policy and the Further Future: The Social Discount Rate," *Energy and the Future*, Douglas MacLean and Peter Brown, eds. (Totowa, N.J.: Rowman and Littlefield, 1983):166–179. For economists' discussions see, in addition to the articles cited in note 14, A. K. Sen, "On Optimizing the Rate of Saving," *The Economic Journal*, vol. 71, Sept. 1961, 479–496, and "Isolation Assurance and the Social Rate of Discount," *Quarterly Journal of Economics*, vol. 81, Feb. 1967, 112–124; also Gordon Tullock, "The Social Rate of Discount and the Optimal Rate of Investment: Comment," *Quarterly Journal of Economics*, vol. 68, May, 1964, 331–336.

# 8

# Ethical Issues in Agriculture

## WILLIAM AIKEN

## I. THE PROBLEM

### §1 INTRODUCTION

Everyone knows the story of "progress" in agriculture. There was that first glorious day when our wandering stone age ancestors settled down to plant fields and domesticate animals, the first step in the long march toward "civilization" with cities, commerce, governments, and culture. This march toward "development" has been accelerated in the last few centuries by a revolution in trade and transportation that has made plantation farming profitable while eliminating the need for locally grown and marketed foodstuffs. The machine revolution produced new efficient implements (plows, reapers, thrashers) and eventually led to self-propelled tractors, combines, and irrigation pivots, tools that vastly expanded the size of farms and at the same time eased the need for back-breaking labor (and laborers). The smell of sweat was replaced by the smell of gasoline. The engineering revolution created new, high-yielding varieties and hybrids, produced insecticides, herbicides, fungicides, fertilizers, growth enhancers, and preservatives which not only increased yields but made large-scale monoculture (repeatedly growing a single crop) practical. The march of progress has resulted in a rather remarkable situation today: Less than 4 percent of the population of the United States not only grows enough to feed the other 96 percent but creates considerable exportable surpluses as well.

The success of this "progress" story is taken for granted by most of us. It shapes our food expectations; we urbanites and suburbanites can go to our neighborhood grocery store and buy cheap, varied, safe, conveniently packaged, easy-to-prepare food in hundreds of forms year round. It fuels our economic expectations; we use foreign sales of grain to balance international payments and we create new markets for our farm-related industries in the "developing" world. It informs our judgments of quality of life; we use the variety of diet and the percentage of income expended on food and extent of urbanization as a basis for ranking levels of modernity and development. It shapes our political motivations; we use gasohol made from corn to be less dependent on political adversaries, we control grain sales (use the food weapon) to help us to get our way in the world. It even informs our humanitarian expectations; from school lunches and food stamps at home to relieving famines abroad, food is a tangible expression of American goodwill. We take the fact of this "progress" which produces abundance for granted.

Of course "progress" means change and will inevitably provoke some nostalgia for earlier ways. We muse on the life of the noble hunter-gatherer who lived so harmoniously with nature. We recall the pioneer days of hardy independence and self-reliance when a family could feed itself. We yearn for the simplicity and serenity of the small family farm of wise Old MacDonald for whom good land, good farming, good food, good family, and good neighbors defined success. We look back to the pre–microwave oven days of homegrown, chemical-free food lovingly "made from scratch" by our forever-busy gramma.

Although some defenders of the practices of modern agriculture dismiss their critics as economically naive, nostalgic romantics ever yearning for an idealized past (as indeed some of these critics are), their most persistent critics are not so politely ignored but are characterized as "far-out environmentalists" who are not only subverting the march of progress in agriculture but are actually turning their backs on human beings. For the sake of unrealistic environmental protection, modern agriculture's defenders claim, these "hunger mongers"[1] are irrationally demanding absolute safety and in effect are placing scenery and a few birds above human beings. Of course the critics can respond in kind. Just look at the devastation caused by your greed—massive destruction of forest, wildlife, watersheds; depletion of ground water; poisoning of surface water, undefendable erosion of topsoil and fertility; elimination of wild species and germ plasm—and for what? All for the sake of chemically saturated and nutritionally questionable "food." You are destroying the ecosphere, driving us to ecological disaster, ruining our very life support system, gambling with the well-being of the earth—all for your own greedy private gain.

The intensity of acrimony accompanying the debate between defenders of modern agriculture and its environmental critics makes it difficult to be judicious and "philosophical" when analyzing and evaluating the ethical issues involved. If the debate is seen as a simple contest between human welfare and environmental welfare, so that you must choose *either* to serve human food demands at all costs to the environment *or* to leave the environment alone at all costs to human welfare, then we have really less of a debate here than a confrontation of ideologies with all the typical name calling, mistrust, distortion, condemnation, defensiveness, and evangelism. Some effort must be made to get beyond the slogans and to resist the quick reduction of very real conflicts to the status of irreconcilable camps. To do this requires the realization that by its very definition agriculture is a means of manipulating environments for human purposes; some intervention with natural ecosystems therefore is inevitable if there is to be any agriculture at all. So the issue is not whether the environment will be altered, but to what degree and how extensive is the resultant damage.

Nor is the issue realistically approached unless we note that we human beings are part of the larger biotic community, so much so that our well-being as a species depends, at least to some extent, upon harmonizing our activity with this larger community. Indeed the very *survival* of the species requires observing the ecological constraints placed upon it by nature. Though the piper can be put off for a while, eventually we must pay for our dancing. So when addressing the problems which agriculture places on the environment we should no more see the environment as pure undisturbed wilderness than as a huge quarry of raw materials for exploitation. Between these extremes we can perhaps find a form of agriculture which is sustainable, harmonious, and compatible with conserving the stability and diversity of the ecosphere and which adequately supplies the food needs of people. It will be toward that goal that I will argue in this essay.

## II. THE ENVIRONMENTAL CRITICS AFFIRM

The environmental problems caused by modern agriculture can be divided into three categories: public health and safety, resource use and depletion, and ecological disturbance. Let us briefly sketch all three in the order just given.

### §2 PUBLIC HEALTH AND SAFETY

The problem for public health and safety has gained the most attention. Since the aspects of the environment which affect us most are its physical properties as they relate to our biological needs, the quality (and sometimes quantity) of air, water, and food are most vital to us. To the extent that agricultural practices alter the availability and quality of these essential goods, there are grounds for legitimate criticism of these practices. Anxiety and public concern in recent years has centered around both chemical inputs (fertilizers, pesticides, preservatives, for example) used in food production and processing and the waste products or unintended by-products of these activities. The sheer quantity of chemical input has raised concern over adequate testing for the safety of these substances and control over proper use of them. Whether it is pesticide residue on fruits and vegetables or pesticides that have been taken up into the food chain, later to appear in milk or meat, there is a concern that these substances may be carcinogenic (when sufficiently concentrated) or even responsible for mutagenic malformations in embryos. It is well known that DDT and other pesticides are absorbed and stored in animal fat and can be found in the milk of nursing mothers throughout the world. In addition there are numerous additives like growth enhancers, preservatives, and dyes whose use is extensive and whose safety is unknown. So the safety of the products of modern agriculture and processing is controversial.[2]

The heavy reliance upon chemical poisons raises other safety issues. The manner in which they are applied can be questioned (for example, carelessly spraying from aircraft can result in wind drift over residential areas). Misuse of these chemicals (too frequent and too much) is a problem since they seep into our water supplies. So too is the frequent lack of appropriate caution; for example, forcing farm workers back into the fields too soon after spraying. The sheer volume of chemical use can create problems since the dangers resulting from human error are multiplied with the volume of use.

In asking about the public health and safety of agricultural products and their production, critics challenge the industry to justify why they are jeopardizing the quality of the food, water, and air which we need for survival. They also ask for justification for the apparent unfairness of placing some citizens at great risk to their health. The focus is upon the industry's polluting the environment in ways that adversely affect human interest.[3]

## §3 RESOURCE USE AND DEPLETION

A second set of problems caused by agriculture focuses upon resource use and depletion. Important resources such as topsoil, water, fossil fuels, and gene pools are being used up. The loss of topsoil to wind and water erosion is immense. Estimates vary, but approximately one inch of topsoil per decade is being lost in Iowa.[4] And that is some of our top farmland. Since it is the topsoil which provides nutrients for crops, this loss dicates increased reliance on chemical replacement. Add to the erosion loss the loss of natural fertility by repeatedly growing the same crop, and you have a real problem with the future of our soils. Another serious threat to natural resources is water depletion caused by massive irrigation in arid regions where underground reservoirs (aquifers) are being drained faster than they are replenished. Surface water is overused causing rivers to virtually dry up (North Platte) or become so chemically laced or salty that they are useless (Colorado).

Because modern agriculture is highly mechanized, it consumes enormous amounts of fossil fuel, for example, to drive gargantuan tractors and harvesting equipment, and to dry grain and to produce fertilizer. By eliminating hedgerows, swamps, and woodlots, wild species are being crowded out, thus eliminating genetic diversity. Moreover, by restricting seed selection to the products of a few companies which supply the entire industry, local varieties are being replaced by infertile, annually purchased hybrids. This negates nature's way of creating locally adaptive diversity through natural mutation. With the narrow focus on only thirty-eight "food" species[5] and the rest of nature's abundance sprayed as weeds, the danger of killing off or crowding out the germ resources necessary for adaptation to new conditions is high.

The rapid depletion of vital environmental resources is of particular significance for those who will live after us. If we knew that the world would end in twenty years, or if we were sure we had no obligation to future peoples, then the depletion of these resources wouldn't bother us too much. But, of course, we are not sure about this and live in the hope that the human species will survive indefinitely.

## §4 ECOLOGICAL DISTURBANCE

The third set of concerns center around the ecosphere—the whole environment including all living things and the resources which support them (water, nutrients, etc.). The impact of modern agriculture on the nonhuman world, its members, its systems, its relationships, is severe. Indiscriminate pesticide use kills off both unwanted pests and beneficial predatory insects—*and* the birds who eat the poisoned insects. It harms soil organisms (which keep the soil fertile, loose, and water absorbent). Leaching into streams, it kills organisms and gains in concentration as it moves up the food chain to the point where it can threaten the very survival of some species (for example, DDT weakens the eggshells of eagles to the point of endangering reproduction). Chemical fertilizer finds its way into lakes and streams, there to cause rapid algae growth which, when decaying, kills fish by robbing the water of oxygen. Silt from erosion and pollution from manure (especially from feed lots where cattle are massed together for fattening before slaughter) change water quality, which affects wildlife. Sheep and cattle grazing crowds out wild species. Small wonder, then, that predators turn to domestic species for food, only to be shot or poisoned by irate ranchers.

All three of these criticisms of modern agriculture are familiar, and detailed documentation abounds. Of course agriculture is not the only environmentally stressing industry. But it has received considerable criticism from environmentalists because of the extent of the industry and its requirement to ever increase productivity. As it has been so poignantly put by Keith Barrons, an agricultural technologist, "Whether we like it or not, farmers are the custodians of a very sizable portion of the world's land surface. Much of the earth's ecological well being depends on how they manage the soil and the vegetation that covers it."[6] A drive through the countryside of virtually any state (or country) will confirm this observation. If new environmentally destructive practices are seen to be necessary for the farmer to remain competitive, they will quickly spread through the land grant extension service and be adopted by farmers, if they can afford the investment costs. Millions of acres can be rapidly affected. When the "soil bank" (land the government paid farmers to leave fallow) was suddenly eliminated, hundreds of acres of pasture, swamp, and fallow land housing numerous wildlife species were suddenly plowed under, *all over the nation*. Perhaps some of the changes were environmentally beneficial, but many were not. The point is that the changes are rapid and extensive. They can affect vast amounts of land, water, wildlife, and ecological balances within a year's time. A particularly destructive practice could spread like an undetected cancer before anyone became fully aware of its danger.

There is another aspect of modern agriculture which makes it of particular concern to environmentalists. There is an ever-increasing demand for agricultural products, but every year there is less and less suitable land on which to expand. The world's frontiers are gone, its peoples are increasing, and urban expansion is taking over much good farmland. The only way, it seems, to meet this growing demand is to intensify production and increase yields on currently used land by adding more inputs (fertilizers, pesticides, etc.) and using more sophisticated technological innovations, an approach to food production being heavily pushed in developing nations. It is current agribusiness gospel for the Third World that

> unless farmers in a traditional subsistence agriculture can be persuaded
> to use fertilizers, pesticides, improved seeds, and other modern inputs to
> increase output, all other efforts to increase food production will fail.[7]

Yet it is the ecological wisdom of these very techniques that is being challenged by environmental critics. When you consider that food is one commodity that we simply cannot "do without," you can see how easy it would be to accept as necessary any environmental abuse resulting from agriculture. But you can also see how easy it would be to appeal to this necessity to justify any and everything, to the point where "food needs" become the carte blanche for whatever agroindustry wants to do (that is, whatever is profitable regardless of the environmental costs). So environmentalists are naturally concerned that zealousness for a good cause does not lead to overkill.

## §5 INITIAL MORAL REACTION

Our initial reaction to reading Rachel Carson's *Silent Spring*,[8] Barry Commoner's *The Closing Circle*,[9] or any other documentation of agricultural abuse of the land, is to feel that we should do something to *stop it*. Regulate chemical additives and stop poisoning our streams. Stop using up ground water. Stop the erosion, the siltation of rivers, the strangling of fish. Stop the big machines torturing the land. Save the hedgerows, the woodlots, the rangeland, the wilderness. Stop it now or we'll pass laws to make you stop it.

Besides the question of how one would go about stopping it (a political question) is the ethical question: Should it be stopped? Is the assumption that environmental damage is wrong always true? What if it is a necessary evil? These are the ethical questions which arise when agriculture is addressed from the perspective of environmental concerns. And they are the questions which we will ultimately examine. But first, it is only fair to let agroindustry respond to its environmental critics, to answer the charges made against it, and to try to justify its practices.

## III. AGROINDUSTRY RESPONDS

Quite naturally, defenders of modern agriculture are unwilling to sit back and take the blame for all of these alleged environmental abuses. Like it or not, they insist, we cannot turn back the clock to earlier days. The call to "stop it" is ill advised for a variety of reasons: Critics are naive about modern agriculture; critics exaggerate the abuses; critics underrate science and the principle of substitution; and critics' priorities are confused. Again, let us consider these ideas in the order given.

### §6 CRITICS ARE NAIVE

The first line of defense is to counterattack. The tactic here is to stress the extent and complexity of modern agroindustry which is, after all, a *business*, not a hobby or a recreational activity. A farm is not a garden or a weekend retreat for professors of ecology. If, to succeed in their chosen business, farmers must be energy, mechanical, and chemical intensive, they will be. If emphasis on growth and production are required, they will emphasize growth and production. They will seek efficiency in machine use and so will seek larger farm size (economy of scale) and will concentrate on that crop most profitable for them to grow (comparative advantage). They will try to avoid paying the "hidden costs" of production which are not priced in the market (so called "externalities," including in this case loss of natural scenery or wildlife) and so will not be overly concerned with the "social loss" of these externalities or others, such as the possible changes in water quality resulting from chemicals in runoff water.

Because farming is a business, it is only reasonable that farmers prioritize business objectives of efficiency, growth, and profit. The purpose of agriculture is not to promote environmental sanctity, ecological stability, or natural resource conservation. It is not different from any other business and so, if judged at all by "ethics," it should be judged by "business ethics" standards (for example, advertising practices, product quality and safety, worker safety, and equitable trade practices) and not by some extraneous "extra" environmental standards specifically aimed at farming. And it is *big* business. How big is it? The combined production, processing, and merchandising activities of agroindustry constitute approximately one-fourth of the GNP of the United States.[10]

Besides, *what* the industry produces, *how much* it produces, and *how* it is produced is largely a result of consumer demand. The demand for cheap, abundant, unblemished fruits and vegetables dictates massive use of irrigation and pesticides. The environmental fallout from the industry is the result of the food preferences and demands of the consumer. If the society wants to stop eating meat, milk, eggs, grains, fruits, and vegetables and live on algae in order to save the environment, then farming would cease to be necessary (or profitable); *then* its damage to the environment would stop. But as long as consumers demand farm products at a low price you can't blame farmers for the resultant damage. And to hamstring the industry with irrational regulations and restrictions will both drive farmers out, thus limiting supply, and raise prices. If you make it profitable for the industry to "conserve" the environment it will. But it is not profitable at present. Those who blame farmers for ecological damage tend to be ignorant of the fact that this is a natural result of market forces as reflected in consumer demand and thus shows the social preference of cheap food over the environment.

This reply of agroindustry is a very common one. It represents the attitude of perhaps the majority of defenders of modern agriculture against the "environmentalist," as is represented in this quote from Keith Campbell, an Australian agricultural economist:

> The world in the late twentieth century is beset by many faddists—the antigrowth lobbyists, the doomsday men, the advocates of the steady state economy, the admirers (and more rarely, part-time practitioners) of antiquated farming methods—who if they had their way, would turn back the clock.[11]

But this litany of the facts about the real world of business and the economic realities of modern agriculture is little more than an appeal to the status quo, not a reply to environmental criticisms. It attempts to excuse what modern farming does by shifting the focus to society at large and thus is an implicit appeal to the authority of consumers whose "choice" for environmental damage is reflected in their preferences and market behavior. But environmental critics are just as likely to challenge the status quo, the culture, and the preferences of consumers and to condemn them along with the practices which result from them. Two wrongs do not make a right. If, as these critics will urge, consumers are wrong to demand the products of an ecologically damaging agriculture, then that agriculture cannot be judged "right" because it satisfies these demands.

## §7 CRITICS EXAGGERATE ABUSES

It is common to reply to environmental critics by challenging their data, discrediting their scientific credentials, and disputing their conclusions. The point is to show that they drastically overstate the abuses and distort the dangers. How extensive is the abuse of, for example, pesticides? A very low percentage of accidents or misapplications occur within the industry as a whole. A few abuses draw national news coverage, but the total amount of abuse is low in proportion to the volume used. An occasional pesticide abuse is within the tolerable limits of human error, especially when you consider the cost to the environment if pesticides were not used since more land would have to be plowed and irrigated, resulting in increased erosion and loss of watersheds.

If it is the widespread use of a pesticide rather than the risk of accidents that is at issue, defenders of agroindustry can challenge the danger involved. For example, no one disputes that DDT has been found throughout the globe in virtually all food chains. But as Keith Campbell replies,

> One of the earliest casualties of administrative intervention was DDT. This insecticide, which quite apart from its agricultural applications made possible a tremendous improvement in public health through the control of malaria, has according to the World Health Organization never been demonstrated to be poisonous to man, though it does accumulate in his fatty tissue.[12]

The *real* danger of agricultural chemicals to humans is a subject of much dispute since results gained from standard testing procedures (massive dosages fed to lab animals) are considered to be of questionable application to humans. Projections of ecological collapse or of uncontrollable widespread breakdowns in ecosystems are considered highly suspect because they are not based on hard data. That there will be a *Silent Spring*, as Rachel Carson warned in her book with that title published in 1962, is considered more science fiction than hard scientific prediction. And the professional ability of its author is ridiculed to this day.[13]

But even if the extent of abuse is high and the impact of widespread use severe, one could still reply that in comparison to *other* industries, agriculture's environmental damage is modest. The industries serving urban populations like steel and chemical refineries all place a heavier burden on the environment by polluting both water and air with highly toxic chemicals and metals. Services which support urban populations like transportation and sewage disposal are more polluting and draining on natural resources (especially energy and water). Topsoil loss due to erosion is not as severe as prime farmland loss to parking lots, highways, suburban developments, and shopping centers. All in all, the volume of environmental damage resulting from agriculture is not incommensurate with, and may be even less than, that from other services and industries that also serve the general public. To isolate agriculture and demand more rigorous standards is not only somewhat unfair, it is unreasonable.

All of this is true, to some extent, and should serve to remind environmental critics to do their homework before leveling charges of abuse. There has indeed been some exaggeration and perhaps distortion. Nonetheless, the environmental problems caused by agriculture are real. They won't go away even if they are less severe than some imagine.

The other tactic, pleading that "everybody else does it too," is about as convincing to an environmentalist critic of agriculture as it would be to the exasperated parents of a naughty child. It would be unfair to allow pollution by the steel and automobile industries, for example, while complaining of agroindustry's pollution. But no environmentalist worthy of the name takes this stand. *All* industrial polluters fall within the scope of the criticisms, not just farming.

## §8 CRITICS UNDERRATE SCIENCE AND THE PRINCIPLE OF SUBSTITUTION

Much of the concern of environmentalists is with conserving natural resources which are currently being heavily exploited and rapidly depleted. They despair over the future when these resources are used up. Defenders of modern agriculture sometimes reply to these "doomsayers" by claiming that they fail to realize the ability of scientific advancements to provide alternatives which, when the scarcity becomes severe enough to make it profitable, will be substituted for the depleted resource. Though topsoil, ground water, and petroleum are being used up—substitutes will be found. We must rely upon "science as talisman,"[14] and we must become "technological optimists" and face the challenge rather than despair the loss. Nuclear-powered desalinization plants will irrigate the desert. Extensive aquaculture will replace depleted natural fisheries. Increased solar conversion efficiency will dramatically increase yields. Breeding will increase protein quality in food grains. Recombinant DNA research will bring us nitrogen-fixing grains, doing away with the need for fertilizer. Single cell protein (from algae) and extracted protein (from leaves and hay) will replace other sources of food. Desert greenhouses, space colony greenhouses, and floating aquaculture factories are all within scientific vision. As traditional resources play out, new efficient methods, new techniques, and new recovery processes will be substituted. Scientific research will point the way, and the market will determine when the new substitutes are to be implemented. The fear of depleted resources and thus an end to adequate food production is the fantasy of antiscientific doom-and-gloomers. We can adapt to changing conditions and we can change conditions to adapt to us.

The force of this response hinges on the extent to which one takes "ecological laws" to be scientific truths and "ecology" to be a science. If there are ecological limits to growth (that is, if there are fixed limits beyond which a natural system cannot be stressed without adverse reaction) then this confidence in always staying ahead of systemic collapse is akin to mere faith. Furthermore, ecologists stress the interdependence of the elements in the biosphere. Throughout nature there is a ripple effect: If you tamper at one end of the system, the whole thing begins to vibrate and undergo change. So scientific innovations which serve as stop-gap measures to push in a bulge here, will end up causing another bulge to stick out over there, demanding other new scientific innovations, and so on. The more drastic the tampering, the greater the risk that there will be a major systemic backlash. So ecologists are dubious about this type of confidence in "engineering the environment" when it ignores basic ecological principles. But, of course, one can imagine an ecologically informed confidence in science which would take into account the impact on the entire system of proposed modifications. So it is possible to be a techno-logical optimist with ecological awareness, one who through technology finds new, less wasteful substitutes for old, more wasteful practices. But whether or not these new technologies will be adopted (presuming that they are discovered) is another matter. Relying on market forces to pro-vide for the substitution can be precarious. Earlier we pointed out that it was precisely those market forces which impel farmers to abuse their land. It seems that the new technologies will not be profitable until the abuse is so severe that it has become too costly to continue farming with-out new technologies to compensate for the loss. Thus the irony of this view is that the market encourages rapid depletion which not only makes the new substitutes profitable, it makes them necessary. The faster the abuse, the more substitutes are needed.

## §9 CRITICS HAVE THEIR PRIORITIES CONFUSED

The response just examined relies upon science and substitution to ensure human welfare when current agricultural resources are used up. The one we are about to examine defends current exploitation of resources and overt environmental abuse and damage on grounds that they are ne-cessary to promote human welfare. Since humans need food, throwing a wrench into modern agriculture for the protection of "nature" is to place nature above human food needs. So the environmentalist who turns his back on people has his priorities confused. He is *misanthropic* (hateful of or against people) and morally blameworthy.

   This response and charge must be understood against the backdrop of projections of population growth rates. Now that most major diseases have been controlled, the death rate has declined rapidly and too many people are being born and surviving. Current trend projections give an astonishing 8 billion people on Earth by the year 2000, nearly double what it is today.[15] Population growth stabilization might not occur until the year 2090, when there would be 11 billion people.[16] Along with this increase in sheer numbers of mouths, there will be an increased demand for food due to rising income (richer people want to eat "better," that is, more meat and varied foods) and due to improved nutritional quality among currently undernourished nations. To meet this drastically in-creased demand requires increased production. As Keith Campbell says, "The key to achieving the increased food output needed to feed the greatly enlarged world population in prospect, and to feed it more ade-quately, is the further application of science and technology."[17] This ap-plication means intensifying efforts in chemical and energy intensive "progressive" agriculture. Humanitarian principles dictate that human needs be met first so the quality of the environment must, if necessary, be sacrificed. Those who advocate otherwise are misanthropic. And those "doomsayers" who prophesy ecological collapse "divert attention from the urgency of the world food situation."[18] Campbell puts productivity, science, reason, progress, benevolence, and humanitarianism on one side and irrationality, faddism, misanthropy, and environmentalism on the other. Barrons puts the point somewhat more cleverly by asking whether what he calls "far out environmentalists" and other "hunger mongers" will influence us so that our "society, seeking a Utopian world of zero risks to health and an idealistic environment; [will] outsmart itself and create the greatest health and environmental hazard of all, a shortage of food."[19]

So agroindustry defenders question environmentalists' values. They are supported by social justice advocates who are concerned that the environmentalists will draw attention away from the plight of the urban poor who depend on cheap, mass-produced food to live, or away from the plight of peasants throughout the world who are excluded from good farming land, land that is underutilized or, in many cases, not utilized at all. As in earlier days, the contemporary equivalents of kings' estates and deer parks are preserved while the masses starve for want of land upon which to grow food. When regulations and controls and environmental sanctity are stressed it is the poor who suffer, not the affluent "appreciators" of nature. Environmentalists may charge that "humanism is arrogant" but they are elitist, misanthropic, morally perverse, "hunger mongers."

This charge by defenders of agroindustry goes right to the heart of the ethical debate concerning agriculture. If human needs are primary, then the environment must be sacrificed whenever human needs require this. If human needs are not primary, then what is? What *could* be a reasonable alternative?

## IV. ANTHROPOCENTRIC ETHICAL CONSIDERATIONS

The questions posed at the end of the previous section capture the deep, foundational ethical worries that arise in the debate over modern agriculture. Since agriculture causes environmental damage as a result of growing food to feed people, there seems to be a still-to-be-resolved conflict between human needs and environmental integrity. How shall this conflict be resolved? The environmentalists' ethical frameworks for approaching this question can be divided into two groups: anthropocentric critics and non-anthropocentric critics. The former evaluate environmental damage exclusively in terms of human welfare. The latter see value in nature independent of human interests and so judge the worth of human actions by their effects on the larger ecosphere.

### §10 WHOM SHALL WE FEED?

Traditionally, ethical thought has been anthropocentric, focusing exclusively on human interests and well-being. The great ethical theories of the past and most of today's deal with the proper relationships between people. Theories which emphasize rights, freedoms, duties, and obligations as well as those which stress the public good or the maximal social benefit deal with human character and action. When agriculture is discussed in this context, the questions will be: How does it relate to humans' interests? How does it benefit or harm them, ennoble or demean them, enhance or detract from their dignity? The focus will be on safe and sufficient production and equitable distribution. To the extent that environmental issues are considered at all, they will be discussed in terms of their relation to human well-being. This anthropocentric framework need not treat the nonhuman world as an inert tool or mere instrument for human exploitation and development. There may be some aesthetic values, recreational values, or character-building qualities in natural environments which may be seen as important and worth retaining. But when there is a conflict between human interests and the maintenance of the environment the former will naturally take precedence.

Different ideas are stressed, depending upon the moral theory. Traditional rights-based theories insist that the moral rights of humans not be violated. For example, they will demand that a person's right not to be harmed is not violated by those who poison surface water with pesticides or that a person's right to an adequate diet is not violated by those who discourage sufficient production or equitable distribution. Utilitarian-oriented theories which seek to maximize the public good are more comfortable with "tradeoffs" which could justify causing a minor harm to all or a high risk to some for the overall good of the society. Since most of our difficult moral decisions seem to involve a conflict of values where we must "weigh" or "balance" benefits and harms, the tradeoff approach has become a popular way of handling moral conflict. Utilitarians share this decision-making method with economists and they often concur in their results (though they may differ on their assessment of the public good). Following this method we could argue that if large, highly mechanized and chemically dependent farming produces more food at a lower cost to consumers than alternative farming methods, and if the need for such abundant and cheap food is crucial to human welfare, then the cost to the environment and even the cost to other human interests (for example, aesthetic delight in unspoiled nature) must be overridden. Modern farming brings more benefit than cost to human beings. The greater the demand for food, the greater the justification for mass production as a benefit. And so too, the greater the amount of risks and harms which can be incurred. Increasing the benefit to human welfare increases the justification for harm to the environment. Adequate food production which is so necessary to human well-being justifies whatever environmental damage is necessary to meet this goal. Environmental concerns are secondary. This utilitarian justification is the theory which lies behind the criticism about moral priorities in §9.

Even within this common, anthropocentric framework there is plenty of room for debate on environmental issues as these relate to agriculture.

Granted that human welfare is to be maximized, we can ask: *Which humans?*

Once we consider this question seriously we are led into the problems of "distant strangers" and "future peoples." In political matters we seldom speak of duties to peoples of other nations. But in moral considerations it is necessary to confront this issue. If one's view of ethics is anthropocentric, human interests determine moral right and wrong, not just the interests of, say, those humans who are Americans. One's ethical principles are universal in scope in the sense that the interests of *every* human being must be considered. Indeed, if our moral duties to respect rights and maximize the well-being of others ended at our political boundaries, then the argument offered earlier by Barrons and Campbell, that we must increase our environmentally damaging production for the sake of the hungry abroad—would not carry any weight. If the only people for whom we are justified in sacrificing our natural resources are United States citizens, then much of the damage done by modern agriculture would not be justified. Without exports we would be justified in taking a major percentage of the land out of production to conserve agricultural resources, on both environmental and economic grounds. But from the more "universal," global perspective, the natural resources and environmental health of some countries may have to be traded off for the food needs and welfare of peoples in some other countries. Where you ask the question, for *which people* (the malnourished in America, or in the Third World, or both?) are we to allow severe environmental harm?, the scope of the answer helps to determine the extent of the environmental damage you will allow. Even within the anthropocentric framework there is considerable debate on the nature of just distribution, on the equitable sharing of burdens, and upon the strength of property rights as they relate to this issue.

A second answer to the question, *Which humans?*, brings up the issue of future generations, those who will follow us. If the duty to meet the food needs of people includes the needs of future people (and not just those currently living) then the problem of environmental damage through agriculture takes on a new light. For the sake of immediate future generations Campbell argues for increased production and consequent increased environmental damage (which he believes can be alleviated by technological substitution). But what about the long run? What will be left of the topsoil and ground water in 200 years if we continue at the present pace of depletion? If we have duties to future persons then conserving the environment for their use may override some of the benefits we derive from the damage done to it by modern agriculture. If these duties are taken seriously, perhaps we ought to take steps to reduce present production levels and begin to preserve farm land currently in use. Perhaps not. The issue has no obvious solution, even judged in exclusively anthropocentric terms.

Notice that these two concerns, distant and future persons, can be combined in various ways: us-now, us-future, them-now, them-future, us-and-them now, us-and-them future, us-and-them now and future. Exploring some of these options will demonstrate the complexity involved in resolving these anthropocentric debates.

Though seldom put so bluntly, much of the motivation behind using current agricultural practices is a concern with us-now, or rather some-of-us-now. Besides the oft-repeated fact that farmers are primarily out to make a profit, much other evidence can be cited. The political motive behind American food aid and food-for-peace programs was to dump surpluses into foreign markets to ensure high farm prices at home.[20] Talk of balancing international payments by planting "fence to fence" and selling our "surplus" is in fact meant to serve "our" (that is, those agribusiness industries which gain) current interests now. The environmental cost is traded off for current economic interests. One could rightly challenge the alleged moral justification of this environmental overkill by raising a concern with increased health risks to most of us-now, and by citing the inequity of risk distribution (for example, workers are subject to high health risk from chemical exposure). Thus one could argue that the moral concern for contemporary, domestic human welfare of the many is being overridden by the economic interests of the few. Not all of us-now really benefit.

The us-future perspective raises other considerations. By acting in severely environmentally damaging ways we are strangling our-future generations. Draining aquifers, sterilizing our soil, eroding our topsoil, even for the sake of distant peoples is to spend our capital funds. It is like going on a wild middle-aged fling of rash generosity to the detriment of our children's health. The duty to conserve our agricultural resources for *our*-future generations, it may be claimed, takes precedence over whatever duty we may have to current distant strangers. Since it has become highly profitable to "export topsoil" by selling grain abroad, the question of saving for *our*-future (that is, for our descendants) is being increasingly raised. Concern here is amplified by world population growth rates. Unlike Campbell, biologist Garrett Hardin does not see the future human population of double or triple its present size as a challenge. Rather it is a threat to the agriculturally wealthy. The pressure will be too great on foreign environments and they will collapse, leading to the death of many millions of people. If the agriculturally wealthy nations try to "feed the world," they too will exhaust the stores in their lifeboat and suffer the consequences. So the welfare of our-future generations dictates conservation of *our* resources and thus ignoring the welfare of distant strangers.[21]

Various other combinations of us-them and now-future can be articulated into ethical positions. A great deal of material has been published on the moral duty to aid distant strangers[22] and the duty to preserve for future generations.[23] Details of these debates would take us too far afield from agriculture. But it is important to realize that the anthropocentric landscape is rich with moral complexity and littered with moral uncertainty. Perhaps it is safe to say that the ideal position would have to be fair to all peoples, both distant and future. If a way could be found to provide sufficiently for the food needs of all persons, this would be better than having to sacrifice or trade off some group. So the ideal objective is to find a way to ensure the well-being of all humans both here and there, now and future. From the anthropocentric perspective it would be morally preferable to achieve this goal instead of intentionally neglecting some group for the sake of some "environmental sanctity" which is unrelated to satisfyiing human needs. But the way to provide for both current distant peoples and future peoples has not been found. To see this more clearly, let us consider the assumptions and implications of a position like Campbell's, one that enjoins us to feed all who now exist by increasing production and that, at the same time, is optimistic about our ability to feed future people.

## §11 FEEDING EVERYONE

Like Campbell, most advocates of the call for increased production assume that current levels of consumption among the affluent will remain constant. Given this assumption, the only way the increased demand caused by population growth can be met is by increasing production. So the dilemma is seen to be one solely involving the environment versus the poor. And the call is to prioritize the poor—that is, to save the poor at whatever cost to the environment is necessary. But this attempted justification for increased production seems blind to the fact that current affluent life-styles and consumption habits *are themselves* responsible for overtaxing the environment and thus robbing future generations and limiting distant strangers' ability to meet their food needs. The same result (that is, prioritizing the poor) could be achieved by *redistributing* the food resources we have. Yet the argument of Campbell and Barrons and other production advocates hinges on supposing that the choice we must make is between stressing the environment or serving the poor, rather than protecting the environment or changing the dietary habits of the affluent. If the affluent cause the environmental overtaxing because of their food preferences then you cannot so easily evoke "humanitarian" priorities to justify increased production. Both Campbell and Barrons pass over this issue, disclaiming any connection between production and distribution. Only, they assume, by increasing production will there be a sufficient amount of food available to "trickle down" to the poor. Alternatives are dismissed. Barrons says:

> When food is short, prices are high and those with money naturally come out with a better diet. It's easy to decry maldistribution, but the world has never found a way to achieve equitable distribution of a short supply. The first step toward good nutrition for the masses is enough nourishing food to go around.[24]

It is questionable, given the exceptionally wasteful diets of the affluent, that there is a real shortage of supply or that there will be one in years to

come. There is a shortage *for the poor* but that is due to economic structures, not absolute shortage of food. Barrons assumes the inevitability of
maldistribution. This covertly takes all responsibility for environmental
damage off the affluent. *They* need not examine their life-style and diets.
It shifts the case for severe environmental damage to the need to minister
to the poor. Thus the poor are the "victims" of environmental regulation
and restrictions on production. No matter that some eat too well for their
own health, unless there is full-tilt growth not enough will "trickle
down." Presumably if I drink my fill of beer, I will leave some sips in the
fifth or sixth can so my impoverished colleague can have a drink too. But
why is it inevitable that we can't split the beers more evenly?

The obvious tack of lowering the consumption level of the affluent to
secure sufficient surplus for the poor, whether present or future generations, without increasing environmentally damaging production is usually
dismissed as economically naive. Such idealists, it is claimed, are obviously ignorant of market factors and the general laws of economics. We
could with equal disdain charge Campbell with a lack of philosophical sophistication when he offers the following undefended normative assertion:

> There seems to be little point in dragging the standard of diets in the
> more advanced countries down toward subsistance levels . . . the
> measures required to implement such a policy would be draconian and
> unacceptable to most citizens.[25]

The argument here seems to rest on the feasibility of political implementation and the opinion of the affluent. But moral arguments do not hinge
on the opinion of those with a vested interest in the status quo. However,
perhaps Campbell's real view is concealed by appearances. Witness his
later claim that acts designed to "drag down" standard diets in advanced
countries would interfere with "economic freedom."[26] Here is a normative claim that ultimately tests the issue. If "economic freedom" is
seen to be the supreme human value, the ultimate norm, the paramount
moral value, then indeed interference with this freedom and the fruits of
this freedom (affluence for some, poverty for others), for the sake of the
food needs of distant strangers, is unjustified. And certainly the protection or conservation of the nonhuman environment would not override
this important freedom. Defense of this much-heralded freedom is rare
but citation of it is not. Consider the words of a vice president of Castle
and Cook (a major grain dealer and exporter):

> Agribusinesses have shown that within the system of a free society at
> work, agriculture can be efficient and profitable. . . . We must assert
> the connection between the free market, political and personal liberty,
> and the economic and social progress made during the past three dec-
> ades by the nations of North America. . . . The world is in a race be-
> tween productivity and catastrophe. There is simply no way for the poor
> people of this planet to achieve either liberty or prosperity through a
> planned system of redistributing wealth. The people of the world can
> only achieve what they want by increasing wealth; and wealth can only
> be increased . . . by a free people responding to the profit motive. . . . It

is time for the world's free prosperous countries to get over their guilt at
being wealthy in a world where most are poor.[27]

But it is not *just* "most (who) are poor" in distant lands who stand to
be harmed by the wasteful dietary habits of the affluent. The quality of
life of our own future generations is threatened. If you ignore the environmental consequences of the actions of the affluent who are mobilized
by the profit motive, you are likely to miss the fact that these advocates
of freedom for maximal extraction and production are in fact engaged in
a very drastic form of redistribution (from rich to poor), not of money
but of *agricultural resources*. The overtaxing of topsoil and ground
water to create exportable surpluses is a way of redistributing water and
soil from the well endowed to the less well endowed. North Africa's fertility was redistributed to Rome; the West Indies' and Africa's to Europe.
The history of colonialism is the history of redistribution of agricultural
resources from those "wealthy" in such resources to those poor in them
but powerful in other ways—all in the name of economic freedom. But
unlike colonialism where "exploitation" of the colony occurred, today
the agriculturally rich are redistributing the resources of *their* future
generations without any cost to themselves. *They* are in fact prospering.
So the redistribution is there but in such a way as to avoid the cost of it.
Our affluence thrives, and we pass the cost on to the future. The future is
discounted by our reliance on substitution, which in turn relies on our
confidence in science and technology to keep ahead of the debt collector
—nature. So those who dismiss redistribution of available food now to
avoid curtailing the wasteful affluence of the rich are simultaneously redistributing the earth's wealth of future generations. Maximizing current interests through economic freedom to seize opportunities and stim-
ulate growth and generate wealth *is* redistributive between generations.
Unless the issue of affluent life-style overconsumption and waste are con-
fronted, the environmental concerns will not be fairly addressed. The
appeal to helping the poor as dictating environmental abuse is a red her-
ring unless the habits of the rich are examined. The call to economic
freedom is not, by itself, enough. If it were, one would be forced to
argue that this freedom overrides *all* environmental concerns, even those
related to the well-being of our own future generations. And this is to argue for too little at the price of too much.

Even remaining within an exclusively anthropocentric framework,
then, the tradeoff between the environment and people's needs is not
nearly so pat as the defenders of agroindustry would have it. How much
more difficult the challenge to defend current agroindustry policies
when we move beyond an anthropocentric framework, is something that
will become clearer in the next section.

## V. NON-ANTHROPOCENTRIC ETHICAL CHALLENGES

Recently there have been numerous calls for a "new ethic," one which does
not restrict itself solely to human welfare but which takes a broader perspec-

tive. This broader perspective is not limited to human concerns or interests but sees the nonhuman world as valuable in its own right, independent of its value for humans. Thus it finds the nonhuman world to be more than a mere tool or instrument for human use and satisfaction. Since the standard defense of agricultural destruction of the environment is to promote human well-being, this new ethic undercuts the defense by challenging the value on which it rests; that is, that human well-being is the *sole* measure of value and so the *exclusive* grounds for moral duty.

Two types of "broader ethic" have emerged: one that focuses on the moral status of some nonhuman animals, and one that focuses upon the moral status of the whole of nature. I will discuss each of these.

## §12 ANIMAL INTERESTS AND RIGHTS

Traditional anthropocentric ethical thinking focuses exclusively upon human concerns. If only human interests are of moral worth then it makes little moral difference how we treat other animals. Provided that human interests are promoted then we can use animals any way we desire. Traditionally, animal husbandry is an important part of agriculture. Animals are raised either for their products (meat, milk, eggs, wool, skins, leather, feathers, musk, etc.) or for their labor (to pull plows or carry loads). Though on anthropocentric grounds we may want to discourage cruelty to animals since this might either spill over into cruelty to people (the animal abusers become desensitized to suffering) or offend the sensitivities of other humans who pity the animals' suffering, still there are no moral reasons to regulate the treatment of animals if these possible side effects can be avoided.

But there is a growing number of critics of this exclusively anthropocentric view who are calling for a moral consideration of the interests of animals and who are advocating that some animals (members of "higher," neurophysiologically more sophisticated species) be included within the moral community (the group of entities between whom moral relationships pertain). These critics, sometimes called Animal Liberationists, are advocating that moral actions not be determined exclusively by human interests. They tend to fall into two groups: the utilitarian-oriented theorists like Australian moralist Peter Singer[28] and the rights-based or justice-oriented theorists like Tom Regan,[29] editor of this volume.

The utilitarians base their arguments on some animals' indisputable sentience (ability to experience pain and pleasure). Since animals experience pain and suffering and since it is wrong (on utilitarian grounds) to intentionally cause suffering without significant justification, then only those who are "speciesists" will subordinate animals' important interests (and cause them to suffer) to trivial human interests (such as the *taste* of meat which nutritionally is unnecessary). A speciesist, like a racist, lets prejudice rule his judgment, and overrides the important interests of others in favor of his own trivial interests. The traditional anthropocentric perspective is speciesist; no wonder then that it is uncritical of our treatment of animals. But a non-anthropocentric, non-speciesist moral perspective condemns most modern methods of animal husbandry precisely because they intentionally cause animals to suffer without any regard for the animals' interests. Modern "factory farming" causes immense suffering to animals. Even though the motive is not sadism but efficiency (e.g., high concentrations of animals to provide economy of scale) or product protection (e.g., clipping beaks of chickens so they won't hurt each other) or product improvement (confining veal calves to keep the meat tender) or mere convenience (driving terrified cattle into the slaughterhouse to avoid transporting corpses)—nonetheless the suffering is willed along with the practice and so is not merely an unintentional by-product. The intense suffering of the animal is unthinkingly traded off for the promotion of a relatively unimportant human interest. This is speciesism and is morally wrong. Thus either the methods used in meat production must be reformed to minimize suffering or this production must, morally, be given up altogether. Peter Singer makes it clear in his famous book *Animal Liberation*[30] that vegetarianism is morally required for us.

But when it comes to animal labor this position is less clear. Much of the world's agriculture relies on using animal labor (bullocks, water buffaloes, donkeys, mules, horses, and camels). These animals pull plows, carry loads, and in addition supply milk, manure (for fertilizer and fuel), and occasionally meat. Many Asian farmers are vegetarians on religious grounds but they still use animal labor. The utilitarian position would seem to require that these animals not be abused, neglected, or made to suffer. Their interest must be taken into account. But since the well-being of the animal is often crucial to the survival of these farmers they are not likely to mistreat them (for instance, by making them work in the hot sun too long or carry too heavy loads). Yet their interests are clearly being subordinated to human interests. It could be argued however that this is justified since the human interest overriding the animals' is not trivial or minor—but is itself of great significance to the well-being or even survival of the humans. So on utilitarian grounds a non-anthropocentric view which includes animals in the moral community could justify the use of animal labor if suffering was minimized even though it could not justify meat production in the factory farms of the agriculturally advanced nations.

The second non-anthropocentric position, the one based on rights, argues that animals have moral rights which limit what humans are morally permitted to do to them. Such rights could include the right not to be harmed (caused to suffer)[31] or the right to life (not to be killed unjustly),[32] or the right of noninterference with their interests (for example their natural proclivities to root, graze, chew the cud, mate, or suckle their young). Since rights are normally ascribed to individuals, then it is individual animals (of some species) who have rights and thus have inherent value or intrinsic worth in their own right. Arguments to support this view usually attempt to show that all criteria used to show a morally relevant difference between humans and some animals fail either because they beg the question, are arbitrary, or fail to apply to all humans and only humans. For example, traditional criteria such as rationality or speech do not include human infants or the retarded, while consciousness not only fails to include comatose humans but does include some animals. Since there is no clear, nonarbitrary, unambiguous criterion, then we should ascribe moral rights to animals who are relevantly similar to humans. Thus we should treat them with the respect they are due, and realize that as centers of inherent value, they cannot be manipulated and used as mere tools for human satisfaction or purposes.

The consequences of adopting this view for agriculture would be extreme since it would seem to require an end to all commercial and noncommercial animal husbandry for food use, as we know these practices. Merely reducing suffering by providing better living conditions would not do. Justice demands the total elimination of practices that treat animals as if they are a renewable resource that exists for us. It would seem that animals could not even be used for labor—since this would be exploitative and not only violative of the right not to be harmed (assuming the work causes some suffering) but the right of noninterference (for it requires retaining animals in captivity and thus restricting their movement). So it would seem that no use of animals is permitted because they are incapable of giving informed consent to being used. The options for agriculture in the underdeveloped nations would be limited to voluntary human labor or mechanical labor, if this view persisted. Either option would place a hardship on farmers since the first would probably be insufficient to do the necessary work and the second too costly. Of course one could argue that animal rights can be overridden by legitimate human interests but this is controversial since it would seem to drastically dilute the rights.

So on either utilitarian grounds or rights grounds these non-anthropocentric views challenge the moral propriety of many of the practices of both technologically developed and "undeveloped" agriculture. Since, they argue, human interests are not the sole measure of value, then animal husbandry for food and perhaps for animal labor are, in all or some instances, morally unjustified.

In broadening the moral community to include some animals, both approaches extend traditional humanistic ethical theories which place value on *individuals*. But what about species? Do animal species have interests or rights which morally limit what humans can do to them? For instance if, in expanding cultivation, some wild species' habitats are being destroyed with the result that these species are threatened, are there any moral restraints on humans to protect or preserve these endangered species? Both of the non-anthropocentric positions we have considered are clear about this. Both Singer and Regan deny interests and rights, respectively, to a collection or whole species.[33] Yet many environmentalists are extremely concerned about protecting the diversity of life, preserving the maximal number of species, and maintaining a broad gene pool. In-dividual members of endangered species are considered more valuable than members of nonendangered species simply because they are rare. It is not because as individuals they have rights but because of their type and their rarity that they are judged to be valuable and worthy of extra protection.[34] Since individual-oriented theories can not account for this "extra" value given to these individuals, many environmentalists have deserted individualistic ethical theories and have turned to a different type of non-anthropocentric theory—one that emphasizes whole groups, relationships, and whole ecosystems as the sources of value.

## §13 ECOCENTRISM

Ecocentrism is a non-anthropocentric position which places value in whole systems. It is evolutionary and ecologically oriented. As a moral position it has grown out of the works of nineteenth century naturalist John Muir, and Wisconsin forester and essayist Aldo Leopold, among others. Leopold's famous chapter "The Land Ethic" in *A Sand County Almanac* has become its scripture. He advocates that we

> enlarge the boundaries of the (moral) community to include soils, waters, plants, and animals, or collectively: the land.[35]

When making ethical decisions we are to use this "key-log":

> A thing is right when it tends to preserve the integrity, stability, and beauty of the biotic community. It is wrong when it tends otherwise.[36]

It is unclear what Leopold means by this provocative maxim, and inter-preters disagree. However, they do agree that the basic organic or eco-logical insight expressed is that *everthing is connected* and that *the good of the parts is dependent upon the good of the whole*. This view is there-fore "holistic" rather than "atomistic" (or "individualistic") and ecocen-tric rather than merely anthropocentric. Ecological equilibrium, stabil-ity, and diversity seem to be "objective" natural goods. But if they are naturally good then we ought to value them. Also we ought to judge an action right or wrong according to whether it increases or diminishes these goods. Nature more or less gives us our moral norms and tells us how we ought to act.[37]

Advocates of this new ecocentric ethic vary from an extreme, which I will call *eco-holism*, to the most moderate view, which I will call *eco-humanism* or ecological humanism. The former interprets Leopold liter-ally, the latter reads him in ways that allow advocates to remain humanists (placing primacy on humans) but not exclusively anthropocentric human-ists. Between these two positions is another I will call *eco-compatibilism* which sees human interests and ecocentric values coinciding. Since the prescriptions each position recommends for agriculture vary greatly with the strictness of the interpretation adopted, it is important to dis-tinguish them. I will proceed from the most extreme ecocentric view to the most moderate.

## §14 ECO-HOLISM

The best articulation of this position I know of was written by philosopher and environmentalist Baird Callicott.[38] He says, "Environmental ethics locates ultimate value in the 'biotic community' and assigns differential moral values to the constitutive individuals relative to that standard." Thus "inanimate entities such as oceans and lakes, mountains, forests, and wetlands are assigned a greater value than individual animals. . . . ." Also, "the biospheric perspective does not exempt *Homo sapiens* from moral evaluation in relation to the well-being of the community of nature taken as a whole." As a result, "the extent of misanthropy in modern environmentalism thus may be taken as a measure of the degree to which it is biocentric." The moral worth of individuals and of species is relative to the collective good—and this includes humans. So "competing individual claims may be adjudicated and relative values and priorities assigned to the myriad components of the biotic community" by looking to the whole.

Here the holistic norm is indeed taken literally to the point that, given human overpopulation, "if one had to choose between a specimen of *Homo sapiens* and a specimen of a rare even if unattractive species, the choice would be moot":[39] The nonhuman would automatically be preferred. Needless to say this type of ethic would leave little room for justification of most of the practices of modern agriculture. Even "organic" agriculture is disruptive of soils, waters, and natural habitats. It is not clear in this strict interpretation that *any* form of agriculture could be justified. If the conflicts between humans and soil, humans and pests, humans and aquifers, and humans and weeds were relative to the health and diversity of the whole biosphere, then it would be difficult to defend saving humans at all. In fact, massive human die backs would be good. Is it our duty to cause them? Is it our species' duty, relative to the whole, to eliminate 90 percent of our numbers? This question is certainly raised by the following thoughts of philosopher Paul Taylor, who contemplates the short epoch of man in the long perspective of evolutionary history:

> Every last man, woman, and child could disappear from the face of the Earth without any significant detrimental consequence for the good of wild animals and plants. On the contrary, many of them would be greatly benefited. . . . If then, the total, final, absolute extermination of our species (by our own hands?) should take place and if we should not carry all the others with us into oblivion, not only would the Earth's community of life continue to exist, but in all probability its well being would be enhanced. Our presence, in short, is not needed. If we were to take the standpoint of the community and give voice to its true interest, the ending of our . . . epoch would most likely be greeted with a healthy "Good riddance."[40]

This extreme eco-holism may not prescribe mass genocide or species suicide but it comes close. Certainly it is difficult to imagine how humans could live according to this norm if taken literally. The only permissible form of food acquisition would seem to be that of primitive hunter-gatherers who live off the land, in harmony with it, by harvesting wild plants and culling weak members of abundant animal herds. I think perhaps Callicott understates the case when he says,

> Implementation of the land ethic would require discipline, sacrifice, retrenchment, and massive economic reform tantamount to a virtual revolution in prevailing attitudes and life styles.[41]

The implication for humans would be astounding, staggering. No wonder that agricultural apologists find it hard not to question the priorities of what they call "far out environmentalists." Indeed, by its own admission, this stance measures its worth by its level of misanthropy. Since only species matter, there are no *individual* rights whatsoever, including human rights. But it is not clear how many environmental critics would want to push environmentalism this far. Many seem to want to stop short of taking Leopold's maxim literally.

## §15   ECO-COMPATIBILISM

Any ecocentric view must advocate a change of attitudes to broaden our concern to more than just human well-being. If the biotic community can be seen to have intrinsic worth in its own right, then more "love, respect and admiration for the land, and a high regard for its value"[42] will follow—or at least should. More care will (or should) be taken in the treatment of nonhuman nature. That humans will disrupt the harmony and cause instability is unfortunate (and perhaps a sign of the sinfulness of the "human condition" after our expulsion from the "Garden of Eden"), but every effort should be made to minimize this violence and disruption. We should strive to restore and enhance the beauty and inherent goodness of the biosphere. Leopold himself seems to be merely recommending that we conform our actions to the larger ecosphere (though this is subject to debate). He suggests that agriculture should attempt to stay within the bounds of nature's limits, so the land can preserve both its "habitability for man and for most of the other natives."[43] He also says that the "less violent the man made changes the greater the probability of successful readjustment in the pyramid" of relationships.[44] He prescribes a minimization of disruption to promote the health of the land which is "its capacity for self renewal."[45] The emphasis should be placed on seeing man as *member*, not as master, of nature.[46] The traditional distinction between intrinsic value (human) and instrumental value (nonhuman) is ill drawn. Man is not opposite nature but part of it. We must harmonize our actions with nature. We must "command nature by obeying her."[47] In farming we should "direct nature round to our goals," but "if we are intelligent, we [should] use only those disruptions that nature can absorb, those appropriate to the resilience of the ecosystem under cultivation."[48] But it is not *merely* a matter of conforming.

"The rural environment is, or ought to be, a place of *symbiosis* between humankind and nature, for we may sometimes improve a biosystem."[49]

What is advocated here is a compatibilism between nature and humans. There should be no conflict. Only actions which promote attunement, cooperation, harmony, and integration are right. In all of our activities, including agriculture, we ought to stay within the constraints of nature which prescribes diversity, decentralization, integration, interdependence, remaining within limitations, and the long-run viewpoint. The moral ideal of this compatibilism between human well-being and biotic well-being does not merely refer to the human species as a whole. It also seems to refer to individual human beings. There is to be no conflict between humans' needs and environmental good. To promote the good of the whole is *simultaneously* to promote the good of each part; they are not in a struggle. And the human parts include future as well as present persons, neighbors as well as those who live in distant lands. By promoting the biotic community's beauty and stability, diversity and integrity, you promote the good of all persons.

The worth, happiness, and ultimate well-being of *all* individuals lies in valuing and acting to promote the ecosystem's integrity. We will regain our dignity,[50] overcome our alienation from nature,[51] and establish "the right relationship between human beings and the Earth" by recapturing a "personal relationship" to it.[52] We even will derive "personal satisfaction."[53] Even more mystically, this could lead to a point of merger between self and nature by expanding the self since

> the preservation of the ecosystem [is] in human self interest, for the "self" has been so extended as to be ecosystemically redefined. The human welfare which we find in the enriched ecosystem is no longer recognizable as that of anthropocentrism.[54]

So we should achieve this compatibilism of interests and thereby eliminate the need for tradeoffs between human needs and the environment. Harmoniously living in cooperation with nature and promoting nature's goals will best serve the needs of human beings.

But what happens when human interests actually do come into conflict with the larger ecosphere? In the long run the species' interest may indeed coincide with the larger whole, but in the short run an *individual's* vital interests (for instance, in survival) often do clash. Eco-compatibilism underplays these conflicts—but they are very real, especially for poor people who are living just at or below subsistence level.

## §16 ECO-HUMANISM

Eco-humanism is a compromise position which attempts to combine (1) eco-compatibilism's emphasis upon harmonizing human activity with ecological principles and promoting the overall well-being of the non-human biosphere with (2) humanism's concern for human individuals. As a humanism, eco-humanism stresses the importance of humans and so

grants priority to the vital interests of humans when they come into irreconcilable conflict with other individuals or the larger biosphere. Individual humans' vital interests and basic rights cannot simply be ignored
or unthinkingly traded off for the sake of the greater human (species) or
nonhuman (animals or ecosystem) good when a conflict arises. But why?
How can this compromise position be defended?

A full defense would ultimately require defending a distinctive
human attribute which would confer on individual humans a greater
degree of value than is derived by occupying a role in or being part of a
larger whole. If pressed I would select *self-conscious creativity* as that
attribute which grounds special significance to vital human interests and
ultimately grounds rights claims in our case. Though *sentience* seems to
grant a creature some special status as an individual (since that individual has interests in avoiding suffering), the interests of creatures which
possess the attribute of self-conscious creativity seem to be of greater significance, in part because of the *awareness* of the future that is involved.
A creature with this attribute is aware of its interests in the actualization
of a plan. It is this aspect more than any other which is responsible for
the development of, reflection upon, and manifestation of ideas in the
world. I hold these abilities to be of distinctive value, conferring upon
creatures who have them greater worth than that conferred by being a
part of a larger whole. But these are difficult matters. Thinking about
them exposes the deep significance of our opinions about what is valuable. Furthermore, whenever a single attribute is isolated as the sole
criterion for conferring special status upon humans, one runs into the
problem of including all and only humans. Since some humans will fail
to have this attribute and some nonhuman animals may have it, clean
distinctions by species will be problematic. But I would judge that the
vital interests of a creature with self-conscious creativity in addition to
sentience should override the interests of a merely sentient creature
though I would not rule out that creatures with mere sentience have
worth as individuals. Note, however, that this debate over the appropriate criterion for ascribing value to individuals is still from *within* the
perspective of individualism or atomism. The eco-holistic perspective
simply treats any distinctive attribute of individuals as irrelevant. Individuals are *only* members of a species, *only* parts of a larger biotic
system. Appeal to *any* special characteristic of individuals to bestow individual worth is ignored. So how do we choose between these two fundamental perspectives?

It is not clear that we could "prove" the rational superiority of one
value framework over its competitor. Perhaps this is why eco-holism's
defenders often appeal to "objective" moral norms dictated by nature.
But this move, for most traditional philosophers, will be seen as falla-
cious reasoning (it confuses facts and values) and thus it provides no real
argument for this view. On the other hand, to defend that humans have
intrinsic worth, or natural rights, or are ends-in-themselves seems to beg
the question (that is, to simply assume what one is trying to prove). To

extend the individualist view to include some nonhuman animals as having intrinsic worth or some natural rights also seems to beg the question. So rationally deciding on one view (that individuals have superior worth) or the other (that individuals are valuable merely as members of the larger biotic community) is difficult. Since *both* seem to contain an element of truth, eco-humanism tries to embody aspects of both. But of course, it cannot fully serve both masters at the same time; so it leans toward the individual human-worth side of the controversy when eco-compatibilism breaks down and fundamental human interests and environmental values are in conflict. Even though it supports the humanist side when push comes to shove, eco-humanism is not exclusively anthropocentric. One must always justify any action that is ecologically disruptive by showing that it is required because of the *vital* interests of some humans. And the short- and long-term effects of such an action are important; it must not jeopardize the possible restoration of harmonious relationship between humans and the ecosphere. To allow acts or policies for the sake of human benefit does not reduce all that is not human to worthlessness. One can still hold ecosystems to be valuable in their own right. To say that human beings and ecosystems are *both* intrinsically valuable is not to say or imply that both are *equal* in intrinsic value. Moreover, to prioritize human welfare does not justify total disregard of nonhuman animals or destruction of the environment. This feature distinguishes eco-humanism from traditional (exclusive) anthropocentric humanisms which seek only to promote human well-being. It is not just for the sake of preserving resources for future humans' use that we should act harmoniously with nature. Nor is it just for our *own* dignity and satisfaction. Some element of what Leopold calls an "ethical relationship to land,"[55] or what we could call an ecosensitive attitude, must be present. When it is necessary to prioritize human welfare it should be done with the least possible amount of environmental damage, destruction, and intervention.

Eco-humanism is a compromise between eco-holism and anthropocentric humanism. Like all compromises it is difficult to keep distinctive. It tends to slip to one side or the other. Finding the "golden mean" between extremes is never easy. Yet we can distinguish it from anthropocentric humanism, even the ones which argue that it is in the enlightened self-interest of humans (both now and future) to maximize environmental integrity. We could ask: Supposing there are other ways to promote our interests? If through technological development we could substitute so as to perpetually avoid the consequences of environmental abuse, wouldn't this equally serve our self-interest? Suppose the so-called laws of ecology turn out not to be scientific laws at all but inconclusive generalizations and thus caution and conservation need not be enacted? What would happen to our duty to respect the environment? An "enlightened anthropocentrism" which asserts that "a healthy environment is *in fact* necessary for the long term satisfaction of human needs and interests"[56] hangs on the truth of this "in fact" claim. If science can indeed deliver us from reliance on nature and create artificial environments, then there would be no further justification to preserve the natural environment, except perhaps for aesthetic or character-building reasons. Yet even here there is no reason to think that human aesthetic tastes would not shift to the artificial (what is "art" after all?) and human character has been seen to be primarily shaped by social interaction ever since the age of the Greeks. A variety of aesthetic or character-building experiences may be lost with the destruction of the enviroment, but certainly not the complete enterprise. So anthropocentric humanism which asserts that "environmental preservation and resource sustainability are goals that should be sought primarily for their human benefit" and that "ecosystem integrity . . . contributes to the long term interests of humans"[57] *contingently* associates environmental integrity and human well-being. It may *not* in fact turn out to be necessary to preserve an ecosystem's integrity in order to promote human interest.

Eco-humanism, on the other hand, does not tie the value of the environment to human interests. Even granting all the scientific substitution required to promote human interests and free us from nature, there would still be value in the natural environment, a value we ought to preserve. But as a humanism, human welfare will be given priority in eco-humanism when there is an irreconcilable conflict with enviromental integrity. What we mean by human welfare is important. Not any old human desire will justify overriding the welfare of the environment. For Heffernan, *survival* is the key meaning of human welfare which can override environmental concerns. He says:

> The survival interests of human beings ought to outweigh those of the rest of the biotic community and the survival interests of the rest of the biotic community ought to outweigh the nonsurvival interests of human beings.[58]

If this definition is adopted then certainly the agricultural practices necessary to ensure subsistence for present and future people are justified. Yet it would not justify luxurious diets, much meat production, or non-food luxury items (coffee, tobacco, tea). Nor would it justify the maldistribution which requires overproduction and gross surplus for some to ensure a trickle down for others. Accepting this *survival criterion* for when human welfare justifiably overrides the welfare of the biotic community is *very* strict and would lead to significant changes in treatment of the environment. But is human welfare limited to survival needs?

Beyond the biological survival interests of humans there are social interests which seem to be necessary if humans are to develop their potential and attain a minimal level of self-fulfillment. As physics and religion professor Ian Barbour says, "A person or society interested only in satisfying biological needs would miss the most distinctive potentialities of human existence."[59] To ensure the development of this potential, certain social goods, beyond mere subsistence level, must be attained (for example, health, security, community, education, leisure, etc.). So if we measure human welfare by a richer standard than mere subsistence, the range of cases in which one would be justified in causing ecological damage is increased. But adequate levels of production to support the attainment of these goals should be set, to as great an extent as possible, within ecological limits and with full attention paid to promotion of the well-being of the ecosphere. Since there is a duty to curtail damage, we cannot simply look at the production side. Once again distribution becomes important. Affluent life-styles and overrich diets, which tax the environment, are not justified by appeal to meeting basic social needs. To see this requires making a distinction between human needs (including social ones) and human wants and desires. Not all human desires or wishes will justify overriding the welfare of an ecosystem. Subsistence, health, and security, yes; but not luxury, waste, or conspicuous consumption. A healthy, balanced, and varied diet, yes; but not the typical meat-based and exotic palate-titillating diet of most of the affluent world. To make this distinction between needs and mere wants or wishes requires that one not accept the economist's equation of subjective preferences (as reflected in consumer behavior) with human "satisfaction" and thereby automatically collapse all distinctions between needs, wants, wishes, and desires. For eco-humanism, *only some* human interests (survival and basic social needs) will justify intentionally damaging the environment. Thus for a nation strapped with severe food shortage, increasing use of environmentally damaging production techniques can be justified (including heavy pesticide use, large irrigation projects, and energy-intensive mechanization). But for a nation creating so much surplus that it must let it rot outside grain elevators, or be "reductively converted" to use up surplus (for example, by use as animal feed, gasohol, retextured protein-imitation meats, etc.), the damage is not justified. Eco-humanism targets its criticism not on the poor, who *are* justified in overusing the environment, but on the rich who *are not*. It cannot accept the trickle down as justifiable. It necessarily calls for redistribution because it is the diet and production requirements of the affluent which unjustifiably overstep the limits of ecological constraints. The contest is environmental integrity versus the rich, not environmental integrity versus the poor.

Eco-humanism, then, is distinct from anthropocentric humanism and eco-holism. Yet it serves the purposes of the environmentalist well since it challenges the three basic moral arguments of the defenders of modern agriculture. First, it does not concur that "human interest," as reflected in market demand, overrides environmental integrity (see §6). Only *some* human interests (which are not usually distinguishable in the market) do. Second, it does not separate production questions from distribution questions (see §11). The moral argument for increased production must be placed in the context of current distribution. Since increased production damages ecosystems, it is *prima facie* wrong and so should be avoided if possible. Redistribution can avoid the necessity for increased production, and can perhaps even reduce the current massive level of environmentally damaging production. Since current food use (and waste) by the affluent is not eco-humanistically justifiable, it follows that current production is not intranationally justified. It can remain at the same level only if necessary for the meeting of basic needs internationally. Yet this cannot be determined until a substantial redistribution has occurred, one that would reduce the consumption level of the affluent and improve the consumption level of the impoverished. Eco-humanism ties production and distribution together. Third, eco-humanism undercuts the claim (see §8) that since science will provide substitutes for environmental damage and resource losses (so that future humans are not being unfairly treated), there is no reason not to fully exploit the environment. Since eco-humanism grants intrinsic (though not absolute) value to the biosphere, any damage is *prima facie* wrong. Even if this damage would not affect the welfare of future persons, it should, nonetheless, be avoided whenever possible. So whether science can provide substitutes is irrelevant to the question: Should we deplete biospheric resources? This does not mean that science and technological innovation are unimportant. Substitution could be used to replace current practices with less environmentally damaging ones. This would promote the fulfilment of both human needs and biospheric needs simultaneously. An ecologically appropriate use of technology to increase food production would be welcomed by eco-humanism since it promotes its two goals—the welfare of both humankind and nature.

Eco-humanism is also compatible with some of the goals of the animal liberationists—in particular, the elimination of intentionally causing sentient creatures to suffer for trivial human purposes. Nonhuman animals are, after all, part of the land, and sentient creatures do seem to have special worth as individuals precisely because they can suffer. So even though eco-humanism grants special worth to the vital interests of individual humans, it is not exclusively anthropocentric and thus it does not ignore nonhuman animals' interests entirely.

I think eco-humanism is the best ethical framework from which to approach the controversy over modern agriculture. As a compromise between two extremes it has the golden ring of a superior position which transcends the limitations of both. It exposes the weaknesses in arguments used by defenders of modern agriculture without trying to "turn back the clock" and without being antiprogress or antiscience. Rather it encourages ecologically sound technological innovation. It values human distinctiveness and recognizes the necessity of sufficient agricultural production to ensure the development of human potential. And it does so in a way that takes into account the needs of all peoples, those living now, wherever they live, and those who will live after us. Eco-humanism also values the environment in its own right and is sufficiently holistic to advocate the virtues of harmony, interdependence, sustainability, diversity, integrity, and permanence, all within naturally set limits. But its valuing of the larger biosphere is not misanthropic. As a compromise between eco-holism and anthropocentrism, it is a reasonable, balanced, normative position which promises to resolve the battle of ideologies alluded to in my opening remarks (see §1). In describing this position I have offered it as a plausible alternative framework, but I have not provided a complete defense of it, developed it to any degree, or dealt with the major objections to it. Leaving these theoretical considerations for a more appropriate forum, I will return to the issue of agriculture and, in the final section, will briefly discuss the principles according to which an eco-humanistic agriculture would be developed.

# VI.  ECO-HUMANISTIC AGRICULTURE

Whenever it is possible, eco-humanistic agriculture should provide food and fiber necessary to fulfill the basic survival and social needs for all humans now and in the future, in ways that are compatible with, and supportive of, the overall health, stability, integrity, and permanence of the biosphere. To approach this goal, agriculture must conform, to as great an extent as possible, to four principles: ecological efficiency, use of complementary technology, no unnecessary use of animals, and embodiment in an appropriate cultural setting. Each principle is discussed in turn.

## §17  ECOLOGICAL EFFICIENCY

Agriculture must not be viewed merely as a production-oriented industry. Its efficiency should not be measured solely in terms of yield per acre, output per input, yield per man hour, or even total profitability. Efficiency for agricultural production should be measured in terms of compatibility with ecological stability and in terms of the long-run sustainability of yields (maximal yield per acre over an indefinitely long time span).

Since all agriculture is by its nature disruptive, the criterion of stability is to be seen as a goal to be approached. To draw close to this goal of ecological stability, agriculture must stay within the environmental limits of both the larger biosphere and the particular local ecosystem.

Not all of the earth's land can be safely cultivated. There is a limited amount of arable land resilient enough to survive human interference. So, to meet the goal of ecological stability on the global scale, some consideration must be given to *how that good land is being used*. Eco-humanism justifies causing some instability to grow food crops (and perhaps some essential fiber crops). But it cannot justify using good land to grow nonfood or luxury food crops, especially when this forces people to use less stable and damage-prone lands for food crops.[60] Thus growing exotic fruits and vegetables, tobacco, beverage crops, and crops for meat production on top grade (damage-resilient) land cannot be justified. From the global perspective, promoting the stability of the ecosphere means not growing crops unnecessary for human survival or social needs. To grow them on good land is wasteful and displaces food crops to bad land, and to grow them on bad land is destructive. Even though luxury crops are "preferred by [affluent] consumers" and are thus good "cash crops," they should not be grown. Economically, it is true, it is "inefficient" not to grow a luxury export crop if you have a "comparative advantage" over other producers (that is, if you can grow it more cheaply). *But ecological efficiency is not economic efficiency.* To use the earth's resources in an ecologically efficient way is to minimize instability and this means growing only necessary (in the sense of "necessary" previously explained) food and fiber crops. If there were an abundance of good (resilient) land then luxury crops could be grown in addition to basic food crops without causing great instability. But the days of abundant choice land are gone. Even in the agriculturally superior United States, top grade farm land is becoming scarce. From the perspective of the global ecosphere, we can no longer justify creating ecological instability for luxury food and nonfood crops.

Furthermore, agriculture cannot be viewed in isolation. High chemical, energy, and irrigation dependence requires dams, wells, and refineries for the manufacture of those inputs. If the production of those inputs causes severe ecological instability then an agriculture which creates a demand for them (thus "causing" their manufacture) is not ecologically efficient. Just as the fashion markets of Europe (for beaver hats or peacock feathers) were responsible for mass extermination of animal populations in the past, so the input market of modern agriculture (pesticides, etc.) is today responsible for the ecological damage due to manufacture of those inputs. Neither fashion nor farming which depends on this damage is ecologically efficient.

In addition to how good land is being used, a second aspect of the goal of stability is *local adaptation.* What is grown, how it is grown, and how much of it is grown depend upon the peculiar conditions of the local ecosystem. Soils, climates, fertility, and water availability vary greatly from area to area. So too does ecosystem fragility. To be ecologically efficient means to finely tune agricultural practices to local conditions. There can be no one prescribed method of farming. General textbooks or agribusiness pamphlets which promote a standardized way to farm (level it, irrigate it, fertilize it to desired standards, spray it, etc.) are ecologically silly—at best. You can't treat farming like fast food chain restaurants with standardized size, method, and procedures all nicely prescribed in advance. What may work in Kansas will not work (ecologically) in tropical Africa. Moreover, the goal of local adaptability is not the goal of maximization of output. Though standardization and modernization may be more economically efficient (and especially more profitable for the suppliers of inputs and mechanical implements), they cannot be ecologically efficient because *nature is not standardized.* Adaptive farming is an art or craft, based on skill, experience, and a sense for one's land.[61] If, to minimize creating instability within local conditions, you should use draft animals, or small two-wheel tractors, or human labor, then it should be done. If frequent fallowing, interplanting, minimal plowing, small plot plowing, or contour plowing are required, then it should be done. In desert conditions, species that thrive in arid climates should be cultivated or desert "weeds" (often the foods of ancient civilizations) should be developed and cultivated.[62] Massive aquifer irrigation is ill adaptive in the desert. But irrigation in river deltas and on flood plains is suitable. Wind erosion in the great prairie region makes fall planting erosive; it may even make row cropping itself ecologically inefficient, and so we should develop and cultivate only perennial grasses on the plains. To a large extent, adapting agriculture to local ecosystems means taking Barry Commoner's third law of ecology seriously; that is, "nature knows best."[63] Since nature presents many faces, we must conform to the individual differences of every visage.

In addition to respecting ecosystem stability, the principle of ecological efficiency dictates that agriculture be sustainable *over a long time period*. This entails that it be regenerative, that it be practiced in a way that replaces the extracted resources in an environmentally safe way and rejuvenates the ecosystem of which it is a part. Techniques used to regenerate (like fallowing) can be supplemented by adding inputs *provided* that the inputs are available and effective over long time periods. An agriculture heavily dependent on inputs from scarce nonrenewable resources (for example, fossil fuels) is not sustainable without constant substitution. So heavy reliance upon petroleum energy, or chemicals derived from petroleum or natural gas, or nonrenewable ground water irrigation, is not sustainable for the long term. Since modern agriculture is highly dependent on these, it is called into question. The rising price of these increasingly scarce inputs is drastically affecting many farmers' ability to continue farming. Traditional farming is more sustainable in this sense. What few inputs it uses to supplement sustainable techniques, such as human and animal labor and manure, are renewable over the long haul. Some farm plots in "undeveloped nations" have continuously and with ecological safety been farmed for *hundreds* of years. Or consider this example of an ecologically efficient integrated recycling system:

> In silkworm production, mulberry leaves are picked and fed to silkworms whose waste products are then fed to fish who are periodically harvested. Silt from the fish pond bottom is used to fertilize the mulberry trees.[64]

Contrast this with the typical American farmer in thousands of dollars of debt because of his purchase of fertilizer, pesticides, gas, water, machinery, and other inputs made from increasingly scarce resources. Which is more sustainable?

Not only should inputs be available over the long run, they should be effective in regenerating the soil. One indication that an input is not effective, in the long run, is the necessity of annually increasing the volume applied in order to produce the same output. If chemical fertilizers must be applied in greater volume year after year, then they are not regenerating the soil; they are masking a deeper environmental problem:

declining natural fertility of the soil due to overuse. This is like taking increasing amounts of painkiller to mask the pain in your mouth when what you ought to do is get the diseased tooth fixed. "Natural" fertilizers like manure, or plowed-in nitrogen-fixing crops, are genuinely regenerative; they keep the microbic life in the soil thriving, which is nature's way of restoring fertility. Another indication that an input is not effective is when it ceases to do its "job" after a short time period. Many pesticides fall into this category. Pesticides are highly effective for a short period of time, but resistant strains of pests evolve rapidly, making the pesticide ineffective. Thus the race is on to develop a new pesticide to kill the new variety of pest that is resistant to the old pesticide. Since pesticides kill off natural predators, their use may in fact increase the pest problem in the long run. A more sustainable method of pest control is use of biological techniques (relying heavily upon predators, timing, and even on interference in the reproduction of pests by releasing sterile males), since these do not result in new resistant mutations. So regenerative agriculture not only uses ecologically stable techniques, it also uses effective and available inputs.

It has often been asserted that traditional methods or even contemporary "organic" methods of farming are simply not capable of producing the volume necessary to meet the food needs of the world's people. Since on eco-humanistic grounds basic human biological and social needs can override considerations about the welfare of the environment, one is tempted to think that "ecological efficiency" simply cannot be adopted as a goal. In response, we could grant that even though a complete adoption of this goal may not be feasible, it should nonetheless be striven for to as great an extent as possible. This means that bigger is not always better, that there is room for traditional farming alongside of more modern techniques, and that various combinations of the two methods should be developed. Just because total ecological efficiency cannot be attained on all farms in all countries does not mean that we should not try to improve our practices to approach this goal. How we might encourage such improvements is discussed in §20.

## §18   USING COMPLEMENTARY TECHNOLOGY

The second guiding principle for an eco-humanistic agriculture requires using only that technology which is complementary to nature. "Complementary" means cooperating with or enriching as opposed to conquering or manipulating. Commoner expresses the basic idea thus:

> Let us hope that we can overcome the myths of omnipotence, and learn that the proper use of science is not to conquer the world, but to live in it.[65]

All scientific innovations and technological alternatives which will increase food production are welcome under eco-humanism when they are compatible with ecological principles and a healthy biosphere. Science can indeed be a talisman. There is no need for ecosensitive critics to reject technology or to "turn back the clock." On the other hand we shouldn't try to "beat the clock" playing a fool's game of "chicken" with nature, hoping to avoid ecological backlash by frantic stop-gap measures. I enjoy, as much as any lover of progress, learning about the exciting new research which promises new production potential (for instance, new corn varieties with more "complete" protein; or new nitrogen-fixing, perennial, or salt-resistant grains; or new ways to produce protein by extracting it from alfalfa leaves, or deriving it from single cell organisms like algae, fungi, even bacteria, or from insects, or even from urea and manure!) The clever ways of biologically controlling insects which are being developed are fascinating. And if a way were found to cheaply remove the salt from sea water, a great burden could be taken off our fresh water supplies. I have great hopes for scientific advancements, provided that they are ecologically compatible. Eco-sensitive scientists like plant breeder Wes Jackson can do far more than we nonscientists in developing ways to reduce the current amount of environmental abuse and at the same time increase *sustainable* yields, thus serving both long-term human welfare and environmental health.[66]

In addition to these "high-tech" solutions, "low-tech" innovations should be encouraged. Better horse-drawn carts, more comfortable oxen harnesses, and more efficient foot plows (shovellike tools) would do more for productivity for the vast majority of farmers in the world than the newest mega-horsepowered, air-conditioned, computer-guided tractor.[67] Attention to small traditional farming is just as important as large farming since the same goals of environmental health and food production guide it. Combining high-tech methods with traditional farming can also show positive eco-humanistic results. For instance, sophisticated breeding techniques can produce locally adapted strains with much higher yields and less harvest loss. Or for nations desperately short on food, rather than push for complete adoption of modern methods which would require jeopardizing a fragile environment, a nudge in the direction of some down-scaled technology (for example, small two-wheel tractors) could permit increased production which is more sensitive to ecological constraints.

From the perspective of eco-humanism, human scientific creativity is a welcomed resource. Certainly we are smart enough to figure out ways to cooperate with and to complement nature. The fact that science and technological innovation have often been the servants of rapers, plunderers, and dominators of nature does not mean they cannot become our allies in a better cause.

## §19 NO UNNECESSARY USE OF ANIMALS

Animal use is a major part of both traditional and modern agriculture. It is compatible with eco-humanistic agriculture, though only in a restricted sense. Eco-humanism is a humanism which places priority on vital human interests and thus does not see nonhuman animals as having a right to life or a right of noninterference equal to such rights in humans. But since some animals clearly are conscious of pain and pleasure and have interests, the utilitarian position (which will not allow animal suffering without significant reason) seems an indisputable first step, even if not the last. Simply because some vital human interests are given greater worth (and are protected by rights) does not mean that nonhuman animals' interests should be *completely* disregarded. The guiding principle for justifiable use of animals in eco-humanistic agriculture is that this use be *necessary* for the meeting of basic human survival and social needs. Just as these human needs can override larger ecosystemic values (within the limits previously described), so they can override the interests of nonhuman animals (within the limit imposed by the command to minimize suffering). What does this mean for eco-humanistic agriculture?

"Factory farming" meat production to satisfy the taste for meat that affluent peoples have acquired is not justified. It causes immense animal suffering and is not necessary for meeting the basic needs of people (since alternative diets are just as nutritious). Add to this the further ecological disvalues caused by factory farming and it becomes even less justified. These disvalues include overtaxing the soil to produce feed for these animals (almost all of the grains grown in this country, such as corn, oats, and sorghum, are fed to animals) and polluting water with the runoff from the wastes of these "factories" (with their high volume of animals concentrated into a small space). Even range-fed meat (from animals which graze) causes some ecological problems in that the domestic animals compete with other species and thus tend to destroy the diversity and stability of the range land. For affluent people any meat production with its use of animals is questionable. Vegetarianism seems inevitable.

But it is different for poor people. If animal protein is required to supplement otherwise protein-deficient diets then animal products (including meat) can be justifiably used provided, of course, that the animals are not caused to suffer unduly. A few egg-laying chickens scratching for their food or a slaughtered pig which was fed on organic (including human) waste can mean the difference between adequate nutrition and malnourishment. Furthermore, if animal labor is essential for meeting subsistence then this use of animals is also justified.

So eco-humanistic agriculture does not autonomatically exclude animal use—it just limits it. Ironically, it reverses the current order of things. Now it is the affluent of the world who use most of the animal products because they can afford to have "improved" diets. Under eco-humanistic principles it would only be the poor who would be justified in using animal products because they need them to survive and to thrive.

## §20 EMBODIMENT IN AN APPROPRIATE CULTURAL SETTING

By far the most difficult goal to attain is the creation of an appropriate cultural setting for eco-humanistic agriculture. I make this a guiding principle, and not merely a means of implementation, not only because a culture is dependent upon its agriculture for its very survival but also because a culture is judged by its agricultural practices. The extravagantly banqueting Romans with their agricultural slaves, the old Plantation South with its slaves and its devastation of topsoil by king cotton, the plunder of the tropics by European colonialism, and the displacement of Irish subsistence farmers by eighteenth century English wool growers—all of these agricultural examples are symbols of a culture's priorities and values. And the "modern agriculture" of our era will carry its historical legacy, symbolizing to future generations the values and priorities of our culture. To attain a cultural setting conducive to eco-humanistic agriculture requires more than a minor adjustment for commercial farmers. It requires a virtual revolution of cultural attitudes, values, organization, and actions.

Nothing illustrates this better than the economic conflict that exists for farmers between ecological efficiency and profitability. To be quite blunt, eco-humanistic farming just doesn't pay off. In an economic framework which heavily discounts the future and which sees "profitability" within a very short time frame, the real return on investment for ecological agriculture (a healthy environment and a well-fed population for centuries to come) is never realized because it is never risked. The blame for this shortsightedness does not lie totally on "free market" economies since many "centrally planned" ones (for example the Soviet Union) have fared no better by eco-humanistic standards. Undoubtedly there will be a gradual move toward more ecological farming as land wears out and as the price of inputs from finite resources soars out of reach. And there are signs that "organic" farming is becoming increasingly profitable, even today.[68] On the other hand, the very cost of maintaining modern extractive farming is leading to centralization and increased reliance on inputs in order to ensure a profit. Earl Butz, former secretary of agriculture, once instructed farmers to "get big or get out," meaning that only very large, energy and chemical intensive operations will be able to make a living at farming. Even though the United States Department of Agriculture acknowledged that small operations are more efficient,[69] they are not as profitable since the larger the size, the smaller return per unit required to make an overall profit. So the economic forces present in our culture are driving even small "modern" farmers out and are turning farming into a large-scale, highly specialized industry. Already the bulk of our nation's food is grown on a small percentage of our farms, a few vast operations.[70]

Yet the type of stewardship and care required to farm ecologically is not compatible with large size. From a perspective of what poet and organic farmer Wendell Berry calls a "propriety of scale"[71] (versus economy of scale), diversity, decentralization, and the nurturing of the land are valued. An eco-humanistic agriculture is inconceivable in a culture which *prides* itself on the fact that only 4 percent of its members grow the food for the other 96 percent. Yet it is hardly profitable, given current practices, for half of that 4 percent to survive. Something is wrong here.

Perhaps the standard stick-and-carrot technique of regulations and incentives could help to make ecological farming more profitable. American agriculture is already heavily influenced by price supports, subsidies, and tax incentives. These devices could be expanded to encourage ecological efficiency. The state could take a more active role in ensuring the health of the environment, though the current mood in the White House is somewhat hostile to this.

But the battle for ecological agriculture is not, at this stage, primarily a political battle. It is a battle over cultural attitudes and priorities. Once value changes occur, the political, economic, and institutional changes will follow. However, cultural attitudes do not easily change independent of institutional modification; political and economic tactics cannot be ignored. I have no grand program, no magic potion to transform our culture overnight into one that is more ecosensitive and more oriented toward future and global distributive justice. But I do think that there is one step which individuals must take. Not only must we realize how closely linked our life-styles are to food production, we must also conform our life-styles to eco-humanistic goals. This involves two aspects: life-style as consumer, and life-style as producer.

First, it is necessary to realize that as consumers our personal dietary habits are linked to the practices and techniques of agricultural production. What kind of food we eat makes a difference: Is it grain-fed meat which causes animal suffering and is high on the food chain? Is it highly processed? Is it produced in an environmentally damaging way? Is it indirectly involved in promoting food shortages abroad or in the future? Our personal link with agriculture is reaffirmed at least three times a day. What we eat expresses the values we hold. Barbour has stated:

> Every lifestyle expresses distinctive values. The dominant pattern in the contemporary United States may be characterized as a high-consumption lifestyle.[72]

In food consumption this is manifested both in our waistlines and in the declining state of our agricultural resources. A serious eco-humanistic evaluation of our own personal life-styles should impel us to change our consumption habits.

Once this change has occurred we as consumers can apply economic leverage to support ecological agriculture and to ensure that "propriety of scale" can remain economically feasible. This means buying from local ecological farmers, part-time farmers, and commercial organic farmers. Agroindustry supposes that we "choose," by our market behavior, environmentally damaging production methods. It is necessary to live a life-style which reflects in its market behavior eco-humanistic goals. In other words, we must "choose" to support ecological agriculture. We must practice what we preach.

Second, we should assess our life-style with respect to production. Barbour says:

Industrial societies have sharply separated production from consumption, isolating work from other activities. The dichotomy of work versus leisure is minimized when there is production for use rather than for wages. . . .[73]

Production for use means growing your own food. This is to de-economize food production because homegrown food never enters the market and is not calculated in the Gross National Product. One sure way to guarantee that ecological agriculture will be practiced is to do it yourself. This doesn't mean that everyone should become a subsistence farmer. But it does mean that there should be more semirural part-time farming and more suburban gardening. All the suburban labor that goes into lawns and shrubs could go into food production. In the cities, vacant lots and rooftops can be converted into gardens. Even something as simple as growing sprouts for a winter salad or cherry tomatoes in a flowerpot can alleviate the winter vegetable crop strain on California's agricultural resources. If gardeners and small-scale, part-time farmers follow regenerative principles, they can not only produce ecologically safe food but also discourage overtaxing of the land by large commercial growers.

Once enough of us realize in our own lives that what we eat (and how and by whom it is grown) and what we morally refuse to eat are intricately tied both to justice for distant and future peoples and to biospheric health, then the basis for a cultural shift in values, practices, and institutions will be laid. Only then can a setting appropriate to eco-humanistic agriculture be created. Let's hope that it won't be too late.

## *NOTES*

I wish to thank Tom Regan for his excellent editorial advice and assistance and Holmes Rolston III, and J. Baird Callicott for their helpful comments.

1. Keith C. Barrons, *The Food in Your Future* (New York: Van Nostrand Reinhold Co., 1975), 67–89.
2. There are numerous books documenting these dangers. See for example Jim Hightower, *Eat Your Heart Out: Food Profiteering in America* (New York: Crown Publishers, 1975) (hereafter cited as *Eat Your Heart Out*).
3. For an excellent challenge of pesticide use, see K. S. Shrader-Frechette, "Pesticide Toxicity: An Ethical Perspective" in her *Environmental Ethics* (Pacific Grove, Calif.: Boxwood Press, 1981), 287–324.
4. Harvey Arden, "Iowa, America's Middle Earth," *National Geographic*, vol. 159, no. 5 (May 1981): 618.
5. Darrel S. Metcalf and Donald M. Elkins, *Crop Production: Principles and Practices* (New York: Macmillan Publishing Co., 1980), 53, quoting Food and Nutrition Board, 1967 (hereafter cited as *Crop Production*).
6. Keith C. Barrons, *The Food in Your Future*, 51.
7. Darrel S. Metcalf, *Crop Production*, 58.
8. Rachel Carson, *Silent Spring* (Cambridge, Mass.: The Riverside Press, 1962).
9. Barry Commoner, *The Closing Circle* (New York: Bantam Books, 1972).
10. Ed Edwin, *Feast or Famine* (New York: Charterhouse, 1974), 263–264. Based on 1972 figures.

11. Keith O. Campbell, *Food for the Future* (Lincoln, Nebr.: University of Nebraska Press, 1979), 82–83.
12. *Ibid.*, 76–77.
13. Since I teach at her *alma mater* I am always interested and surprised by the overreaction her name evokes among agroindustry defenders.
14. Keith O. Campbell, *Food for the Future*, 58–71.
15. According to British Broadcasting Company's television special "Global Report" aired on Public Broadcasting System, projections based on 1981 figures revise the estimate to 6 billion by the turn of the next century.
16. The high figures estimated here are from Keith O. Campbell, *Food for the Future*, 13.
17. *Ibid.*, 58.
18. *Ibid.*, 83.
19. Keith C. Barrons, *The Food in Your Future*, 153.
20. William and Paul Paddock, *Famine 1975* (Boston: Little, Brown, 1967), 166–190.
21. Garrett Hardin, "Carrying Capacity as an Ethical Concept" in *Lifeboat Ethics: The Moral Dilemmas of World Hunger*, ed. George R. Lucas, Jr., and Thomas W. Ogletree (New York: Harper and Row, 1976), 120–137, and also his "Lifeboat Ethics: The Case Against Helping the Poor," *Psychology Today*, 8 (1974): 38–43, 123–126.
22. See for example William Aiken and Hugh LaFollette, eds., *World Hunger and Moral Obligation* (Englewood Cliffs, N.J.: Prentice-Hall, 1977).
23. See Ernest Partridge, ed., *Responsibilities to Future Generations* (Buffalo, N.Y.: Prometheus Books, 1981).
24. Keith C. Barrons, *The Food in Your Future*, 116.
25. Keith O. Campbell, *Food for the Future*, 29.
26. *Ibid.*, 30.
27. Rafael D. Pagan, Jr., "A System That Works," *Vital Speeches of the Day*, vol. 46, no. 19 (July 15, 1980):594–595.
28. Peter Singer, "All Animals Are Equal," in *Animal Rights and Human Obligations*, Tom Regan and Peter Singer, eds. (Englewood Cliffs, N.J.: Prentice-Hall, 1976), 148–162. See also "Utilitarianism and Vegetarianism," *Philosophy and Public Affairs*, vol. 9, no. 4 (Summer 1980):325–337.
29. Tom Regan, "Do Animals Have a Right to Life," in Regan and Singer, 197–204. Also "Animal Rights, Human Wrongs," in *Environmental Ethics*, vol. 2, no. 2 (Summer 1980):99–120. Also "Utilitarianism, Vegetarianism, and Animal Rights" in *Philosophy and Public Affairs*, vol. 9, no. 4 (Summer 1980):305–324.
30. Peter Singer, *Animal Liberation* (New York: *New York Review of Books*, 1975).
31. Tom Regan, "Animal Rights, Human Wrongs," *Environmental Ethics*, vol. 2, no. 2 (Summer 1980):116.
32. Tom Regan, "Do Animals Have a Right to Life" in Regan and Singer, *Animal Rights*, 197–204.
33. See Peter Singer, "Not for Humans Only: The Place of Nonhumans in Environmental Issues," in *Ethics and Problems of the 21st Century*, K. E. Goodpaster and K. M. Sayre, eds. (Notre Dame, Ind.: University of Notre Dame Press, 1979), 191–206. Also see Tom Regan, *The Case for Animal Rights* (Berkeley, Calif.: University of California Press, 1983), chap. 9. 3.
34. On this controversy see Alastair S. Gunn, "Why Should We Care About Rare Species?" *Environmental Ethics*, vol. 2, no. 1 (Spring 1980):17–37, and Lily-Marlene Russow, "Why Do Species Matter?" *Environmental Ethics*, vol. 3, no. 2 (Summer 1981):101–112.
35. Aldo Leopold, *A Sand County Almanac* (New York: Ballantine Books, 1966), 239.

36. *Ibid.*, 262.
37. For an interesting, influential discussion of this point, see Holmes Rolston, III, "Is There an Ecological Ethic?," *Ethics*, vol. 85, no. 2 (January 1975): 93–109.
38. J. Baird Callicott, "Animal Liberation: A Triangular Affair," *Environmental Ethics*, vol. 2, no. 4 (Winter 1980):311–338. Quotes from pp. 326, 337, 338 (hereafter cited as "Animal Liberation").
39. *Ibid.*, 326.
40. Paul W. Taylor, "The Ethics of Respect for Nature," *Environmental Ethics*, vol. 3, no. 3 (Fall 1981):208–209.
41. J. Baird Callicott, "Animal Liberation," 338.
42. Aldo Leopold, *Sand County Almanac*, 261.
43. *Ibid.*, 256.
44. *Ibid.*, 257.
45. *Ibid.*, 258.
46. Ernest Partridge, "Are We Ready for an Ecological Morality?," *Environmental Ethics*, vol. 4, no. 2 (Summer 1982):176.
47. Holmes Rolston, III, "Can and Ought We to Follow Nature?," *Environmental Ethics*, vol. 1, no. 1 (Spring 1979):20.
48. *Ibid.*, 20.
49. *Ibid.*, 21.
50. E. F. Schumacher, *Small Is Beautiful* (New York: Harper and Row, 1973), 117.
51. Robert C. Oelhaf, "Environmental Ethics: Atomistic Abstraction or Holistic Affection?," *Environmental Ethics*, vol. 1, no. 4 (Winter 1979):337.
52. *Ibid.*, 337–338.
53. Wendell Berry, *The Gift of Good Land* (San Francisco, Calif.: North Point Press, 1981), 183–188.
54. Holmes Rolston, III, "Is There an Ecological Ethic?," *Ethics*, vol. 85, no. 2 (January 1975):105.
55. Aldo Leopold, *Sand County Almanac*, 261.
56. Milton H. Snoeyenbos, "A Critique of Ehrenfeld's Views on Humanism and the Environment," *Environmental Ethics*, vol. 3, no. 3 (Fall 1981):234.
57. Ian G. Barbour, *Technology, Environment, and Human Values* (New York: Praeger Publishers, 1980), 96–97.
58. James D. Heffernan, "The Land Ethic: A Critical Appraisal," *Environmental Ethics*, vol. 4, no. 3 (Fall 1982):246.
59. Ian G. Barbour, *Technology, Environment, and Human Values*, 94.
60. Numerous international instances of this practice are documented by Francis Lappé and Joseph Collins, *Food First* (Boston: Houghton Mifflin Company, 1977).
61. Wendell Berry's essays in *The Gift of Good Land*, *op. cit.*, reiterate this point.
62. See Noel D. Vietmeyer, "Rediscovering America's Forgotten Crops," *National Geographic*, vol. 159, no. 5 (May 1981):702–712.
63. Barry Commoner, *The Closing Circle*, 37–41.
64. Medard Gabel, *Ho-ping: Food for Everyone* (Garden City, N.Y.: Doubleday, 1979), 216 (hereafter cited as *Ho-ping*).
65. Cited in Ed Edwin, *Feast or Famine*, 136.
66. See the work of Wes Jackson at the Land Institute (Salina, Kansas).
67. Noel D. Vietmeyer, "Animal Power Muscles Ahead," *International Wildlife*, vol. 12, no. 5 (September–October 1982):38–41.
68. Medard Gabel, *Ho-ping*, 135.
69. Jim Hightower, *Eat Your Heart Out*, 132.
70. Lindsay Thomas, "America's Changing Farm Structure," *Vital Speeches of the Day*, vol. 46, no. 10 (March 1, 1980):304.

71.   Wendell Berry, *The Gift of Good Land* (San Francisco, Calif.: North Point Press, 1981), xi.
72.   Ian G. Barbour, *Technology, Environment, and Human Values*, 304.
73.   *Ibid.*, 307.

## SUGGESTIONS FOR FURTHER READING

For further reading on the issues discussed in this essay, the reader is encouraged to consult the sources cited in the footnotes as well as those that follow.

§2   For an ecological understanding of the effect of pesticides see Robert L. Rudd, *Pesticides and the Living Landscape* (Madison: University of Wisconsin Press, 1966). Robert van den Bosch, *The Pesticide Conspiracy* (Garden City, N.Y.: Doubleday, 1978) details the political aspects of pesticide regulation.

§§10 and 11   Future world food demand and strategies to cope with it are analyzed in the Rockefeller Foundation's *Strategy Toward the Conquest of Hunger* (New York, 1966) and the Presidential Commission on World Hunger Report, *Overcoming World Hunger* (Washington, D.C.: U.S. Government Printing Office, 1980). Some works critical of these strategies are Frances Moore Lappé et al., *Aid As Obstacle* (San Francisco: Institute for Food and Development Policy, 1980), and Michael Perelman, *Farming for Profit in a Hungry World: Capital and the Crisis in Agriculture* (Montclair, N.J.: Allanheld, Osmun and Co., 1977).

§12   The literature on animal rights and interests is extensive. For a good introduction and a helpful bibliography see Peter Singer, "Animals and the Value of Life" in Tom Regan, ed., *Matters of Life and Death* (New York: Random House, 1980). For additional bibliographies, see Tom Regan, *All That Dwell Therein: Essays on Animal Rights and Environmental Ethics* (Berkeley: University of California Press, 1982), 241–246, and Charles Magel, *A Bibliography on Animal Rights and Related Matters* (Washington, D.C.: University Press of America, 1981).

§§13, 14, 15, and 16   On the philosophical problems raised by a "new" ecocentric ethics see the entire issue of *Environmental Ethics* (vol. 4, no. 2, Summer 1982) on "Environmental Ethics and Contemporary Ethical Theory." The essays in this volume discuss the fact-value problem, the subjective-objective problem, and the atomistic-holistic problem. They also contain many helpful citations in the footnotes.

§§17 and 18   A highly readable and informative criticism of contemporary farming and an alternative vision of regenerative farming are presented in Wendell Berry, *The Unsettling of America* (San Francisco: Sierra Club, 1977). Rodale Press is developing an extensive critique and alternative vision of sustainable agriculture in *The Cornucopia Project* (Emmaus, Penn.). For another alternative see Wes Jackson, *New Roots for Agriculture* (San Francisco: Friends of the Earth, 1980).

# 9

# *Preserving Rare Species*

## ALASTAIR S. GUNN

## I. INTRODUCTION

Most of the species that have ever lived are now extinct.[1] This is hardly surprising. The earliest life forms emerged on earth about 3.5 billion years ago, and since that time there have been innumerable climatic variations, geologic upheavals, and other major environmental changes. The dinosaurs became extinct around 70 million years ago. During the subsequent "tertiary period," characterized by the rise of warm-blooded animals, around 70,000 mammal and bird species have died out—a rate of about 1 per 1,000 years.[2]

Many present-day lists of endangered species seem relatively insignificant (see §8). Humans have brought about the extinction of a few species in the past, of course, but given the explosive increase in human population and the pace of industrialization, this is hardly surprising. Many countries protect rare wildlife by law, and establish reserves, national parks, and wildlife refuges. International treaties regulate the killing of migratory animals and the trade in live animals and animal products. It is tempting to believe that we have learned from the exploitative ways of the past, and that most endangered species will soon make a comeback.

The picture presented so far is seriously misleading, however, in several respects.

- It implies that extinction via human agency is limited to relatively modern, more or less industrialized societies, and ignores the destruction wrought by stone age humans.
- It underestimates the number of species presently or potentially at risk.

- It is overoptimistic in assuming that most threatened species can be saved by passing legislation or by creating a few parks and reserves.
- It implies that ethical issues arise only in connection with rare and endangered species, whereas common species give rise to most of the same issues as do rare ones.
- It encourages a species-oriented approach to conservation, drawing attention away from the need to protect ecosystems.

In this essay I try to correct these mistaken beliefs, and I examine a number of arguments for species protection. Part II presents information on the scale and causes of species extermination and briefly discusses attempts to protect species. This part, while (I hope) interesting in itself, is intended as factual, background material, as a context in which to discuss the moral issues of species protection. In Part III I examine two approaches to species protection, which I label *preservationist* and *conservationist*, contrasting both with *consumption*. The point of these distinctions is to contrast a view of species as a resource (likely to be associated with a "management" ethic) with a view of species as having intrinsic or inherent value (likely to be associated with an environmental or ecological ethic). In Part IV I present and evaluate a number of arguments for the protection of species. Rationales for species protection are examined in the light of claims that individual living things are entitled to moral consideration (for example, that they have rights); that *rare* species are especially to be valued; and that the utility of species to humans should be a decisive factor. Some common conservationist arguments are presented, and criticized, in Part V. Finally, I argue that a purely species-oriented approach to environmental protection, even a preservationist one, may be too narrow, that the protection of ecosystems is a more important environmental goal.

## II.  EXTINCTIONS—PAST AND FUTURE

### §1  WHAT IS A SPECIES?

The systematic naming and classifying of plants and animals, known as *taxonomy*, began with the Swedish scientist Linnaeus (1707–1778). The basic unit of taxonomy is the species. In the Linnaean system, each species is given a two-word name which indicates also the genus to which the species belongs. Thus the tiger is known as *Panthera tigris*: It is a member of the genus *Panthera*, which also includes the lion (*Panthera leo*), leopard (*Panthera pardus*), and jaguar (*Panthera onca*), among others. Groups of genera are grouped into families and so on into progressively larger units. Each taxonomic unit is called a *taxum*.

The Linnaean system has two great advantages: It is universally understood, and each species has a unique name. "Common" names such as "blackbird," "little tern," and the like may be locally applied to different species in different regions. The same species may have a variety of different local names, adding further to the confusion: For example, *Felis concolor* is known variously as cougar, panther, puma, mountain lion, or even, in parts of Florida, tiger! In this essay the Linnaean or "Latin" name is given in addition to the prevalent "common" name whenever a species is mentioned for the first time.

## §2 SPECIES, SUB-SPECIES, AND POPULATIONS

A *species* may be defined as "a natural biological group sharing a common pool of genes."[3] All members of a species can successfully interbreed —that is, can produce fertile offspring. Some species are divided into *sub-species* (or *races*): groups within a species, sometimes but not always with well-marked morphological differences such as color, and typically geographically isolated from other sub-species. Sub-species are considered to have evolved from a common ancestor, the differences being due to adaptation to local conditions: Geographic isolation prevents breeding with other populations of the species. When for some reason sub-species cease to be reproductively isolated, they often interbreed freely. For example the different races of the common flicker (*Colaptes auratus*)—the gilded (*C.a. chrysoides*), red-shafted (*C.a. colaptes*), and yellow-shafted (*C.a. auratus*) flickers—once considered to be separate species, have now been reclassified. Ecological barriers such as the tree-less Great Plains formerly isolated these tree nesters, but European settlement and tree planting have led to population mixing, with "hybrid" forms occurring where the ranges of sub-species overlap.[4]

Some related species are capable of interbreeding, but the offspring are commonly infertile. A well-known example is the mule, an infertile cross between the horse (*Equus caballus*) and one of the several species of ass or donkey (*Equus* species). The criterion of reproductive capability is not perfect, however, since some closely related species can successfully interbreed. For example the mallard (*Anas platyrhynchos*) successfully hybridizes with the grey duck (*Anas superciliosa*) of New Zealand. The difficulty of defining a species with any degree of precision sometimes raises difficult policy questions; endangered species protection legislation often protects species from habitat destruction, so that the taxonomic status of a population may be crucial in determining whether a proposed development is allowed to go ahead.

Modern taxonomy is more than just a system of naming. The divisions of living things are also meant to exhibit presumed evolutionary relationships. Evolution is a continuous process, however, and most species are capable of further evolution. Except for highly specialized species with a narrow genetic base, most species represent a point along the evolutionary process, not an endpoint. (Exceptions include species whose populations have sunk to a very low level, and which may be genetically almost uniform.) To protect the evolutionary potential of a species it is necessary to maintain a large range of genetic characteristics, that is, a large number of individuals. The *future* of a species includes the potential of some of its members to be the ancestors of new forms. To maintain only a remnant, or even a larger but inbred group, is to "freeze" the species into its present form.

## §3 EXTINCTION AND RARITY

A species becomes extinct when it has no members alive. Rarely do we know precisely when a species has become extinct: or rather, we know that it has *become* extinct, but we don't often know when that happened. An example of an exception is the death of what was almost certainly the last passenger pigeon (*Ectopistes migratorius*), named Martha, in the Cincinatti Zoo in 1914. But of course the species was effectively extinct when the last (unrecorded) male died. The death of Martha therefore has a symbolic significance only.

The International Union for the Conservation of Nature and Natural Resources (IUCN), an independent international organization based in Switzerland, publishes and regularly updates lists and information on species considered at risk. This work, known as the *Red Data Book*,[5] employs the following status classifications:

Endangered: "Taxa in danger of extinction and whose survival is unlikely if the causal factors continue operating."

Vulnerable: "Taxa believed likely to move into the endangered category in the near future if the causal factors continue operating."

Rare: "Taxa with small world populations that are not at present endangered or vulnerable, but are at risk."

## §4 NATURAL EXTINCTIONS

To what extent human behavior is "natural" is controversial. If it is "natural" for humans to kill animals for food, then the extermination of a species by overhunting might be natural. Here I include under "natural causes" only those extinctions *not* caused by human activity. Often, we do not know the explanation for a natural extinction. The reasons for the disappearance of the dinosaurs, for example, are a perennial and fascinating source of speculation.

The "natural life" of a species is the period from its evolution into a distinct species until its final demise or evolution into a new species. According to the IUCN,[6] no species has ever lived for more than a few million years: The mean "natural life" of a bird species is estimated at 2 million years, and of a mammal 600,000 years. Most extinctions, then, have been the natural result of changed conditions from those in which the species evolved and to which it was adapted—changes to which the species was unable to make a new adaptation, because its requirements were insufficiently flexible, or because it lacked the genetic potential to develop new traits, or because the changes were sudden and catastrophic. Wholesale changes of this order, such as the periodic glaciations or ice ages of the last million years, may have wiped out whole complex faunas several times as the ice spread and retreated. The fauna of England during the glaciations included arctic animals such as reindeer (*Rangifer tarandus*) and arctic foxes (*Alopex lagopus*). These species have survived by moving northward to permanently cold regions, as the climate warmed. During the warm, interglacial periods, now extinct species of elephant, lion, hippopotamus, spotted hyena, and other tropical fauna inhabited England.

Other natural causes of extinction have included changes in habitat and food supply, and competition or predation by newly evolved species or species extending their geographical range. These factors may themselves have been a response to climatic changes. Cataclysmic events such as volcanic eruptions, tidal waves, hurricanes, disease and parasite epidemics, increases or decreases in solar radiation, and even intense meteor bombardments may have wiped out many species.

## §5 EARLY HUMAN EXTERMINATIONS

Human impacts on species have mostly been *indirect*, such as habitat destruction (see §6). Early humans, however, had *direct* adverse effects, mainly by overhunting. The theory that stone age hunters acted as "superpredators" on the giant animals of Africa, Asia, the Americas, Australia, New Zealand, and Madagascar challenges the alternative view that these megafauna died out naturally due to climatic changes. Advocates of the superpredator theory argue that the hunting techniques of early humans permitted an "overkill" of large mammals and birds which were killed at a faster rate than they could reproduce. In all the areas mentioned above, it seems, sudden extinctions coincided with the arrival of human hunting cultures. For example, thirty-one genera of large animals disappeared at the end of the last ice age in North America. The theory does not deny indirect factors such as destruction of habitat through fire, and the introduction of dogs, but concludes that around 11,000 years ago, a hunting culture of less than one million could have exterminated these animals within a few hundred years.[7]

Fossil and subfossil remains found in association with human settlements provide physical evidence of stone age hunting. Such remains are found in the area of the La Brea "tarpits" in Los Angeles.[8] Of the 56 mammal species fossils found at La Brea, 24 are now extinct, as are 22 of the 113 bird species. These fossils date from 1,800 to 4,500 years ago, and hunters were certainly ensconced in the region for much of that time. Humans were probably responsible for the extinction of some European species too, including elephants, rhinoceroses, bison, giant deer, and others.

## §6 EXTINCTIONS OF THE RECENT PAST

The year 1600 is usually taken as the beginning of the "modern" period of species extinction, mainly because only since that time has reasonably complete information become available. Estimates of the number of extinctions since 1600 vary, and mostly do not include species which are very likely extinct but which may conceivably survive in remote locations. Nor, of course, do they include plants, invertebrates, and perhaps reptiles, and fishes, whose presence or absence no one noticed or bothered to record. Ronald Lockley,[9] a naturalist based in New Zealand, puts the total of higher animals extinct in modern times at over 200, while *Wildlife in Danger*[10] gives figures of 94 birds and 36 mammals, representing 1 percent of the total number of higher animal species in 1600. This source adds that of full species still surviving, 164 races of birds and 64 of mammals have become extinct during this period.

Most of these extinctions are the result of human pressures. There is not much evidence that *any* losses of full species since 1600 can be explained by natural causes, though *Wildlife in Danger* cautiously allows that 25 percent may be explained in this way. Some recent extinctions were a direct result of hunting for food, for example Steller's sea-cow (*Hydrodamalis stelleri*), a marine mammal discovered in 1741 and wiped out by 1768. Others, such as the passenger pigeon, formerly numbering up to 5 billion, may have been extirpated by a combination of hunting pressures and habitat destruction. Ecologist George Uetz and geographer Donald Lee Johnson[11] note that whereas 86 percent of the seventeenth century extinctions can be attributed to the direct effects of human actions, mostly hunting, and 14 percent to indirect effects such as habitat destruction, by the nineteenth century the proportions are almost reversed: 24 percent being attributed to hunting and 76 percent to indirect effects (including the effects of introduced animals). In the period 1900–1970, around half, or more than 60, extinctions are attributed by these authors to introduced species. For the whole period, *Wildlife in Danger* gives figures for birds of 24 percent natural causes, 42 percent hunting, and 34 percent indirect, while the figures for mammals are 25 percent, 33 percent, and 36 percent, respectively.

Regardless of these figures, which to me at least seem if anything to underestimate the indirect effects, there are many instances of extinctions caused by introductions of new animals and habitat destruction. Examples include

- The grey dodo (*Raphus cuncillatus*), a giant flightless pigeon of Mauritius, discovered in 1599, and last seen in 1681. Many were killed by sailors for food, but the principal causes of its loss were the introduction of pigs and monkeys to Mauritius, which destroyed the breeding potential of this ground-nesting species.
- The solitaire (*Pezophaps solitarius*), another giant flightless pigeon, was discovered on remote Rodriguez Island in 1691. By 1791 it was certainly extinct. The causes are uncertain: Hunting

for food must have reduced the population, but loss of habitat via forest destruction, and predation by feral introduced cats, were probably the main causes of its extinction. The cats, incidentally, were brought in to control accidentally introduced rats.

- New Zealand has lost at least seven full species since the coming of the Europeans. In almost all cases, including a quail, a honey-eater, and at least one wren, the cause was mainly predation or environmental destruction wrought by the bewildering variety of introduced species: mice, brown and black rats, pigs, goats, deer, marsupial opossums, hedgehogs, rabbits, feral cats and dogs, and mustelids—ferrets, stoats, and weasels. The most striking example is the Stephen Island wren (*Xenicus lyalli*), the entire population of which was exterminated by a cat belonging to the lighthouse keeper. This man saw the species alive on only two occasions. The cat, which presented its owner with twenty-two dead specimens in 1894, may thus be credited with both the discovery and the extermination of the species in a single year.

- The American chestnut (*Castenea dentala*), a valuable and formerly widespread hardwood, has become virtually extinct due to a fungus disease which arrived with the introduced Chinese chestnut (C. *mollissima*) early this century.

## §7 RICH AND POOR NATIONS

Most developed countries have lost a number of species over the years, and all contain at least some endangered species today. But comparatively few extinctions are likely in these countries in the near future. Most have passed protectionist legislation and have established more or less adequate parks and reserves to protect species.

The United States lost five species of vertebrates between 1600 and 1850, and fifty-seven from 1850 to 1975. Several species and races will likely follow them into extinction, but United States species protection is among the most comprehensive in the world.

The situation in many Third World countries is quite different. These mostly tropical countries contain an increasing proportion of the world's human population. They also contain most of the world's species.[12] The pressures to develop new food and energy sources, to urbanize and industrialize, are very strong, and in the context of widespread disease and starvation, protection of species and ecosystems inevitably receives a low priority.

It is doubly unfortunate that the poorest countries with the worst problems often contain the richest and most diverse ecosystems, and that these tropical ecosystems are often very vulnerable. Norman Myers, an environmental consultant based in Nairobi, Kenya, has made extensive studies of tropical ecosystems. He notes that "a single hectare of Brazilian Amazonia has been found to contain 235 tree species; the same area of temperate forest has about 10. A square mile of Costa Rican forest has been found to contain 264 bird species, more than wildlife-rich Alaska, an area 500,000 times larger."[13]

The developed countries can easily afford to protect their own native species. These countries already have resources available beyond the basic needs of their people and can therefore choose to spend money, or forego opportunities, in order to protect species and ecosystems. This is obviously not the case in many poor countries, except where protection can be shown to have some value to humans, for example the setting up of national parks to attract tourists.

## §8 THE FUTURE OF SPECIES

No one knows how many species there will be by, say, the year 2000. This is partly because the actual number of species is not known. It probably never will be, since fragile, unique, species-rich tropical rain forest habitats are being destroyed before biologists have a chance to study them. Norman Myers's estimate, commonly quoted, is that there are between 5 and 10 million living species, of which 1.6 million have been identified so far.[14] Most of these are invertebrates, particularly insects. Birds and mammals comprise only a tiny fraction, less than 13,000 species. Because they are mostly relatively large and also more interesting to many biologists, it is likely that almost all bird, mammal, and larger reptilian species have been discovered. Some isolated areas doubtless contain as yet undiscovered races, however, and occasionally nature springs a surprise, as in the discovery of the Fijian crested iguana (*Brachyloplus vitiensis*) in 1981.[15]

The main source of data on rare and endangered species, the *Red Data Book*, lists only vetebrates (1088 in 1979). In 1970, according to the calculations of Uetz and Johnson,[16] *Red Data Book* information yields the conclusion that 185 species will probably be extinct by the year 2000, while 718 may possibly be extinct. Much larger estimates have been offered, covering nonvertebrate and plant species and based on extrapolations and (sometimes) speculation. One recent estimate[17] is that around 600,000 extinctions of plants and animals will occur by the year 2000. The U.S. Council on Environmental Quality, in 1975, guessed that 10 percent of the existing (known?) 1.6 million species were "threatened with extinction within the next generation." In 1980, the council was quoting the view that, if present trends continue, 20 to 25 percent of the estimated 5 to 10 million species will have gone by the end of the century—a range of 1–2.5 million.[18]

Whether present trends will continue, and if so what will be the result, is of course in doubt. That very many extinctions will occur is not, and the main cause will be habitat destruction. Few species will become extinct naturally, because natural extinction is relatively infrequent. Probably hunting or other deliberate killing will account for few species. This is partly because subsistence hunting cultures have largely been extinguished, while recreational hunting is increasingly controlled with "game" species managed as a resource on a sustained yield basis. The trade in skins, furs, horns, and tusks may account for a number of mammals, and possibly some birds and reptiles, but again there is a trend toward sustained yield management policies while international conventions have helped to reduce, if not prevent, the trade. Zoo, museum, and private hobby collection pressure is diminishing. Zoologist William G. Conway, in his study of the international wildlife trade, notes that "zoos contribute remarkably little to the (wildlife) trade,"[19] and that most zoos no longer seek to obtain specimens of rarities. Peru, for example, in 1964, was able to find markets for only 174 of the then-unprotected ocelot (*Felis pardalis*), while exporting 11,244 ocelot skins.

It is not easy to say which species are most threatened. Population numbers are not a good guide, for some very numerous species have been exterminated in a short period—for example, the passenger pigeon. Other rare, localized species may survive indefinitely provided their habitat is not altered. But certain highly specialized species, or species living in fragile, isolated environments, are obviously under more threat than widespread, adaptable species.

David Ehrenfeld,[20] a biologist at Rutgers University, has constructed a hypothetical example of what a "most endangered" species might be like. It would be large, able to survive only in a restricted area, but migratory across international boundaries. It would reproduce slowly and because of its specialized behavior patterns would be vulnerable to environmental change. It would be hunted but not properly managed as a game species. Finally, it would travel and reproduce in groups and be intolerant of humans. The nearest species to the model is the polar bear (*Thalarctos maritimus*).

Relatively nonvulnerable species would be those likely to survive any conceivable environmental change in the foreseeable future. These species would be tolerant of or even parasitic on humans, abundant, adaptable, rapid breeders, and of no economic value. Uetz and Johnson cite the house sparrow (*Passer domesticus*), grey squirrel (*Sciurus carolinensis*), Virginia opossum (*Didurus marsupialis*), and Norway or brown rat (*Rattus norvegicus*). A group of Soviet scientists[21] likewise considered the brown rat to have the best chance of survival in a world dominated by humans: They gave a similarly high survival rating to the rock pigeon (*Columbia livia*), cockroach (*Blattidae* family), and dandelion (*Taraxacum officinale*).

## §9 LIMITS TO SPECIES PROTECTION

A number of arguments in favor of species protection are presented in Part IV. Here I present a number of reasons for believing that even if we become convinced that *all* species ought to be protected, we shall almost certainly fail: With the best will in the world we shall be unable to protect them all. It is important to realize that this is so, and why it is so, because it forces us to make choices about *which* species to protect.

*Public Opinion*   A recent survey of public attitudes to endangered species in the United States[22] suggests that even in such an environmentally conscious and prosperous society, public support for species protection is rather selective. The survey showed that Americans tend to favor measures to protect species which are beautiful, are historically or culturally important, or are perceived as biologically "close" to humans. Snakes, insects, and lowly plants are not so favored. It may prove impossible to mobilize public opinion to save an endangered species of fly or ant.

*Lack of Data*   It was suggested earlier (§8) that there are 5 to 10 million species on earth, of which only 1.6 million have been discovered. Some species will die out, undoubtedly, before they are even discovered. Even to protect an identified species requires detailed knowledge of habitat requirements, which we cannot possibly acquire for all species.

*Limited Resources*   The lack of resources to carry out any goal may be a "practical" problem that could, in theory, be solved if we were willing to divert resources from other goals. For example, in East Africa some fish species are threatened by programs to eradicate waterborne diseases such as sleeping sickness and bilharzia: The insecticides which kill the hosts of these diseases also kill the fish. Indigenous fishes of Lake Victoria, again, have declined through overfishing, and the only practical way to restore the fishery is to introduce other, more vigorous species which in many cases will result in the disappearance of the native species.[23] The people of these areas are unlikely to adopt the heroic course of preferring to starve, or die of disease, in order to protect endangered fish species, and (political realities aside) it seems unjust to expect their governments to impose such a value on them.

  In other cases, the resources simply do not exist. For example, at least forty-five taxa of New Zealand snails are endangered, mainly due to predation and overgrazing by introduced mammals. Several species have been saved by transfer to offshore islands. But there are not enough islands to secure *all* the sub-species: For example, no two races of the flax snail (*Plactostylus ambagrosus*) are naturally found together in the same locality, and it is likely that they would hybridize, thus destroying two sub-species.[24]

*Doomed Species*   The populations of some species have sunk to such a low level that the species perhaps cannot be restored, because its genetic base has become too narrow. Myers[25] notes that the Nene or Hawaiian goose (*Branta sandvicensis*) has recovered from a low of forty-three in 1940 to a wild population of several thousand, thanks to captive breeding. But there is "a high level of infertility among males, apparently associated with inbreeding. This problem bears out the rule of thumb that a vertebrate breeding stock with fewer than fifty individuals is liable to carry a built-in potential for its own destruction, since inbreeding brings together the harmful genes that larger pools can accommodate." The same may be said of the California condor (*Gymmogyps californianus*)[26] and of several species of whales.[27] We might do better to use scarce resources to protect species which still have a chance, rather than spend vast sums on species which may already be past the point of no return.

## §10 RECREATING SPECIES: SELECTIVE BREEDING AND GENETIC ENGINEERING

A species that is reduced to only a few individuals, or, conceivably, an extinct species, could perhaps be recreated or restored by selectively breeding from·survivors or from closely related species, or by advanced biotechnology.

Captive breeding has its dangers, as explained in the preceding section: Inbreeding in a very small population often leads to degeneracy. Breeding programs need to be selective, therefore, with a view to avoiding a concentration of harmful recessive genes. Breeding programs for rare breeds of horse and cattle, for example, require the careful accumulation of data in a stud book, and extensive chromosome analysis.[28] Such programs raise difficult moral issues. For example, is it right to kill off "unsatisfactory" offspring in order to maintain a pure, viable breeding stock? Arguments which defend species protection on the grounds that members have a right to life could face a difficulty here (see Part IV).

If a population has fallen to a very low level and its genetic base is excessively narrow, an infusion of new blood from rediscovered wild specimens might be the only means to save the species. The approximately 7,000 specimens of the only surviving true wild horse, Przewalski's horse (*Equus przewalskii*), are descended from only thirteen animals, so a recently reputed sighting of the species in the wild could help the species immeasurably.[29] But if *no* further specimens are discovered, it would seem that much of the genetic material which originally made up the species must be irretrievably lost.

It is in cases such as this that genetic engineering might be suggested.[30] The most promising development, known as recombinant DNA technology, is advancing rapidly. It has been applied successfully to produce new strains of bacteria: More complex organisms, such as agricultural plants and even mammals, could perhaps be created eventually. The "missing genes" could be provided in this way to replace those lost by near-extinct species; an extinct species could even be restored by genetic manipulation of a closely related species.

Some of the problems of this approach are of a practical nature. For example, we do not have the genetic information on extinct species and so do not know what to aim at. Such programs would also be very costly, and the reintroduction of species to an environment is fraught with problems.[31] But there are also ethical issues. It might be argued that a recreated passenger pigeon would not be a *real* pigeon (and therefore not *worth* recreating), perhaps because it has not evolved naturally. Robert Elliott,[32] a philosopher from Queensland, Australia, has argued that the restoration of natural environments (say, a clear-felled forest) by environmental engineering does not have the same value as the original, because the value of a natural area is partly a function of its history, its natural development, its origins, its continuity with past and present plant communities. A regenerated or restored forest might contain much of value, then, but not of the same value as a primeval forest. Elliott draws extensively on analogies with works of art to show that a copy or recreation is not as valuable as the real, original work: "The difference of course lies in the painting's genesis."

A further objection to genetic engineering is that to employ it is to "play God." Not only are there great risks (because, for example, virulent disease organisms might accidentally be created), but the enterprise itself is unjustified. The basis for this claim might be overtly religious ("only God has the right to create") or secular ("we do not have the right to interfere with evolution").

I do not have the space here to deal fully with either of these objections, though it will be clear where my own sympathies lie. To begin with, defenders of species recreation, by either of the means under discussion, would note that the endangered status of many species is itself a result of previous human interference, so that by "interfering" on behalf of the species we would simply be trying to undo the harm. Even if a recreated species is not quite as good as an "original," it is a lot better than nothing. More fundamentally, it is worth pointing out that humans, very likely, have had a considerable influence on many—perhaps most—species, in some cases to the apparent advantage of the species. We cannot very well argue that all, and only, those species whose evolution has been *completely unaffected by human actions* are "real" and have value as "natural" objects. Almost every area on earth has been affected in some way by human activity. For example, traces of persistent pesticides and PCBs have been discovered in arctic walruses and antarctic penguins through the general dispersion of these substances. Most areas of the globe have experienced some human interference, thus tipping the survival balance in favor of both adaptable or resilient species *and* individuals, with unknown evolutionary consequences. Palaeolithic exterminations of large fauna in the Americas and Europe left niches to be filled by other species. The American bison (*Bison bison*) or "buffalo" presumably owed its huge pre-European population to the extermination (by humans) of larger competitors. Some species appear to have evolved along with humans, as parasites and scavengers—for example, the house or English sparrow (*Passer domesticus*). Human activity has diminished the range and numbers of many species but has provided increased habitat for others. Ignoring deliberate or accidental introductions, there are still many species which have increased due to land-use changes and other human-induced factors—for example the European starling (*Sturnus vulgaris*), originally a bird of the Russian steppe, spread throughout Europe as the forests were cut; many gulls (*Larus spp*) and other scavenging seabirds and landbirds received an increased food supply from human garbage; and the creation of artificial ponds and lakes and reservoirs via quarry and gravel pit flooding and development for water supply and power generation provides habitat for transient and sometimes permanent waterfowl.

Indirectly, then, humans have reduced the population and distribution of many species while we have also increased that of others. In various ways we have altered the genetic characteristics and their distribution within species, and therefore the course of evolution. But we do not say that gulls and starlings do not *belong* in their expanded range, or that the house sparrow is not a *real* species. If, as we might, we are able to recreate an extinct species by use of genetic engineering, would not this also count as a real species? *Perhaps*, after all, extinct is not necessarily forever?

## III. PRESERVATION, CONSERVATION, AND CONSUMPTION

Traditional western attitudes to the rest of nature have been exploitative. Land, water, air, and living things have been viewed, and treated, as a resource, often as an inexhaustible resource. These attitudes have begun to change in recent years. The recognition that natural resources are not infinite has led increasingly to management policies designed to ensure that there will still be resources for future generations: *Conservation* is replacing *consumption*. A more fundamental shift in attitudes has also taken place: Some people have questioned the view of nature as a resource, arguing that animals, for example, have value in themselves and should be accorded a moral standing. In this view, *preservation* should replace *conservation*. In this part of the essay, I try to make these distinctions clearer and to relate them to species protection.

### §11 CONSUMPTION

To consume a resource is to use it up, to destroy it so that it will not, in the foreseeable future, be available again. Strip mining for coal is an obvious example of consumption: The land is destroyed in the mining process, and the coal is consumed by burning. Both coal and land are nonrenewable; as a friend put it, they stopped making them a long time ago. The coal and land resources are therefore finite and irreplaceable: To consume any part of the resource is to diminish the total resource. If all existing coal is consumed, the resource itself will have been consumed. Land is consumed, usually, in less obvious ways: The characteristics which give it value, such as soil fertility, drainage, and stability, may be destroyed by overgrazing, removal of vegetation cover, or paving over, leading to damage such as erosion, topsoil loss through wind action, nutrient loss, and pollution. Land, then, may be said to be consumed to the extent that its valuable qualities are destroyed.

The industrial revolution treated resources in a consumptive way. Coal and iron ore were extracted and processed at the fastest possible rates. Human beings were treated as a resource and men, women, and children were worked to death (often literally) in mines and factories, just as horses were worked to death hauling coaches and omnibuses. The ability of natural systems—air, water, and land—to absorb pollutants and contain wastes was also consumed, in that the pollution burden was in a quantity and of a type which went beyond the capacity of those systems and often destroyed them.

Twentieth century discussion of our use of nature, particularly in former European colonies, has taken place against the backdrop of earlier consumption—a reckless, wasteful exploitation of nature which used up materials, felled forests, decimated wildlife, and destroyed indigenous cultures. Everywhere that the European conquerors went—Latin America, North America, Australia, New Zealand, India, Africa, the Pacific, and Southeast Asia—they found apparently endless resources for the taking. Land, gold, forests, wildlife, slaves, all were there in great profusion compared with the cramped conditions and scarce resources of the old countries from which the explorers, buccaneers, missionaries, traders, and settlers came. Most non-European societies were relatively undeveloped technologically; for this reason, and sometimes because it was deeply rooted in their culture, most indigenous peoples lived in reasonable enough harmony with their environment. Enough has already been said to dispel the myth of "primitive man, the conservationist" (see §5); even so, most areas of the world were fairly thinly settled and ecologically stable.

European settlement changed all that. Emotive terms such as loot, rape, and pillage come naturally when considering European exploitation of the rest of the world since the sixteenth century. The wealth of nations—precious metals, art objects, and sometimes people—was stolen and shipped overseas. The land was often cleared and exhausted, forests being left to rot and the organic content of soils exhausted, to leave eroded slopes and dustbowls. In the Americas and elsewhere native peoples were enslaved, massacred, poisoned, and displaced.

The effects on animals were often equally devastating: Wildlife was consumed as if it were just another inexhaustible resource. Many species of birds were almost exterminated by the demand for their feathers for the millinery trade—most of America's herons and terns were vulnerable or even on the way to extinction by the time the trade was stopped early this century. Other extinctions or near extinctions resulted from a combination of factors including habitat destruction, hunting pressure, competition or predation from introduced species, introduced diseases or parasites. Island faunas such as those of New Zealand and Hawaii have suffered particularly in these ways.

## §12 CONSERVATION

An infinite, or practically infinite, resource can be consumed at a very high rate for as long as we wish to consume it. The early colonists in North

America and other areas perceived resources as superabundant. Thomas Jefferson referred to America as "a Chosen Country, with room enough for all descendants to the hundredth and thousandth generation."[33] There are no intrinsic constraints on the rate of consumption of such a resource; or rather, we can never consume the resource itself however rapidly we consume its parts. The only limits will be extrinsic: For example, even if energy resources were unlimited there would be good reasons for restraining our use of them, because the waste heat generated in fuel use would have serious environmental effects.

Conservation policies are a response to the recognition that resources are limited, coupled with a desire that the resources be available in future. Conservation, then, is linked to consumption in this way: It is "the saving of resources for our later consumption."[34] Conservation, strictly, can only be applied to renewable resources since consumption of nonrenewable materials and energy sources eventually results in the total destruction of the resource. But to use a very large nonrenewable resource sparingly is effectively conservationist if the resource will last for, say, thousands of years at present rates of extraction. To convert oil into gasoline and burn it in automobiles, or to burn it for space heating or electricity generation, is consumptive, since (whatever optimists may say) oil reserves *are* limited and the rising cost of extraction of much of the remaining oil reserves will tend to preclude their use. But to use oil for lubrication and petrochemicals is conservationist, because the rate of extraction of the resource would be very much lower if it was used only for these purposes.

To conserve a species is to use it in such a way that it will be possible to go on using it for the indefinite future. The use made of *members* of the species may be consumptive, for example, eating them. But if consumption is restrained by killing, say, only the proportion of "surplus" animals or plants beyond those necessary to maintain a stable population, then the resource—the species—is not consumed but conserved.

Conservationists, then, regard species as resources, and the language of wildlife management is remarkably similar to that used in discussions of minerals extraction or agricultural production. The population is the "resource"; the annual kill is the "crop" or "harvest"; the optimal harvest is the "maximum sustainable yield." This approach to species protection has become widespread: The IUCN adopts a thoroughly conservationist view to the point of faintly condemning those who would even consider a different approach: "Many people still find it hard to understand that the ultimate protection of nature, and all its ecological systems, and all its endangered forms of life, demands a plan, in which the core is *a management of the wilderness, and an enlightened exploitation of its wild resources* based on scientific research and measurement" (emphasis added).[35]

Conservationists advocate species protection in order that we may continue to consume members of the species indefinitely. They object to the extinction of a species because the resource is thereby destroyed. Noting that the abundant mourning dove (*Zenalda macroura*) of the United

States is intensively hunted[36] with no discernible effect on populations, the conservationist will regret the extinction of the passenger pigeon from which an even larger annual "harvest" could have been taken. Conservationists approve the protection of rare species and measures to build up populations if they have an interest in these species as a resource and these steps will yield a regular harvest. Several species of crocodile, formerly threatened or endangered, have been rescued by the establishment of crocodile farms in Australia and Papua–New Guinea. The Papua–New Guinea scheme, sponsored by the government and the United Nations Food and Agriculture Organization, provides legal protection for breeding-age animals in the wild, while allowing the sale of captured hatchlings to the farms. Animals bred or raised on the farms are mostly slaughtered for their hides, but some are returned to the wild. The skin trade brings in around $2 million per annum, the profits being returned to the local community. Similar schemes are proposed for India and the Philippines.[37]

## §13  PRESERVATION

Preservation of nature is "the saving of species and wilderness from damage and destruction."[38] Preservationists, therefore, hold fundamentally different views from conservationists on species protection. The conservationist regrets the loss of the passenger pigeon as a lost resource: "What the conservationist opposes is not the harnessing of nature for man's economic purposes but carelessness and wastefulness in doing so."[39] To exterminate a harvestable species is wasteful and shortsighted, like burning oil inefficiently for personal transportation, or eating the seed corn. Thus Conway writes, "It is not . . . well-managed farming of wild species . . . that troubles me . . . but the unmanaged, unregulated slaughter of diminishing wild animals in the world's few remaining wild areas. The carefully supervised utilization of the fur seal herd in Alaska's Pribilof Islands can scarcely attract criticism. . . ."[40] The reason why Conway thinks that the annual killing of thousands of seals for their fur "can scarcely attract criticism" is that he sees seals, and other wildlife, as "immense renewable resources." The preservationist, broadly speaking, *denies* the legitimacy of any destructive use of natural objects, at least where there is an alternative. Fur seals might be a legitimate prey for traditional Eskimo subsistence hunters, who would starve or freeze without seals, but not for modern commercial hunters who by and large provide luxuries for the wealthy. To the preservationist, "excessive" commercial hunting of seals does not merely waste a resource: *The very conception and treatment of these animals as a resource is illegitimate.*

   Broadly preservationist justifications for the protection of threatened species, and the maintenance of common ones, generally appeal to *inherent* or *intrinsic values*: the value of the lives of individual animals, or of whole species, or of ecological wholes. Sometimes this view is presented as, ultimately, self-evident—or at least not supportable by evidence or reasons. Stanford University biologists Paul and Anne Ehrlich assert that the ". . . argument [sic] is simply that our fellow passengers on Spaceship Earth, who are quite possibly our only living companions in the entire Universe, *have a right to exist*."[41] The French author Romain Gary sees the giving of reasons (which he identifies with the efficient pursuit of self-interest) as antithetical to saving species: ". . . as far as hard reason goes, killer takes all. The heart either speaks or it does not. The reason why has about as much to do with rationality as does beauty."[42] In contrast, Tom Regan[43] presents a carefully reasoned case for valuing the lives of nonhuman animals, though not for valuing species as such. Regan's views are considered in §19.

## §14 CONSERVATION VERSUS PRESERVATION

American history is full of arguments about the appropriate attitude toward the environment. Early in the twentieth century a debate—often bitter and drawn out—continued for years between two different schools of thought,[44] the chief protagonists being John Muir (1838–1914) and Gifford Pinchot (1865–1914). Pinchot himself summarized the conservationist view in these words: "The object of our forest policy is not to preserve the forests because they are beautiful . . . or because they are refuges for the wild creatures of the wilderness . . . but . . . the making of prosperous homes. . . . Every other consideration comes as secondary." Muir wrote, in messianic vein, "the present flourishing triumphant growth of the wealthy wicked, the . . . Pinchots and their hirelings, will not thrive forever . . . truth and right must prevail at last."

Muir, founder of the Sierra Club and, by his influence on the first President Roosevelt, an instigator of the National Parks System, was presented by his opponents as a proud, aloof, misanthropic figure, who, disliking human company and unable to fit into society, strove to "lock up" useful resources in order to benefit trees and wildlife. In turn, Muir's supporters accused Pinchot, the first United States Conservator of Forests, of wanting to hand over America's irreplaceable natural wonders to the railroad companies, the lumbermen, and the utilities. The debate has never really stopped, and was typified, both in substance and in style, in the policy disagreements and sometimes heated exchanges in the early 1980s between President Reagan's secretary of the interior, James Watt, and the spokespeople and supporters of organizations such as Friends of the Earth, the Sierra Club, and the Environmental Defense Society.

Conservationists and preservationists may on occasion support the same policies: Especially, they may be united in opposing destructive, consumptionist policies. To take an extreme example, both would oppose the clear-felling of the Amazonian forests. But their reasons, as I have explained, would be very different. The policies which they would advocate *instead* of clear-felling would also be different. The conservationist would advocate the careful development of the biotic resources of the forest, particularly its timber resources, via selective logging and re-planting (perhaps with exotic species), the clearing of some land for agriculture, and perhaps the creation of large reserves, both for tourism and to protect potentially useful species. The preservationist, in contrast, would be more likely to support polices to maintain very large areas completely untouched by human activity. More importantly for this essay, the justifications that would be advanced for these policies would differ considerably, as will be seen in the next section.

## §15  CONSEQUENTIALISM AND NONCONSEQUENTIALISM

The central disagreement between the two views I have been discussing arises from a disagreement about a basic question of value which has the widest possible implications for ethics in general.

Ethical theories, in the western tradition, may be divided broadly into two types. On the one hand are *consequentialist* (or *teleological*) theories, according to which actions (or, perhaps, rules, principles, policies, and institutions) are evaluated according to their consequences. In this type of view, a right action, roughly speaking, is one which has good consequences; a wrong action one which has bad consequences. Such a theory may be referred to as an *extrinsic* theory of value, because it locates value not in the act itself but in the consequences of that act. A common theory is *utilitarianism*, the most widely accepted version of which holds that "actions are right in proportion as they tend to promote happiness, wrong as they tend to produce the reverse of happiness."[45] Consequentialists would evaluate proposals to protect species on the likely consequences of suggested policies; utilitarians would, normally, evaluate policies on the specific ground of their effects on happiness.

*Nonconsequentialist* theories are frequently referred to as *deontological* theories. Deontologists hold that the rightness or wrongness of actions is *not* reducible to the value of their consequences. Deontologists do not necessarily argue that the consequences of an action are irrelevant to determining its obligatoriness, but they do deny that obligation can be *reduced* to consequences. The debate about capital punishment provides a useful illustration of the contrast between these two types of theory: The utilitarian supporter of the death penalty will argue that capital punishment is justified because of its good effects, for instance its alleged deterrent effect. The deontologist, in contrast, argues that murder is such an intrinsically evil crime that the murderer *deserves* to die, the consequences of a capital punishment system being largely or wholly ir-relevant. In the case of species protection, the deontologist is likely to defend protection policies on the grounds that they protect what is valu-able in itself, rather than advancing claims that good consequences will result from protection. Thus Nicholas Rescher, a philosopher at the University of Pittsburgh, argues that "when a species vanishes from nature, the world is thereby diminished. Species do not just have an instrumental value . . . they also have a value in their own right—an intrinsic value."[46]

## §16 SPECIESISM VERSUS EQUALITY

Traditional ethical systems in the west have not attributed independent value to animals, plants, or the land. Rather, the rest of nature has been seen as having only an extrinsic or resource value—having value only as a means to human ends and not for its own sake. Richard Routley, a philosopher from the Australian National University, has called this attitude "human chauvinism"[47]; the well-known Australian philosopher Peter Singer has popularized the term "speciesism,"[48] which I shall use here. Singer defines speciesism as "a prejudice or attitude of bias towards the members of one's own species and against members of other species."[49] The speciesist evaluates the treatment of nonhumans solely in terms of their fitness to human ends. Speciesism, according to Singer, is wrong for much the same reasons that racism and sexism are wrong: It fails to take account of the interests of nonhumans, treating them as if they were of no account, just as sexism fails to recognize the interests of women. Singer, a utilitarian, argues that all sentient beings have an interest in not suffering; that suffering is an evil no matter what the species of the being which undergoes the suffering; and that the infliction of suffering on any being is therefore wrong except in extreme and rare cases where the infliction of relatively trivial suffering on one being will result in relatively great gains which quite clearly outweigh that suffering. It is not that Singer is advocating identical *treatment* for all animals, of course; rather, he argues for equal *consideration*, so that the interest of an animal in avoiding suffering must always be counted equally with the comparable interest of a human.

Singer, then, is a consequentialist, and would evaluate policies of species protection on the bases of their tendency to reduce suffering and promote happiness. But whereas the conservationist considers only the effects on *human* welfare, the "animal liberationist" considers, equally, the effect on the welfare of animals too. Many of the arguments for species conservation presented in Part V of this essay, such as the value of species for food, would be rejected by Singer since they are based on the assumption that humans are morally entitled to exploit animals by eating them.

It is not easy to apply Singer's version of utilitarianism to species protection, because the extermination of species, or their replacement by introduced species, need not cause any suffering at all. A program to eradicate a species by painlessly sterilizing each member (placing a contraceptive substance in the water holes they use, for instance) would cause no direct suffering, and the introduction of an exotic species which would fill the vacant ecological niche could ensure the welfare of the predators and parasites which depended on the now extinct species. Singer has indicated that in his view, "Members of common and rare species of, say, whales have exactly the same moral standing *qua* individual animals."[50] To harm *individual* animals is wrong, regardless of their species; so if the extermination of a species caused no loss of utility or ecological damage, it would not be wrong.

I have argued elsewhere[51] that utilitarian accounts of the moral status of animals, and of species, are seriously deficient. If the extermination of a species can be achieved without causing suffering then we might as well develop a wilderness area, if there are definite net benefits to doing so, or dam a wild river to produce hydroelectricity. Utilitarian defenses of species protection when proffered will tend to be conservationist, therefore: Provided that we do not cause suffering, species should be protected (or not protected) only to the extent that there are beneficial consequences.

## §17   ANIMAL RIGHTS

The most complete and persuasive argument in favor of animal rights is offered by Tom Regan. He argues that animals "are to be treated with respect *and* that respectful treatment is their due"[52]: that such respect, or recognition of them as right holders, is a matter of *justice*. The reason why animals are entitled to respect is that they are "subjects of a life"; they have a life of their own, and therefore have value apart from anyone else's interests. Animals have this right equally with humans, so that it is always wrong to disregard their rights, though they may sometimes, for reasons too complex to explain here, be overridden. Regan concludes, as does Singer, that it is wrong to raise animals for food, to hunt or trap them, commercially or for sport, and to use them for research.

The apparent similarities between the views of Regan and Singer, however, are in some ways less important than the differences. The theoretical bases of their positions are of course quite different, in that Singer is a consequentialist while Regan is not. But this fundamental difference also yields quite different practical conclusions. For Singer, as for any utilitarian, policies must be evaluated in terms of their consequences, and as I noted in the previous section, the best policy for a utilitarian could be one which causes some suffering or death to animals provided that the best possible result overall is achieved with the least possible suffering. *Painless* commercial animal farming might well be the best agricultural practice for Singer, in certain instances, for example on marginal land unsuited to crop production in a country where the population was underfed. The rights view espoused by Regan rules out *all* painful or destructive use of animals in principle.

The rights view, then, implies that conservationist arguments must be rejected. Thus Regan writes, "A practice, institution, enterprise, or similar undertaking is unjust if it permits or requires treating individuals with inherent value as if they were *renewable resources* . . ." If species protection policies are justified, in this view, they would be preservationist policies and their justification would not be that good consequences would follow from protection, but that the rights of individual animals would be protected. The defense of species preservation would be that members of rare species, like those of common species, have rights which we ought to respect. Differ though they do, however, Regan, like Singer, argues that the *species* of a being is irrelevant to its moral status. Species *as such* do not have any value, so there is no duty to preserve species as such. I shall return to this question in Part IV.

# IV. WHY PROTECT SPECIES?

## §18 INTRODUCTION

Parts II and III of this essay surveyed the past and likely future status of species, and briefly examined some important general principles relevant to species protection. It is now time to study the central question of the essay. I discuss, first (in §19), the claim that species as such have a moral status, for instance that species have rights, concluding that such claims cannot serve as a basis for species protection. The conventional emphasis on rare species is then examined (§20); I argue that plausible justifications for species protection will apply equally to both common and rare species. A rather lengthy section (Part V) follows, in which a number of case-by-case conservationist arguments are evaluated, and this is followed by a general critique of a species-oriented approach to environmental management. Finally (Part VI), I defend the view that conservationists cannot provide a general answer to the question "Why should we care about species?" and that, if any general account can be given, it will have to be a preservationist one. Also in Part VI I discuss some problems this position must face, including how best to protect species.

## §19 RIGHTS FOR SPECIES?

If species have value, then they ought to be protected; at least, they ought not to be harmed or destroyed. If it is wrong to harm or destroy individuals, it might be argued, then it is also wrong to harm or destroy species, which are but collections of individuals. The two main justifications of an equal moral status for animals and humans do not support this view, however.

Singer, first, bases his claim that animals should be accorded equal moral consideration on the fact that animals suffer, and the principle that it is wrong to inflict suffering. Species as such cannot suffer, and so cannot be harmed: They do not have an interest in avoiding suffering, therefore. To exterminate a species would be wrong only if it caused suffering, whether directly to the animals that died, or indirectly by depriving other animals of food. But the harm would then be done to individual animals, not to the species. A second feature of utilitarianism is that it is limited to sentient beings, since only they can suffer. To exterminate a plant species, then, would be wrong *only* to the extent that the loss of the species would deprive animals (or humans) of the benefits of eating or otherwise utilizing the species. To replace an indigenous forest with an exotic one, capable of supporting the same population of sentient beings as formerly occurred, would not be wrong, even if as a result several indigenous plant species became extinct. If the new ecosystem was able to support a larger number of sentient beings, and if it better provided for human wants, it might even be a duty to make the change. Utilitarians, then, cannot value plants *at all* except as a resource.

The view that animals have rights, as noted earlier, is not transferable to the claim that species have rights. Regan writes[53] "The rights view is a view about the moral rights of individuals. Species are not individuals, and the rights view does not recognize the moral rights of species to anything." It is therefore no worse to kill a member of an endangered species than of a common species, other things being equal. Indeed, Regan argues, "If we had to choose between saving the last two members of an endangered species, or saving another individual who belonged to a species that was plentiful but whose death would be a greater prima facie harm to that individual than the harm that death would be to the two then the rights view requires that we save that individual"—even though the endangered species would thereby become extinct. Regan emphasizes that the rights view does not oppose the protection of endangered species —indeed, it supports such efforts, but primarily in order to protect the rights of individual members. Regan accepts, also, that human interests in preserving rare species for cultural, aesthetic, or other nondestructive reasons are also important, but these interests would not necessarily justify preservation of an endangered species, as in the example referred to earlier in this paragraph. Finally, plants do not qualify as right holders on Regan's view, so to exterminate a plant species would be wrong only if it destroyed the natural habitat of an animal species. Seriously endangered plants are not essential to any animal, usually,[54] and so there is no compelling reason, based on animals' rights, to preserve them.

It seems unlikely to me that the value of species could ever be explained in terms of rights. University of Arizona philosopher Joel Feinberg[55] notes that the typical criteria for attributing rights to individuals, such as ability to suffer or possession of interests, could not possibly apply to species.

Christopher Stone,[56] a law professor at the University of Southern California, has argued that nonhuman entities such as natural features, trees, or lakes could be given a legal standing just as corporations, by a legal fiction, are treated as persons for certain purposes. Corporations can sue and be sued and can be held liable for breaches of the criminal law; the "interests" of corporations are represented legally by actual persons such as company officials or attorneys. Stone argues that a lake, for example, could be granted a legal status, too: It could be granted certain legal rights against those who would damage it by pollution, for instance, and persons could be appointed to represent it in court. The New Zealand practice of appointing boards of guardians for certain lakes is along those lines. A legally protected species, as are most birds in the United States, could be treated similarly.

To grant legal rights to a species, against developers, hunters, or others who threaten its existence, would be one method of species protection. But Stone's suggestion is not a *reason* for protecting species; it is not as if he was arguing that *since* species have legal rights then they *ought* to be protected. He argues, rather, that natural objects *ought* to be granted an enhanced moral status, and that the best way to protect a natural feature is to grant it legal standing. To grant legal rights to lakes, trees, or species, is a *consequence* of recognizing their moral status, not a reason for their moral status. The rights of nonpersons in law are, in any case, not necessarily a recognition of moral status. We do not endow a corporation with legal rights because we believe that it is morally entitled to respect for its interests; we do not really believe that corporations are persons. Rather, we treat them as if they *were* persons, in certain limited ways, because our legal system has grown up to deal with persons: Persons are the subject of law, and the law relating to corporations, trusts, societies, clubs, and the like is simply an extension of the law relating to persons. It is not clear to me that fictional persons are really regarded as having interests at all; we allow General Motors to bring suit in court because we wish to give expression to the legitimate economic activities of its stockholders, not because we want to protect "its" rights. A corporation is an artificial entity, set up at the will of its members, and it may be altered, expanded, sold, merged, or wound up if they wish. Species are not means to the ends of their members, nor are they artificial entities. The point of asserting their rights, if one is inclined to assert them, is to protect them from being treated as *merely* means to an end.

Stone's analogy with fictitious legal persons such as corporations, then, provides a *mechanism* for species protection but not a *reason* for valuing species. One final argument for species' rights needs to be considered. It may be argued that groups of persons have legal (and moral) rights, which are the sum of the members' rights taken collectively. My business partners and I have rights to pursue our legitimate commercial activities within the law, and the partnership may be said to have rights as a whole which are the sum of the rights of the individual partners. If it is recognized that individual peregrines, for instance, have rights, then species (the set comprising all peregrines) could be said to have rights, too. Peregrine falcons, perhaps, have the right to live their lives undisturbed—therefore a right not to be killed or injured, to an undisturbed habitat, to eat, sleep, mate, and raise a family without hindrance. The species *Falco peregrinus* may be said to have rights in the sense that its members have rights.

I do not think that this argument will do the job, however. First, it is still a fiction, for it is *individuals* which really have interests; and to say that a species is suffering a painful death, or that its ability to reproduce is threatened by pesticides, is only to say that *individuals* are suffering or are having difficulty in reproducing. Were we to say that a "species is suffering," then, we would be saying no more than that individuals are suffering, but in a rather misleading way. There are some things which are true of species but not of their members—for example, a species may have evolved 20 million years ago, and may be said to be 20 million years old, therefore, but obviously no individual is 20 million years old. It is thus not clear how a species can have interests other than those of its members.

A further difficulty, as Regan notes, is that the rights of a member of a rare species are no greater than those of a common species. To kill one of the few remaining California condors, painlessly, would be *less* wrong than to kill a common bird by slow torture. To kill the last few condors would have little ecological effect since their numbers are so reduced that they no longer play an important ecological role, so again it would be worse to torture a dozen common sparrows than to kill, painlessly, all the condors that survive. A member of a rare species does not have special rights merely because it is rare, if rights are based on the interests of an individual in living its life well. Rare species are not necessarily more valuable than common ones (see §20) but they are in need of protection if they are to survive. Measures to protect *all* rare species, including plants, cannot, however, be justified on the basis of the rights of their individual members.

## §20  RARITY AND VALUE

Ethical questions about protecting species arise, usually, only about rare and endangered species. This is not surprising, perhaps, since the point of ethics is to help us to decide what do do, and we do not need to do anything to protect common species. The purpose of conservationist legislation and government policy is often to protect species whose continued existence is threatened by past or present human action; some countries protect *only* species believed to be threatened, permitting the killing or capturing of common species even where they are not seen as "pests." The implication is that it is morally acceptable to kill, destroy, or capture individuals, so long as that individual is not a member of a rare taxum. Such policies are clearly speciesist and conservationist (see §16) and imply a view of nonhuman animals and plants as resources to be used rather than as individuals meriting respect.

Our concern with rare species as such raises several puzzling questions. I discuss three in the remainder of this section.[57]

First, there is the problem of characterizing rare species. To say that a species is rare, and therefore ought to be protected, sounds like a judgment that a species has some particular characteristic in virtue of which it has some special claim on our attention. Rarity, however, is not a characteristic or property of a species, nor of its individual members. The properties of a species are the biological facts about typical members of the species. These are not precise descriptions of the appearance, structure, or behavior of any individual. Field guides give general descriptions including approximate sizes and colors; feeding, mating, and nesting behavior; and range, which is to say that an individual's dimensions are most likely to fall within the measurements listed, that it is most likely to be found somewhere in the range described, and will probably exhibit some of the behaviors specified. An individual will not just be "between twenty and twenty-five centimeters in length," nor will it exhibit "a range of variable color patterns," but will be of a *precise* length and color.

The name of a species designates those individuals having a combination of properties falling within a general range. But *rarity* is not one of those properties. To say that a species is rare is not like saying that it is green or long legged, that it lays between five and seven eggs, or that it inhabits pinyon-juniper associations. To say that tigers are rare is to say that there are few tigers. When they were more common, they had the same properties as they have today. Perhaps the statement "tigers are rare" is a description of the world (it contains few tigers), but not a description of tigers.

A second puzzle arises from the value that many people attach to rare, as opposed to common species. It is not merely that our actions can make a difference to the survival of the species, whereas at the moment we do not need to worry about our effects on common species. Many people also value *encounters* with rare species.[58] As an enthusiastic birder, I actively seek encounters with rare species of birds; but the reason cannot merely be that such encounters are infrequent. Encounters with muggers or leprosy are infrequent, and we do not value them.

I suggest that we do not, in fact, value anything *merely* on account of its rarity: that we do not attach value to rarities *as such*. Rather, rarity seems to function as an *intensifier* of value, so that the pleasure (or pain) of an experience is increased according to the unlikelihood of the experience. Thus birders, or stamp collectors, value birds and stamps in general, and especially rare birds and stamps; no one wishes to contract any disease, but especially not a rare disease. Thus it is "lucky" to see a rare bird, "unlucky" to contract a rare disease.

Third, although we may value encounters with rare species more than encounters with common species, we wish that rare species were *not* rare. I have seen a peregrine falcon on but one occasion, and am very glad that I did so. To observe this rare species was a good, but I wish that there were more peregrines, that they were not rare. To value rare species is not to wish that they continue to be rare, but to wish that they would become more common. The purpose of the captive breeding and release program is to increase the numbers of peregrines so that they will no longer be rare.[59] If they do become common, an encounter with a peregrine will presumably lose some of its special value. It is possible, of course, that some birders will therefore regret the fact that peregrines are no longer rare. This possibility suggests, once again, a view of species as a resource.

To say that falcons ought to be protected because they are rare is not like saying that they should be protected because they are beautiful or unique, fierce or strong, or necessary to maintain balanced ecosystems. I suggest that the rarity of a species is not, in fact, a proper ground for valuing it, though it may be a good reason for doing something to protect it. In the remainder of this essay, therefore, I discuss problems of the value of species in general, alluding to rare species as such only when the question of special measures for species in need of protection is relevant.

## V. A CRITIQUE OF CONSERVATIONIST ARGUMENTS

Conservationist defenses of species protection take many forms—not surprisingly, since animals and plants are useful or agreeable to humans in many different ways. Arguments in favor of protecting, or not exterminating, species or populations appeal to their economic, medicinal, scientific, educational, or aesthetic value, their potential to provide genetic diversity, food or energy sources, tourist revenues, ecological health, indicators of environmental quality, or (often unspecified) benefits to future generations; their cultural or religious significance, their contribution to our understanding of ourselves or even to our ultimate survival. Finally, even where there are manifestly no benefits to present or (conceivably) future generations, it is sometimes argued that we should protect all species because if we allow exceptions it makes the general case for protection that much weaker.

Some of the arguments discussed in this section might appear to be preservationist rather than conservationist. To protect wild geese for the aesthetic pleasure gained by observing huge migratory flocks at twilight, it is necessary to avoid harming or disturbing the geese, perhaps. Birders and others value these experiences, and if flocks are disturbed, or if the social behavior of many of the geese are disrupted (as it is by hunting since geese mate for life and individuals who lose a mate often behave abnormally), the aesthetic experience would be diminished. The best way to protect the interests of birders, then, is to avoid harming individual geese at all, which is a policy of preservation. In the case of a naturally rare species, too, each member may need to be protected in order to save the species for aesthetic or scientific interest.

We should not confuse the practical details of policy with the justifications or motives for policy, however. It is true that in some cases, because of certain contingent features of the world, preservationists and conservationists may support the same policies. Those who value a species for its own sake, and those who value it for its aesthetic or scientific interest, may support absolute protection for the species, but their reasons are different. The one values it for itself, the other as a resource, and while preservationists may also derive enjoyment from studying a species, the preservationist case does not depend on the resource value of a species. Rescher,[60] for example, argues that while the instrumental value of species is a valid reason for protecting them, it is not the whole story: that natural kinds of thing have an intrinsic or inherent value which it is wrong to destroy.

I now proceed to examine a number of arguments for species protection which are conservationist in that species are valued ultimately as a resource, even if the use of that resource is nondestructive.

## §21 FOOD

The conservation of suitable species may provide a cheap, high production food source. In East Africa the eland (*Taurotragus oryx*) and on the Scottish island of Rum the red deer (*Cervus elaphus*) have been shown to produce more marketable meat than could be obtained by ranching sheep or cattle.[61] These species, being native to the area, are adapted to local climatic conditions, diseases, and parasites. American bison, usually crossed with domestic breeds of cattle to produce "beefalo" steaks, are also highly productive, easily managed sources of meat.

The vegetarian will not find this argument very persuasive, of course, and in any case not all animals are tasty or nutritious. Economically, only gregarious species can be raised for food; perhaps many social invertebrates, such as ants, fall into this category, but for cultural reasons are unlikely to be adopted as a food source by most people.

It is sometimes argued that many plant species could provide new food sources if developed into crops. Our food supply would certainly be poorer if earlier generations had exterminated the grasses which are the ancestors of our modern grains, for example. "Who knows," F. Nigel Hepper, a botanist from England's Royal Botanic gardens asks rhetorically, "which of today's weeds and wild seeds will become the progenitor of tomorrow's crop plants?"[62] No one knows, of course, and therefore, so some conclude, we ought to avoid destroying plant species. A similar argument is also raised for the potential medicinal value of plants which might, for example, yield new drugs for birth control, painkillers, or cancer-curing agents.[63]

Like all arguments about the unknown consequences of actions, this one is vulnerable to the counterclaim that we cannot pursue all logically possible good things at once. Most plants will *not* produce benefits which could not have been produced any other way, while the opportunity cost of preserving *all* plant species is considerable. Sometimes we simply have to forgo potential unproven benefits in order to reap actual, proven benefits, as when one spends one's money on groceries rather than using it to play roulette or to buy lottery tickets. Furthermore, many plant species could be protected by storing seeds in "banks" around the world.[64]

Sometimes animals are direct competitors for food with humans—by eating food that humans or domestic animals would otherwise eat; by occupying land which if cleared could grow crops; by damaging cropland; or by predating livestock. The African elephant eats several hundred pounds of vegetable matter and drinks up to 50 gallons of water per day. The million or more African elephants of today therefore may consume up to 250,000 tons of food and 50 million gallons of water per day, as well as occasionally damaging cropland and breaking down fences.[65]

There is no simple answer to the present world food shortage. If population growth is outstripping increase in food supply, the eventual solution is to reduce population growth. There is some evidence that this is happening, though for demographic reasons growth will continue for some years yet. We could reduce food wastage by storing it more efficiently and thus preventing losses to rodents, by ceasing to overconsume as most inhabitants of Western countries do, by feeding grains to people instead of to livestock, and by growing crops on some of the land now given over to stockraising. We could follow the examples of China and India and meet much of our protein needs from fish "farms."[66] We could, perhaps, synthesize food in factories, or even research the science fiction proposal in F. Pohl and C. Kornbluth's *The Space Merchants*,[67] in which chicken tissue biomass, known as "Chicken Little," is allowed to spread through underground caverns and is mined like coal. In any event it is not clear that we need to save all, or even very many species in order to feed the earth's population; nor is it clear that putting efforts into protecting as many species as possible will provide more food in the long run. So species protection based on present and foreseeable interests in food will not yield a satisfactory general policy.

## §22 ECONOMIC ARGUMENTS

Some species have an actual or potential economic benefit to humans. Determinations of the economic value of a species can be made only on a basis of benefit-cost analysis and it is often argued that such calculations fail to take account of moral or aesthetic values on which a dollar price cannot be put. A philosopher at the University of Maryland, Bryan Norton,[68] describes the method of "shadow pricing": "The dollar amount assigned a value is determined by what people would be willing to pay to obtain it, and the dollar amount assigned a loss in value is determined by what people would pay to prevent the damage involved"; but he accepts that this may be inadequate as a measure of these values. There is also the problem of deciding how much reliance to put on people's assertions about what they would pay, when they are not actually being asked to pay anything right now. Norton points out that benefit-cost analysis also depends on the assumption that the best policy is the one which satisfies the most desires of a group. Even if it is possible to determine objectively what would have this effect (thus permitting us to ignore people's mistaken or ill-informed beliefs about what would make them happy), this would not provide a reason for saving very many species. The rewards may be high, and opportunity costs low, of saving bald eagles or tigers, but most people will *not* lose utility if many obscure species disappear, while the aggregate cost of protecting *all* species would be very high.

Even where a straight economic value can be placed on a species, other values may need to be considered. For example bobcats (*Lynx rufus*) predate livestock to which a market value can easily be assigned. On the other hand, their pelts are worth up to $400 each. In 1979 a study was underway of the economic value of the bobcat to the Navajo, on whose reservation they occur, to determine the "optimum sustainable yield" of the bobcat as a "harvestable species." But the species also has religious and cultural value to the Navajo.[69] It is difficult to imagine a bobcat management policy which could accommodate these values as well as turning the maximum profit.

The appeal to economic value is a dangerous weapon, and may rebound, for we cannot defend conservation of species on economic grounds without being prepared to accept that economics will sometimes point the other way. David Ehrenfeld argues that many species simply do not have an appreciable money value and therefore cannot properly be viewed as resources. To defend the protection of presently nonuseful species as if they were really useful (which they may turn out to be in the long term) is to court disaster. As Ehrenfeld notes, "In a capitalist society, any private individual or corporation that treats non-resources as if they were resources is likely to go bankrupt. In a socialist society, the result will be non-fulfillment of growth quotas."[70] The well-known biologist and author Garrett Hardin[71] has pointed out, similarly, that no one would grow a redwood tree for profit. For an outlay of $1 on a seedling, a 300-foot redwood tree would eventually be produced, containing $14,000 worth of timber. Unfortunately, the investment would take 2,000 years to mature, yielding a return of less than one-half of 1 percent per year.

The human benefits of species protection, then, need to be conceived more broadly. At the same time, one cannot merely ignore economics. Many people would not accept the bald claim that "no food, no clothing, no shelter, no land, and certainly no luxury or technology is worth the irreplaceable loss of any species."[72] Argument is needed to persuade people that they should give up luxuries and technology, and perhaps food, clothing, and shelter, in order to protect species, especially when people are starving to death. There is also the practical problem that even if the claim under consideration is a justifiable one, the public will need to be convinced of its truth before it can become policy.

## §23 AESTHETIC ARGUMENTS

Many species are conventionally regarded as beautiful or otherwise visually appealing. Sometimes, as in the case of spotted cats, their beauty has been their downfall. But these animals, and others, are also aesthetically valuable because of their grace, the way they move, and their stillness in repose. Aesthetic value has been claimed to be intrinsic to, for example, works of art, and perhaps by extension to natural objects too. This view is discussed, and rejected by Elliott.[73] Elliott argues that the value of works of art lies in their potential to produce enjoyment and pleasure in onlookers, and that it would therefore not be wrong for the last human on earth to destroy works of art. If this is accepted, it follows that the last human (if humans are the only beings with aesthetic sensibilities) would likewise not do wrong to destroy species of animals or plants if their only value was aesthetic.

Whether or not aesthetic values are intrinsic to works of art or natural objects, not all living things are aesthetically valuable in themselves. Some endangered animals in the United States, such as the celebrated snail darter (*Percina tanasi*), are aesthetically insignificant, while the Houston toad (*Trichechus manatus*) and Florida manatee (*Bufo houstonensis*) are regarded by most people as downright ugly. Fashions in aesthetics change, of course (which is not to say that aesthetic value is merely a matter of fashion). The educated classes in eighteenth century England had a horror of wild nature, which they regarded as visually unappealing; mysteriously, they also held Shakespeare's *Hamlet* in low esteem. Future generations may hold quite different views from our own (see §29); perhaps they will find elephants hideous and Houston toads exquisitely beautiful.

The appeal to aesthetic value, then, may justify the protection, for the time being, of a small number of species, but will not provide a rationale for general protection. It will also be vulnerable to competing claims such as the economic value of *not* protecting a species, as well as the argument that no one needs to experience *all* the potentially aesthetic objects that there are, so that adequate choice can be left by sacrificing some of the present oversupply. Thus even the view that "unattractive" species contribute to diversity, which is a component in aesthetic value,[74] does not in itself justify species protection in general.

## §24  THE VALUE OF GENETIC DIVERSITY

Many arguments for conserving species which may possibly be of use as sources of food, drugs, or other materials are claims that we should protect potentially useful genotypes. Common plants or animals instantly provide us with resources once their value is recognized. Rare and endangered ones cannot do this until they have multiplied sufficiently to be nonvulnerable. We cannot maintain large populations of all species, and all species are at least potentially useful for something. Many species have probably never been common; some, such as the unfortunate Stephen Island wren discussed in §6, or many species of invertebrates and plants, have always been restricted to a small area. Others have become rare due to habitat loss, and a vast effort would be required to restore the lost habitat—much of it, today, agricultural, urban, or industrial.

One of the rarest species in the world is the endangered plant *Phacelia argillaceae*[75] of Utah. The total population is four plants: There used to be seven, but three were trampled by sheep. These four, now enclosed by a fence, represent the total gene pool of *P. argillaceae*. In case these plants should turn out to be useful, we should protect them, like any other genotype. Many other species or varieties of plants *known* to be useful have already died out, due to the excessive concentration of modern agriculture on the pursuit of high yields via genetic uniformity. Many native varieties of wild flax, maize, and wheat, including the ancestors of some of our modern varieties, are now extinct.

The argument from genetic diversity is a compelling one, but still we cannot protect large populations of all species. As our knowledge of genetics increases, it may be possible to predict just what proportion of a species is necessary to preserve its entire genetic range. Should it turn out that the only way to be *sure* that we do not extinguish a genotype is to protect each individual, then we shall have to establish an order of priority. More than likely, such a complete study is not practically possible, given the huge number of species existing. We will probably have to be content with conserving what we hope is a reasonable genetic cross-section of as many species as possible, and putting more effort into genetic engineering research so as to increase the gene pool if necessary. To conserve a reasonable variety of genotypes, in the case of very rare species such as *P. argillaceae*, requires us to save, and increase, the entire population. To conserve the genetic potential, or most of it, of more common species does not. Indeed, it may not require us to save many, or even any actual members in the wild. In many cases we can (more safely perhaps) maintain individuals in captivity or store the genetic materials in some kind of gene bank. Eventually we may be able to recreate genotypes at will, so that we will need to keep only formulae, much as a cook keeps files of recipes rather than storing the dishes themselves.

A final point on genetic diversity: There could not be an absolute principle that it is always wrong to reduce genetic diversity. The reason is that we almost certainly cannot avoid doing so. Every time we kill an animal or plant for food, pull a weed from the garden, or chop a tree, we *may* be destroying a unique genotype. We probably are not, since even if an individual's genetic *combination* is unique, the genes it contains are not, individually. But collectively, even if we restrict our impact on nature as much as possible, we probably *do* destroy unique genetic potential from time to time. Since we can hardly be expected to submit for genetic analysis every weed in the garden, we must be prepared for some losses. Our obligation is to avoid destroying genetic diversity needlessly; but of course this principle would have to be interpreted, depending as it does on what is to count as a need.

## §25 EDUCATION, SCIENCE, AND THE PURSUIT OF KNOWLEDGE

To exterminate a species is to lose, forever, the possibility of finding out information about it. Even intensively studied species may have secrets for later generations to discover, while the extinction of an unknown species represents a considerable loss of knowledge. Knowledge and understanding of the world are commonly accepted to be components of or contributors to the good life, and we ought to maintain or increase opportunities for them rather than permanently foreclosing them.

Why should we concern ourselves with the loss of potential subjects of knowledge? The answer depends on why we think that knowledge is valuable. If it is because all knowledge is, or might turn out to be useful, then this argument is really only a variant of other, resource-oriented arguments already discussed. Alternatively, as Elliott points out,[76] it may be that the argument is appealing to a view of knowledge as good in itself. Hepper, writing on plants in *Wildlife in Danger*,[77] notes that many species of great scientific interest "are seldom spectacular and may not attract popular interest, but scientifically they can be far more important than others of horticultural merit."

Knowledge is indeed good, I suggest, but it is not *the* good. Andrew Belsey,[78] a philosopher from University College, Cardiff, Wales, argues that even if we accept that scientific research is good in itself it is still proper to urge that it be directed toward useful (and certainly not toward destructive) ends—for there are more possible areas for research than can conceivably be completed in the foreseeable future. The scientist cannot claim that his or her desire to further knowledge should automatically have priority over other interests and needs. This is one reason why we do not approve of painful, degrading, or dangerous research on human subjects, often even consenting ones. Much scientific research on animals appears to have no value except to extend knowledge for its own sake (and often, thereby the career and prestige of the researcher), at the expense of animal suffering.[79]

If we do not place absolute and overriding value on the pursuit of knowledge for its own sake, we cannot urge that species protection be given the highest priority merely in order to preserve potential fields for research. I suggest that the desire of scientists to study a species of beetle or fish, for example, would not by itself override the interest of persons who need to alter the habitat of that creature, thus exterminating it, in order to avoid starvation.

## §26 ENVIRONMENTAL INDICATORS

The state of an ecosystem is typically reflected in the state of its members. Declines (or increases) in the populations of a species or changes in their behavior and health may be the first visible indication of ecological change. Chinese scientists are reportedly studying folk beliefs about the unusual behavior of some domestic animals prior to earthquakes, and some animals were observed to dive for cover shortly before the eruption of Mount St. Helens in May 1980.[80]

Less spectacularly, animals or plants may provide early warnings of environmental deterioration. Purdue University philosopher Lily-Marlene Russow[81] points out that the decline of predatory birds due to their eggshells being weakened through DDT absorption is an indication of the level of environmental contamination. We might add that the detection of persistent substances in Antarctic fauna provided a similar warning of the wide dispersal of these substances. The practice of old-time miners of taking caged canaries into the mines (these birds being sensitive to the presence of toxic or explosive gases) is well known. Many species of fish are much more sensitive to damage by waterborne pollutants than are humans. (As a result the purity standards for game fish water under clean water legislation are more stringent than those for human swimmers.) Dead fish in a river are an early warning of pollution; and it is becoming standard practice to monitor the purity of factory wastewater discharges by passing samples through a fish tank.

Ecological indicators, then, enable us to detect (and therefore to treat, if possible) problems early on. They are therefore of considerable indirect benefit, in helping us to protect ourselves from threats, and enabling us to increase resources. As William Ramsay, of Resources for the Future, puts it, "Ecological indicators function like fever thermometers in that their high sensitivity to ecological change aids ecologists in planning species management on a large scale for the conservation of other species in a region or community."[82]

For all that, we can hardly conclude that all species ought to be protected in case they turn out to be useful indicators. It is easy to argue from selected examples but sub-species need not be protected if other varieties will do the same job.[83] In cases where we plan to develop, destroy, or replace an ecosystem, as by damming a river, we do not need the indicators which were relevant to the old ecosystem. The quality of the water behind the Tellico Dam will be assessed by the health of introduced trout, not by the snail darters and fresh water mussels which occupied the undammed river.

## §27 THE LIMITATIONS OF CONSERVATION

The conservationist case for species protection is, as David Ehrenfeld points out, ultimately inadequate. He writes, "The difficulty is that the humanistic world accepts the conservation of Nature only piecemeal and at a price: there must be a *logical*, *practical* reason for saving each and every part of the natural world that we wish to preserve."[84] Yet many threatened species are, in Ehrenfeld's terms, "non-resources": They have *no* economic, aesthetic, recreational, or other resource value. The pioneer ecologist-philosopher Aldo Leopold[85] was perhaps the first to note the limitations of conservationist policies. His view, often quoted, was that "one basic weakness in a conservation system based wholly on economic motives is that most members of the land community have no economic value." Conservationists, says Leopold, "invent subterfuges" to show that apparently "useless" species really do have economic value, for example to claim that wild predators are necessary for the health of game populations. Leopold suggests that "of the 22,000 higher plants and animals native to Wisconsin, it is doubtful whether more than five per cent can be sold, fed, eaten, or otherwise put to commercial use." Even if we add on other species perceived as valuable for aesthetic, recreational, or other resource reasons, there would still be very many non-resource species. In this section I present five arguments designed to cast further doubts on conservationist species protection.

First, conservationists often argue that the resource potential of most species is unknown at present. For example, Peter Steinhart,[86] a prolific writer on environmental subjects, asserts that a strong Endangered Species Act is necessary: "For until we can actually answer the question ["What good are they?"]—until we can honestly and accurately say that the northern monkshood holds the secret of eternal life or the Santa Catalina bushmallow is no good now and never will be—we must do what we can to save them all." But, of course, we cannot be sure that *anything* is useless. Many people (including myself) hoard apparently useless items of junk in the hope that they might come in handy one day. To fill one's house with material of this sort is to sacrifice tangible uses for intangible, speculative benefits. If the value of species is only their resource value, then at some point we are entitled to clear out the "useless" species in order to make better use of the useful ones, or other natural resources.

Second, utilitarian conservationists[87] are committed to approving of schemes which raise the overall level of human well-being. They should approve, therefore, of policies designed to create the highest *net* utility, including, sometimes, the replacement of indigenous species by introduced ones. Several species of trout and salmon are highly esteemed for their fighting qualities as a sport fish, and for their flavor. They have been introduced to streams and rivers around the world, sometimes displacing indigenous species without apparent ecological damage. The introduction of a new species usually causes ecological *change* but the modified system may be just as stable and diverse, and may have a higher utility value. The New Zealand grayling (*Prototractes oxyrhynchus*) is almost certainly extinct; predation by introduced trout is probably a cause of its extinction.[88] Trout have the same food value as grayling, and also contribute to the New Zealand economy by attracting overseas trout fishermen. If utility is the sole ground for species protection, then it would seem rational to introduce species which are *more* useful, even at the expense of indigenous species. In such a case the utilitarian approach appears to be committed to policies resulting in species extermination.

Third, the previous argument has especial force when we consider that the ecosystems of most developed countries (and, increasingly, of developing ones) are already seriously modified. Changes in water quality may reduce the populations of specialized, indigenous species to the point where their resource value is seriously reduced. The New Zealand grayling's decline may also have been caused in part by a deterioration in water quality which does not affect the more adaptable trout. The only way to maintain the utility of the fishery, then, may have been to introduce competitors (see §9). Once again, utility may dictate policies which will at least hasten the decline of a species.

Fourth, a commitment to resource conservation, with its philosophy of maximum sustainable yield, may imply the reduction or elimination of competitors or predators, by direct killing or habitat modifications. Several state fish and game departments have experimented with predator elimination policies in areas set aside for hunting, so as to increase the survival rate of species favored by hunters. The result may be to increase the resource value of an area (more ducks to kill) without any offsetting resource loss: The game population is maintained at optimal level, and a balance between ducks and food supply is maintained by open seasons, bag limits, licensing, habitat management, and artificial feeding. In this instance the resource value of some species is enhanced by reducing the population of others, perhaps to the point of local extinction.

Fifth, to conserve a species as a resource may be effectively to destroy the qualities for which preservationists (or even some conservationists) value it. Africa's large quadrupeds have considerable value as tourist attractions: Millions of tourists visit many African countries specifically to look at wildlife.[89] Elephants attract flocks of tourists; elephant tusks, hides, and meat are valuable, too. The Kruger National Park, which contains most of South Africa's 7,800 elephants, is described as "rigidly managed," and even has a modern abattoir to process culled animals.

Careful management is necessary to maintain populations within the resources available, to protect herds from poachers, and to ensure that enough animals of impressive size are easily viewed by tourists. At Addo National Park, also in South Africa, about 100 elephants live, protected behind a steel fence. "From slaughter to strict preservation of a tiny fragment—this South African example may foreshadow the future of most of Africa's elephants."[90]

The price of protecting these animals is high. Their nomadic instincts are frustrated and may be bred out eventually; the most aggressive animals, which may damage perimeter fences or attack wardens and tourists, will be culled; surplus baby elephants are sold to circuses and zoos; temporarily sick or disabled animals, which provide an outlet for elephants' altruistic, supportive behavioral needs, will be culled instead of being healed or dying a proper death within their own society. These selective pressures, and the genetic isolation of small populations, will alter the gene pool, probably detrimentally. Something of the *value* of elephants will be lost, precisely *because* the elephants are protected as a resource.

## VI. PROBLEMS FOR THE PRESERVATIONIST

In the previous section I discussed a number of conservationist arguments for species protection: claims that the continued existence of various species is necessary or might be necessary, or at any rate contributes to human welfare. None of them, on its own, justifies a commitment to preserving species as such. It is tempting, though, to conclude that even though each of these arguments has flaws, taken together they are conclusive. This will not do. Michael Scriven, writing about arguments intended to demonstrate the existence of God, refers to an old story about a theologian who said, "None of my arguments is any good by itself, but taken together they constitute an overwhelming proof."[91]

The conservationist, though, may argue that the attack mounted so far is unfair. It is not as if conservationists are arguing for deliberate or casual destruction of species. On the contrary, they urge restraint on the grounds that species represent irreplaceable resources. The variety of benefits which we do, or might expect, to gain from a variety of species, ought to make us hesitate to destroy or threaten any species unless there is some clear and considerable benefit which could not be gained by any less destructive means. Our knowledge of animal behavior, genetics, and ecology is still very incomplete; we should proceed with caution.

The preservationist critique advanced in the previous section was largely negative: It was intended to cast doubt on the claim that conservationist arguments, *taken together*, provide a sound case for species protection. I do not doubt that in many cases the two approaches will yield similar practical conclusions, even though for quite different reasons. It is in those cases where no conceivable use can be imagined for a species that the two approaches will yield differing conclusions. A good example is the case of species whose existence is actually harmful to human interests, and it is to this problem that we now turn.

## §28  HARMFUL SPECIES

Some species are, or may be useful; many are almost certainly not. Worse, some species have a *negative* value for humans. If the *only* value of a species is as a resource, then "harmful" species presumably can be exterminated with a clear conscience. Such cases pose difficulties for the preservationist who advocates the protection of *all* species. The smallpox virus (*Poxvirus variolae*) is probably extinct "in the wild," thanks to a systematic vaccination campaign by the World Health Organization. British microbiologist Bernard Dixon[92] notes that "this is the first time in history when man has been able to obliterate—for all time and by conscious, rational choice—a particular form of life," and he asks, "Should the WHO be applauded for pioneering this new form of genocide? or is there a call for the preservationists to call a halt?" Dixon goes on to argue that the virus should indeed be preserved, both because knowledge of it might be useful in fighting related diseases, and because of its potential use in genetic engineering. But these are arguments for protecting it only in laboratories: The virologists who wish to maintain it do not wish to preserve it in its ecological role, presumably. The risks of maintaining the species are enormous, since fairly soon there will be no natural or acquired immunity in the human population; an accidental or deliberate release could cause millions of deaths.[93]

There are less dramatic "problem species," including agricultural and other "pests": fruit flies, boll weevils, fire ants, rats, mice, silverfish, and termites, for instance. These species have a wider ecological role than disease organisms, whose only function appears to be to keep down the human population by (presumably) unacceptable deaths. There are also behavioral and technological solutions to prevent "pests" from seriously harming human interests while not threatening populations in areas where they do *not* harm human interests. The preservationist will be prepared to pay the price of such measures, even though extermination might be cheaper; the conservationist will not. More importantly, the preservationist seems to be committed to accepting some human deaths as the price to be paid for saving species. University of Wisconsin environmental philosopher J. Baird Callicott refers to Edward Abbey's statement that he would sooner shoot a man than a snake; while not going so far himself, Callicott writes that "the preciousness of individual [animals] . . . is inversely proportional to the population of the species" and at least implies his agreement with the view that "the human population has become so disproportionate from the biological point of view that if one had to choose between a specimen of *Homo sapiens* and a specimen of a rare even if unattractive species, the choice would be moot."[94]

The adoption of a view such as Callicott's requires a revolution in our ethical thinking, and probably a much wider conceptual revision. The conservationist, in contrast, can appeal to concepts of the place of humans in nature and the value of human life which are familiar to and accepted by most people. To make a general case for the preservation of all species as such, therefore, presents a considerable challenge—especially when the existence of the species in question threatens the existence of some humans.

## §29 FUTURE GENERATIONS

The conservationist case has a further dimension which I have not yet considered: that we are not (presumably) the last generation of humans. Even if we do not perceive a species as a valuable resource, it may be that future generations will, and it might be thought that we ought not to cut off the option of enjoying or utilizing a species merely because we happen not to value it. This argument appeals to a duty to conserve resources of all kinds for future generations, which in turn is part of a generally accepted duty to make some sacrifices of present enjoyment for the sake of benefits to future generations.

Accepting, for argument's sake, that these duties should be taken seriously, the conservationist could argue that we ought not to deny future generations the use of species for which we have no use at present. Indeed, perhaps we ought even to consider the possibility that *they* might be preservationists, who will place inherent value on all species! This argument appears to reduce the practical differences between the two positions to zero. In fact, it is seriously deficient, for three reasons.

First, it requires us to speculate about the wants, needs, and values of future generations but provides no basis for such speculation. We cannot *know* everything they will value, and, like us, they will have to choose from what is available.

Second, the conservationist will certainly support policies designed to protect species with a view to the needs of future generations, unless strong reasons to the contrary are presented, because conservation implies the saving of resources, even potential resources. But in some cases there may be good, perhaps overwhelming reasons for proceeding with developments which destroy the habitats of rare species, precisely in order to provide benefits for future generations. For example, our duty to provide energy or materials for future generations may require us to begin today projects which will not yield benefits for decades, such as forestry planting. Some developments of this sort may destroy the habitats of endangered species.

Third, our obligations to the future do not automatically override our other obligations. We also have duties to our contemporaries, and in carrying them out we may sometimes be using up resources and thereby denying the benefits to future generations. The nature and scope of our obligations to the future, then, pose difficulties for both the conservationist and the preservationist: for the former, because it is not easy to decide which resources should be used now and which saved for the future; for the latter, because failure to proceed with developments may harm the interests of future as well as present generations. Once again, the preservationist may be forced to accept a considerable loss to humans as the price to be paid for protecting species.

## §30 BEYOND SPECIES PROTECTION

So far I have mostly been considering species as isolated units, whose claims to protection must be based on their own properties. The value and interest of many species has often been conceived in this way. Old-fashioned zoos exhibited separate animals in cages for people to look at. Biology has studied the physiology, morphology, and (more recently) behavior of species in isolation. Propaganda for species protection focuses on individual species, often spectacular or beautiful ones such as tigers, bald eagles, or giant panda. Legislation is often species oriented: Most countries have their lists of species which it is forbidden to harm.

I suggest that a better way to approach the problem is to focus on the protection of ecosystems. This approach is not an original one, of course, and is behind the creation of many national parks, reserves, and protected habitats around the world. The topics of wilderness preservation and environmental law are covered elsewhere in this volume, so I shall make only brief comments.[95]

The following five considerations may be urged in favor of the protection of large areas of land and thus of protecting species. First, natural systems are interrelated—or rather, there are not separate systems. Ecological areas overlap; they gradually merge into each other; what happens in one part affects what happens elsewhere. The smaller and more isolated the areas which are protected in their natural state, the more tenuous become the global ecological links which serve to maintain the whole biosphere. Massive ecological collapse could mean the end of the human race; therefore we should preserve large, diverse ecosystems around the world.

Second, the protection of ecosystems provides hope for saving more species. Many species do not breed or even survive in captivity; some need huge tracts of land to migrate, to engage in display fights as an essential precondition of mating, or just to achieve psychological health. No animals are indefinitely adaptable: Rare ones are (tautologously) relatively nonadaptable.

Third, to attempt to save a species in captivity is justified, generally, only on the grounds that the eventual intention is to release it back into the wild. For various reasons, this is not always possible.[96] Most species behave differently in captivity than in the wild, and some captive populations undergo genetic changes in response to the special conditions of captivity (see §27). The "saved" species may turn out to be different than the one with which one started. There is already some evidence of significant genetic change among captive lion populations, for example. Moreover, captive animals often develop behavior traits which make their survival in the wild unlikely. If an animal is exterminated in one area, other species will often fill the vacant niche thus created. The reintroduced species may find, therefore, that it has nowhere to go; in any case, during its absence a new ecological balance may have been struck which the reintroduction will upset.

Fourth, most of the benefits from the protection of individual species can also be gained from ecosystem protection. The charm, aesthetic appeal, and scientific interest of animals and plants is as great or greater in natural systems than in zoos, parks, or small reserves. The dynamics of population change, interspecific competition, and the like can often be observed and understood only in large areas. Genetic variation and natural hybridization are protected in the wild, with the added advantage that nature both provides the product and tests it. Recreational hunting and fishing are (or ought to be) more satisfying, because it is more challenging, when the quarry is wild animals and birds living in a natural environment than in a carefully managed state park.

Finally, to adopt an ecological approach is to avoid the difficulties of trying to justify the protection of uninteresting, ugly, inedible, useless, or dangerous species. Almost all species play an important role in their environment. There may be some exceptions: Orchids and other aerophytic plants seem to interact very little with the rest of their environment; but it would be rash to conclude that therefore we may safely remove such species.

None of these arguments is meant to imply that the entire earth should be restored to wilderness (which may be a conceptual or at least practical impossibility). It is meant to show that many of the human interests in protecting species can be met best by preserving large natural areas. The interests of many animals themselves will also be protected too, of course. I have had little to say on this subject since, along with many supporters of an enhanced moral status for animals (see §19), I do not believe that a commitment to animal liberation or animal rights has much relevance to the protection of species as such. Wilderness preservation, in any case, does not imply that we should cease to exploit individual animals for food, or in other ways.

I have argued that the best way to justify species protection, and the best way to do it, is to protect large natural areas. There are benefits to humans and to animals (and plants, if one can benefit plants) from adopting protectionist policies. I cannot here present a full case for protecting large natural areas, which is not in any case the subject of this essay. But I am sure that it is a great deal easier to justify the protection of large areas of Amazon rain forest, Sonoran desert, or coastal marshland than it is to defend measures to protect each of the varieties of plants and animals inhabiting these areas. It is certainly easier to defend the maintenance of environmental quality globally than to provide separate arguments for saving each of the 5 or more million species which live here.

## VII.  CONCLUSION

The claim, commonly made, that species as such possess inherent value, in virtue of which they ought to be protected, has been examined from a number of perspectives. In this final section I summarize these perspectives and their practical implications for species protection.

1. The *consequentialist*, committed to the view that the right act is the one with the best results, cannot consistently regard the protection of species as such as an obligation. Most consequentialists, being humanistic (or anthropocentric) utilitarians, believe that the right action in any situation is the one which produces the highest net balance of human happiness. They value the nonhuman world only as a resource; to the extent that they take the long view, they support conservationist policies. Non-anthropocentric utilitarians, such as Singer, insist that the interests of nonhuman animals in avoiding suffering must be taken into account equally with the similar interests of humans. They deplore the extermination of a species, therefore, only to the extent that avoidable suffering is caused, or happiness avoidably lost, regardless of the species of the being whose interests are affected. The interest of a member of an endangered species in avoiding suffering is no greater than that of a common one, so that it is no worse to cause a given degree of harm to the latter than to the former.

The indirect effects of exterminating a species must be taken into account as well, because the loss of one species may harm other species on which it depends, but in the case of very rare species these effects will be negligible. Plants cannot be harmed, since they are nonsentient; their value is only as a resource for sentient beings. Very rare plants, again, are not essential to the well-being of any sentient beings.

Finally, utilitarians value the total utility of a system. The extermination of a species (especially if carried out painlessly) could be an obligation, if as a result the greatest net utility could be achieved. The destruction of an entire ecosystem, and its replacement by something else, could be justified on utilitarian grounds: For example, if all life in an area of the Lower Sonoran desert in the Southwestern United States could be destroyed instantly without any suffering, and the desert somehow turned into woodland, the result would be a net gain in utility, with many more sentient beings thriving than formerly. The loss of several species of plants and invertebrates would not matter to the utilitarian, since no suffering was caused. Utilitarians, then, are committed to ecosystem protection only to the extent that protectionist policies yield the highest net level of utility.

2. The proponent of the *rights* view likewise does not regard the protection of species as such as an obligation. Regan argues that, special considerations aside, it is wrong to kill or injure an animal because to harm an animal is unjustly to harm its interests. The rights view deplores the extermination of a species, therefore, only to the extent that the interests of individual animals are unjustly harmed, regardless of the species of the being whose interests are affected. The interests of a member of an endangered species are entitled to equal consideration with those of a common one, so that it is no worse to cause a given degree of harm to the latter than to the former.

The rights view likewise takes into account the indirect effects of exterminating a species, but again the effects of exterminating a very rare species will be negligible. The remarks made about utilitarians' attitude to plant species apply equally to the rights view. The two views differ, though, in a very important respect: The rights view does not require— indeed, does not permit—the sacrifice of some animals in order to provide a net overall benefit. To replace an indigenous species with an introduced species is wrong, in the rights view, because it unjustly violates the rights of the members of the indigenous species; that the replacement would result in a net gain in utility does not justify the injustice. The proponent of the rights view has a stronger reason for preserving ecosystems, therefore. Another practical difference stems from the fact that the rights view appears to recognize a wider range of interests. The utilitarian recognizes but one interest of sentient beings, the interest in avoiding suffering. To kill an animal painlessly and replace it with another which will enjoy the same level of utility is not wrong, therefore; nor is it wrong to domesticate, selectively breed, or otherwise transform an animal even if as a result a species is effectively exterminated. If, as Regan argues, all animals have a right to live their own proper lives, then to distort an animal's behavior, and perhaps also to interfere deliberately with its natural breeding patterns, would be wrong.

Singer's and Regan's theoretical positions have in common a concern for the interests of individuals: The basis for both positions is a claim about the wrongfulness of harming animals by violating their individual interests. In this respect their positions differ from both the preservationist and the holistic positions. In practice, the rights view, because it requires respect for the rights of individual animals, will lead to the preservation of many species and of ecosystems, even in the case of very rare species. The rights theory, however, does not require us to make efforts to save endangered species *as such*, for example, whooping cranes and California condors, though it does require us not to harm individuals, and the use of massive resources to save an endangered species might even be considered wrong in the rights theory if, for example, resources were thereby diverted away from measures which would protect from harm larger numbers of common species. Finally, an ecosystem containing no sentient beings at all would not contain any beings with interests. The rights view could not explain why it would be wrong, by appeal to the notions of rights and justice, to destroy an ecosystem which included only plants and very primitive nonsentient animals, even if the species were unique to that area.

3. The *preservationist* values the existence of species, perhaps of all natural kinds, for their own sake. Despite my evident preservationist sympathies, I must concede that there are various objections to this position. It seems impossible to provide *reasons* for valuing natural kinds. It seems to me that the world would be a worse place if we were to lose the tiger, the bald eagle, or the various species of whale, but I do not know how to justify this view to someone who disagrees. Preservationists also have difficulties in the case of species which are harmful to human interests, and there are further problems regarding our obligations to future generations.

Preservationists are quite clear on one point—that it is always wrong to exterminate any species—and, in my view, are also committed to positive measures to rescue species which, through human action, have become endangered. That a species is very rare, that its members are nonsentient, or that it is ecologically insignificant, are not relevant considerations. Where a species is becoming extinct naturally, the preservationist would probably have to permit it to die out, since the characteristics which make it unable to adapt to, say, climatic change are, after all, *its* characteristics. The preservationist values each species as it is, and presumably what it is includes its evolutionary potential—even if its future is to become extinct.

4. Finally, the *ecological* or *holistic* perspective yields the same practical conclusion as the preservationist—that no species should be exterminated—but for different reasons. An ecosystem is not a collection of individuals or of natural kinds, a series of parts forming a whole, or a number of living beings in a place. It *is* a whole, and to ask whether the beings, processes, and interactions which comprise it are good and merit protection is to miss the point. We should preserve ecosystems because

they are good, if anything is, and therefore we should not exterminate or threaten species, because we might thereby threaten ecosystems. It would be misleading, then, to say that an ecological ethic provides a reason for valuing species *as such*.

In practice, the preservationist and holistic positions yield similar conclusions, because to preserve an ecosystem is, necessarily, to preserve the species which partially comprise it, while on the other hand the best — often the only — way to perserve a species is to preserve its habitat. This does not mean that every ecosystem must be preserved. It does mean, at the very least, that representatives of every type of ecosystem must be given protection.

# NOTES

1.  There are few estimates of the total number of species since life began. G. C. Simpson, in "How Many Species?" *Evolution* 6 (1952): 342, estimates 500 million while Norman Myers, *The Sinking Ark* (New York: Pergamon Press, 1979), 29, suggests a range of 100–250 million.
2.  R. M. Lockley, *New Zealand Endangered Species* (Auckland, N.Z.: Cassell N.Z. Ltd., 1980), 112.
3.  Myers, *Sinking Ark*, 14–15.
4.  They may be mere color variations: M. D. F. Urvardy, *The Audubon Society Field Guide to North American Birds—Western Region* (New York: Alfred A. Knopf, 1977), 643.
5.  IUCN, *Red Data Book* (Morges, Switzerland: IUCN, 1966, 1972–78).
6.  James Fisher et al., *The Red Book: Wildlife in Danger* (London: Collins, 1969), 12. This book (hereafter cited as *Wildlife in Danger*) was also prepared under IUCN auspices.
7.  See G. Uetz and D. L. Johnson, "Breaking the Web," *Environment* 16 (1974): 31–39; Paul Martin, "The Discovery of America," *Science* 179 (March 9, 1973): 969–974.
8.  The figures that follow are taken from *Wildlife in Danger*, 15.
9.  *N.Z. Endangered Species*, 112.
10. *Wildlife in Danger*, 11.
11. "Breaking the Web," 35.
12. *Sinking Ark*, 21–24.
13. Myers, *Sinking Ark*, quoted in *Environmental Quality 1980: 11th Annual Report of the Council on Environmental Quality* (Washington, D.C.: U.S. Government Printing Office, 1980): 54.
14. *Sinking Ark*, 18.
15. Fergus Clunie (Director, Fiji Museum), personal communication.
16. "Breaking the Web," 32.
17. G. Meadows, "Mammoth Task Saving Species," *N.Z. Herald*, March 12, 1980.
18. *Environmental Quality*, 6th (1975) and 11th (1980) Annual Reports. The second figure is taken from *Sinking Ark*, 5.
19. W. G. Conway, "The Consumption of Wildlife by Man," *Animal Kingdom*, June 1968, reprinted in W. Anderson (ed.), *Politics and Environment* (Pacific Palisades, Calif.: Goodyear Pub. Co., 1975), 116–7.
20. See "Breaking the Web," 37–38.
21. Yelena Presnyakova, Novosti Press Agency syndicated feature 1981.

22. The study, which was carried out for the U.S. Fish and Wildlife Service 1977–79, was based on 3,107 interviews, and is reported in the Service's *Endangered Species Technical Bulletin* 5 (January 1980), 9.

23. See Ethelwynn Trewavas, "Freshwater Fishes of Africa," in *Wildlife in Danger*, 344–50. The author asserts that "conservation of a species cannot be given priority over maintenance of a fishery in such an area of expanding population."

24. *N.Z. Endangered Species*, 104–105.

25. *Sinking Ark*, 219–220.

26. David C. Phillips, Friends of the Earth, letter to *New Scientist*, March 12, 1981: 701.

27. *Greenpeace News* (N.Z.) 23 (Winter 1982).

28. The Rare Breeds Survival Trust, of Kenilworth, England, which deals with domestic breeds rather than wild animals, is active in these areas.

29. *New Scientist*, May 7, 1981: 336.

30. A good discussion of ethical issues in this field is found in Stephen P. Stich, "Genetic Engineering: Should Science Be Controlled?" in Tom Regan and Donald VanDeVeer (eds.), *And Justice For All* (Totowa, N.J.: Rowman and Littlefield, 1982), 86–115.

31. See James A. Kushlan, "Reintroduction of Indigenous Species to Natural Ecosystems," *Environmental Management* 4 (1980): 93–94.

32. Robert Elliott, "Faking Nature," *Inquiry* 25 (1982): 81–93. The quotation is from p. 85.

33. Jefferson, Inaugural Address (1801), as quoted in Roderick Nash, *Wilderness and the American Mind* (New Haven: Yale University Press, 1967).

34. John Passmore, *Man's Responsibility for Nature* (London: Duckworth, 1974), 73.

35. *Wildlife in Danger*, 19.

36. The annual "harvest" in North Carolina alone is around 3 million, according to an article in *Wildlife in Carolina* 42 (August 1978): 20.

37. Information on crocodiles from *Red Data Book*, Philippines Bureau of Animal Industry; and Rupert Grey, "Shed No More Crocodile Tears," *New Scientist*, October 19, 1981: 328.

38. Passmore, *Man's Responsibility*, 73.

39. Passmore, *Man's Responsibility*, 74.

40. "Consumption of Wildlife," 119 (see note 19).

41. Paul and Anne Ehrlich, *Extinction* (New York: Random House, 1981), 48.

42. Romain Gary, in Time-Life, *Vanishing Species* (New York: Time-Life Inc., 1974), 15.

43. Tom Regan, *The Case for Animal Rights* (Berkeley: University of California Press, 1983).

44. See Samuel P. Hays, *Conservation and the Gospel of Efficiency* (Cambridge, Mass.: Harvard University Press, 1975). The quotations from Muir and Pinchot below are taken from pp. 41–2, 193–4.

45. John Stuart Mill, *Utilitarianism* (1863, numerous editions), Chap. 2.

46. Nicholas Rescher, *Unpopular Essays on Technological Progress* (Pittsburgh: University of Pittsburgh Press, 1980), 79.

47. Richard Routley, "Is There a Need for a New, an Environmental Ethic?" *Proceedings, 15th World Congress of Philosophy* I (1973): 205–210.

48. The term was coined by Richard Ryder: *Speciesism: the Ethics of Vivisection* (Edinburgh: Scottish Society for the Prevention of Vivisection, 1974).

49. Peter Singer, *Animal Liberation* (New York: Avon Books, 1978), 7.

50. Peter Singer, personal communication.

51. See my "Why Should We Care About Rare Species?" *Environmental Ethics* 2 (1980): 17–37, and "Traditional Ethics and the Moral Status of Animals," *Environmental Ethics* 5 (1983).

52. Regan, *The Case for Animal Rights*, 7.8. The quotation in the second paragraph below is from 9.1.

53. *Animal Rights*, 9.3.

54. For example the plant discussed at note 75 below.

55. Joel Feinberg, "The Rights of Animals and Unborn Generations," in William T. Blackstone, ed., *Philosophy and Environmental Crisis* (Athens: University of Georgia Press, 1974).

56. Christopher D. Stone, *Should Trees Have Standing?* (Los Altos, Calif.: William Kaufman, 1974).

57. For a more detailed discussion see my "Why Should We Care About Rare Species?"

58. See Lily-Marlene Russow, "Why Do Species Matter?" *Environmental Ethics* 3 (1981): 101–112.

59. See John Kaufman, "Soaring Free Again," *National Wildlife* 14 (1976): 4–11; Donna Finley, "The Incredible Peregrine—On the Rebound?," *Endangered Species Technical Bulletin* 5 (August 1980): 7–9, 16.

60. See note 46.

61. Ehrenfeld notes "the danger of assuming, with an air of infallibility, that one knows what the ecological effects of game ranching will be. This again is a manifestation of the arrogance of humanism: if the animals are to be considered resources and worthy of being saved, they must be available for exploitation." *Arrogance of Humanism* (New York: Oxford University Press, 1978), 197–198.

62. F. Nigel Hepper, "The Conservation of Rare and Vanishing Species of Plants," *Wildlife in Danger*, 354.

63. Myers, *Sinking Ark*, 68–72.

64. See P. R. Mooney, *Seeds of the Earth* (Ottawa: Canadian Council for International Cooperation, 1979). Gene banks have serious disadvantages however: Myers, *Sinking Ark*, 220–221.

65. See Sylvia K. Sikes, *The Natural History of the African Elephant* (London: Weidenfeld and Nicholson, 1971).

66. Freshwater aquaculture provides about 40% of the fish harvest in those nations: D. N. Lapedes, ed., *McGraw-Hill Encyclopedia of Food, Agriculture and Nutrition* (New York: McGraw-Hill, 1977).

67. Frederick Pohl and Cyril Kornbluth, *The Space Merchants* (New York: Ballantine, 1953).

68. Bryan G. Norton, "Endangered Species: Why Save Them?" (unpublished manuscript, Center for Philosophy and Public Policy, University of Maryland, September 1981), 8.

69. "Endangered Species: New Challenge for the Navajo," *Endangered Species Technical Bulletin* 4 (January 1979): 7–11.

70. David W. Ehrenfeld, "The Conservation of Non-Resources," *American Scientist* 64 (1976): 651.

71. Garrett Hardin, "Why Plant a Redwood Tree?," in G. Tyler Miller, Jr., ed., *Living in the Environment* (Belmont, Calif.: Wadsworth, 1975), 154.

72. Editorial, *Oceans* 12 (September 1979): 8.

73. Elliott, *Faking Nature* (see note 32).

74. Russow, "Why Do Species Matter?": 109.

75. *Endangered Species Technical Bulletin* 5 (August 1980): 2.

76. Robert Elliott, "Why Preserve Species?" in Don Mannison et al., *Environmental Philosophy* (Canberra, Australia: Australian National University, 1980): 12–13.

77. Hepper, "Conservation of Plants": 357.

78. A. Belsey, "The Moral Responsibility of the Scientist," *Philosophy* 53 (1978): 113–118.

79. For a lengthy account of many grisly and apparently pointless experiments on animals see Singer, *Animal Liberation*, Ch. 2.

80.    Scientists in the People's Republic of China are reported to be studying the behavior of animals as a method of earthquake prediction.

81.    "Why Do Species Matter?": 107.

82.    William Ramsay, "Priorities in Species Preservation," *Environmental Affairs* 5 (1976):615.

83.    Russow, "Why Do Species Matter?": 107.

84.    David Ehrenfeld, *The Arrogance of Humanism* (New York: Oxford University Press, 1978):177 (emphasis in original).

85.    Aldo Leopold, "The Land Ethic," in *A Sand County Almanac* (New York: Oxford University Press, 1949):201–226.

86.    Peter Steinhart, "Those Endangered Species: What Good Are They?" *Los Angeles Times*, July 2, 1978.

87.    Other than non-speciesists such as Peter Singer.

88.    Lockley, *N.Z. Endangered Species*: 101.

89.    The value to tourism of one lion in Kenya has been estimated at $7¾ million over its lifetime; in contrast, a hunter would pay only $8,500 for a license to kill it. Norman Myers, "Roaring Success," *New Scientist*, March 12, 1981: 697.

90.    Oria Douglas-Hamilton, "Africa's Elephants: Can They Survive?" *National Geographic* 158 (November 1980):590–591.

91.    Michael Scriven, *Primary Philosophy* (New York: McGraw-Hill, 1966): 107.

92.    Bernard Dixon, "Smallpox—Imminent Extinction and an Unresolved Dilemma," *New Scientist*, February 27, 1976: 430–432.

93.    A worker in a British medical school died in 1978 of infection from smallpox virus being studied elsewhere in the school. See Lawrence McGinty, "Smallpox Laboratories, What Are the Risks?" *New Scientist*, January 4, 1979: 8–14.

94.    J. Baird Callicott, "Animal Liberation: A Triangular Affair," *Environmental Ethics* 2 (1980):326. The reference is to Abbey's *Desert Solitaire* (New York: Ballantine Books, 1980):20.

95.    The protection of environmental wholes needs to be justified, in my view, as part of an ecological or holistic ethic. It is obviously beyond the scope of this essay to deal with such a large question. An ecological ethic would certainly value wholes rather than individuals or species. See my "Traditional Ethics and the Moral Status of Animals," *Environmental Ethics* 5 (1983) and Callicott, "Animal Liberation."

96.    See note 31.

# SUGGESTIONS FOR FURTHER READING

*Parts I–II (General):*

There are many books on rare and endangered species; most are picture books with little information or argument. Two good general works dealing with a range of questions are: Paul and Anne Ehrlich, *Extinction* (New York: Random House, 1981), and Norman Myers, *The Sinking Ark* (New York: Pergamon Press, 1979). Updated reports on the status of endangered species are found in: *Endangered Species Technical Bulletin*, a regular publication of the U.S. Fish and Wildlife Service; *Environmental Quality*, the Annual Report of the U.S. Council on Environmental Quality; *The Red Data Books*, published by the International Union for the Conservation of Nature in Morges, Switzerland.

*Parts III–V—Conservation and Preservation:*

A good historical study of the conflict between conservationists and preservationists in the United States is Samuel P. Hays, *Conservation and the Gospel of Efficiency* (Cambridge, Mass.: Harvard University Press, 1975). There is not a great deal of material by philosophers directly on the conservation/preservation distinction; see John Passmore, *Man's Responsibility for Nature* (London: Duckworth, 1974):73–126. The following material contains useful discussions, mostly from a standpoint hostile to conservation as I have characterized it: William Devall, "Reformist Environmentalism," *Humboldt Journal of Social Relations* 6 (1979):129–157; David Ehrenfeld, "The Conservation of Non-Resources," *American Scientist* 64 (November–December 1976):648–656; David Ehrenfeld, *The Arrogance of Humanism* (New York: Oxford University Press, 1978); A. Naess, "The Shallow and the Deep, Long-Range Ecology Movement," *Inquiry* 16 (1973):95–100; Ernest Partridge, "Sea Otters as a Moral Resource," in "Proceedings, Management of Sea Otters and Shellfish Fisheries in California: Policy Issues and Management Alternatives," University of California, Santa Barbara, 1981; R. and V. Routley, "Human Chauvinism and Environmental Ethics," in D. Mannison et al., eds., *Environmental Philosophy* (Canberra, Australia: Australian National University, 1980):96–189; George Sessions, "Ecological Consciousness and Paradigm Change," in Michael Tobias, ed., *Humanity and Radical Will* (San Diego, Calif.: Avant Books, 1981).

*Parts III–VI—Moral Questions of Species Protection:*

Arguments for species protection are discussed in the books by the Ehrlichs and Myers noted above. The following articles provide detailed discussion of such arguments: Robert Elliot, "Why Preserve Species?" in D. Mannison et al., *Environmental Philosophy* (Canberra, Australia: Australian National University, 1980):8–29; Alastair Gunn, "Why Should We Care About Rare Species?," *Environmental Ethics* 2 (1980):17–37; Edwin Pfister, "Endangered Species: Costs and Benefits," *Environmental Ethics* 1 (1979):341–352; William Ramsay, "Priorities in Species Preservation," *Environmental Affairs* 5 (1976):595–616; Nicholas Rescher, "Why Save Endangered Species?" in his *Unpopular Essays On Technological Progress* (Pittsburgh: University of Pittsburgh Press, 1980):79–92; Lily-Marlene Russow, "Why Do Species Matter?," *Environmental Ethics* 3 (1981):101–112.

# Treating the Dirt: Environmental Ethics and Moral Theory

## EDWARD JOHNSON

《〉》

## I. WHO COUNTS MORALLY?

It is difficult to deny that societies have made some terrible mistakes about who counts morally. Most of us would agree, for example, that treating women, children, or slaves as so much property is morally wrong. The present century has seen the triumph (rhetorically and in principle, if not politically and in practice) of the ideal of "universal" moral franchise: Every human being is supposed to count, to have her or his interests, or rights, given due regard.

Each fresh extension of the moral franchise has seemed to be a confession of earlier moral oversight. If the history of morality is seen as the story of an "expanding circle," it is inevitable that philosophers wonder how far that circle, the "moral community," can extend. After pioneer English feminist Mary Wollstonecraft published her *Vindication of the Rights of Woman* in 1792, her countryman Thomas Taylor wrote a satirical reply, entitled *Vindication of the Rights of Brutes*, in which he announced, tongue in cheek: "There is some reason to hope that this essay will soon be followed by treatises on the rights of vegetables and minerals, and that thus the doctrine of perfect equality will become universal." Taylor meant to ridicule Wollstonecraft's argument that women have rights by suggesting that similar arguments would lead to the absurd conclusion that rights are possessed by brute animals—indeed, even by clods of dirt! But one age's satire is another's cliche. Pursuit of the belief that no human should be treated like dirt has led us to reconsider how we should treat the dirt.

What sorts of creatures count, morally? We answer this question by our actions every day, though we perhaps only rarely consider it explicitly. Here is an example. In January 1974, a schooner sank off the eastern coast of the United States. The captain, his wife, their 80-pound Labrador retriever, and an injured crewman occupied a lifeboat to which two youths, aged nineteen and twenty, as well as a forty-seven-year-old Navy veteran, tied themselves with ropes while floating in the freezing waters. The captain refused repeated requests by the swimmers that he throw the dog overboard to make room for (some of) those in the water. He later explained that he could not bear to do it. After nine hours, the youths perished from exposure and the veteran struggled aboard. (Why not earlier?) All the occupants of the lifeboat, dog included, were subsequently rescued. After an initial investigation, the Coast Guard recommended that no criminal action be brought. However, in May 1975, the captain was indicted in a federal court for manslaughter, for refusing to eject his dog in lieu of (some of) the swimmers who died.[1]

What sort of moral consideration do we owe the dog in such a tragic case? If the passengers had drowned because the lifeboat space was preempted by the captain's *wardrobe*, we would feel pretty clearly that this was unjustified, a preference of property to people. But a *dog*? Can a dog count morally, count directly, for its own sake, rather than because of some human's interest in it? This is the problem of moral patiency. *Moral patients* are those beings who are members of the moral community, who deserve, or are owed, direct moral consideration.[2] On lifeboat Earth, what is cargo and who is passenger? Moral patients are passengers, rather than cargo. But *which* creatures are moral patients?

One popular answer has been that only (and, perhaps, all) *humans* are moral patients, or that humans are specially important moral patients (§1). This answer has appealed to many moral philosophers, who have of course been human themselves. Recently, this view has been powerfully attacked by animal liberationists such as Peter Singer (§2) and Tom Regan (§3). If the inclusion of nonhumans in the moral community is justified, as it seems to be, the question arises whether the moral community can be extended yet further, to include nonsentient environmental objects (such as rocks and trees, rivers and rainbows). According to one theory, all *living* things deserve moral consideration or respect. This view is popularly associated with Albert Schweitzer (§4), but more interesting versions of it have been developed by Paul Taylor (§5) and Kenneth Goodpaster (§6). This extension of the moral community to include all living things is harder to justify than the liberation of animals, but it still seems insufficient to some, who wish to include the land or earth as a whole (§7–8).

## II. SPECIESISM AND ANIMAL LIBERATION

### §1 HUMAN CHAUVINISM

Obviously, we need to be concerned about issues in environmental ethics (such as the destruction of natural habitats) both for our own sake, in the short run, and for the sake of our descendants, in the long run. But are these the only things that need to be taken into account, in our moral reflection, or do nonhuman things count too? Do animals? Do trees, or stones, or "eco-systems"?

The short answer to such questions is to insist that *only* humans count, or that humans count *immeasurably more* than others. Its adherents think of this view as a kind of humanism; its critics call it *human chauvinism* or, more broadly, *speciesism*. Whatever label is preferred, the view implies that nonhumans count for nothing morally, or count for little as compared with humans. This human chauvinism has been by far the dominant view among moral theorists. Often the human species is simply *assumed* to be morally special. My favorite example of this is found in the earnest *Treatise on the Moral Ideals* (1876) by British philosopher John Grote (1813–1866).

> Now we ourselves are the highest and worthiest kind of beings that we know of. It may be difficult, if I am asked to say what highest and worthiest means here, to say it: but I think the proposition is one which every one, whatever his views, would allow in some sense: allowed in this way, the proposition is in a manner a definition of what is meant by high and worthy.[3]

This passage, in effect, merely appeals to the reader's intuition that he, or she, is indeed the "highest" and "worthiest" sort of being *we* know of. But since this claim is made *by* humans and *to* humans, it looks suspiciously self-serving. The sad fact is that, when whites enslaved blacks, many "honestly" thought that slaves were morally inferior to their masters. When males legally enslaved females, many "sincerely" believed that wives were morally inferior to their husbands. But men, talking to men about their inferior women, were wrong: To think otherwise is sexism. And whites, talking to whites about their inferior blacks, were wrong: To think otherwise is racism. Now, what about humans, talking to humans about "the inferior creatures"? Reflection along the lines just sketched leads one to refuse to *assume* that humans must be morally special just because they are human. Are there any *reasons* to believe that humans have such special moral worth? What do *all* and *only* humans have that is morally significant?

Reasons have been offered over the centuries, but none is convincing to an unprejudiced thinker, and most are ridiculously inadequate. Space does not permit detailed discussion of these failures; the last decade has seen the publication of dozens of books and essays about the moral status of animals.[4] This sudden proliferation of arguments, pro and con, bears witness to the fact that the old assumption of human moral superiority can no longer be taken for granted.

Human chauvinism is easy to question if it claims that *all* humans count morally, as well as claiming that *only* humans count. It is easy to question because *species* is the only criterion that will include all humans and exclude all nonhumans; yet discrimination merely on the basis of species seems arbitrary from a moral point of view.

Some human chauvinists, however, are quite prepared to give up the *all humans* clause, so as to keep the *only humans* clause. One can, after all, hold that "marginal" humans (such as the severely mentally retarded) *don't* really count morally, in themselves and for their own sake, directly. It was fear of this possibility that led an early reviewer of Australian moral philosopher Peter Singer's influential book, *Animal Liberation*, to object that

> these kinds of comparisons [between nonhuman animals and "marginal" humans] are not only morally repugnant, but also dangerously irresponsible. They are less likely to extend men's moral sympathies to pigs or rats than to weaken the inhibitions that restrain their behavior toward other human beings.[5]

This kind of criticism can be made of every extension of moral franchise; presumably it cannot be correct in every instance. Insofar as the criticism amounts to the claim that the animal liberation movement is futile, it begs the question politically. Furthermore, it is possible that pigs and rats might *deserve* to be represented in moral deliberation, even if that imposed costs on humans; to dismiss this possibility out of hand is nothing more than the very speciesism that Singer attacks. Despite these weaknesses, however, the criticism nevertheless makes an important point. If consistency requires us to treat beings at the same mental level similarly, as Singer suggests, it still leaves it open whether we should treat beasts better or human retarded worse. This shows that the *negative* arguments of animal liberationists, which question the alleged justification for treating human and nonhuman animals *differently*, are not enough to determine our treatment of nonhumans; we need also to be provided with *positive* reasons to treat nonhumans better than we do, rather than humans worse.

In the case of the nonhuman animals, such reasons have been presented from each of the two leading perspectives in contemporary moral theory—utilitarianism and rights theory; these will be examined in the next two sections (§§2 and 3). In the case of other nonhuman objects —e.g., the "environment"—compelling positive theory is harder to come by, as we shall see in later sections.

## §2 PETER SINGER AND RESPECT FOR INTERESTS

Singer's account of why nonhuman animals count morally is based on his commitment to utilitarian doctrine, according to which what moral agents ought to do is that act which, directly or indirectly, can most reasonably be expected to result in the best consequences (where goodness of consequence is measured by the extent to which satisfaction of preference is maximized, and dissatisfaction minimized). The goal, according to utilitarians, is to achieve, or make likely, the best balance of total (or, perhaps, average) good over bad in the world. We are supposed to take into account *all* interests, regardless of *who* has them. Animals, like humans, have interests and preferences; at least, it is plausible to believe that the animals we commonly exploit and abuse do. Every interest is just what it is, and counts just for its own weight: Whether it is human or not becomes secondary or irrelevant. Singer employs this line of argument with dexterity, candor, and a keen eye for practical implications. However, the argument is, in its theoretical core, traditional utilitarian doctrine.

Early utilitarians such as Jeremy Bentham (1748–1832) insisted that the pleasures and pains of nonhuman animals should be included in the total good to be maximized. The question, says Bentham, "is not, Can they *reason?* nor, Can they *talk?* but, Can they *suffer?*"[6] He rejects the idea that animals are mere things. Nevertheless, Bentham allows that there may be a "difference in point of sensibility" between humans and nonhumans. Bentham's eminent disciple John Stuart Mill (1806–1873) agrees that animals count. Indeed, he is willing to let this matter be a test of the truth of his utilitarian doctrine. "Granted that any practice causes more pain to animals than it gives pleasure to man; is that practice moral or immoral?"[7] It is immoral according to Mill's utilitarianism. Nevertheless, Mill allows that it is "better to be a human being dissatisfied than a pig satisfied."[8] Pleasures alleged to be distinctively human (such as intellectual pleasures) are assumed by Mill to be more important in the utilitarian calculation than nonhuman pleasures.

Singer, in his influential briefs for animal liberation, continues this utilitarian tradition of assertion and qualification. Insofar as animals can suffer equally with humans, they have equal claim to relief, since pain is pain. Nevertheless, Singer allows that "a rejection of speciesism does not imply that all lives are of equal worth."[9] The typical human life is more important than the typical nonhuman life.

> It is not arbitrary to hold that the life of a self-aware being, capable of abstract thought, of planning for the future, of complex acts of communication, and so on, is more valuable than the life of a being without these capacities.[10]

The foundation for such a judgment is obscure. Singer does offer the following argument:

> In general it does seem that the more highly developed the conscious life of the being, the greater the degree of self-awareness and rationality, the more one would prefer that kind of life, if one were choosing between it and a being at a lower level of awareness.[11]

This is, perhaps, not a great advance on John Stuart Mill ranking dissatisfied Socrates above any satisfied pig. But these are difficult issues: Singer faces them candidly and tries to give consistently utilitarian answers. Like notable earlier utilitarians, Singer is led by theoretical reasons to extend moral consideration beyond the limits of the human species. Like them, he allows the conviction, that the *kind* of being we are has moral importance, to elevate most human lives above most nonhuman ones. Like other utilitarians, he is a "sentientist": Only conscious beings count morally.

> Suppose that we apply the test of imagining living the life of the weed I
> am about to pull out of my garden. I then have to imagine living a life
> with no conscious experiences at all. Such a life is a complete blank; I
> would not in the least regret the shortening of this subjectively barren
> form of existence. This test suggests, therefore, that the life of a being
> that has no conscious experiences is of no intrinsic value.[12]

Singer's utilitarian case for animal liberation thus seems to rule out any
*radically* environmental ethics, which would recognize inherent value in
nonsentient environmental objects or systems. The adequacy of utilitarianism as a moral theory is a key issue in contemporary moral philosophy; no proper discussion of that general question is possible here.[13]
The case for animal rights, however, is independent of utilitarianism, as
can be seen from the work of Tom Regan.

## §3 TOM REGAN AND RESPECT FOR INHERENT VALUE

Regan agrees with Singer's practical conclusions about animal liberation,
but disagrees with Singer's theoretical arguments. Regan rejects utilitarianism as inadequate both for humans and for nonhumans. Unlike
Singer, Regan is attracted to the idea that one of the things an acceptable
moral theory must do is to yield results that agree with our considered
judgments or reflective intuitions. Regan starts from the intuition that
"marginal cases," such as humans who are severely mentally enfeebled,
are moral patients, creatures to whom we have direct duties, including
duties not to exploit or abuse them.

Singer is also inclined to offer the argument from marginal cases,[14]
but he and Regan disagree about its full significance. For Singer, the argument often seems to be one whose force is primarily rhetorical. For
Regan, no utilitarian account can do justice to the *depth* of the intuition.

> It is only, I think, if rights are postulated *even* in the case of morons that
> we can give a sufficiently firm theoretical basis for our conviction that it
> is wrong to treat them in the ways in question [that is, to harm them for
> our purposes].[15]

Utilitarians have no choice but to link this intuited wrongness up to bad
consequences; if the consequences were otherwise, the action (exploiting
morons) would not be wrong. But a change in consequences would not
cause us to change our judgment, says Regan, so utilitarianism must be
mistaken.[16]

This disagreement between Regan and Singer involves tough questions about how a moral theory is justified. In order to account for our
feeling that the mentally retarded ought not be exploited, Regan argues,
we need to postulate rights. Utilitarian accounts, he seems to hold, fail
to make the obligation *deep* enough. We need not discuss here whether
utilitarian theorists can give an adequate account of the obligation in
question, since even if they fail, they can still reject the intuition that
there is such an obligation. (If, like Bentham, you consider the concept

of rights to be "nonsense on stilts," then you might regard the alleged fact, that the intuition about morons could only be accounted for by appeal to rights, as a reduction to absurdity.) Singer stands in the classic line of utilitarian thought when he says:

> Our moral convictions are not reliable data for testing ethical theories. We should work from sound theories to practical judgments, not from our judgments to our theories.[17]

The idea, popularized by Harvard philosopher John Rawls, that "testing" goes both ways, is rejected by Singer as a procedure "liable to take relics of our cultural history as the touchstone of morality."[18]

This issue, about the proper role of intuitions in moral theory, is not easy to settle.[19] Elusive as it is, however, it remains a palpable obstacle to settling the debate between Singer and Regan over the adequacy of utilitarianism. This debate obviously affects how plausible appeals to inherent value can be, since, in Regan's view, the attribution of non-utilitarian rights is accounted for by appeal to inherent value. This matter, in turn, will be central to deciding whether environmental ethics is really viable, if, as Regan holds, "the development of what can properly be called an environmental ethic requires that we postulate inherent value in nature."[20]

In order to do justice to our intuition about morons we must, Regan holds, recognize that they have rights, rights grounded in their possession of inherent value. They have inherent value because they "not only are alive but are *subjects* of a life that itself has value (is better or worse) for the individual whose life it is."[21] This subject-of-a-life criterion is offered by Regan as a *sufficient* condition for having inherent value, not a *necessary* condition. This leaves open the possibility that nonconscious beings, environmental objects, could have inherent value.

Is sentience, or consciousness, or awareness necessary for having a sake, a good of one's own? Singer says *yes*: "A stone does not have interests because it cannot suffer. Nothing that we can do to it could possibly make any difference to its welfare."[22] Regan, however, observes: "The reason we cannot make sense of the idea that something might be in a stone's interests is not that it cannot suffer; it is that we cannot form an intelligible conception of what its good could be."[23] A stone may not have a good of its own, but other nonsentient objects do, in a sense. A tree, an engine, even the finish on a table, can each have a good of its own, in the sense that events can be good for it or bad for it, benefit or harm it. It can be a good object *of its kind*, or not so. Nevertheless, in the end this good-of-its-kind argument is not able to constrain action. "Recognizing that something is good of its kind does not call forth my admiring respect," says Regan. "Recognizing its being inherently good does."[24] Therefore, though a tree may have a good of its own, it does not follow that it has inherent value.

To see how serious a problem this is, it is useful to recall the great Good Roots controversy between Prescriptivists and Descriptivists that has raged in meta-ethics for the last quarter century. Prescriptivism's leading theorist, British moral philosopher R. M. Hare, holds that "good" is a general term of commendation and recommendation used to prescribe actions. According to this view, you need criteria in order to call something "good," but you get to choose your own criteria, with no constraint except that you are required to apply your chosen criteria universally and evenhandedly.[25] Descriptivists, such as British philosopher Philippa Foot, argue that "good" has specific senses tied conceptually to specific criteria, which are determined by language, tradition, or something. (This attitude is influenced by Aristotle's use of the concept of *health* as his model for moral concepts: Health is natural, in some sense, and is to a considerable extent fixed for the species.) Foot writes:

> We say, in a straightforward way, that a tree has good roots, meaning by this that they are well suited to the performance of their function, serving the plant by anchoring it and drawing moisture out of the soil. Our interests are not involved, and only someone in the grip of a theory would insist that when we speak of a good root we commit ourselves in some way to choosing a root like that.[26]

We might, after all, have unusual purposes: When we collect tomatoes to throw, we want *rotten* ones, not good ones.

Hare can keep the connection between calling something "good" and valuing it, but only at the cost of giving up almost all constraints on *what* is valued and so called "good." Foot can anchor "good" to specific natural criteria, but only at the cost of being unable to insist that rationality *requires* one to value what is good. Neither of these positions provides what philosphers have dreamt of: a sense of "good" that is tied *both* to specific natural criteria (so that arguments over whether something is good can be rationally settled) *and* to the speaker's motivations and evaluations (so that agreeing that something is good rationally compels one to value it); in sum, a good whose recognition calls forth one's admiring respect.

This distinction between good of its kind and inherent, respect-eliciting good is comparable to the distinction between good *from a point of view* and good *all things considered*.[27] What is good from a point of view is defined in terms of the point of view in question, whereas what is good all things considered is what is good when all points of view have been taken into account. Moral philosophers have long debated whether morality should be seen as one particular point of view (with its distinctive subject matter) or as our judgments *all* things considered (not just those pertaining to a specific subject matter). If morality consists of all-things-considered judgments, then it will be easy to get from the theoretical judgment that *x* is the best action morally (i.e., all things considered) to the practical judgment that *x* is what I ought to do; what I *ought* to do, after all, is what is best all things considered. The problem with this approach is that it is difficult to be specific about *what it is* that is best all things considered. On the other hand, if morality is one particular point of view (contrasted with others: the *legal* point of view, the *aesthetic* point of view, etc.), then it will be easy to say what it is that is best morally, since morality according to this view has a specific subject matter. The problem with this approach is that it becomes difficult to insist convincingly that this specific moral content is really best all things considered.

It has seemed to some philosophers that *having a good of its own* is where the line of moral patiency must be drawn: If a being has no good of its own, then what we do to that being is a matter of indifference—except insofar as the good of some other creature is also involved. In response to this view, some critics urge that nonconscious objects *do* have a good: A tree has a good, an automobile has a good, the finish on a desk, and so on.

I think it must be granted that, as our ordinary-language uncles used to say, it is "correct English" to speak of a tree's *good*, or at least of things being *good or bad for* the tree, as an entity, independent of human purpose. The big question, though, is what conclusions this admission invites. If a tree has a good, does it also have needs? Interests? Wants? *Rights*? Something may be good-of-its-kind without being good in any way that, as Regan puts it, calls forth our respect.

Good-of-its-kind judgments seem to be tied to fairly specific facts about community purposes and judgments. An apple that poisons someone is not *a good apple*, even if it is selected with malice aforethought. But we seem to be under no rational constraint to desire or select only good apples (rather than apples good-for-*our*-purposes). That we can agree that a tree has a good-of-its-kind is not sufficient to compel us rationally to respect that good.

Similarly, it seems possible to determine what is good from any given particular point of view (legal, religious, aesthetic, that of etiquette, etc.), by reference to shared social criteria—after all, our communication with one another seems to require broad agreement on social essentials.[28] But what is to be done all-things-considered (if this judgment actually determines action) seems not reducible to such considerations. The criteria invoked by different points of view clash. Ethics tries to make sense of this clash of criteria.

The foregoing discussion gives some indication, I hope, of how deeply the question of moral patiency is embedded in abstract and difficult issues in moral theory. The word "good," for example, often serves in practice to facilitate a transition in reasoning from the *factual* judgment that a particular thing *is* good-of-its-kind—or has a good (as the kind of thing that it is), or is good judged from a particular point of view—to the *value* judgment (or decision, or commitment) that such a good *ought* to be respected (or admired, or chosen). Scottish philosopher David Hume (1711–1776) famously questioned this apparent gap between claims about descriptive facts (usually expressed by talk about what *is* the case) and normative judgments or decisions (usually expressed by talk about what *ought* to be the case). Regan agrees that "Hume's famous observation in his *Treatise*, about the mystery of the passage from *is* to *ought*, points to one of the fundamental problems that a philosophically sophisticated environmental ethic must address."[29] When Regan says elsewhere that "the development of what can properly be called an environmental ethic requires that we postulate inherent value in nature,"[30] one expects that he believes that postulating inherent value (in humans, nonhumans, or natural objects) would function to license the mysterious passage from *is* to *ought*. Whether—and under what circumstances—it is possible rationally to move from the one to the other is a central issue in recent moral theory, and one whose outcome must closely concern those who wish to demonstrate the need in moral theory for the concept of *inherent value*.

It is difficult to see how we could have a useful notion of inherent value without first solving these traditional problems of moral theory, and that is a large task indeed. On the other hand, it is at least arguable that *some* inherent or intrinsic value *must* be recognized by any cogent moral theory.[31]

Proponents of animal liberation have, to a large extent, been able to proceed without resolution of these theoretical issues. Regan's argument, at least in his early essays, is *conditional*: If humans have rights then (some) nonhumans do too. If human rights recognize the inherent value of humans, then nonhuman rights can recognize the inherent value of nonhumans; talk about "inherent value" is no more questionable in the latter case than in the former.

But how far can such a conditional argument be stretched? The step from human to nonhuman animals seems easy to make because both are conscious individuals. This "atomism" and "sentientism" has been attacked, however, by those who want to attribute inherent value to nonconscious environmental objects, if they are living, or even to the planet as a whole, living or not.

## III. RESPECT FOR LIFE

The idea behind the respect-for-life theories is that something about the nature of *living* organisms requires our respect. That sounds simple enough, but two questions immediately arise. First, what is this requirement based on: What is it about a living organism that demands respect, and why should such a demand apply to us if we just don't care? Second, what does this requirement really require: What does it mean, in practice, to show respect for life?

### §4 ALBERT SCHWEITZER AND REVERENCE FOR LIFE

A very crude version of this sort of theory can be found in Albert Schweitzer's well-known reflections concerning reverence for life.

A man is truly ethical only when he obeys the compulsion to help all life which he is able to assist, and shrinks from injuring anything that lives. He does not ask how far this or that life deserves one's sympathy as being valuable, nor, beyond that, whether and to what degree it is capable of feeling. Life as such is sacred to him.[32]

*Why* should we feel that life is sacred, and *how* does this feeling affect our decisions and actions? Unfortunately, Schweitzer has no satisfactory answer to either question. The *basis* of ethics, for him, lies in mysticism[33]—apparently in a mystical and irrational fellow-feeling that humans have, or are supposed to have, with the will to live in every living organism.[34] Schweitzer does mention some of the *implications* of his ethical view. We are to tear no leaf, pluck no flower, crush no insect. Indeed, we are called upon to carry out little rescue operations for stranded insects.[35] Further reading reveals, however, that Schweitzer is really only concerned to attack "thoughtless" injury to life.[36] If the injury is "necessary" —for what, he does not say—then it is permitted. Schweitzer simply assumes the necessity of experimentation on nonhuman animals. Such experimentation establishes "a new and special relation of solidarity" between these animals and us, which apparently requires us to do good deeds for animals other than those we experiment on. "By helping an insect when it is in difficulties, I am only attempting to cancel part of man's ever new debt to the animal world."[37]

Schweitzer says a good deal more about reverence for life, and his view has been oddly popular (probably because of his image as a saint and sage), but in the end it just doesn't come to much. Its basis is obscure and its implications are useless, at best, and incoherent, at worst. Though Schweitzer seems to say that we are not to rank lives, that is, practically, impossible. As Peter Singer remarks:

> His life as a doctor in Africa makes no sense except on the assumption that the lives of the human beings he was saving are more valuable than the lives of the germs and parasites he was destroying in their bodies, not to mention the plants and probably animals that those humans would kill and eat after Schweitzer had cured them.[38]

The lesson of Schweitzer's failure as an ethical theorist is that, if we try to go beyond sentience to embrace all living things in the moral community, we have some difficult questions to answer. It is worth keeping this lesson in mind as we examine the more interesting respect-for-life ethic being developed by Paul Taylor, a well-known moral theorist who teaches at Brooklyn College of the City University of New York.

## §5 PAUL TAYLOR AND RESPECT FOR NATURE

Taylor believes that "the relevant characteristic for having the status of a moral patient is not the capacity for pleasure or suffering but the fact that the being has a good of its own which can be furthered or damaged by moral agents."[39] Something can have a good of its own, according to Taylor, without being sentient, but not without being animate; trees and flowers are in, rocks and water are out. Moral agents are required to be concerned about the good of sentient creatures—human and nonhuman animals—but also about the good of nonsentient living creatures, that is, plants and various "lower" organisms.

To pass from speciesism to sentientism, we must take seriously the possibility that it may be necessary to sacrifice the good of humans to the good of nonhumans. Similarly, according to Taylor, to move beyond sentientism we must take seriously the possibility that it may be necessary to sacrifice the good of sentient animals to the good of nonsentient creatures, such as plants.

> The conscious suffering of a sentient creature is indeed intrinsically bad from that creature's standpoint . . . But cannot that intrinsic evil be outweighed by consideration for the creature's overall well-being? And if so, why may it not be outweighed by consideration for another creature's well-being, even if it is not sentient?[40]

The natural answer would be that the sentient creature *cares* whether its good is sacrificed, while the living-but-nonsentient creature doesn't. This answer, and the controversy surrounding it, leads us to the heart of the issue. Living organisms certainly have a good, can be benefited and harmed, have interests (in a suitably broad sense of "interests"), and so on. The same may be true for inanimate things. But does morality require us to pursue a creature's good, if that creature does not *care* about its good? This question is not easy to answer. Sentientists, such as Peter Singer, say *no*: The creature must care, or at least be able to care. Anti-sentientists say *yes*: Caring is not what is at issue. Those anti-sentientists who, like Taylor, emphasize respect for life appeal to a natural goal-seeking ability in living organisms. This goal-seeking, or teleological, character is manifested in the way animals and plants seek out certain elements of their environment and turn away from other elements, as when a dog pulls its paw from the fire or a plant turns toward the sun. Taylor says that

> a teleological center of life is an entity whose "world" can be viewed from the perspective of *its* life . . . [W]e can conceive of a teleological center of life as a being whose standpoint we can take in making judgments about what events in the world are good or evil, desirable or undesirable . . . [T]he entity itself need not have any (conscious) *interest* in what is happening to it for such judgments to be meaningful and true . . . But conscious or not, all are equally teleological centers of life in the sense that each is a unified system of goal-oriented activities directed toward their preservation and well-being.[41]

Taylor's emphasis on natural teleology has important consequences. One consequence is that it provides, he thinks, a foothold for moral obligation:

> We begin to look at other species as we look at ourselves, seeing them as beings which have a good they are striving to realize just as we have a good we are striving to realize. We accordingly develop the disposition to view the world from the standpoint of their good as well as from the standpoint of our own good.[42]

Once we see clearly that human claims to moral superiority are groundless, Taylor thinks, we will be inclined to adopt a doctrine of species impartiality.

> One who accepts that doctrine regards all living things as possessing inherent worth—the *same* inherent worth, since no one species has been shown to be either 'higher' or 'lower' than any other . . . Once we reject the claim that humans are superior either in merit or in worth to other living things, we are ready to adopt the attitude of respect.[43]

Once we adopt what Taylor calls the "biocentric outlook" on nature, and realize that humans, animals, and plants are all members of "the Earth's community of life," we will recognize "the attitude of respect to be the only *suitable* or *fitting* attitude to take toward all wild forms of life."[44] Having adopted this attitude of respect, we will see living entities as possessing "inherent worth" and will place "intrinsic value on the promotion and protection of their good."[45] This will lead to a moral commitment to certain rules of duty and standards of character, which in turn will affect how we treat living entities.

What is the theoretical basis of this view, and what are its practical implications? If the basis of Taylor's view is less obscure than Schweitzer's mysticism, that is partly because Taylor is willing to settle for less. The attitude of respect for nature, like that of respect for persons, is, he thinks, an ultimate attitude. There are "two senses in which an attitude can be justified: showing that it is *not unjustified* for anyone to take it, and showing that it is *unjustified* for anyone *not* to take it."[46] Taylor thinks that the former can be done for the ultimate attitude of respect, but not the latter, because an ultimate attitude involves "commitment to certain normative principles" but does not involve "a statement of fact whose truth or falsity can be ascertained by some kind of empirical test."[47] Thus, the attitude of respect for nature is said to be "suitable" or "fitting," and we are told that

> the biocentric outlook recommends itself as an acceptable system of concepts and beliefs to anyone who is clearminded, unbiased, and factually enlightened, and who has a developed capacity of reality awareness with regard to the lives of individual organisms. This, I submit, is as good a reason for making the moral commitment involved in adopting the attitude of respect for nature as any theory of environmental ethics could possibly have.[48]

Maybe. But is that good enough? The importance of this question is heightened by the fact that the practical implications of respect for nature are unclear. Taylor is not unaware of the problem. He asks:

> If we accept the biocentric outlook and accordingly adopt the attitude of respect for nature as our ultimate moral attitude, how do we resolve conflicts that arise from our respect for persons in the domain of human ethics and our respect for nature in the domain of environmental ethics?[49]

The question is acute, but Taylor does not answer it. Perhaps we may hope for an answer in the future. In the meantime, the practical implications of Taylor's view are obscure, since conflicts between persons and nature seem unavoidable. Shall we save the snail darter, or build the dam? Shall we preserve wilderness, or drill for oil? To resolve such practical disputes, we need to know when respect for persons is more important than respect for nature. Does it really make sense to attribute *equal* inherent worth to *all* living creatures, as Taylor does?[50] Peter Miller, of the University of Winnipeg, objects to Taylor's view on the ground that

> there is little room for ambivalence, it would seem, if an individual human life weighs in no more heavily than any of the myriad its existence causes to terminate. I am not sure what keeps him [i.e., Taylor] from advocating human genocide as the moral policy that, on balance, best respects living nature.[51]

Though some thinkers *have* advocated human genocide,[52] what keeps Taylor from agreeing with them is presumably his commitment to the attitude of respect for persons. But if we have more than one ultimate principle, and these cannot be ranked or reduced one to another, then is it possible to avoid ultimate incoherence?[53] Should we not attempt to abandon one of these incompatible ultimate attitudes? It is not hard to guess which one would go.

## §6 KENNETH GOODPASTER AND RESPECT FOR SELF-SUSTAINING ORGANIZATION

Kenneth Goodpaster, of the Harvard Business School, has also defended a version of respect for life. Rejecting both forms of sentientism (human chauvinism and animal liberation), he says:

> Neither rationality nor the capacity to experience pleasure and pain seem to me necessary (even though they may be sufficient) conditions on moral considerability. . . . Nothing short of the condition of *being alive* seems to me to be a plausible and nonarbitrary criterion.[54]

Goodpaster attacks what he considers "the best defense of the sentience criterion in recent literature,"[55] the argument given by the well-known moral and legal theorist Joel Feinberg. Feinberg admits that nonsentient living creatures such as plants have a good, can be benefited and harmed, and so on. But the same is true of your automobile, or the finish on my desk. We tend to think, however, that the "good" of such things is importantly different from the good of human and nonhuman animals. Feinberg insists that the possession of interests in the full sense requires wants or aims or desires. Goodpaster finds this requirement implausible. "In the face of their obvious tendencies to maintain and heal themselves, it is very difficult to reject the idea of interests on the part of trees (and plants generally) in remaining alive."[56] Furthermore, these interests "are clearly those of the living things themselves, not simply those of the owners or users or other human persons involved."[57] Why, then, Goodpaster asks, is there "reluctance to acknowledge in nonsentient living beings the presence of independent needs, capacities for benefit and harm, etc."?[58] The roots of this reluctance he locates in the fact that "there is an affinity between hedonism or some variation on hedonism and a predilection for the sentience criterion of considerability or some variation on it."[59] What is the nature of this affinity between hedonism (the view that pleasure is the only good) and sentientism? It is not that one view logically implies the other. Goodpaster's claim is that "if one's conception of the good is *hedonistic* in character, one's conception of a beneficiary will quite naturally be restricted to beings who are capable of pleasure and pain."[60] This association of sentientism with hedonism is misleading. The advocates of sentientism do not make sentience the criterion of moral patiency because they think pleasure the only value. Rather, they just do not see what point there could be in worrying about how we treat things, living or not, if they cannot feel and do not care.[61]

I am willing to believe that trees have a good, a good not dependent on the purpose of humans or other sentient creatures.[62] In light of this good, we may want to attribute to them purposes, needs, interests, and the like. The crucial question, though, is: Does the tree *care* whether its "purposes" are fulfilled or frustrated? Does it *matter* to the tree whether its interests are well or ill served? The problem is *not* just: Why should I, as a moral agent, be concerned about the good of another being? (That skeptical question is hard to answer adequately even for the human case. If the only way to avoid obligations to trees were to resort to general moral skepticism, the cause of tree liberation would be much advanced.) The problem is: *Given* willingness on my part to attend to the good of other humans, even other animals, who *care* about what happens to them, why should I care for the tree's good when the tree does not and cannot?

The finish on my desk has a good, in the sense that various kinds of treatment can be good or bad for it, but no one would suggest that it is a moral patient. How is a tree different? Two answers spring to mind: The tree is "natural" and the finish is not; the tree "strives" to maintain itself and the finish does not. Neither answer seems very convincing. That the tree is "natural" does not make it a moral patient; rocks are equally natural. That the tree "strives" to maintain itself does not make it a moral patient, unless a machine with similar talents would also qualify—but why should it? The world is full of feedback mechanisms that "strive" to do their thing, yet there seems to be nothing wrong with interrupting a mechanism because, despite the "striving" of the machine, there is no frustration; the machine doesn't care if its "purposes" are thwarted, so why should we?

It is here, on the matter of machines, that mystical versions of respect for life, such as Schweitzer's, are most sharply distinguished from nonmystical versions, such as the views of Taylor and Goodpaster. For Schweitzer, life is something mysterious, and he counts on this mystery to gloss over the gap between fact (*x* is a living creature) and value (*x* should be respected). Goodpaster, in contrast, seems quite content to define living systems in terms of homeostatic feedback processes. He says, in fact, that "the core of moral concern lies in respect for self-sustaining organization and integration in the face of pressures toward high entropy," that is, toward disorganization.[63] Taylor leaves

> open the question of whether machines—in particular, those which are not only goal-directed, but also self-regulating—can properly be said to have a good of their own. . . . When machines are developed that function in the way our brains do, we may well come to deem them proper subjects of moral consideration.[64]

But why should we have to wait for machines *that* complicated? Why don't simpler machines, goal-directed and self-regulating, deserve moral consideration already, if living things do? Even if we might someday want to recognize the civil rights of complex computers and robots, as some have imagined,[65] it seems clear that we would have little concern for machines no more sophisticated than trees. If that is so, then why should we be concerned about trees, or other environmental objects that, because they lack consciousness of any kind, don't care what happens to them?

Besides machines, is not the great globe itself a kind of self-sustaining organization? Shall we say that the earth as a whole is a single organism (or, perhaps, a goddess), called *Gaia*?[66] Our treatment of the earth would then in many respects fall under the notion of respect for life. (The problem of which lives are more important would persist.) Or shall we say that moral consideration is not restricted to objects that are alive? In that case, perhaps the distinction between *living* and *nonliving* will cease to possess central moral significance. Have we been missing the planet for the trees?

## IV. THE LAND ETHIC

The land ethic is a collection of views which recognize as moral patients entities that are not sentient, or not individual, or both. Proponents of such views often call themselves *holists* (emphasizing both the *whole* and the *holy*) and see the earth as, metaphorically if not literally, one organism. Some holists go so far as to attribute to this totality a kind of "planetary consciousness,"[67] but other holists reject such cosmic mind–mongering and insist that we can view "landscape as an articulate unity (without the least hint of mysticism or ineffability)."[68] There may be much to be said for ineffability, but it is best, in the present context, to ignore the versions of holism that hint at mysticism, and stick instead to theories that appeal to what might be called ecological politics. Two examples will be considered. The land ethic of Aldo Leopold (§7) emphasizes the inadequacy of moral individualism in the light of ecological interdependence, while the view of John Rodman (§8) puts most emphasis on the inadequacy of sentientism.

## §7 ALDO LEOPOLD AND RESPECT FOR LAND

The term "land ethic" comes from Aldo Leopold (1887–1948), an expert in forestry and game management, and an essayist whose most famous book, *A Sand County Almanac*, appeared in 1949. In March of 1948, Leopold wrote:

> We abuse land because we regard it as a commodity belonging to us. When we see land as a community to which we belong, we may begin to use it with love and respect. . . . Perhaps such a shift in values can be achieved by reappraising things unnatural, tame and confined in terms of things natural, wild, and free.[69]

Later that year, Leopold died fighting a grass fire on a neighbor's farm. The ideas in that posthumous book have exerted considerable influence; indeed, Leopold is "universally recognized as the father . . . of recent environmental ethics."[70] Leopold's arguments turn around three key concepts: land, community, and health.

*Land*, for Leopold, means more than just inanimate dirt. The land, he says, "is not merely soil; it is a fountain of energy flowing through a circuit of soils, plants, and animals."[71] Energy is transformed and passed on, up and down the food chains. The soil is full of animals. The water is full of "little animals." Our bodies are habitats for creatures, many of whom are indispensable to bodily functions. Indeed, our very cells are inhabited. These invisible fauna and flora can now, thanks to microphotography, be seen. In light of such facts, it may be easier to see land not just as meaningless dirt, but as a *community* of interdependent parts; that is the ecological vision of things: The ways of one life form depend on the ways of many other life forms, large and small, sentient and not. Humans, like other creatures, are part of "a community of interdependent parts."[72] Ethics is about such communities, Leopold thinks. "The land ethic simply enlarges the boundaries of the community to include soils, waters, plants, and animals, or collectively: the land."[73] Instead of speaking of "the land," Leopold sometimes calls it "the biotic community." Here, for example, is Leopold's famous account of right and wrong: "A thing is right when it tends to preserve the integrity, stability, and beauty of the biotic community. It is wrong when it tends otherwise."[74] We are also to preserve the *health* of the land. "Health is the capacity of the land for self-renewal."[75]

Appreciation of the interdependence ecological science has revealed may well suggest to us that we should mend our ways lest we, or those we care about, come to grief. This *prudential* consideration supports one kind of environmentalism, sometimes referred to as "shallow." Sometimes Leopold's arguments seem to make this kind of prudential appeal,[76] but it is clear that Leopold is really a partisan of the "deep" environmental movement, according to which the ethics of how we treat the environment depends on more than *our* interests, economic or other. Thus, he says that "predators are members of the community, and . . . no special interest has the right to exterminate them for the sake of a benefit, real or fancied, to itself."[77]

Why, then, should we not be content with purely prudential considerations in our dealings with the environment? Do we need an ethics *of* the environment, or just an ethics *about* the environment (i.e., the usual ethics *applied to* the environment)?[78] Why should the perception of interdependence make us not only mend our practical policies, but alter our conception of who, or what, is a moral patient? How do we argue from the *facts* revealed by ecological science to the *value* of the land, "value in the philosophical sense,"[79] as Leopold says?

The problem of how to get from the *is* of description to the *ought* of moral injunction has been thought a central, if not *the* central, problem in moral philosophy, especially in the twentieth century.[80] Leopold was not unaware of the apparent gap. "That land is a community is the basic concept of ecology," he says, "but that land is to be loved and respected is an extension of ethics."[81] Why, then, should this extension be made?

Leopold's brief and scattered remarks on this matter are elusive. He tells us that this extension of ethics is "an evolutionary possibility and an ecological necessity."[82] One is tempted to ask both *why?* and *so what?* That the extension of ethics to the land is an evolutionary *possibility* is no reason why the extension should be made. That it is an ecological necessity *might* be a reason, if it could be made clearer why it's a necessity. What is it necessary *for?* Leopold goes on to say something about "social expediency" and "community instinct," and elsewhere mentions "a sense of kinship with fellow-creatures,"[83] but his rationale is obscure.

It is possible that Leopold is trying to argue that we will (or should?) make the extension of ethics, once we come to appreciate the ecological facts, in light of our psychological attachment to communities. This kind of line is certainly taken by J. Baird Callicott, a philosopher at the University of Wisconsin much influenced by Leopold's views, who writes: "The biotic community is a proper object of that passion which is actuated by the contemplation of the complexity, diversity, integrity, and stability of the *community* to which we belong."[84] Two comments need to be made about this position.

First, whether or not Callicott's argument shows that the justification of moral treatment of the land is no more problematic than the justification of moral treatment of our fellow citizens (*given* that we are well disposed psychologically toward members of "our community"), this does not show that we *should* have (or develop, or keep ) such a disposition. But even if we believe that moral reason is (and ought to be?) the slave of the passion for community, public weal, or whatever, there remain worries: How strong a hold does this particular passion have on us? Can it be displaced by other feelings? What is the precise content of this passion? Hume, to whose theories Callicott appeals, repeatedly emphasizes the way in which our personal passions—not just our selfishness, but the chauvinism of our altruistic feelings—are at war with any general sense of social justice.[85] He also emphasizes that when interest diminishes (or is perceived as diminishing) moral obligation relaxes.[86]

Second, the idea of "a community" is ambiguous. A political or moral community consists in individual *members* joined together by shared *rights and obligations*. The land, however, is uncontroversially a community only in the different sense of interdependent *parts* with interlocking *functions*.[87] Recognizing that we and the land form a community, in the latter sense, does not imply that we have any moral obligations to the land. Appeal to the concept of community cannot ameliorate our "moral atomism," nor has it shown that such amendment is desirable.

## §8 JOHN RODMAN AND RESPECT FOR THE WILD

An alternative version of the land ethic has been formulated by American political theorist John Rodman, from whom I have taken the term *sentientism*. Rodman criticizes Peter Singer's attack on speciesism as itself a case of sentientism:

> The rest of nature is left in a state of thinghood, having no intrinsic worth, acquiring instrumental value only as resources for the well-being of an elite of sentient beings. Homocentrist rationalism has widened out into a kind of zoöcentrist sentientism . . . If it would seem arbitrary to a visitor from Mars to find one species claiming a monopoly of intrinsic value by virtue of its allegedly exclusive possession of reason, free will, soul, or some other occult quality, would it not seem almost as arbitrary to find that same species claiming a monopoly of intrinsic value for itself and those species most resembling it (e.g. in type of nervous system and behavior) by virtue of their common and allegedly exclusive possession of sentience?[88]

The word "allegedly" serves to remind us not to conflate two separate issues: (1) whether sentientism—the view that being sentient is the necessary (and possibly sufficient) condition for moral patiency or considerability—is a correct view; (2) whether humans, and those animals closely resembling humans in certain physical or behavioral traits, are the only sentient creatures. Though Rodman's remarks sometimes bear on the latter issue—Who *is* sentient?—it is clear that his main concern is to reject sentientism as a moral view. He writes, for example:

> I confess that I need only to stand in the midst of a clear-cut forest, a strip-mined hillside, a defoliated jungle, or a dammed canyon to feel uneasy with assumptions that could yield the conclusion that no human action can make any difference to the welfare of anything but sentient animals. I am agnostic as to whether or not plants, rocks, and rivers have subjective experience, and I am not sure that it really matters. I strongly suspect that the same basic principles are manifested in quite diverse forms—e.g. in damming a wild river and repressing an animal instinct (whether human or nonhuman), in clear-cutting a forest and bombing a city, in Dachau and a university research laboratory, in censoring an idea, liquidating a religious or racial group, and exterminating a species of flora or fauna.[89]

Can creatures lacking "subjective experience" *have* a welfare, a welfare that calls for moral respect? Drying up is no doubt bad *for* a river, but such desiccation is not bad *to* it, since the river does not seem to care whether it continues to flow, or is evaporated into clouds. If the river doesn't care, why should you or I? Why should we be more concerned to preserve the river that is than to hasten the arrival of the desert that will be?

Rodman's real concern is not with welfare, however, but with *domestication*. He says:

> My view of the domestication of nonhuman animals clearly presupposes that it is a fundamentally coercive and exploitative institution. This view is not refuted . . . by imagining how much better off certain animals are in the servitude or captivity that they have become habituated to than they would be if we simply turned them loose to fend for themselves.[90]

What is wrong with domestication? Apparently, what is wrong is not that it is contrary to the welfare of domesticated creatures; rather, it threatens the *existence* of, or at least the *experience* of, the Wild: wildlife and wilderness.

> Either what is preserved is so successfully segregated from the impact of human civilization that it cannot be experienced in a participatory way, or else it is transformed by the impact of human overuse due to its very scarcity, or else human use is methodically rationed as part of a deliberate plan of "wilderness management" that eliminates much of the quality of the authentic wilderness experience. . . . Tame birds in a zoo; substitute pines in a National Forest; bureaucratic permits to use a Wilderness Area, asking where the backpacker intends to spend each night; detribalized Indians on reservations: they are all parts of the same historic policy.[91]

Why is the Wild so important? This question may be interpreted in two ways.

If the question means, Why is the Wild important *in itself*?, the answer seems to be that "nonhuman species exist 'in their own right' (have their own origin, structure, tendencies, etc.) and not simply 'for us.'"[92] Rodman argues that natural entities are degraded

> by our failure to respect them for having their own existence, their own character and potentialities, their own forms of excellence, their own integrity, their own grandeur—and by our tendency to relate to them either by reducing them to the status of instruments for our own ends or by 'giving' them rights by assimilating them to the status of inferior human beings.[93]

If, on the other hand, the question means, Why is the Wild important *to us*?, then Rodman's answer is this:

> The need for wilderness grows more acute every moment because it is, among other things, the need to experience a realm of reality beyond the manipulations of commodity production and technology, the need for a

norm given 'in the nature of things', the need for realities that function as symbols of otherness that can arouse a response from the suppressed potentialities of human nature.[94]

The essence of wildness seems to consist in independence and otherness, whose metaphysics is freedom and whose epistemology is mystery. Rodman is certainly not alone in his feeling that human morality ought to be responsive to nonhuman value.[95] But can such value be found apart from the attribution of "subjective experience"? In answering *yes*, the land ethic seems to require almost a new way of doing ethics. Discussing Leopold's *Sand County Almanac*, Rodman says that

> we cannot simply abstract from the last part of this carefully-composed book the notion of extending ethics to the land and its inhabitants. The land ethic emerges in the course of the book as an integral part of a sensibility developed through observation, participatory experience, and reflection. It is an 'ethic' in the almost forgotten sense of a 'way of life'. For this reason it would be pretentious to talk of a land ethic until we have let our curiosity follow the skunk as it emerges from hibernation, listened with wonder at the calls of the wild geese arriving at the pond, sawed the fallen ancient tree while meditating its history, shot a wolf (once) and looked into its eyes as it died, recognized the fish in ourselves, and strained to see the world from the perspective of a muskrat eye-deep in the swamp only to realize that in the end the mind of the muskrat holds for us a mystery we cannot fathom.[96]

It is here, meditating on the mystery of the muskrat's mind, that the difference between Singer and Rodman comes out most clearly. Rodman attacks the idea that judgments of moral obligations should be based on the moral agent's "capacity for putting himself in the victim's place." He thinks that "the location of value in the subjective experience of sentient entities allows for no small amount of subjectivity in our moral appraisals."[97] For Singer, on the contrary, such putting-oneself-in-the-patient's-place is the essence of moral agency. In his view,

> the limits of sentience are not really limits at all, for applying the test of imagining ourselves in the position of those affected by our actions shows that in the case of nonsentient things there is nothing at all to be taken into account. We need not deliberately exclude nonsentient things from the scope of the principle of equal consideration of interests: it is just that including them within the scope of this principle leads to results identical with excluding them, since they have no preferences—and therefore no interests, strictly speaking—to be considered. There is nothing we can do that matters to them.[98]

While Leopold and Rodman are quite happy to talk about "thinking like a mountain,"[99] Singer argues that "imagining myself in the position of the tree or mountain will not help me to see why their destruction is wrong; for such imagining yields a perfect blank."[100] Imaginative projection has often seemed to be the key tool of ethics; well-known American moral philosopher Thomas Nagel has called it "the primary form of moral argument."[101] Rodman attacks such imaginative projection, presumably because he believes that it falsifies its object. Singer defends it, presumably because he thinks that it is unclear just what the alternative could be. Judging the inner experience of others, says Rodman, depends either on "our criteria of evidence" or on "our imaginative/emotional capacity . . . to put ourselves in their place."[102] Singer would say, I suppose, *What else*!

Any version of the land ethic must answer several questions. First, we can ask what is wrong with interrupting natural processes, or disrupting the wild. We cannot, as a matter of fact, avoid such interruptions. If there is nothing wrong with kicking a stone out of its spot, or burning a piece of wood, why should things be morally different if we change the course of a river (excluding, of course, the effects of such a change on humans and other sentient creatures)? Anyway, aren't human interruptions themselves natural actions? If it is all right for a landslide or a glacier to change the course of a river, why not a bulldozer? Even if humans are a "planetary disease,"[103] are we not at least as *natural* as a disease? (What we call *disease* is, ecologically, just a conflict between forms of life whose optimal conditions are at odds.)

Second, we must not forget that many of the environments we now *consider* "natural" or "wild" are in fact products, at least in part, of human intervention long ago.[104] How important is the truly wild—in itself, or to us?

Third, we must recognize that life forms and natural objects adapt to new circumstances.

> The biotic community changes over time; the environment alters; forms of flora and fauna appear and disappear; deserts become oceans and oceans dry up, with all the attendant metamorphoses. The crucial question is: why isn't *whatever* happens integral, stable and beautiful? Any arrangement of parts will be just what it is, and last as long as it does.[105]

What makes the old circumstances any more "natural," or any more morally valuable, or any more worth preserving, than the new disposition of things?

If these questions cannot be satisfactorily answered, the land ethic will seem no more compelling than respect for life, about which similar questions arise. We have not yet, I think, been given conclusive reason to believe that it is necessary, or even possible, to go beyond individualism and sentientism in moral theory. To that extent, it remains in question whether any *radically* environmental ethic is either possible or desirable.

## V. CONCLUSION

Modern moral philosophy has often been attacked for its "individualism" or "moral atomism." Such attacks play a significant role in contemporary moral theory,[106] but the attack has been particularly pronounced in connection with environmental ethics. A typical complaint is the following remark, from the conclusion to an excellent essay by philosopher Bryan G. Norton, currently at the University of Maryland's Center for Philosophy and Public Policy:

> The animal liberation movement is based upon an analogy between human and animal suffering and its main thrust is *not* to provide a means to adjudicate between conflicting demands that human individuals make on the environment, but rather it introduces a whole new category of demands—the demands of animals. . . . Expanding the number and types of rights holders does not address the problem of deciding which individual claims have priority over others—it only increases these demands and makes it more and more difficult to satisfy them. The basic problem, then, lies precisely in the emphasis on individual claims and interests. An environmental ethic must support the holistic functioning of an ongoing system.[107]

This attack is not simply on rights, but on "claims and interests" generally as an adequate basis for an environmental ethic; it raises questions about Peter Singer's utilitarian arguments for animal liberation as much as about Tom Regan's rights-based approach.

The problems pointed out by Norton, and by other proponents of holism,[108] are real ones, but the gestures made by such critics toward a solution are both theoretically unclear and politically worrisome. It is hard to guess what considerations could compel us to want to "support the holistic functioning of an ongoing system," or even what such functioning or such support could amount to. Norton himself shrewdly observes that "the ascription of rights to collectives is an inherently odd idea because every environmental collective is a part of a larger such collective";[109] that "the relationship between the individual interests of organisms, individual plants, and nonliving objects, on the one hand, and the healthy functioning and integrity of the ecosystem, on the other hand, is a contingent one";[110] and that "it is unclear whether it is in the species' interest to survive in its present form or to be allowed to evolve in response to changing environmental situations."[111] Reflection on the truth of such observations might suggest that any attempt to "support the holistic functioning of an ongoing system" will face similar problems. Are we to support "the entire ecosystem which makes up the universe"[112]—the ecocosmos, so to speak—or one of the many ongoing systems it contains? Won't our actions, "destructive" or not, be part of the way the whole ongoing system in fact works? Should we aspire to survive in our present form, or allow the humanufactured environment to select those among our progeny who thrive under changing environmental situations? These are difficult questions, but it is hard to see how holism can provide answers any more satisfactory than individualistic theories such as sentientism.

Besides these theoretical unclarities, there are political worries that are worth mentioning, though space does not permit detailed discussion. The utilitarian concept of interests and the post-Kantian concept of rights—unsatisfactory as these concepts in many respects are—have both served a vital political and social function in providing a vocabulary for criticizing the accepted rules of the community by reference to the way those rules impinge on the needs and dignities of individual moral patients. The suggestion that these devices be abandoned in favor of support for the functioning of the ongoing system inspires understandable worries that this prefigures a resurgence of totalitarian thinking: 1984 and all that.

One need not be paranoid about the environmental protection hustle[113] to be uneasy about the possible political consequences of the loss of the rhetoric of claims, rights, interests, the value of the individual, and so on. Perhaps "loss" is too strong a word. Perhaps the holist view is only that claims and interests, and the like, are inadequate for environmental ethics, however necessary for social theory; so that some new sort of moral theory, a less "atomistic" one, is necessary for dealing with the environment. Maybe. But easy conjunction of this "new ethic" with the old one is hard to imagine: All the "priority" problems will appear again. When does respect for nature trump respect for persons? Is preserving wilderness, for example, more important than creating jobs?

Every step we take raises questions in environmental ethics, questions to which moral theory has so far offered no adequate answers. These answers will not be easy to find in the future; at present, it is not even clear whether they are to be looked for with the tools of traditional ethics.

What is a token of respect in one culture may be a gesture of contempt in another, so if you want to show respect to a member of a different culture, you had better do something that will be interpreted in the right way. But how can we show respect to the earth, since it will do no interpreting? It is said that "Apaches moved stealthily about the land . . . not to be sneaky but because to leave footprints everywhere was a mark of arrogance."[114] The earth doesn't *care* whether you leave footprints, so why not tread where you please? Does it *matter* whether we step lightly?

As we leap into the rest of the universe, these questions, questions of environmental ethical theory, become more and more pressing. Already scientists are talking about transforming the environments of *other* planets.[115] For good or evil, we will not be earthbound forever.

## *NOTES*

My essay has benefited from comments by Tom Regan, Carolyn Morillo, Norton Nelkin, and David Johnson.

1. These (somewhat murky) details are taken from accounts of the incident published in the *New York Times*: "Captain Indicted in Deaths at Sea," May 21, 1975, p. 93; "Captain Says He Feared Lifeboat Would Capsize," May 13, 1976, p. 39.
2. I have discussed the notion of moral patiency more fully in *Species and Morality* (Ph.D. Diss., Princeton University, 1976). The term has been used independently by other philosophers in a similar sense. Tom Regan, how-

ever, uses the term in a very different sense in *The Case for Animal Rights* (Berkeley Calif.: University of California Press, 1983).

3.  John Grote, *A Treatise on the Moral Ideals* (Cambridge, England: Deighton, Bell & Co., 1876), 356.

4.  A partial bibliography, prepared by Tom Regan and Charles Magel, appears in Regan's *All That Dwell Therein: Animal Rights and Environmental Ethics* (Berkeley, Calif.: University of California Press, 1982). See also Magel's *A Bibliography of Animal Rights and Related Matters* (Lanham, Md.: University Press of America, 1981).

5.  Marc F. Plattner, "Speciesism," *Commentary* (March 1976):78.

6.  See Tom Regan and Peter Singer, eds., *Animal Rights and Human Obligations* (Englewood Cliffs, N.J.: Prentice-Hall, 1975), 129–130.

7.  *Ibid.*, 132.

8.  John Stuart Mill, *Utilitarianism* (1863), Chap. 2. For discussion, see my essay, "Life, Death, and Animals," in Harlan B. Miller and William Williams, eds., *Ethics and Animals* (Clifton, N.J.: Humana Press, 1983), 123–133.

9.  Peter Singer, *Animal Liberation* (New York: New York Review/Random House, 1975), 23.

10.  *Ibid.*

11.  Peter Singer, *Practical Ethics* (Cambridge, England: Cambridge University Press, 1979), 90.

12.  *Ibid.*, 92.

13.  See, e.g., John Rawls, *A Theory of Justice* (Cambridge, Mass.: Harvard University Press, 1971); J. J. C. Smart and Bernard Williams, *Utilitariansim: For and Against* (Cambridge, England: Cambridge University Press, 1973); Amartya Sen and Bernard Williams, eds., *Utilitarianism and Beyond* (Cambridge, England: Cambridge University Press, 1982); Samuel Scheffler, *The Rejection of Consequentialism* (New York: Oxford University Press, 1982); also my "Ignoring Persons," *Tulane Studies in Philosophy* 31 (1982):91–105.

14.  See, e.g., *Practical Ethics*, 65ff.

15.  Tom Regan, *All That Dwell Therein*, 56

16.  *Ibid.*, 54.

17.  Peter Singer, "Utilitarianism and Vegetarianism," *Philosophy and Public Affairs* 9 (1979–1980):325–337, at p. 327. Cf. J. J. C. Smart and Williams, *Utilitarianism: For and Against*, 69.

18.  Peter Singer, "Utilitarianism and Vegetarianism," 326. Cf. Singer's "Sidgwick and Reflective Equilibrium," *Monist* 58 (1974):490–517.

19.  This is part of a larger issue about the role of intuitions as data for philosophical theories. This issue stands out clearly if you compare Thomas Nagel's *Mortal Questions* (Cambridge, England: Cambridge University Press, 1979) with Richard Rorty's *Philosophy and the Mirror of Nature* (Princeton, N.J.: Princeton University Press, 1979). More explicit still is Rorty's introduction to *Consequences of Pragmatism* (Minneapolis: University of Minnesota Press, 1982); also his essay "Mind as Ineffable," in Richard Q. Elvee, ed., *Mind in Nature* (San Francisco: Harper & Row, 1982), 60–95.

20.  Tom Regan, *All That Dwell Therein*, 203.

21.  *Ibid.*, 135.

22.  Peter Singer, *Animal Liberation*, 9.

23.  Tom Regan, *All That Dwell Therein*, 183.

24.  *Ibid.*, 205; cf. 133.

25.  R.M. Hare's theory can be found in *The Language of Morals* (New York: Oxford University Press, 1952); *Freedom and Reason* (New York: Oxford

University Press, 1963); and *Moral Thinking* (New York: Oxford University Press, 1981).

26. Philippa Foot, *Virtues and Vices and Other Essays in Moral Philosophy* (Oxford, England: Blackwell, 1978), 145. Cf. G. E. M. Anscombe, *Collected Philosophical Papers*, vol. 3 (Minneapolis: University of Minnesota Press, 1981), 31.

27. See, e.g., James Rachels, "Evaluating from a Point of View," *Journal of Value Inquiry* 6 (1972):144–157; Lawrence C. Becker, "The Finality of Moral Judgments," *Philosophical Review* 82 (1973):364–370; Robert Brandom, "Points of View and Practical Reasoning," *Canadian Journal of Philosophy* 12 (1982):321–333; M. S. Quinn, "Good of a Kind and Good from a Point of View," *Philosophical Studies* 26 (1974):239–246.

28. The classic expression of this point is Donald Davidson's "On the Very Idea of a Conceptual Scheme," *Proceedings of the American Philosophical Association* 47 (1973–1974):5–20. See also Richard Rorty's *Philosophy and the Mirror of Nature* (Princeton: Princeton University Press, 1979).

29. David Hume, *A Treatise of Human Nature*, ed. Selby-Bigge (Oxford, England: Oxford University Press, 1888), 469; Tom Regan, "On the Connection Between Environmental Science and Environmental Ethics," *Environmental Ethics* 2 (1980):363.

30. *All That Dwell Therein*, 203.

31. See, e.g., R. and V. Routley, "Against the Inevitability of Human Chauvinism," in K. E. Goodpaster and K. M. Sayre, eds., *Ethics and Problems of the 21st Century* (Notre Dame, Ind.: University of Notre Dame Press, 1979), 36–59.

32. Albert Schweitzer, *The Philosophy of Civilization* (New York: Macmillan, 1959), 310.

33. *Ibid.*, 304.

34. *Ibid.*, 311.

35. *Ibid.*, 310.

36. *Ibid.*, 311.

37. *Ibid.*, 318.

38. Peter Singer, *Practical Ethics*, 92.

39. Paul Taylor, "Frankena on Environmental Ethics," *Monist* 64 (1981): 313–325, at p. 314.

40. *Ibid.*, 318.

41. Paul Taylor, "The Ethics of Respect for Nature," *Environmental Ethics* 3 (1981):197–218, at pp. 211, 210. Grateful acknowledgment is made to Professor Taylor for permission to quote from his paper.

42. *Ibid.*, 217.

43. *Ibid.*

44. *Ibid.*, 206. For Taylor's separation of issues about wild animals from issues about domesticated animals, see p. 200.

45. *Ibid.*, 206.

46. Paul Taylor, "On Taking the Moral Point of View," *Midwest Studies in Philosophy* 3 (1978):35–61, at p. 58.

47. *Ibid.*, 59–60.

48. Paul Taylor, "The Ethics of Respect for Nature," 218.

49. *Ibid.*

50. *Ibid.*, 217.

51. Peter Miller, "Value as Richness: Toward a Value Theory for the Expanded Naturalism in Environmental Ethics," *Environmental Ethics* 4 (1982): 101–114, at p. 113.

52. John Aspinall, for example, in "Man's Place in Nature," in David Paterson and Richard D. Ryder, eds., *Animals' Rights–a Symposium* (London: Centaur Press, 1979), 20.

53.    The fear that morality (or practical reason) might be incoherent has troubled many moral philosophers. Brooding on this subject can be found in Henry Sidgwick's *Methods of Ethics* (7th ed., London: Macmillan, 1907; New York: Dover, 1966); Thomas Nagel's *Mortal Questions* (Cambridge, England: Cambridge University Press, 1979); and Alisdair MacIntyre's *After Virtue* (Notre Dame, Ind.: University of Notre Dame Press, 1981).

54.    "On Being Morally Considerable," *Journal of Philosophy* 75 (1978): 308–325, at p. 310. Grateful acknowledgment is made to Professor Goodpaster and the editors of the *Journal of Philosophy* for permission to quote from this paper.

55.    *Ibid.*, 318. See Joel Feinberg, *Rights, Justice, and the Bounds of Liberty* (Princeton, N.J.: Princeton University Press, 1980), 159–206.

56.    *Ibid.*, 319.

57.    *Ibid.*

58.    *Ibid.*, 320.

59.    *Ibid.*, 321–322.

60.    *Ibid.*, 321.

61.    I have discussed this misinterpretation of animal liberation in "Animal Liberation Versus the Land Ethic," *Environmental Ethics* 3 (1981): 265–273. I consider how animals might have an interest in life, even if they are unable to conceive of (and so care about) death, in "Life, Death, and Animals," in Harlan B. Miller and William Williams, eds., *Ethics and Animals* (Clifton, N.J.: Humana Press, 1983):123–133.

62.    Besides the work of Taylor and Goodpaster, see Robin Attfield, "The Good of Trees," *Journal of Value Inquiry* 15 (1981):35–54. Also relevant is the Good Roots controversy discussed above in §II.3.

63.    Kenneth Goodpaster, "On Being Morally Considerable," 323.

64.    Paul Taylor, "The Ethics of Respect for Nature," 200.

65.    For relevant discussion, see Hilary Putnam, *Philosophical Papers*, vol. 2 (London: Cambridge University Press, 1975), 386–407; Frank R. Harrison, III, "What Kind of Beings Can Have Rights?" *Philosophy Forum* 12 (1972):113–129; Daniel Dennett, *Brainstorms* (Bradford Books, 1978), esp. Chap. 14; Richard Rorty, "Mind as Ineffable," in Richard Q. Elvee, ed., *Mind in Nature* (San Francisco: Harper and Row, 1982), 92.

66.    For a serious attempt by a scientist to view the earth as a single organism, see J. E. Lovelock, *Gaia* (New York: Oxford University Press, 1979). See also Guy Murchie, *The Seven Mysteries of Life* (Boston: Houghton Mifflin, 1978).

67.    See, e.g., the quotation in Christopher D. Stone, *Should Trees Have Standing?: Toward Legal Rights for Natural Objects* (Los Altos, Calif.: William Kaufmann, 1974), 52.

68.    J. Baird Callicott, "Animal Liberation: A Triangular Affair," *Environmental Ethics* 2 (1980):311–338, at p. 321.

69.    Aldo Leopold, *A Sand County Almanac* (New York: Oxford University Press, 1949), pp. viii, ix.

70.    J. Baird Callicott, "Animal Liberation: A Triangular Affair," 311.

71.    Aldo Leopold, *A Sand County Almanac*, 216.

72.    *Ibid.*, 203.

73.    *Ibid.*, 204.

74.    *Ibid.*, 224–225.

75.    *Ibid.*, 221.

76.    *Ibid.*, 214.

77.    *Ibid.*, 211–212.

78.    See, e.g., Holmes Rolston, III, "Is There an Ecological Ethic?," *Ethics* 85 (1974–1975):93–109.

79.    See Aldo Leopold, *A Sand County Almanac*, 223.

80. W. D. Hudson, ed., *The Is/Ought Question* (London: Macmillan, 1969). For balance, see Peter Singer, "The Triviality of the Debate Over 'Is-Ought' and the Definition of 'Moral,'" *American Philosophical Quarterly* 10 (1973):51–56.
81. Aldo Leopold, *A Sand County Almanac*, viii–ix.
82. *Ibid.*, 203.
83. *Ibid.*, 109.
84. J. Baird Callicott, "Hume's *Is/Ought* Dichotomy and the Relation of Ecology to Leopold's Land Ethic," *Environmental Ethics* 4 (1982):163–174, at p. 173. Callicott has expounded his version of the land ethic in a number of essays in *Environmental Ethics*. See especially his essay, "Animal Liberation: A Triangular Affair," and my critique of it in "Animal Liberation Versus the Land Ethic."
85. David Hume, *A Treatise of Human Nature* (Oxford, England: Oxford University Press, 1888), 484, 487.
86. *Ibid.*, 569.
87. Cf. John Rodman, "The Liberation of Nature?," *Inquiry* 20 (1977): 83–131, at p. 126. Grateful acknowledgment is made to Professor Rodman and the editors of *Inquiry* for permission to quote from this article.
88. *Ibid.*, 91.
89. *Ibid.*, 89–90.
90. *Ibid.*, 127.
91. *Ibid.*, 111,112.
92. *Ibid.*, 109.
93. *Ibid.*, 94.
94. *Ibid.*, 113.
95. See, e.g., Henry Beston, *The Outermost House* (New York: Holt, Rinehart & Winston, 1928), Chap. 2, sect. 1; Barry Holstun Lopez, *Of Wolves and Men* (New York: Charles Scribner's Sons, 1978), 249; Mary Midgley, *Beast and Man: The Roots of Human Nature* (Ithaca: Cornell University Press, 1978), 358–362.
96. John Rodman, "The Liberation of Nature?," 110–111.
97. *Ibid.*, 90.
98. Peter Singer, *The Expanding Circle: Ethics and Sociobiology* (New York: Farrar, Straus & Giroux, 1981), 123–124.
99. Aldo Leopold, *A Sand County Almanac*, 129ff; John Rodman "The Liberation of Nature?," 110.
100. Peter Singer, *The Expanding Circle*, 123.
101. Thomas Nagel, *The Possibility of Altruism* (New York: Oxford University Press, 1970), 145.
102. John Rodman, "The Liberation of Nature?," 90.
103. Cf., e.g., Ian L. McHarg, "Man: Planetary Disease," in Robert T. Roelofs et al., eds., *Environment and Society* (Englewood Cliffs, N.J.: Prentice-Hall, 1974), 303ff.
104. See Rene Dubos, *The Wooing of Earth* (New York: Charles Scribner's Sons, 1980), 84ff.
105. Edward Johnson, "Animal Liberation Versus the Land Ethic," 270.
106. See, e.g., Alisdair MacIntyre, *After Virtue*; Herbert Fingarette, *Confucius—the Secular as Sacred* (New York: Harper & Row, 1972), especially Chap. 5.
107. "Environmental Ethics and Nonhuman Rights," *Environmental Ethics* 4 (1982):17–36, at p. 36. Grateful acknowledgment is made to Professor Norton and Environmental Philosophy, Inc., for permission to quote from this article.
108. See K. E. Goodpaster, "From Egoism to Environmentalism," in K. E. Goodpaster and K. M. Sayre, eds., *Ethics and Problems of the 21st Century*

(Notre Dame, Ind.: University of Notre Dame Press, 1979), 21–35; John Rodman, "The Liberation of Nature?," esp. p. 89; Alistair S. Gunn, "Why Should We Care about Rare Species?," *Environmental Ethics* 2 (1980):17–37, esp. p. 36; J. Baird Callicott, "Animal Liberation: A Triangular Affair," esp. p. 324.

109.   Bryan Norton, "Environmental Ethics and Nonhuman Rights," 36.
110.   *Ibid.*, 32.
111.   *Ibid.*, 35.
112.   *Ibid.*, 36.
113.   See Bill Devall's review of Bernard Frieden's book *The Environmental Protection Hustle*, in *Environmental Ethics* 3 (1981):85–94.
114.   Barry Holstun Lopez, quoted by Tom Regan, *All That Dwell Therein*, 237–238.
115.   See, e.g., Larry Sessions, "Preparing Mars for Life," *Science Digest* (November/December 1980):128–129.

# SUGGESTIONS FOR FURTHER READING

§2.   Peter Singer's writing in ethics is extensive. The key article on nonhuman animals is "Animal Liberation," *New York Review of Books*, April 5, 1973, pp. 17–21. The arguments in this essay are repeated, with slight amplification and extensive factual documentation, in *Animal Liberation* (New York: New York Review/Random House, 1975). Important later treatments are found in "Animals and the Value of Life," in Tom Regan, ed., *Matters of Life and Death* (New York: Random House, 1980), 218–259; *Animal Factories* (written with Jim Mason) (New York: Crown, 1980); *Practical Ethics* (Cambridge: Mass.: Cambridge University Press, 1979), especially Chaps. 3–5; "Not for Humans Only: The Place of Nonhumans in Environmental Issues," in K. E. Goodpaster and K. M. Sayre, eds., *Ethics and Problems of the 21st Century* (Notre Dame, Ind.: University of Notre Dame Press, 1979), 191–206. A larger picture is painted in *The Expanding Circle: Ethics and Sociobiology* (New York: Farrar, Straus & Giroux, 1981).

§3.   Tom Regan's chief early essays on animal rights are gathered in *All That Dwell Therein: Animal Rights and Environmental Ethics* (Berkeley: University of California Press, 1982). Later work includes his essay with Dale Jamieson, "On the Ethics of the Use of Animals in Science," in Tom Regan and Donald Van De Veer, eds., *And Justice for All* (Totowa, N.J.: Rowman & Littlefield, 1982), 169–196. His most extensive and systematic treatment is found in *The Case for Animal Rights* (Berkeley: University of California Press, 1983).

§4.   For more on Albert Schweitzer's view, see William T. Blackstone's useful essay, "The Search for an Environmental Ethic," in Tom Regan, ed., *Matters of Life and Death* (New York: Random House, 1980), 299–335.

§5.   Paul Taylor's views are found in "Frankena on Environmental Ethics," *Monist* 64 (1981):313–325; "The Ethics of Respect for Nature," *Environmental Ethics* 3 (1981):197–218; "On Taking the Moral Point of View," *Midwest Studies in Philosophy* 3 (1978):35–61.

§6.   Kenneth Goodpaster's views are found in "On Being Morally Considerable," *Journal of Philosophy* 75 (1978):308–325; "From Egoism to Environmentalism," in K. E. Goodpaster and K. M. Sayre, eds., *Ethics and Problems of the 21st Century*, 21–35; "Morality as a System of Categorical Imperatives," *Journal of Value Inquiry* 15 (1981):179–197.

§7.　Aldo Leopold's main work on environmental ethics is *A Sand County Almanac* (Oxford, England: Oxford University Press, 1949); it is also available in an enlarged edition with additional essays (New York: Sierra Club/Ballantine, 1970).

§8.　John Rodman's views are found in "The Liberation of Nature?," *Inquiry* 20 (1977):83–131; "The Dolphin Papers," *The North American Review*, (Spring 1974), 13–26; "Animal Justice: The Counter-revolution in Natural Right and Law," *Inquiry* 22 (1979):3–22.

# INDEX

# ABOUT THE AUTHORS

―――――――――――――――― ⟨⟩ ――――――――――――――――

WILLIAM AIKEN was born in 1947 and was educated at Carleton College, Yale University, and Vanderbilt University. He is co-editor of *World Hunger and Moral Obligation* and *Whose Child? Children's Rights, Parental Authority, and State Power.* Though he has published essays primarily in the area of applied ethics, he prefers the title of generalist and enjoys teaching a wide range of courses at Chatham College, a liberal arts college for women in Pittsburgh.

ANNETTE C. BAIER was born in Queenstown, New Zealand, in 1929. She received a B.A. and M.A. from the University of Otago, and a B. Phil. from Oxford University. She taught at the universities of Aberdeen, Auckland, and Sydney before moving to the United States in 1962. She taught at Carnegie-Mellon University until 1973, and since then at the University of Pittsburgh. Her interests are the history of modern philosophy, especially Hume's philosophy, ethics, and philosophy of mind. She has published in philosophical journals in these areas.

ALASTAIR GUNN was born in the north of England in 1945. He did his undergraduate work at the University of Sussex in England. He has taught at North Carolina State University and has twice been Visiting Scholar at Duke University. He is at present Senior Lecturer at the University of Waikato. His main professional interests are in environmental and social ethics and policy aspects of engineering, and he has published numerous articles on these topics. He is the editor of a regional environmental journal in New Zealand, *Waikato Environment.*

DALE JAMIESON was born in Iowa in 1947, raised in California, and now lives in inner-city Boulder, Colorado. After ten years in the San Francisco Bay area he retreated to North Carolina where he built a house in the country and became deeply involved in rural life-styles. In 1976 he received a Ph.D. in Philosophy from the University of North Carolina at Chapel Hill. He is now assistant professor at the University of Colorado where he is associated with the Center for the Study of Values and Social Policy. He has published articles on issues in ethics, aesthetics, and philosophy of language, and is currently editing a book on philosophical issues in film, and co-editing another on the contemporary visual arts.

EDWARD JOHNSON was born in Lincoln, Nebraska, in 1950. He received his B.A. from the University of Nebraska (Lincoln) in 1972, and his Ph.D. from Princeton University in 1976. Since 1976, he has taught at the University of New Orleans where he is currently chair of the philosophy department. He has published a number of essays on ethical theory, environmental ethics, the moral status of nonhuman animals, and the ethical limits of technology. He is a poet. He accumulates books and records in large numbers.

TIBOR R. MACHAN is associate professor of philosophy at the State University College of New York, Fredonia, New York. He was born in Budapest, Hungary, from where he escaped in 1953 and then lived in Munich, Germany, until he settled in the United States in 1956. Machan earned his B.A. degree at Claremont Men's College, his M.A. degree at New York University, and his Ph.D. at the University of California, Santa Barbara. His works in philosophy have appeared in such journals as *Inquiry*, *Theory and Decision*, the *Journal of Value Inquiry*, and the *American Philosophical Quarterly*. He has written for law reviews and several collections edited by other scholars, as well as for general magazines, newspapers, and reviews (*The Humanist*, *The New York Times*, *The Los Angeles Times*, *Libertarian Review*). He is a senior editor of *Reason* magazine and director of educational programs of the Reason Foundation, Santa Barbara, California. He is married to Marty Zupan and they have one daughter.

TOM REGAN, a native of Pittsburgh, Pennsylvania, received his undergraduate education at Thiel College and was awarded the M.A. and Ph.D. degrees from the University of Virginia. Since 1967 he has taught philosophy at North Carolina State University, where he has twice been elected Outstanding Teacher and, in 1977, was named Alumni Distinguished Professor. He has lectured extensively on moral issues and has served as Distinguished Visiting Scholar, University of Calgary, and Distinguished Visiting Professor of Philosophy, Brooklyn College. He is co-editor, with Peter Singer, of *Animal Rights and Human Obligations* and, with Donald VanDeVeer, of *And Justice for All: New Introductory Essays in Ethics and Public Policy*, and sole editor of *Matters of Life and*

*Death: New Introductory Essays in Moral Philosophy* and *Just Business: New Introductory Essays in Business Ethics*. His other books include *Understanding Philosophy, All That Dwell Therein: Essays on Animal Rights and Environmental Ethics*, and, most recently, *The Case for Animal Rights*.

MARK SAGOFF has his A.B. from Harvard College and Ph.D. in Philosophy from the University of Rochester. He has taught at several universities, including Princeton, Pennsylvania, Wisconsin (Madison), and Cornell. At present, he holds appointments as research associate at the Center for Philosophy and Public Policy at the University of Maryland, lecturer at the Maryland Law School, and visiting investigator at the Center for Environmental and Estuarine Studies in Cambridge, Maryland. His articles appear in many leading law reviews and philosophy journals, and his work has been supported in recent years by grants from the National Endowment for the Humanities and the National Science Foundation.

K. S. SHRADER-FRECHETTE was born and raised in Louisville, Kentucky. She received her undergraduate degree in mathematics and physics in 1967 and her Ph.D. in philosophy of science from the University of Notre Dame in 1972. Until 1982, she taught philosophy at the University of Louisville, where she won the "Outstanding Teacher" award in 1977. She is the author of *Nuclear Power and Public Policy, Environmental Ethics*, and (soon to appear) *Risks of Risk Assessment*, and has also published a number of articles on philosophy of high-energy physics. She is currently professor of philosophy of science and environmental studies at the University of California, Santa Barbara. She, her mathematician-husband, and their two preschoolers enjoy building sand castles and flying kites at the beach.

ROBERT L. SIMON was born in Brooklyn, New York, in 1941, virtually in the shadow of Ebbetts Field. He received his undergraduate degree from Lafayette College and his Ph.D. from the University of Pennsylvania. He currently is William R. Kenan Professor of Philosophy at Hamilton College. He is co-author of *The Individual and the Political Order* and has written on a variety of topics in political, social, and legal philosophy, including affirmative action, merit and desert, and the ethical implications of sociobiology. Influenced no doubt by his early environment, he is now completing a book on ethical issues in sports.